SELECTED REPORTS IN ETHNOMUSICOLOGY

VOLUME X

MUSICAL AESTHETICS AND MULTICULTURALISM IN LOS ANGELES

UNIVERSITY OF CALIFORNIA
LOS ANGELES

SELECTED REPORTS IN ETHNOMUSICOLOGY

VOLUME X

MUSICAL AESTHETICS AND MULTICULTURALISM IN LOS ANGELES

Editor
Steven Loza

Assistant Editors
Paulette Gershen
Eddie Huckaby

Editorial Assistant
Jay Keister

DEPARTMENT OF ETHNOMUSICOLOGY AND SYSTEMATIC MUSICOLOGY
UNIVERSITY OF CALIFORNIA, LOS ANGELES
1994

Cover: *The Other Side of East L.A.*, by Robert Gutierrez

Selected Reports in Ethnomusicology is a refereed journal published by the Department of Ethnomusicology and Systematic Musicology, University of California, Los Angeles. All communications regarding *Selected Reports in Ethnomusicology* should be addressed to:

Managing Editor
Ethnomusicology Publications
Department of Ethnomusicology and Systematic Musicology
UCLA
405 Hilgard Avenue
Los Angeles, California 90024-1657

ISBN: 0-88287-051-3

CONTENTS

PREFACE

It is with extended gratitude that I acknowledge my colleagues on the faculty and staff of the Department of Ethnomusicology and Systematic Musicology for their academic and administrative support in the publication of this volume of *Selected Reports in Ethnomusicology*. I also wish to make special mention of the UCLA César Chávez Center for providing extra funds which have enabled me to contract extra editing services for the volume.

I would especially like to thank the many scholars who have lent their expertise in the evaluation, research assistance, editing, and proofreading of the manuscripts. I make special acknowledgment of the following colleagues: Teshome Gabriel, Juan Gómez-Quiñones, Carlos Grijalva, Manuel de Jesús Hernández-G, Cheryl Keyes, Manuel Peña, James Porter, Jihad Racy, Roger Savage, Daniel Sheehy, Theodore Solís, Fernando Soriano, and Robert Stevenson.

Finally, I thank my assistant editors, Paulette Gershen and Eddie Huckaby, for their invaluable role in the publication; Jay Keister, for technical assistance; and Betty Price, for her administrative support.

SL

MUSICAL AESTHETICS AND MULTICULTURALISM IN LOS ANGELES:

AN INTRODUCTION

Steven Loza

Every mother tells men—her husband and her sons—what men cannot quite believe: Birth is traumatic. It is messy, it is slimy, it is painful beyond pain. There is blood. Birth begins with a scream. I tell you, Los Angeles is being born.

Richard Rodriguez (1993)

WITH THIS TENTH VOLUME OF *Selected Reports in Ethnomusicology*, we at UCLA have finally decided to explore the land and culture that surrounds our oftentimes isolated university in the city of Los Angeles and its vast array of musical culture. As a native of this exciting and glamorous, yet segregated and problematic metropolis, I have welcomed the opportunity to edit this volume, a project that has given me a great feeling of creative purpose. It also comes at a timely juncture for all of us working and living in a city that in many ways has begun to reach many of its social limits. In probing some musical questions concerning this human complex of multicultural motives and values, perhaps we can at least address a selection of problems in a way that goes beyond the weighted, dominant academic practice of socioeconomic, non-aesthetic studies of urban culture.

The original strategy for compiling these essays was related to the issue of musical aesthetics, primarily generated through the curricular development of a course I have been teaching through the last three years in the Department of Ethnomusicology and Systematic Musicology (Musical Aesthetics in Los Angeles). The decision to add the concept of multiculturalism to the volume title was one that enabled me to accept particular articles that do not necessarily apply a line of aesthetic analysis, but that nevertheless signify a contribution to the aesthetic questions that form the basis of this inquiry.

Why Los Angeles?

The city of Los Angeles and its suburbs provide a contemporary laboratory for what can be called the multicultural urban reality of the last years of the twentieth century. Zena Pearlstone, in the preface of her book *Ethnic LA*, makes the following note:

> Los Angeles is today on the cutting edge of
> the twenty-first century as a result of the
> waves of migration which have brought
> diverse peoples into the Los Angeles area
> in the last 25 years. In the nineteenth
> century, European immigrants fleeing wars,
> famines and lack of economic opportunity
> poured into New York and other Eastern
> cities and made their way in the Industrial
> Revolution. In the late twentieth century,
> Asian and Latin immigrants fleeing wars,
> famines and lack of economic opportunity
> are arriving in Los Angeles in record num-
> bers and struggling to find a place in the
> Electronic Revolution. And Los Angeles's
> immigrants, because of the climate and the
> sprawling nature of the area, seem more
> visible than those in the East. Ethnic vari-
> ety is celebrated from the small items that
> people place in their windows or on their
> front lawns to large architectural monu-
> ments. (1990:13)

Los Angeles, however, has in some ways always represented the multicultural model. Various American Indian groups inhabited the area at
the time that the first non-indigenous settlers arrived in 1781 from Mexico. That group reportedly
consisted of 44 Spanish-speaking individuals who
were recorded in documents as *indios*, *mestizos*,
negros, *criollos*, and *mulatos*, signifying heritages
of African, American Indian, and European background.

Such diversity has since consistently been a
basic characteristic of Los Angeles. Following the
acquisition of the majority of the present U.S.
Southwest from Mexico after the Mexican-Ameri-
can War ending in 1848, intercultural exchange
was highly active, losing momentum however, by
the turn of the century. By the end of World War
I and the Mexican Revolution of 1910, however,
new equations of a multicultural life in Los Angeles acquired a variety of phases and faces. Early

twentieth century Los Angeles was not a familiar
model of immigration, migration, and intercultural
context as largely experienced by other U.S. cities.
In his highly acclaimed book, *City of Quartz*, Mike
Davis assesses the unique circumstance of Los
Angeles, citing the perspective of Robert Fogelson
in *The Fragmented Metropolis*.

> Unlike most eastern and midwestern me-
> tropolises, which were divided between
> native American and European immigrants,
> Los Angeles was divided between an over-
> whelming native white majority and a siz-
> able colored minority. Nowhere on the
> Pacific coast, not even in cosmopolitan San
> Francisco, was there so diverse a mixture
> of racial groups, so visible a contrast and so
> pronounced a separation among people, in
> the 1920s. (Fogelson 1967:83)

As of the early 1990s, Los Angeles had become
the first metropolis in the continental United States
where whites were no longer the predominant
majority. Estimates project that the combined
Latino and Asian population will soon become a
majority. It has also been estimated that over 140
countries are represented by inhabitants of Los
Angeles County. Los Angeles is also the second
largest populated Mexican, Armenian, Korean,
Filipino, Salvadoran, and Guatemalan city in the
world. Among world cities, it also comprises the
third largest Canadian city, as well as including the
largest Japanese, Iranian, Cambodian, and Gypsy
communities in the U.S. There are more Samoans
in Los Angeles than in American Samoa. Finally,
an estimated 100 different languages are spoken by
the 600,000 children enrolled in the Los Angeles
Unified School District. As of 1988, more than
500,000 of these students were classified as "non-
white" (see Pearlstone 1990:27–34). In 1994, the
current official estimate of students enrolled in Los
Angeles public schools resonates with an especially significant figure: 67% Latino.[1] Also of
interest are the languages following Spanish in
order of preponderance among these students:

Armenian and Korean. The list, of course, continues in international fashion. Statistics of the current student population at UCLA reveal the following: In 1980, two-thirds of the first-year students were Anglo; in 1992, two-thirds of the first-year class were students of color (Asian American, Latino, African American, and Native American). UCLA and UC Berkeley are now the most ethnically diverse research universities in the United States.

The Los Angeles of twenty years hence thus looms not as a mystery, but more as an exciting, albeit continuing problematic, human complex of networks. An optimistic viewpoint predicts intercultural convergence and creativity in order to manage the challenge of multiculturalism.

On the Notion of Aesthetics

In a city that has, on various levels and at different points in time, spawned an eclectic field of musical artists ranging from rock acts such as The Doors, Frank Zappa, Eddie Van Halen, and Los Lobos to other innovators including John Cage, Ornette Coleman, Eric Dolphy, and Charles Mingus, what can be said of any forms of collective musical aesthetics in a metropolis so physically expansive and culturally diverse?

An answer lies in the rejection of any sort of collective aesthetic formula at one level, while on another, recognizing an actual sociopolitical oneness of Los Angeles, e.g., government, transportation, economy, pollution, natural disasters and crime. The problems that have emerged due to a multicultural society characterized by such expanded ranges of cultural practices do not easily access a dominant ideological, political, or religious system, much less an artistic one. The problem is not an easy one, and it represents a human challenge. It is for this reason, among others, including their largely nonverbal nature, that the arts oftentimes emerge uncritically *assessed* and randomly *accessed*. But how do we evaluate these arts of multiplicity from a frequently not-so-multiple academic sphere?

In my estimation, we must consider a diversity of philosophical perspectives. How, for example, are we perceiving "art," the experience we refer to as the "aesthetic," and the study, the branch of philosophy, that we have entitled "aesthetics?" And on a much more significant level, how do we evaluate art according to different and intercultural standards of meaning, quality, and value?

One of the classical definitions of art that has always caught my fancy is that of Benedetto Croce, who defied the current definitions of his era. Reacting against the positivists whom he viewed as negating knowledge through art, he also dismissed the modernist concept of art as "play" (unfortunately, a concept still employed by some contemporary anthropologists and aestheticians). Croce considered aesthetics as centrifugal, as a philosophy of art. Art is thus not "intellectualistic." To defend his interpretation, Croce relied upon both his own aesthetic senses as well as formal exercises from philosophy. To Croce, therefore, art was most simply and perfectly defined as *intuition* (1921).

One conceptualization of "aesthetics" that I have found useful in teaching and conveying my own ideas is that of "the study of the cognition of sensation." This derives largely from earlier European philosophy, and has been interpreted through various schools of thought, from Kant to Adorno. Francis Sparshott has provided a useful contemporary perspective by writing that "aesthetics investigates the rational basis of artistic appreciation on the understanding that the objects to be appreciated are isolated as aesthetic objects, in abstraction both from their context of use and their context of production" (1983:3). In addressing the semantic issue of the term "aesthetic" and the problems germane to cross-cultural studies of musical meaning, Judith Becker reminds us that "the descendent word *aesthetic* may, as it did in the eighteenth century, take on new fields of meanings" (1983:76).

In his development of the field of aesthetic anthropology, Jacques Maquet recognizes forms of both "instrumental" (utilitarian) and "non-instrumental" art as "aesthetic phenomena." Because anthropology is empirical, Maquet posits that "aesthetic phenomena must be defined so that they can be identified by the usual techniques of anthropological observation" (1979:4). In terms of a definition of aesthetic phenomena, Maquet implies "not so much a statement on their 'nature' or 'essence' but primarily observable *criteria* which permit us to identify them among other phenomena" (ibid.).

> Since anthropology is comparative, the validity of the definition is not to be restricted to one civilization, or to a few civilizations of the same type—the literate or non-literate cultures, the industrial or non-industrial societies. It is not *a priori* claimed that artistic or aesthetic phenomena are found everywhere, but their definition would not preclude that possibility... Anthropology's scope encompasses the cultural phenomena of any human collectivity. Consequently our basic definitions have to be cross-cultural. (ibid.)

But what of current definitions or non-definitions that actually break the pattern and tradition of so-called "western" aesthetics? One scholar radically challenging the "meaning of aesthetic" is Marimba Ani (1994). Recognizing the two senses of "the European aesthetic," that of the "experience" and that of the "objectification," Ani rejects the idea that art and the aesthetic (and religion) can be merged with rationalism. Following a critique of Kant's *Critique of Judgment*, she offers the following assessment:

> The analytical and the "rational" are so valued that they become a part of the emotional experience of pleasure among a select group of people. There is no doubt that the undergraduate who is required to read the *Critique of Judgment* gets no pleasure from the experience and in fact may regard it as punishment; but the power of the

sanctions in the culture should not be underestimated, for if the student pursues philosophy until the end of her college career and into graduate school, she will no doubt begin to consider the *Critique* a "work of art" and be convinced therefore of the pleasure it should convey, at least to "understand" it (if not to read it). (202)

Thus, in addition to questioning the universal concept and interpretation of aesthetics, Ani also alludes to the idea of critical studies and scholarship themselves as part of the aesthetic, and as "art." I have posited such a notion in a recent article (Loza, in press).

In his book *Sound and Sentiment* (1982), Steven Feld refers to a concept of an "ideology of emotions." In assessing art, and especially throughout the multicultural ambit of contemporary world society, fresh and innovative discourse on aesthetics, beyond the academic tradition of what is rational and scientific, is a necessary consideration for expansion in scholarship. This is especially appropriate in the field of ethnomusicology, which has served as a conduit for the study of diverse artistic cultures throughout the world.

On the Notion of Multiculturalism

There has existed an inordinate amount of debate on the virtues and non-virtues of "multiculturalism" in the United States and Canada since the inception of the term itself. With the growing diversity of numerous urban centers in these countries, both educators and marketing executives have sought new methods and strategies. Conversely, a segment of society has questioned the subsequent deconstruction of many previous cultural standards. These standards include the issues of language, education, economics, immigration, and the arts.

Unlike the political and social rhetoric and reactions to attempts to adjust to a multicultural society, it is cultural practices, and especially the arts, that penetrate the issue on a much different, and perhaps more meaningful, level. In examining a city such as Los Angeles, the concept of multiculturalism is simply a reality. Food, religion, sports, and music all interact on a material network of streets, freeways, and various urban sectors. Downtown Los Angeles serves as an illustrative metaphor, where business executives walk during their lunch hours alongside the highly ethnic cross-section of Latinos, African Americans, and Asians. The foods being eaten for lunch reflect the walk.

On the Research and Teaching of the Course

As previously cited, the idea of this volume actually grew out of an undergraduate course that I initiated in the winter of 1992, and which I had been developing prior to that as part of a team of UCLA faculty, working under the auspices of a Ford Foundation grant. The goal of the project was that of expanding existing university curriculum to include a wider crosscultural base, especially that of American cultures. I used the opportunity to develop the class "Musical Aesthetics in Los Angeles."

The opportunity to develop the class served the kind of need that ethnomusicology curricula have, of course, served at certain levels in various universities, especially at UCLA. However, this opportunity enabled me to develop a course that could be structured crossculturally within itself, and within a focus on a city that I had already examined extensively through my research that had led to the publication of my book on the music of Mexican Americans in Los Angeles (Loza 1993). The idea of expanding the cultural referents of my research in Los Angeles seemed to be a logical and useful step.

Another goal that I hoped to incorporate was that of converting much of my teaching into my actual research, versus the usual research-teaching chronology. For the first two (of three) years of the course, I had the majority of classes videotaped, most of which were enhanced by guest artists, scholars, or individuals representing the music industry.

The class has also served as a way to emphasize the need for expansion within the predominant music curricula throughout universities in the United States. One perspective that I have often voiced in emphasizing the importance of such expansion is the fact that for a student in any U.S. university music program, it would be almost impossible to graduate without a knowledge of the music of Bach; yet that same student can usually graduate without knowledge of the music of Ellington. The study of music has grossly lagged even behind the cultural diversity of the social sciences. What, for example, might be the case of history if it had focused thus far on such a limited cultural-geographic domain as that of historical musicology?

At the outset of my classes, I have purposely commented on such rationale for developing the course. An example is the following transcript from my winter 1993 course:

> One of the problems we've had in musical curricula throughout the country and probably throughout the world, is that we've really limited the parameters of what is music, and how we think about music, and therefore how we philosophize about music. The majority of musical programs in this country basically focus on some five to ten European countries before the twentieth century. So as Americans, we haven't even examined our own music here on this continent, regardless of what cultural background we might represent—black, white, brown, red, yellow, etc. We also find, or at least I have found, that we're really running out of adjectives to describe ourselves culturally. What is it to be black, what is it to be brown? Here in Los Angeles, ideally we would all be living together, and therefore understanding cultures better than we have done thus far. One of the problems is that we haven't really attempted to do this in

our curriculum, in our course work, especially in the area of music. I believe that not only do we have a problem of discrimination in terms of different cultures here in this country, but that we discriminate in one of the strongest parts of all cultures, music, musical culture. Music and the arts, I feel, are the most discriminated areas of study in the University. This class is a case in point. There's probably only about five or, I would say, how many here are music majors? Or ethnomusicology majors? OK, I was going to say between five and ten, so I was pretty close.

The majority of you are not music majors. To me, looking at culture cross-sectionally is something that all students should do, but especially music students. But yet we haven't done it. Most of the degrees in music in this country are still based on pre-twentieth century European music. Which is fine—I had to go through the same process as an undergraduate. But it's time for us to start catching up with reality, especially in this country which is a multicultural country. I started this class before the riots last April. In fact this course literally ended about a week before the riots erupted. And interestingly, we were examining things like Ice Cube and Ice T—rappers from South Central Los Angeles. We were discussing the problems of censorship in the music industry. The contexts of the different groups in Los Angeles, Asian Americans, black Americans, Latin Americans. And not just the so-called ethnic enclave. Remember, everything is ethnic. Rock music is ethnic. We looked at rock culture, we looked at classical music. We looked at the film music industry.

So Los Angeles, in my book, is in a way a microcosm of the world, because we have over a hundred speaking languages on a daily basis throughout the schools of Los Angeles. We have over a hundred and forty cultures living here, not only immigrants, but cultures of first, second, third, and beyond generations. All of you have some kind of ethnic background. But even when you identify that ethnic background, remember there was some ethnic background before that. What is it to be German American? What is it to be German? Germans were not always Germans. They also were an enclave that came together and formed a particular nation. So we have to start looking at ethnicity and beyond the five colors that we always use to describe ourselves. If you live in Los Angeles, you're white, you're black, you're brown, you're everything, because you are affected by everybody else. If you live in Los Angeles you are part of L.A.. And if you have that spirit, then you'll learn about that part of your culture.

The above represents the basic framework that I use as my basic definition of "multiculturalism" within the context of not only the course, but in terms of the social reality we are studying—and from what philosophical perspective we might study that reality.

The structure of the course has followed a set of cross-cultural examinations of diverse musical contexts within Los Angeles. These cultural inquiries have focused on various musical networks and specific experiences of the African American, Asian, Chicano/Latino, Native American, rock culture, Western art music tradition, and the commercial music industry. With each of the three years I have taught the course, I have made various modifications to this basic framework.

On a theoretical basis, I have attempted to expose students to various modes of thought and analysis applicable to the diverse aesthetic dimensions of the examined musical/cultural contexts. Assigned readings have included the previously cited sources by Maquet (1979, 1990) and Croce in addition to others including Davis (1990), Rieff (1991), Kitano and Daniels (1988), Riddle (1985), Merriam (1964), Wilbert (1976), Kroeber (1963), Loza (1992, 1993), Lipsitz (1990), Dje Dje (1989), Spencer (1991), Dyson (1991), Jones (Baraka)(1970), Huntley (1970), and Pearlstone (1990). Also included in the course reader have been various journalistic articles and reviews.

Readings, however, have not constituted the only analytical fodder for the course. Live performances and lectures by guest artists have been as important as my own lectures, and I have made extensive use of recordings and video materials (commercial and field produced). Invited artists/lecturers have included the following:

Herb Boyd, professor of African American studies, College of New Rochelle, Marist College, New York City Technical College

Bobby Bradford, jazz musician, college instructor

Phyllis Chang, Korean American songwriter, folklorist

Billy Childs, jazz/contemporary pianist and composer

Teresa Covarrubias, songwriter, composer, musician

Jacqueline Dje Dje, professor of ethnomusicology, UCLA

Ernest Fleischmann, Executive Director, Los Angeles Philharmonic

Michael Greene, president, National Academy of Recording Arts and Sciences

Steve Hochman, pop music critic, *Los Angeles Times*

James Horner, film composer

Cynthia Hsiang, Chinese musician, ethnomusicologist

Isaiah Jones, gospel music director

Jessica Kim, Korean American musician, ethnomusicologist

Ira Koslo, Peter Asher Artists Management

Dan Kuramoto, June Kuramoto, Johnny Mori—members of musical group Hiroshima

Guangming Li, Chinese musician, ethnomusicologist

Scott Lipscomb, musicologist (film music specialist)

Charles Moore, ethnomusicologist (African American specialist)

Raul Perez, Vice-President, Music Administration, Sony Pictures

David Reyes, composer, journalist

Rudy Salas, musical director of the group Tierra

Dorrance Stalvey, composer, director of Monday Evening Concerts, Los Angeles County Museum of Art

David Torres, pianist/composer/arranger

Gerald Wilson, jazz band leader and composer

Devising the described course has thus led me to a whole new line of research. This decision, in effect, has motivated me to ponder the useful progression of one's research, and what direction such progression should take. Expanding my research matrix of Chicano/Latino music in Los Angeles becomes a valuable springboard for comparative and individual juxtapositions of the complex and multiple interworkings of musical culture in such a cosmopolis.

The course has also directed me to other curricular projects at UCLA. Largely because of the success of the course in addition to my membership on the UCLA Council for Undergraduate Education, I was asked to facilitate a faculty seminar based on curricular expansion. Titled "Arts in America: Cross-cultural Aesthetics and Education," the seminar was held in Winter 1994. Teshome Gabriel, professor of film studies, served as co-facilitator, and the seminar was made available to twelve faculty members and five graduate students within the School of the Arts. It proved to be a most worthwhile effort. Fifteen new courses were designed by the faculty, and group discussions coupled with various presentations and readings generated significantly positive results.

The Essays

The essays comprising this volume represent an eclectic sampling of the multiple possibilities in assessing musical aesthetics and multiculturalism in Los Angeles. The articles presented are constructed on conceptual, contextual, or historical frameworks, or combinations thereof. While the majority of the pieces are written by established scholars and professionals, three are done by graduate students at UCLA, with another one initiated by two undergraduates. It is my conviction that all the essays represent important scholastic contributions to the field of ethnomusicology.

The first three articles project some essential theoretical concerns in the formulation of a musical aesthetic, all of which provide insightful considerations for the ensuing essays in the volume.

Jacques Maquet has been a pioneer in the conceptualization of aesthetic anthropology, and his work has directly impacted my own approach to aesthetics, especially in my research and teaching of musical culture in Los Angeles. In his refreshingly new essay included in this anthology, Maquet reflects not only on the multicultural interpretation of Los Angeles, but also on the notion of L.A. as "one single society." Recognizing that culture is based on society, he notes that "the multicultural interpretation is focused on the diversity of the artistic and less tangible aspects of Los Angeles and neglects the fact that Los Angeles is societally one." On an analytical plane, Maquet adapts a framework of culture layered by the productive, the societal, and the ideational. Through these levels, Los Angeles is fluid and ever-changing through new musics, ideas, trends, cuisine—all expansively extending what Maquet refers to as "options." Innovation in a culture is highly generated by external penetration by way of reinterpretation and "naturalization." But Maquet also cautions those of us who might leap too quickly and uncritically upon the multicultural model, focusing only on the influence of cultures, while ignoring both the panhuman and individual component of all that "we make, feel, and think."

In his role as a philosopher, and particularly in his treatment of aesthetics, *Roger Savage* has had a profound influence upon both students and faculty in the Department of Ethnomusicology and Systematic Musicology at UCLA. Here, in his philosophical consideration of music and the cultural imagination, he specifies that questions of aesthetic significance and cultural meaning impinge upon music's valuation as an aesthetic and cultural phenomenon. Applying some of the concepts of Paul Ricouer, he addresses a "hermeneutics of culture," implying that the non-representational character of music is no longer opposed to an interpretation of its cultural significance. In recognizing the pluralistic world we live in, Savage critiques the concepts of music as a work of culture that transcends the reductionist analyses of the culture industry.

In confronting the multicultural reality of Los Angeles, *Angeles Sancho-Velázquez* raises the timely question as to whether an aesthetic approach is suitable to address cross-cultural musical phenomena. In her essay, she argues in favor of cross-cultural aesthetics from an ontological position, whereby she asserts that "knowing is always derivative of a mode of being." In her conceptualization, she borrows largely from the hermeneutic work of both Gadamer and Ricouer, in addition to that of her mentor, Roger Savage. In considering the possibilities of a new aesthetic theory, Sancho-Velázquez critiques Alan Merriam's views on the adaptability of Western aesthetics to ethnomusicology. She argues that "the supposed incompatibility between ethnomusicology and aesthetics is the result of the narrow views of how both disciplines are to be defined." Concepts of appropriation, the transformation of self, and distanciation form part of Ricouer's theory of interpretation, which Sancho-Velázquez detects as a much more meaningful aesthetic approach, one that "opens doors for the overlapping of aesthetics and ethics, and places aesthetics on a common ground with other forms of knowledge and general communication.

My paper examining identity, nationalism, and aesthetics among Chicano/Mexicano musicians in Los Angeles was originally presented at a 1994 conference titled "Aquí: A Key to Chicano Identity Through the Humanities and the Arts," sponsored by the Hispanic Research Center at Arizona State University. In the article, I focus my analysis on four general musical styles adapted and stylized by Chicano/Mexicano musicians—rhythm and blues/rock, rap, mariachi, and banda. Ultimately, such artistic "movements" must be considered from the aesthetic viewpoint. A major factor in my analysis is the consideration of tradition as a cyclical, regenerative process involving the experiences of both reinterpretation and innovation. I also suggest that the issues of identity, nationalism, and aesthetics are congruent to both social and artistic motives— motives that are inevitably interactive and interdependent in any viable or successful artistic movement.

Following is an article by *Carlos Manuel Haro* and me on the evolution of banda, presently a musical/dance phenomenon that does not seem to have artistic precedence in the city of Los Angeles. As an extension of my article abstracted above, this study focuses on the musical heritage of banda and its development to its current stage of popularity in Los Angeles, presently its major location of identity. The article also provides a review of several bandas and their recorded music, thus offering much data that can be useful for further study of this current movement of extensive social and media interest.

Timothy Rice has conceptualized and developed an innovative field study for the volume. In conjunction with a graduate seminar that he conducts on ethnomusicological fieldwork at UCLA, Rice has incorporated his students' field projects based on the music festival organized for the 1993 Los Angeles Marathon. Rice's students survey musical performances and their contexts, which included musical expressions representing Japanese American, Chinese American, Mexican/Chicano/Latino, Jewish, African American, and Native American communities. As Rice notes, the timing of the 1993 L.A. Marathon was significant, for it "occurred a little less than a year after the civil unrest, looting, and burning in the wake of the innocent verdict in the L.A. County trial of the police officers who beat Rodney King and during the closing moments of the federal trial of the same officers on charges of violating King's civil rights."

Guangming Li provides a valuable survey of the Chinese musical community in Los Angeles, beginning with some explanation on the two principal cultural centers, the older downtown Chinatown and the more recently extensively developed Monterey Park, which he refers to as the "suburban Chinatown." As an active musician in the community and ethnomusicologist, Li relies on a considerable amount of rich field data and his own professional participation to portray a cross-section of musical activity. Contexts critiqued range from the some fifteen Beijing Opera clubs and a variety of instrumental ensembles and orchestras to performance settings and organizations. Chinese and Western music are both surveyed, and viewpoints regarding the various forms of musical instruction are incorporated into the essay, as well as an assessment of local music production, businesses, television and radio.

Citing the lack of and need for biographical and historical data of ethnomusicologists and folklorists, and specifically those of Latin American specialists, *Robert Stevenson* provides a caringly assembled survey of the musical research of Eleanor Hague. This scholar produced a substantial body of manuscripts on the music of Latin America and the U.S. Southwest, including articles in the *Journal of American Folklore* as early as 1911, in addition to monographs such as *Latin American Music, Past and Present*, and *Spanish-American Folk Songs*. Hague is associated with Los Angeles by virtue of her residence in Pasadena, from where she based her work from 1920 to her death in 1954. Additionally, a collection of her manuscripts are archived at the Southwest Museum in Los Angeles.

George Lipsitz offers a perspective of Las Tres and Goddess 13, Chicana groups that he interprets as progressive, postmodern contexts of musical style. The feminist, eclectic, and bilingual format of the groups lend well to Lipsitz's analytical play with *mestizaje* sensibility, ethnicity, gender, sexuality, class, and the music industry. Referring to various comparative modes of Chicana and Chicano musical life in Los Angeles, Lipsitz posits that Las Tres and Goddess 13 do not signify the modernists who create totally new forms of expression. Rather, the groups approximate more aptly the role of the postmodernists, e.g., those artists that deploy forms from the past in such a way "as to problematize the present." Part of this latter concept includes the notion that postmodernists deploy the methods of immanent critique, immersing themselves in the contradictions of their time and working through them, building the "society of tomorrow out of the contradictions, ruptures, and non-equivalences of today."

Included in this anthology is an article on Los Angeles "gangsta" rap that has evolved out of an undergraduate student paper submitted for my Musical Aesthetics in Los Angeles class. The final collaborative result here has been collectively prepared by *Milo Alvarez, Josefina Santiago, Charles Moore* (my graduate teaching assistant in the course) and me. Upon reading the original paper by Alvarez and Santiago (which basically encompasses the first half of the final essay, that of a survey of gangsta rap and two case studies in Los Angeles), I was moved to apply the idea of an "aesthetics of violence" as an analytical option for the topic of the study. The violent acts as imaged through the gangsta rap genre as created by artists such as African American Ice Cube and Chicano ALT can be considered as metaphors of an experiential aesthetic that corresponds to the expressions of gang life and gang warfare, be they gang colors, clothes, language, or styles of brutal and violent physical behavior. The "aesthetics of violence" concept is developed as a point of analysis in the assessment of issues such as peer pressure, socio-

political empowerment within a group, the possession of a materialist expression, the simulation of violence, morality, the representative, and the intellectual. Also applied and critiqued in the essay are some of the ideas of Marimba Ani, Bell Hooks, and Cornel West.

With a population exceeding 250,000, the Iranian community and its music in Los Angeles has for some time merited a serious study. *Behzad Allahyar* offers a socio-historical critique of the various levels of musical activity within this significant community. Iranian music has grown extensively since the 1979 Revolution in the form of media, recording, marketing, and performances. Categorizing musical practice into the popular and traditional, Allahyar surveys various musical contexts in Los Angeles. Among the different themes that he probes are issues related to song text, Iranian politics, nationalism, musical instruction, concert tours, the local Iranian music industry, improvisation, costume, instrumentation, and musical philosophy.

Steven Pearlman offers an analysis based on a "context-dependent aesthetics" of mariachi music in Los Angeles. In the United States, mariachi music has become an important focus of ethnic identification for both Mexicanos and Chicanos, although each of these groups brings different levels of familiarity and expectation to their understanding of the art form, which has also become an important experience for the non-Latino community. Each of these groups, Mexicanos, Chicanos and non-Latinos have their own ideas as to where mariachi music should be heard, and what constitutes "authenticity." In Los Angeles, the result is a variable aesthetic of mariachi music performance which is linked to context and performance style.

In her study of the social role of European-based concert music in Los Angeles at the turn of the century, *Catherine Parsons Smith* investigates the period of open and competitive concert-giving that occurred between 1899 and 1905. Smith substantiates considerable data into a thesis that, largely due to the open ambiance of this musical period, a concert music tradition in Los Angeles became firmly established with particular class, race, and gender associations, distinct from the more established traditions of public entertainment and enlightenment in church and theater.

In the final essay of the volume, *Grace M* provides an ethnographic sketch of Los Angeles-based jazz artist and educator Bobby Bradford, based on an interview conducted by her in addition to a formidable lecture given by the artist in the previously cited Musical Aesthetics in Los Angeles class at UCLA. Bradford has received international acclaim as one of the principal musicians (trumpet/cornet) in the formulation of the "free jazz" movement initiated in Los Angeles by Ornette Coleman. It was in Los Angeles that Bradford first began performing with Coleman during the early 1950s. In 1964, Bradford began his important musical association with Los Angeles-based clarinetist/saxophonist John Carter, with whom he was closely identified until Carter's death in 1991. Throughout this highly personal profile, Bradford makes prolific commentary on his musical philosophy, musical style, politics, race, identity, the recording industry, performance contexts, and education. The essay represents a seminal piece of data and thought.

This set of essays does not attempt to "paint a picture" of Los Angeles musical culture. Rather, the essays may be thought of as separate "pictures" of a complex city with many problems, many cultures, and a diversity and plenitude of music.

Forward Thoughts

On the back cover of Mike Davis's book, *City of Quartz*, it is declared that "no metropolis has been more loved or more hated" than Los Angeles, and that "to detractors, L.A. is a sunlit mortuary where 'you can rot without feeling it.'" Davis begins the book referring to the common complaint that "Los Angeles's truly indigenous intellectual history seems a barren shelf" (1990:17). But Davis also recognizes an important fact: that "this essentially deracinated city has become the world capital of an

immense culture industry, which since the 1920s has imported myriads of the most talented writers, filmmakers, artists and visionaries" (ibid.). In an interesting manner, David Rieff titled his 1991 book on the city *Los Angeles: Capital of the Third World*, published the year after Davis's *City of Quartz*. The juxtaposition of these descriptions—Los Angeles as capital of both the culture industry and the Third World—can lead to much speculation and analysis of culture in its international scheme.

In what directions can we proceed with an assessment of Los Angeles culture and its art-making persona? Is the city, as Mark Slobin (1993) might suggest, a micromusical culture of the west, or a macrocultural microcosm of the world? Or either? Or neither? Are such questions valid, or even useful?

Los Angeles does represent a society and culture well beyond its physical bounds. In critiquing the 1992 Los Angeles Rebellion, Cornel West has expressed the perspective that "what we witnessed in Los Angeles was the consequence of a lethal linkage of economic decline, cultural decay, and political lethargy in American life. Race was the visible catalyst, not the underlying cause" (1993:1).

What the present anthology is perhaps addressed to more than any particular city or people is an encroaching reality. The U.S. and the world at large are becoming, by way of technology and economics, not only "smaller" through lines of communication, trade, and transportation, but even "smaller" with respect to separate cultures and the larger, collective world culture. Interaction, in both its fluid and conflictual patterns, is very likely the most dynamic trait of late twentieth century Earth.

There is also the perspective of optimism that can be used in the making of philosophies pertaining to our contemporary world. West (1993) senses the need for new leadership in a diversity of social roles. The role of the artist must not be devalued nor underestimated as cultural change earmarks our present and continuing history. This volume, in its non-comprehensive way, represents such change and dynamics in contemporary culture. Through this cross-sectional sampling of intercultural sections of music making in Los Angeles and its various aesthetical dimensions, perhaps some models for further thought and action can be forwarded.

NOTES

1. Communicated to me in May 1994, by Manuel Ponce of the Los Angeles Unified School District.

REFERENCES CITED

Ani, Marimba
  1994   *Yurugu: An African-Centered Critique of European Cultural Thought and Behavior*. Trenton, New Jersey: Africa World Press, Inc.
Becker, Judith
  1983   "'Aesthetics' in Late 20th Century Scholarship." *The World of Music* 25(3): 65–79.
Croce, Benedetto
  1965 (1913) *Guide to Aesthetics*. Indianapolis: Babbs-Merrill Co.
Davis, Mike
  1990   *City of Quartz*. New York: Vintage Books.
Dje Dje, Jacqueline Cogdell
  1989   "Gospel Music in the Los Angeles Black Community: A Historical Overview." *Black Music Research Journal* 9(1): 35–79.
Dyson, Michael Eric
  1991   "Performance, Protest, and Prophecy in the Culture of Hip-Hop." *The Emergency of Black and the Emergence of Rap*. A Special Issue of *Black Sacred Music: A Journal of Theomusicology* 5(1): 12–24.
Feld, Steven
  1982   *Sound and Sentiment*. Philadelphia: University of Pennsylvania Press.
Fogelson, Robert
  1967   *The Fragmented Metropolis: Los Angeles 1850–1930*. Cambridge, Massachusetts: Harvard University Press.
Huntley, H. E.
  1970   *The Divine Proportion: A Study in Mathematical Beauty*. New York: Dover Publications.

Jones, LeRoi (Amiri Baraka)
  1970   *Black Music*. New York: William Morrow & Co.
Kitano, Harry H. L., and Roger Daniels
  1988   *Asian Americans: Emerging Minorities*. Englewood Cliffs, New Jersey: Prentice Hall.
Kroeber, A. L.
  1963   *Style and Civilizations*. Berkeley and Los Angeles: University of California Press.
Lipsitz, George
  1990   "Cruising Around the Historical Bloc: Postmodernism and Popular Music in East Los Angeles." In G. Lipsitz, *Time Passages: Collective Memory and American Popular Culture*: (133–160). Minneapolis: University of Minnesota Press.
Loza, Steven
  1993   *Barrio Rhythm: Mexican American Music in Los Angeles*. Urbana and Chicago: University of Illinois Press.
  1992   "From Veracruz to Los Angeles: The Reinterpretation of the *Son Jorocho*." *Latin American Music Review* 13(2): 179–194.
Maquet, Jacques
  1990   "Perennial Modernity: Forms as Aesthetic and Symbolic." *Journal of Aesthetic Education* 24(4):47–58.
  1979   *Introduction to Aesthetic Anthropology*. Malibu: Undena Publications.
Pearlstone, Zena
  1990   *Ethnic L.A.* Beverly Hills, California: Hillcrest Press.
Riddle, Ronald
  1985   "Korean Musical Culture in Los Angeles." *Selected Reports in Ethnomusicology* 6: 189–196.
Rieff, David
  1991   *Los Angeles: Capital of the Third World*. New York: Simon & Schuster.
Rodríguez, Richard
  1993   "Slouching Towards Los Angeles: Removing the Blindfold, the 'Cities of Angels' Begin to See Themselves as One." *Los Angeles Times*, April 11.
Sparshott, Francis
  1983   "Prospects for Aesthetics." *The World of Music* 25(3):3–14.
Slobin, Mark
  1992   "Micromusics of the West: A Comparative Approach." *Ethnomusicology* 36(1):1–87.

Spencer, Jon Michael
    1991   "Introduction." *The Emergency of Black and
            the Emergence of Rap.* A Special Issue of
            *Black Sacred Music: A Journal of
            Theomusicology* 5(1): 1–11.

West, Cornel
    1993   *Race Matters.* Boston: Beacon Press.

L.A.: ONE SOCIETY, ONE CULTURE, MANY OPTIONS

Jacques Maquet

WHEN WE TRY TO understand the contemporary musical scene of Los Angeles, the most often recurring word is "multicultural." Media experts and local authorities tell us with increasing frequency and conviction that Los Angeles is multicultural, and so is its music. Their statements seem, at first sight, plain enough, evident, and uncontroversial. Indeed many items in the L.A. culture, particularly in the performing and visual arts, language and religion, foodstuffs and cuisines, originated in a diversity of traditions.

Yet the multicultural interpretation of L.A. also implies that L.A. has no culture of its own, or only a fragmentary culture made of the traditions of its ethnic groups. It further implies that the differences in the aesthetics and significations of each culture makes understanding them very difficult if not impossible for outsiders. Cultural diversity is extolled as richness, but this richness seems inaccessible; thus, it separates rather than unites.

There is another interpretation of the L.A. situation. It starts from the observation that L.A. is one single society.

- 1 -

The "Los Angeles" we refer to is not only the City of Los Angeles, nor the County of Los Angeles, but the megalopolis that includes, in addition to the County of Los Angeles, parts of the counties of Orange, Riverside, San Bernardino, and Ventura. It covers an area of 34,000 square miles with a population of approximately 13.5 million (Pearlstone 1990:10).

This megalopolis—an urban complex made of several cities and suburbs in close proximity—is a society in the full anthropological sense of the word. Society, as a concept, is a lasting collectivity whose members' activities are complementary and provide them with all that is necessary for survival and development. From birth to death we can find within our society education, work and protection, partners for marriage and enterprise, established ways to share goods, solve conflicts, live together. There are many forms of societies from tribal chiefdoms and kingdoms, to empires of the past, to contemporary national states.

Los Angeles is not a national state: it does not deliver passports, has no embassies abroad, no army, and no money of its own. Yet it is a total society. In Los Angeles, one can be born and educated, one can (or one could until recently) find employment, start a family, develop one's manual and intellectual skills, be taken care of by the health industry, retire and die. It is an all-encompassing framework for the activities of its inhabitants.

Ethnic groups organize some common activities for their members such as annual celebrations and publication of periodicals in their languages. Sometimes they provide assistance to their members in need. So do churches and other nonethnic groupings, such as political or professional organizations. Neither ethnic groups, nor these affinity-based associations are total or full-scale societies: their scope is limited to special functions.

For Angelenos there is only one total society, Los Angeles. It is a fact that does not depend on what we feel about it. Many of us, perhaps most of us, prefer another identification. The first identification we like to choose may be ethnic ("I am a Nisei," "I am a Chicano"), professional ("I am an academic," "I am a photographer"), religious ("I am an Adventist," "I am a Muslim"), national ("I am an American citizen," "I am British") or whatever category we think should define us for ourselves and for others.

Yet because we live, work, and play in Los Angeles, we are submitted to the same traffic and property regulations, we appear in the same courts, we share in the expenses of running schools and services by paying local taxes, and on the same day, we elect officials. We are involved in an array of interdependent economic relationships in which the waxing and waning of the aerospace and military industries affect taxes, employment, and income for all Angelenos. When depression in one industry spreads over the whole megalopolis, we certainly experience that L.A. is one society.

The multicultural interpretation is focused on the diversity of the artistic and less tangible aspects of Los Angeles and neglects the fact that Los Angeles is societally one.

- 2 -

Culture is based on society. It is the way a society is lived by its members. In order to be a competent member of one's society, one has to know the instructions. A culture is the set of instructions, elaborated by past and present generations. It constitutes a collective heritage that is in constant process. A culture changes when its supporting society changes, for instance by receiving a large number of immigrants, by losing or gaining markets, by facing a rise in unemployment, or by waging a war.

The contents of a culture have been described and analyzed by some anthropologists in a three-layer framework: the productive (use of tools and techniques), the societal (proper interactions between forebears and descendants, husbands and wives, employers and employees, teachers and students, sellers and buyers, priests and congregations), the ideational (ideas and beliefs, worldviews and philosophies, myths and sciences, and the arts) (Maquet 1979:58; 1986:180).

A society is an organization of people; a culture is the parallel system of things and ideas. This parallel system is like a mirror-image of the society. Los Angeles being one society, it has one culture. As the L.A. society is complex and includes many different activities carried out by different specialists, the L.A. culture is also complex and variegated.

The multicultural interpretation has two flaws: it neglects the society facet of L.A. and it does not take into account the complete culture of L.A. It limits culture to its expressive part: theater and dance, music and poetry, philosophy and the visual arts. This narrow sense of culture is rooted in a 16th century usage: in the Renaissance, culture referred to the cultivation of intellectual and artistic abilities aimed at developing an informed and refined taste. In the perspective adopted here, the expressive culture is located on the ideational level of the three-layer model.

The full culture of Los Angeles—productive, societal and ideational—is one. But is it not so varied and fragmented that it amounts to a plurality of cultures?

- 3 -

Anthropologists, on the basis of their field observations of nonliterate, technologically simple, and numerically small societies "re-invented" the concept of culture in the second half of the nineteenth century and the first half of the twentieth century—let's say from Tylor to Malinowski. The model they built was characterized by uniformity (everybody grew the same crops and ate the same foods), stability (they changed so little that they were said to be "without history"), and tight integration (all their parts were interdependent). This model was valid for the cultures of isolated societies that do not exist any longer; it certainly does not fit the cultures of contemporary urban post-industrial large-scale societies like L.A. The L.A. culture is fluid and ever-changing: constantly there are new musics, new ideas, new trends, new dishes that extend the range of our options.

What is new in a culture results rarely from internal innovation. Usually it comes from outside by diffusion. But the foreign item does not remain foreign: it is adopted, adapted, reinterpreted, "naturalized" as it were. It becomes a part of the receiving culture.

An anecdote in Steven Loza's book *Barrio Rhythm* illustrates perfectly the diffusion of a musical item from one tradition to another. Walking on the campus of the University of Notre Dame, in South Bend, Indiana, he heard a rehearsal of the percussion section of Notre Dame's marching band. He recognized the rhythms of *Tequila*, a piece characteristic of the Chicano music of East L.A. in the fifties (it was composed in 1958 by Chuck Rio of "The Champs"). "The kids in the band didn't care where the music came from. They just dug playing it...and they played it well" (Loza 1993: 82, 279).

Diffusion—moving a cultural item from its context of origin to its context of adoption and giving it a new meaning—is a frequent process. At the turn of the century, tango was popular in Argentina with the Italian immigrants; it was mainly danced in brothels. Later, tango rhythms were adopted in ballroom dancing along with the waltz, quick step, and fox trot. The *tango argentino* was reinterpreted by professional dancers and became the international-style tango (Azzi 1992a, and b).

During the first decade of this century, the French cubist painters discovered the formal significance of traditional African carvings. Within a few years, Senufo masks, Bambara headdresses, and Dogon ancestral figurines were adopted in the cultures of Europe and America not as ritual objects but as art objects (Maquet 1986: 74).

Similar diffusion happens with modest cultural items. Quesadilla is very popular in L.A. restaurants. A dish of Mexican origin, it has become a part of the L.A. food culture; it is one more culinary option offered here. Of course, the quesadillas made and eaten in Mexico remain a part of the Mexican food culture. Pizza and croissant, chop suey and tempura are examples of the same process.

Cultural items, either material such as carvings, or nonmaterial such as music, coming from other cultures are added to the L.A. culture as new options. In the small and isolated societies studied in early anthropology, there were few options, if any. There was only one style in sculpture, one worldview, one adult status: spouse. What characterizes contemporary urban cultures is their range of options; they could be called "multioption cultures."

The foreign origin of the options does not make the receiving culture multicultural. It makes it more exciting.

- 4 -

There are many ethnic groups in Los Angeles. Does this make L.A. multicultural?

In her book, *Ethnic L.A.*, Zena Pearlstone (1990) does not define what ethnicity means for her. She describes briefly, or merely mentions, 44 ethnic groups: 6 Hispanic, 10 Asian, 14 European, 5 Middle Eastern, 3 African, 4 "invisible" immigrant groups (Australians, New Zealanders, South Africans, and Canadians "because they look, act, and sound so much like Americans" (Pearlstone 1990: 123), and 2 U.S. migrant groups (Native Americans, African Americans). This strange classification implies that there are only two categories among the Angelenos: Americans and ethnics. For Pearlstone, to qualify as American seems to be a matter of generation (ibid.:9) and looking, acting, and sounding like Americans (ibid.: 123). As she classifies African Americans and Native Americans among ethnics, one must conclude that the generation criterion is less important than the appearance criterion. And to look like an American amounts to looking like a white! This is absurd and offensive.

In the current usage, "ethnicity" connotes a social group, membership in it by birth, some common cultural features, and a focus for identity. An ethnic group is a society reduced to a few collective activities such as festivals, dances, solidarity committees, political forums. It is not a group that one can decide to join; one has to be born in it. I may master perfectly the Spanish language, be familiar with the Mexican culture, and have Chicano friends; I cannot become a Chicano if I am not born from parents recognized as Mexicans or Chicanos.

Not being a total society, an ethnic group cannot be the carrier of a complete culture but of some cultural features: language and literature, myths and religion, visual and performing arts, preferred foodstuffs and distinctive cuisine.

The most important function of an ethnic group is that it can be the focus of identity for its members. As said earlier when discussing the L.A. identity, the group with which one likes to identify is a matter of choice. When the "melting pot" approach was dominant, many second or third generation immigrants wanted to identify themselves as "American." Now, the ethnic identity is primary for many. Yet, those who successfully blend into the L.A. culture still may quietly distance themselves from their ethnic roots if they choose to do so.

As ethnic groups are not total societies, and do not have complete cultures, when referring to the ethnic diversity of L.A., it is more appropriate to say that Los Angeles is multiethnic than multicultural.

Because ethnic groups are not open to people of another ancestry, they create distinctions that separate Angelenos. The diffusion of ethnic items is not always welcome. The playing of ethnic music on traditional instruments by outsiders may be felt as an undue appropriation of signs of ethnic identity.

Rarely, this concern is overtly expressed in L.A. Yet, in other places, some Native Americans have forcefully denounced the adoption of Indians' ways by New Age movements as "cultural robbery." John Lavelle, the Sioux director of the Center for Support and Protection of Indian Religions and Indigenous Traditions, said to David Johnston of *The New York Times*: "This is the final phase of genocide. First whites took the land and all that was physical. Now they're going after what is intangible" (Johnston 1993:A1).

Ethnic items are not options for the mainstream as long as they are not made available to outsiders. Are they also outside the understanding of the mainstream?

- 5 -

This question—understanding the expressive part of another culture—is not new. But it is pressing in today's L.A. During the last two decades, massive immigrations of peoples coming directly from their native countries have occurred. This brings us—and them—in contact with so many foreign things that we wonder if we can make sense of it all.

A first step is to realize that artifacts, behaviors, ideas are not entirely and purely cultural: they are not related only to their traditions of origin. They are also related to what is common to all human beings, and to what is particular to the individual who has created them.

Anthropologists discovered the importance of culture: our actions are to be understood not only with reference to human nature (what eighteenth-century philosophers used to do) and to an individual personality (what romantic novelists used to do), but also—and for many anthropologists, mainly—with reference to a specific culture. We act in a certain way because we are members of a certain society. This perspective has spread beyond the social sciences; it has become one of the main categories through which all of us try to understand others and ourselves.

In fact, the cultural factor has been granted such importance—"Tchaikovsky's lyricism is Russian"—that the other factors, the panhuman and the individual, are minimized or neglected altogether. Yet, in all artifacts, productions, and actions, the three components are always present.

Let's take a simple example, food. This fettucine dish meets our common need for nourishing and tasty food: it is the human component. It was created in, and belongs to Italian cuisine: it is the cultural component. This fettucine is prepared in a way characteristic of a particular cook: it is the individual component.

The three components cannot be materially dissociated. There is no dish that is only human food without cultural or individual determinations: it has to be prepared according to a cultural recipe interpreted by an individual cook. No dish is only cultural (the stuff it is made of has to be biologically appropriate to human consumption), neither is it only singular (a cook cannot create a new dish outside of any culinary tradition).

A way to figure out the relations between the three components is to imagine on an horizontal line the whole range of what is within the limits of the biological, psychological, and societal possibilities of human nature. For instance, all the foodstuffs (grains, legumes, meat, and other substances) that can be eaten, digested, and assimilated by the human organism; or, all the sounds (vibrations of certain frequencies) that can be perceived by the human ear; or, all the government institutions (hereditary monarch, elected ruler, national, regional, and local assemblies) that can organize social cooperation.

Any society includes in its culture some—never all—of the foodstuffs, sounds, and institutions that meet human needs. Reported on the horizontal line, they cover only a segment of the human possibilities. Each individual further shortens the segment by selecting the cultural possibilities she or he prefers. The three components, from human nature to culture, and from culture to individual, are related by a restrictive process.

In music, the human range covers all the audible variables of sounds. Each musical tradition has developed a segment of this range: one or several combinations of these variables. For example, the five-pitch scale in Japan, the seven and later twelve-pitch scale in Western tradition, and the seventeen one in the Middle East. Within a cultural style of music, each composer creates pieces in his or her individual style.

Thus, the restricted cultural segment is not the only dimension of music to take into account. This conclusion is directly relevant to the understanding of foreign musics we can listen to in L.A. If musics were only cultural, those developed in the segment we are familiar with would be the only ones directly accessible; the other ones would remain opaque until we master their cultural system through an arduous training. Fortunately, all these musics are also rooted in the metacultural human ground, so we have a direct access to them.

I can enjoy a Mexican dish the first time I eat it because its combination of tastes and smells belongs to the human repertory and thus may be directly experienced as pleasant.

The human component present in any artifact and production, idea and gesture reminds us that deeper than cultures that divide us as groups, and singularities that make us distinct as individuals, there is a grounding in a common humanity that unites us. As it was said by Terence, the African Roman playwright and philosopher of the second century B.C., *nihil humanum alienum* (nothing human is foreign). A quotation useful to remember in L.A.

- 6 -

How far can we go in our understanding and appreciation of the foreign? Is it just a superficial impression ("This is nice") or can we have access to a deeper comprehension?

Culinary analogies throw only some light on the appreciation of unfamiliar art. Let's consider directly the listening experience of other musics. In this experience, can we gain a significant understanding of the aesthetic quality and symbolic meanings of works from other traditions?

The aesthetic quality of a work is located, as it were, in its formal elements: it results from the way these elements are integrated in a compelling whole. This applies to all the arts, visual, literary, and other. The formal elements in music, such as rhythm, tempo, dynamics, tone color, pitch, melody, and texture, are related so as to constitute a composition, a structure, a Gestalt. In the listening experience, structures are directly apprehended through intuition, not analysis.

Is this intuition possible for outsiders to the tradition? When audiences are enthusiastic about foreign musics they listen to for the first time, we know this intuition is possible. Every day in L.A. this is experienced by general audiences—not made only of ethnomusicologists. The capacity to perceive musical Gestalts—and to compose them—is rooted in the panhuman mental ground.

Certainly insiders who are familiar with the formal arrangements preferred in their traditions— the "styles"—are likely to have a more refined intuition: they may perceive this piece as better composed in a certain style than another one they remember. These differences do not matter as listening experiences are individual anyway; what matters is that the aesthetic quality of a piece does not remain inaccessible to outsiders to the tradition.

The aesthetic quality is not the only dimension of a musical piece. To listeners, music conveys significations. Gestalts of sounds stand for something else than themselves: an emotion (joy, fear), a feeling (pleasant, unpleasant, neutral), an image (sea, mountain, meadow), an idea (liberty, destiny), a belief (a requiem stands for the belief in an after-death life), a society (a national anthem stands for a country).

Some of these significations are conventional. In 1879, the French government decided that *La Marseillaise* would be the national anthem; it is by convention that *La Marseillaise* stands for France. For those who do not know the convention, this music does not stand for that country.

Other significations are symbolic. The relationship between symbol and what it symbolizes is based, not on a convention but on a natural correspondence between the music (symbol) and what it represents (signified). In Bizet's *Carmen*, an orchestral motif symbolizes the foreboding of an impending disaster. Just listening to the few bars of the motif, even without attending the opera or knowing the story, is sufficient for intuitively grasping a nearing threat.

Are symbolic meanings the same for insiders and outsiders? Some are, and some are not, just as symbolic meanings differ among insiders. Conventional significations are like messages in words that are expected to mean the same for senders and receivers. Symbolic significations are not messages from composers and performers to listeners; they result from an encounter of particular listeners (having their own individual histories and mental characteristics) with the music, not with the intentions of its creators (Maquet 1986:93–117; 1993: 10–12).

Any listening experience is made essentially of intuitive apprehensions of the aesthetic excellence and the symbolic significations of a music. There is no barrier when the music is part of another tradition. The only difference is that formal compositions may be perceived by insiders on the basis of a wider past acquaintance with similar pieces, and symbolic meanings on the basis of their common cultural worldviews.

Conventional meanings remain opaque for outsiders if they do not learn them. Outside listeners may not know in what context the *habanera* is played and danced. Does it matter if one is not an anthropologist or an ethnomusicologist?

- 7 -

To present an interpretation of contemporary Los Angeles as "one society, one culture," and to disagree with the prevailing interpretation of Los Angeles as multicultural has not been done here for paradox's sake.

Because of its emphasis on culture, multiculturalism forgets that culture is only one facet of living together, the other facet being society. A collectivity of people, even if it is a 13.5 million collectivity, cannot be a multisociety without falling into chaos. Certainly there is more dysfunction in the L.A. society than we, Angelenos, like to see. Yet we move around the megapolis, we find commodities in stores, our children go to school, public services operate. We live in one society, we are on the same boat.

Because it restricts culture to expressive culture, multiculturalism does not take enough into account the societal and productive levels. And it is there, in the system of production and the network of institutions, that our culture is clearly one culture. Again, what unites us is forgotten.

Thanks to communication and diffusion, the ideational level of our culture is rich in options. Our culture offers us choices between many alternatives. They come from other cultures but are not "foreign" any longer, having been adopted and reinterpreted.

Anthropologists have been so mesmerized by their discovery of the pervasive influence of culture on everything we make, feel, and think, that they have come to ignore the panhuman component which is also present in everything we make, feel, and think. The multiculturalist approach shares this anthropological narrowness.

It is a significant shortcoming as the grounding in human nature is the basis of our understanding of other musics.

And of our realization that others are not "other" that much.

REFERENCES CITED

Azzi, Maria Susana
  1992a   "Tango, A Universal Language." *Buenos Aires Herald* (Buenos Aires) Nov. 2.
  1992b   "Tango: How It Came To Be." *Buenos Aires Herald* (Buenos Aires) Nov. 9.
Johnston, David
  1993   "Spiritual Seekers Borrow Indians' Ways." *The New York Times* (New York) Dec. 27: A1, A10.
Loza, Steven
  1993   *Barrio Rhythm: Mexican American Music in Los Angeles.* Urbana and Chicago: University of Illinois Press.
Maquet, Jacques
  1993   "Chose vue, forme regardée." *Initiations* (Brussels) 10:7–14.
  1986   *The Aesthetic Experience: An Anthropologist Looks at the Visual Arts.* New Haven and London: Yale University Press.
  1979   *Introduction to Aesthetic Anthropology.* Malibu: Undena Publications.
Pearlstone, Zena
  1990   *Ethnic L.A.* Beverly Hills, California: Hillcrest Press.

MUSIC AND THE CULTURAL IMAGINATION

Roger W. H. Savage

[W]ithout a Utopian image, however faded...society could not endure.

> Theodor W. Adorno

[A] social group without ideology and utopia would be without a plan, without a distance from itself, without a self-representation. It would be a society without a global project, consigned to a history fragmented into events which are all equal and insignificant.

> Paul Ricoeur

[M]usic is the supreme art of utopian venturing beyond....No art is as socially conditioned[;]....no art has so much surplus over the respective time and ideology in which it exists.

> Ernst Bloch

IT HAS BEEN SUGGESTED that among the activities that distinguish the life of a culture, music has a unique place. Within the Western tradition, the expressive power attributed to music has in the past been linked with the cult of the creative genius. Today we recognize that behind this aesthetics of genius stands a tradition of metaphysics that reached something of an apex in the Romantic fascination with music. The privileged status of music as a *lingua franca*, too, has its heritage in this tradition, specifically in the universality of reason codified by the Enlightenment. However much music might appear to be a language that transcends all cultural and historical boundaries, this understanding is itself one that belongs to the history of Western aesthetics. Yet does the pervasiveness of music as a cultural phenomenon not suggest that music has a uniquely expressive power? And does the diversity of the musics which are the objects of cultural and ethnomusicological studies not bear witness to a different universality, that is, the universality of culturally informed practices that lie at the heart of a way of life?

The notion that music might have a privileged significance, however, is made immediately problematic by the fact of its being non-representational. The perplexity to which this gives rise is nowhere more forcefully evidenced than by the place music and its aesthetics occupies within different philosophical discourses. Where for Immanuel Kant music as an art of the beautiful play of sensations ranks as the lowest of the fine arts, for

G.W.F. Hegel music is one of the most ideal mediums for the presentation of the Idea in purely sensuous form. Of all the arts, only poetry transcends the limitations of music's subjectively sounding inwardness to have a higher aesthetic value. In a more contemporary formulation, the question of music's non-representational status has led to a dichotomy, disastrous for aesthetics in my opinion, between an intra-musical meaning and an extra-musical one. Clearly, questions of aesthetic significance and cultural meaning impinge upon music's valuation as an aesthetic and cultural phenomenon. Yet it is not immediately evident how music's non-representational character relates to its aesthetic phenomenality, nor is it clear how music grounds its cultural significance in a way that might be said to be privileged.

The question of music's cultural significance, to my way of thinking, is inextricably bound to its power to represent a meaning. If its problematic non-representational character divides formalist and expressivist aesthetic theories, the unique mode of the musical work's presentation, which in my opinion is the positive counterpart of this problematic, is the critical touchstone for an inquiry that seeks to understand aesthetics in terms of the cultural efficacy of musical works. Two theses support this inquiry. The first is that as an art of time, music brings to presentation the temporal cadencing which, poetically speaking, raises the time of human existence above itself. Following this thesis, I will suggest that the mimetic power of music is the productive counterpart to its efficacy as an aesthetic phenomenon. The second thesis is that the cultural imagination, inasmuch as it is irreducible to an imago which founds the construction of a cultural identity, is at work in the mimetic processes through which a cultural self-representation is effected. Cultural identity, in other words, assumes the character of a tradition through the cultural interpretation of the signs and works objectified as the signs and works of the cultural imagination. In the light of this understanding of the cultural imaginary, it will be possible to ask in conclusion whether the hegemonic function of the culture industry cannot be understood in terms of the instrumental co-option of the cultural imaginary in the coercive construction of an ideologically distorted identity.

Music as a cultural work

The first of my theses concerns the efficacy of the musical work as a cultural phenomenon. In opposition to a theory of aesthetic significance that adopts a contemplative attitude toward the aesthetic object, this thesis stresses the efficacy of the work and its power to project a world.[1]

However much the claim that music is a cultural phenomenon might be accepted *prima facie*, its meaning in this regard is in no way self-evident. Even more, its non-representational character seems to be an obstacle to deciphering the cultural meanings encoded within it. Like all signifying human phenomena, music is fundamentally symbolic. Yet unlike ordinary language the exchange in music of signs for things, which is the foundation of the symbolic function as such, has no obvious correlate. Music is both like a language and yet is unlike it in this important respect. Further, music's mode of presentation is fundamentally temporal, whereas the analytic paradigms used to explicate its formal structural attributes tend to reduce its temporal charge to terms amenable to a spatio-durational representation. The resulting reification undercuts the most fundamental dimension of the aesthetic experience which the musical work affords. A related problematic, to which I will return, concerns a consideration of culture itself. Inasmuch as a tradition is always a living tradition, how are we to understand the link between culture and tradition as constituting a reality animated from within? Moreover, are the cultural works that provide for a cultural self-representation themselves susceptible to ideological distortion? Later, I will consider how the reality of culture has a possible aesthetic counterpart in the temporalizing attributes of musical works by drawing together reflections on the aesthetic efficacy of music with those on the mediated cultural self-representation effected by the cultural imagination.

By claiming that music is a cultural work, I by no means intend to prejudice a reflection on its aesthetic significance. On the contrary, I want to give the notion of *work* its full anthropological breadth. However much traditional aesthetic categories have reduced the *work* of art to an object to be contemplated in an attitude of aesthetic disinterest, the concept of a work is one that is animated by the notion of a human laboring. Without some form of labor, there is in fact no objectification of cultural life in works and signs. Works of culture, in other words, have as their counterpart the work that is performed in the creation, production, transmission, and preservation of meanings and values that are at the heart of a way of life. As an anthropological category, *work* belongs first of all to that practical field in which humanity distinguishes itself. "Only human beings work," claims Paul Ricouer, following Marx (Ricouer 1986: 43). In fact as Ricoeur points out, it is only because of "the human vocation to be self-creative, self-asserting [that] the fact of alienation cuts very deeply" (ibid.:44). Without this objectification and signification in works of the effort to exist, hegemonic distortion and ideological subreption would not threaten the cultural identity that both individuates and unites a people. But neither would there be a radical plurality of cultures—a reality among cultural realities effected by the unique and irreplaceable labor of a people to achieve an identity and a self-representation that distinguishes them in their ownmost way of life.

If *work* is fundamentally an anthropological concept, the labour that we as human beings perform is at the same time a task that we both choose and that confronts us. This task is perhaps nowhere more forcefully evidenced than in the creative effort required to bring a work of art into being. Yet it is no less evident in the phenomenon of culture. If we are to give the concept of work its fullest meaning, should we not also recognize in the life of culture the effort required to exist in productive

and meaningful ways? If the work of culture has an analogue, could we not say that it is in the effort objectified in the signs and works of the cultural life they signify? Cultural signs and works would then be the signs of the work of culture on itself. We understand ourselves, Ricouer tells us, "only through the long detour of the signs of humanity deposited in cultural works" (Ricoeur 1981: 143). Cultural self-representation, on this reading, is always already an interpretation that through the detour of cultural signs and works completes the circle in which the reality of culture is concretized in the effort to realize a meaningful way of being in the world.

In what sense does music as a cultural work participate in the creation of such a meaningful reality? The cultural significance of music becomes at once both apparent and elusive. On the one hand, the fact that the traditions and cultures to which different musics belong can be identified according to stylistic and ethnic traits is self-evident. How such works contribute to a culture's self-representation, on the other hand, is decidedly more difficult to determine. Yet is it not the spirit of such works, and the power they bear within themselves to represent a cultural reality that ultimately draws us to them? This power, to my way of thinking, legitimizes an inquiry into their cultural significance and meaning. Yet such an inquiry invariably is problematized by the horizontal structures that it brings into play.[2] If in order to take hold of the works of culture we deprive them of their signifying power, the analytic project is jeopardized by its own methods. If this practice is wide-spread in the human sciences, it is particularly devastating for a reflective inquiry into the significance of music as a cultural phenomenon. The dichotomy between a distancing analytic approach and one that stresses the immediacy of the musical experience does justice to neither. Opposing the immediacy of experience to the distancing objectification of analytic discourse sustains this dichotomy at the expense of an interpretation that would recognize in an aesthetic experience both its pre-predicative kernel and the surplus of meaning that is the mark of its temporal charge. In any event, true immediacy is not the blind immediacy of a so-called spontaneous momentary experience but is already mediated by the symbols that structure the effective reality of which it is a part.

Music, it has been said, is an art of time. Its significance as a performative art is undoubtedly tied to the fact that its mode of presentation is one that could be said to be temporal. It should therefore not surprise us that it is in playing music that the aesthetic experience so intimately related with this particular art is effected. The phenomenon of play, as Hans-Georg Gadamer tells us, is after all more an *event of being* than it is an object for consciousness. Could we not say that music is experienced aesthetically as the temporal play that in its most profound sense is constitutive of the very essence of music? Is the cadencing in music of an unfolding temporal whole not the occasion or the event by virtue of which music's aesthetic phenomenality gains its fullest presentation? And could we not also say that in view of this aesthetic *poiesis a se*, in which a temporal cadencing shapes the work as a self-actualizing entity, the *work* of music consists in the predicative action that forms its temporal contours and that shapes our aesthetic experiences? As an object for analysis, of consciousness, we tend to reduce this temporal action to the rectilinear order of time for the purposes of explicating a work's structural arrangement. But if only playing music brings to presentation what the music is, it is because, as Gadamer tells us, the mode of presentation of play is that of self-presentation. The phenomenon of play, in other words, is that of the structuring of a movement that shapes and forms itself as it unfolds. Its essence is constitutive of the very existence of the musical work as an aesthetic phenomenon. We only encounter the work, Gadamer explains, "in the performance" that structures the experience we have of it (Gadamer 1991:116). If "ultimately music must resound" (ibid.:116), then is it not, as Gadamer

asks, for the sake of "the *event of being that occurs in presentation*, and [which] belongs essentially to play as play?" Is it not, in the final analysis, for the sake of the reality to which only the *work* of music in its mode of play can uniquely attest?

Is it not in the performance that we truly encounter the work in the way in which it speaks to us? Is it not in the playing of music that we hear a cadencing that resonates with a sense of being that surpasses the world of mundane experiences?

Privileging musical works specifically, and works of art in general can only be rejected as ethnocentric by denying the fundamental ontological significance that Gadamer here identifies with the phenomenon of play. If, with Gadamer, we recognize that the art work "does not owe its real meaning to…an act of institution…[but] is already a structure with a signifying function of its own" (1991:155), are we not also ready to recognize in the phenomenon of the play of art its significance as a *work*? Undoubtedly, the term *art* has a canonic force that is culturally specific and tradition dependent. Yet if, following Gadamer, we too acknowledge that in the play of art, the representation in the *work* of art of a meaning is an event that enlarges one's experience of being (ibid.:159), should we not also acknowledge that event as the locus of the work's aesthetic efficacy? Gadamer claims that at root there is "no conceptual difference between being and playing" (1976:55). He explains that "where reality is understood as a play…the reality of play [emerges], which we call the play of art" (1991:113). It is here that the aesthetic ideal that privileges art works in terms of their contemplative value is shattered. No longer the object of an embodied contemplative beauty, but a *work* the power of which is manifested in its own specific mode of being addresses us. Is it not also here that the breadth of the concept of work as signifying the effort to exist gains its fullest meaning? Inasmuch as the art work's mode of being is that of play, the seriousness of the play of art has as its counterpart the effort we make to exist in meaningful ways. Not only is the work of art exemplary of the symbolic character of reality; the work itself is the representation, not of a thing, but of a meaning that comes to presentation and that in a transcendence within the immanence of the work enables us to play with real possibilities. If Gadamer defends the special ontological status of works of art against aesthetic leveling, he is in no way deferring to a modern aesthetic religion of art. Rather, he recognizes in the aesthetic phenomenality of the art work the protest against all profanation by alienating consciousness (see Gadamer 1991:149 ff). The sacral character of art he identifies with the advent of a meaning that by enlarging our self-understanding in front of the work enlarges our being. Because representation in the art work is the coming to presentation of a possible way of being it is, Gadamer tells us, a "universal ontological structural element of the aesthetic" (1991:159). It follows, therefore, that reality itself stands in a horizon of possibilities that take shape in the light of the personal, social, and cultural self-understandings to which such works give rise.

By displacing the question of art's representational power from the epistemological level onto its properly ontological plane, the locus of the problematic of music's non-representational character is also shifted. The understanding of art's originary purpose as an event that enlarges our ways of being recognizes the primacy of the art work's aesthetic efficacy. The question of aesthetic meaning which underlies the non-representational problematic is on this reading secondary to the question of the efficacy of the work in structuring an aesthetic experience. As a work, the aesthetic phenomenon exists to do some *work*. But what is its work? If we recognize in the phenomenon of work a labor that transforms the world in which we live, then we could say that the *work* of art consists in transfiguring our understanding of reality. Ultimately, the efficacy of the art work consists in this power to mediate reality. The work is truly a *work* on the one hand only insofar as it structures the experience the reader or listener has in a meaningful way. What it brings to representa-

tion for the reader or listener on the other hand is already a mediation between an existent world and a prospective one.[3]

The reenactment of a ritual, which it might be objected is intended only to preserve a traditional way of life, following this interpretation of the efficacy of cultural works, is already more than that. In the ritual performance of a traditional rite, does the performance not affirm a cultural self-understanding in the light of the many possibilities and even uncertainties that the future holds? And does this affirmation of a cultural self-understanding through the practice of a ritual not provide us with an important clue to understanding the phenomenon of culture? Is it not the very essence of cultural works that their surplus of meaning is unfolded along with the preservation and creation of a tradition? No work is exhausted by the experience of it any more than can the meaning of a rite that perhaps has a place at the very heart of a cultural way of life be circumscribed by what is said about it. Tradition, if it is lived at all, cannot be conceived of apart from the continuing work of culture on itself. Like the *work* of art, the phenomenon of tradition erodes all reifying pretense when in its very existence it unfolds a cultural world the significance of which is fundamentally irreducible to any epistemological explanation.

Far from ethnocentric, privileging the ontological status of cultural works undermines the egocentric claim to know what a work means apart from any culturally situated and tradition-dependent experience. Displaced onto its properly ontological plane, the question of aesthetic meaning is one of the effective aesthetic significance that a work has. Is the power a work has to engender a cultural self-understanding not in the final analysis a power to which the reality of culture attests? If following Paul Ricouer we recognize in this hermeneutics of culture the "detour of understanding [through]...cultural signs" (Ricouer 1981:158), then the representations in cultural works of a cultural reality is at the same time a self-representation mediated by the power of such works to unfold a world to which a people belongs—a world which however alien it initially might be for me, is a world in which I, too, might realize my ownmost possibilities and to which I, too, might ultimately belong.

In the light of this hermeneutics of culture, the non-representational character of music is no longer opposed to an interpretation of its cultural significance. On the contrary, if the occasion of the performance of a traditional rite or a cultural work has as its counterpart a representation that by raising everyday reality above itself affirms and enlarges a cultural self-understanding, one might be tempted to privilege music in a particular way. Privileging music on the basis of its affective significance however would in my opinion be misleading if it directs us away from the more fundamental relation between music's aesthetic efficacy and its mimetic power. *Mimesis*, Ricouer explains, "is a kind of metaphor of reality" (1981: 292). The metaphorical usage of a word, as we know, is one in which a literal sense is superseded by a figurative meaning. Hence the origin of the metaphorical effect "lies in a contextual action which places the semantic fields of several words in interaction" (ibid.:169). Metaphor, in other words, is a work in miniature, the meaning of which is formed in the interstices of the semantic clash it constructs. *Mimesis*, too, is a poetic activity that is productive of a meaning. In a way analogous to that of metaphor, the process of imitating reality in mimetic activity effects a transposition through the imaginative configurations of cultural works and works of art. Displaced from itself, reality appears higher than it is. The transformation that takes place, according to Gadamer, "is a transformation into the true" (Gadamer 1991: 112). Ricouer, too, recognizes in the mimetic process a poetic activity at work that "leads us to what is essential in reality" (Ricoeur 1981: 296). I would hasten to add that the efficacy of cultural works and traditional rites, in abolishing the everyday and raising the mundane above itself in a way in which the true essence at the heart of a cultural

self-understanding is illumined, attests to their mimetic power. The non-metamorphosed reality of the everyday is transformed and transfigured in a way that in the final analysis shatters the aesthetic pretense of a contemplative attitude and opens the path to an interpretation of the significance of cultural works for the reality of culture.

If *mimesis* brings to aesthetic presentation the meaningfulness of a reality raised above itself, then music, too, is a mimetic activity. In fact, I would say it is only as a *mimesis* of the temporal condition of human existence that music's aesthetic efficacy can be adequately understood. For music is a *mimesis* of the time in which the effort to exist is made meaningful in the light of the time of tradition and of the preservation of a way of life. In music, the cadencing of human existence gains a representation of what it means to live according to the time against which life itself is measured. If *mimesis* is a productive, creative activity that by making "human actions appear higher than they are in reality" (Ricouer 1981: 181) releases their meaning from the contingencies of everyday life, then by the same token the aesthetic experience that music effects supersedes the time of ordinary experience in the experience of the time of sacred events, of ritual performances, and of traditional rites.

Could we say that music is truly an *art* of time only insofar as it raises the time of everyday life to a higher order? If we are prepared to recognize in the transformative power of cultural works the *mimesis* of reality, we should also be prepared to recognize in the playing of music a metamorphosis of the temporal ordering of experience into the time of the true, in which the power of music to shape a cultural self-understanding reveals a temporal imago of a world in the making.

The cultural self-understanding of a people is also such a world in the making, the aesthetic imago of which can be represented as the artful play of time. All traditions, if they are living traditions, are lived by someone. All cultural self-understandings are already interpretations in front of those cultural works that preserve the signs of our efforts to exist. If music can be privileged in any way, it is because the power of the musical work to unfold a world in front of itself bears an uncanny resemblance to the temporalizing of all human experience. Its own mode of presentation raises the order of time above itself, as if by forming a temporal whole it gives shape to the reality of a cultural experience of time. Traditional musical structures attest to this narrative quality. Even anti-narrativist strategies evidenced by postmodern minimalist works configure time, albeit in a way that puts its temporal character radically into question. In fact the "eternity experience" attributed to repetitive music is in my opinion the structuring of a possible limit experience that owes its semblance of ecstasy to an aestheticizing deontology of sempiternal presence.[4] Other musics that employ repetitive patternings undoubtedly structure "eternity experiences" the cultural significances of which are markedly different. However profitable this line of inquiry might be, it is not my intention to pursue it here. Yet the possibility of a musical work disclosing a limit experience that founds a cultural self-understanding and that transcends the time of everyday life is fundamental to an understanding of its mimetic power. For ultimately it is the sounding in music of a call to a different understanding and to a more authentic experience of the time of being itself that in the end sets this *art of time* apart.

Let us be clear on this point: a more authentic experience is not one in which the listener is transposed into an original situation, as is sometimes attempted in cultural reconstruction or in the reconstruction of historical performance practices and period instruments. On the contrary, I understand the authenticity of an experience to be inseparable from the transformative power and the mimetic action of cultural works and works of art. Ernst Bloch has suggested that music is an aesthetic analogue of the dialectic of morality (see Bloch 1986 vol. 3:1015–1016; 1080). As the aesthetic imago of a *poiesis a se*, the temporalizing

dynamic that in music structures an immanently unfolding totality has as its analogical counterpart the concretizing mediation through human work of a cultural and social reality. Bloch tells us that as a forming of expression, music aims at the *"shaping of a...call"* (Bloch 1986 vol. 3:1067), which has as its proper counterpart the dynamic of hope. Far from a contemplative object in which the play of forms elicits the sensation of beauty, music is the aesthetic figure of a productive mediation that in its aesthetic self-presentation is the *mimesis* of the time of human experience.

But all cultural realities have their time. Culture itself is the mediation that invests a way of being in the world with meaning. If in music the shaping of a call has as its counterpart the experience of culture itself, it is because in music, as in culture, the call to a way of life is inseparable from the future that addresses us and the past we are called to remember. Is this hermeneutics of hearing not fundamental both to the aesthetic experience of music and to the experience of cultural life as a living reality? Is hearing music as an expression of the wellspring of cultural existence not also the sounding of a call to a way of being in which one's ownmost possibility is linked to that of the community to which one belongs? And does the aesthetic response to a work of music not have an ethical complement in the common reality for which culture frees us?

With these questions, we are led to consider the significance of a cultural self-understanding in the light of the imagination which animates it.

The cultural imagination as productive mediation

To the extent that the significance of music is inseparable from the call to a uniquely individuated way of life, its mimetic power and its meaning as a cultural phenomenon intertwine. Hearing music as an expression of the wellspring of one's cultural existence and as a call to a way of life, as we have said, undercuts the pretense of an aesthetic attitude that embraces cultural works as the objectification of an essential truth. In the light of this hermeneutics of culture, we can acknowledge that the reality of culture itself is charged with possibilities that give its horizonal structure its true significance that its works hold in readiness. If we recognize in the power of music to shape a temporal imago of a world in the making a *mimesis* of the time in which our ownmost possibilities shows itself, then we should admit that the reality of cultural life too, if it is a living reality, is as much a reality of as yet undecided possibilities as it is a present way of living that preserves an inherited and cherished past.

Is the reality of a cultural way of life, in other words, not as much distinguished by the possibilities it holds out as it is by the preservation of a heritage and a tradition? Yet if in this interplay of preservation and possibility culture mediates itself to itself as a tradition, what, in effect, constitutes the mediations that lie at the heart of its ownmost reality?

The constitution of a cultural and social realm in which practices are instituted and in which a way of life is meaningfully constructed can be the methodological focus for cultural research. Yet insofar as the cultural reality that gives meaning to a way of life is its object, such research is faced with a difficult but in my opinion not insurmountable problematic. If the object of cultural inquiry ultimately is directed toward discerning the innervating force that animates the life of culture, then the task ultimately is one of identifying what is at work at the heart of a cultural self-understanding. In other words, the task is one of discerning in the lineaments of a received tradition the efficacy of the cultural imagination at work in cultural works.

The notion that the cultural imagination is at work in configuring a cultural identity forms a counterpart to my thesis that music is a *mimesis* of the temporal condition of human existence. If through its mimetic power music raises the order of time in which life is lived above itself, the cultural imagination is at work in the processes through which the self-representation of a people as a distinctive and individual group is formed. This self-representation undoubtedly has a certain methodological priority. It is only because a cultural group has first identified itself in terms of the way of life that founds it that a methodologically specific mode of cultural inquiry is possible. Yet the more cultural inquiry attempts to positively identify its object and to hold it firmly in place, the more the effective action of the cultural imaginary at the heart of a way of life eludes it.

Just as the way of life to which the reality of a culture attests is no less temporally charged than is the aesthetic phenomenality of music, the question of cultural identity is more productively situated in the light of the problematic that its temporal constitution introduces. Displacing the question of music's representational status onto its properly ontological plane therefore has a counterpart in a critical consideration of the temporal character of the phenomenon of culture. The identity of a culture is on the one hand bound to its self-representation in signs and works. Yet this self-representation on the other hand already belongs to the creation, transmission, and preservation of values, practices, and meanings. Tradition, says Gadamer, is "essentially preservation...active in all historical change" (Gadamer 1991: 281). It is, he tells us, the ground of the validity of the values and practices the authority of which is recognized by those for whom the tradition holds true. Tradition, in other words, is the primary phenomenon in which sedimented practices and cultural values also hold the promise of the continuing meaning and relevance of a way of life. Is the heritage that culture bequeaths and the reality to which it continues to attest not a living legacy at the heart of a people's identity? And is this identity not also a prospective one that is reshaped and refashioned in the retelling of narratives, the reenactment of ritual performances and the preservation of significant cultural works? Could we not therefore say that tradition is this living dialectic between the reality of culture and the forming of its identity?

In view of this living dialectic, cultural identity

is not so much a permanent construct as it is a quest. The tradition or traditions to which we belong orient us toward values and practices, grounding our experiences in a meaningful way by mediating the contingencies of time and place to which all human *being* is subject. Just as the aesthetic efficacy of the musical work gains its significance in the *mimesis* of the temporal action of our effort to exist, so tradition has its meaning in a history the effects of which are inscribed in the life of a culture. Gadamer's insight that "we are always situated within traditions" (1991:282) also recognizes that the historicality of our tradition-dependent experiences is at the same time the condition of possibility for an experience that is open to new horizons. The failure to recognize in the phenomenon of culture the radically temporal root of this living dialectic is perhaps due as much to a lack of reflection as it is attributable to an objectifying attitude. It is ironic that the same attitude of cultural self-effacement in the interest of an unimpeded and ostensibly more authentic reading of culture both binds us all the more securely to the Enlightenment prejudice against prejudice and also blinds us to the fundamentally horizonal structure of the experience to which all cultural realities attest. Culture, we could say, is the primary phenomenon in which the symbolic power of signs and works is both sedimented in the creation of a meaningful way of life and opens onto a horizon that is the true mark of the vitality of cultural life.

It might be objected that since reality is always already a construction of significative relations, a semiotics of culture fully does justice to its symbolic character. It would be difficult not to recognize in language and cultural works the social constitution of their symbolic significance. Semiological analyses stemming from the work of Ferdinand de Saussure and following in the structuralist tradition of Claude Lévi-Strauss evidence the fundamentally social dimension of the systems they explicate. Moreover, the model of semiological explanation is not one that is borrowed from the domain of the natural sciences but is one that is derived from the phenomenon of language itself and applied to social institutions, practices and cultural works. Yet if the symbolic function of such institutions, practices and works is the very foundation of social life, then should we not also say, following Ricouer, that "social reality [too] is fundamentally symbolic" (1981:219), that is, that the reality to which our social and cultural ways of life attest is always already mediated symbolically by the signs of our effort to exist?

The power of the symbol is nowhere more forcefully evidenced than in this mediation of reality. All symbolic systems, Ricouer tells us, "have a cognitive value: they make reality appear in such and such a way" (1981:293). Unlike the instrumental value accorded objectifying knowledge in which we gain a power over things, the value that symbolism confers is that of bringing before us a reality in which we participate and to which we first belong. The power of symbols to assimilate us "to that which is symbolized without our being able to master the similitude intellectually" (Ricoeur 1967:16) means that reality itself, because it is always already mediated by works and signs, is an interpretation. Our attempts to orient ourselves meaningfully in circumstances we did not create precedes any objectification of the symbolic networks that we employ and that first encompass us. Whatever force a semiotic explanation of the symbolic networks of a culture might have, it is derivative of the initial readability of the symbolism through which a culture understands itself.[5] Moreover, we too understand only because we encounter in the symbol a meaning which might otherwise remain hidden. Gadamer tells us that "the distinctive mark of the language of art is that the individual work gathers into itself and expresses the symbolic character that, hermeneutically regarded, belongs to all beings" (1976:104). Recalling the fundamentally ontological significance of the *work* of art, we might add that the cognitive value of symbolic systems has as its primordial counterpart an interpretation where the meaningfulness of a cultural way of existing is concretized as a unique and particular reality.

How is the reality of culture concretized? How, in the light of its symbolic constitution, is culture a living reality? I would say that insofar as culture is the primary phenomenon in which a meaningful way of life shows itself, the reality of culture is the concrete counterpart in which the productive operations of the cultural imaginary can be read. Like the analogical relation that cannot be seen directly but is nevertheless graspable in the lineaments of its symbolism, the cultural imagination is only discernable in terms of the mediations it effects. It is only disclosed, in other words, in the mimetic activity/predicative activity of the cultural imaginary through those works and signs by virtue of which the identity of a people gains a cultural self-representation. Imagination, according to Ricouer, is a "predicative assimilation" (Ricoeur 1991A: 173) that in a sudden insight grasps the pertinence of a new semantic attribution. Following a tensive theory that recognizes in metaphor the emergence of a new meaning, Ricouer argues that imagination is at work in the operation of grasping the predicative pertinence that answers to the "initial semantic shock" (ibid.) structured by the figure of the metaphor. Just as the meaning of a novel metaphor is not drawn from anywhere, but is an imaginative resolution to the logical absurdity that the metaphorical word introduces, the work of imagination, Ricouer tells us, "gives an image to an emerging meaning" (ibid.) which refigures the entire semantic field to which it applies.

It would seem that the cultural imaginary works in an analogous way. If it is true that the meaning of a way of life is represented in cultural works, practices, rites, and rituals, it is also true that this meaning is animated for those for whom the symbolic significance of such works, practices, rites, and rituals is culturally charged. Yet the cultural charge itself is evidenced only indirectly, in the reality of a tradition in which the mimetic activity of the cultural imaginary is at work. Henceforth, we could say that it is through the work of the cultural imagination that the identity at the heart of a culture is represented. The reality of culture itself is the imaginative attribution through cultural signs and works of a meaningful way of existing. Ricouer tells us that the aporias and ambiguities which condition and constrain existence "are constitutive of the very *phenomenon* of imagination" (1991A: 169). At the level at which the cultural imagination is at work in preserving and creating values through cultural works, culture provides an answer to questions of being human through the imaginative attribution of a way of existing that is meaningful in the light of the aporias and perplexities to which the works of culture respond.

Imagination, on this reading, is always already a productive mediation. The predicative attribution that in the metaphorical usage of a word marks the emergence of a new meaning and which has its origin in the imaginative assimilation of conflicting semantic fields has its counterpart in the effective action of the cultural imaginary. Is the reply of culture to the aporias and perplexities of existence any less a productive mediation than that effected by the work of metaphor? Clifford Geertz claims that reflecting upon the fundamentally symbolic constitution of social action plunges us into the midst of those existential dilemmas that are at the heart of culture (Geertz 1973: 30). If we recognize in this understanding of the poetic imagination an efficacy at the heart of culture, we should also recognize in the phenomenon of tradition the production of a meaning to which a cultural self-representation in signs and works attests. If in the end the identity of a culture cannot be equated with its objects, it is because cultural identity does not exist apart from the efficacy of the cultural imaginary at work in the creation and preservation of a way of life.

To my way of thinking, the reality of culture is the material counterpart—or better, the concretized ethos—of the cultural imaginary at work. The paradox that this theory of the cultural imagination presents is theoretically insurmountable. It is as if the cultural imagination is sealed so that the work of the cultural imaginary can only be discerned in the lineaments of those productive mediations which we recognize in the creation, transmission, and preservation of values and meanings. In the light of this paradox, any attempt to identify the cultural imagination other than through the detour of the dialectic of tradition is in vain. There is henceforth no need, as Ricouer tells us "to search, under the title of 'sphere of belonging', for some sort of brute experience which would be preserved at the heart of my experience of culture, but rather for an antecedent which is never given in itself" (Ricoeur 1981:127). Every experience of culture, in short, is always already a mediated one. Hence "in spite of its intuitive kernel, this experience remains an interpretation" (ibid.:127–128).

If the true antecedent at the heart of a culture is a sealed core, I would venture to say that it is the *work* of the cultural imagination that by giving body, shape, and form to a culture's mytho-poetic core constitutes a cultural self-representation. Cultural self-understanding, on this reading, is ultimately a self-representation that follows the detour of understanding in front of cultural signs and works. It is only by virtue of this detour that culture mediates itself to itself. As a living reality, culture has both a history and a horizon along which its ownmost possibilities can by played out. This reality is the reality of the open space between a fully integrated self-understanding and a utopian imago that places such an ideological representation of the identity of people into question.[6] In this cultural space, in which cherished values are handed down and preserved for the sake of those not yet born, the antecedent that is never given in itself becomes visible through the mediations that the cultural imaginary effects. In the final analysis, the identity of a culture as it is lived can never be grasped completely. To the extent that the identity of a people is an imaginative questioning of and response to an antecedent which is never given in itself, it is as much a prospective response that answers to the question of what it means to be a people as it is an inherited reply. However much

the cultural identity and the destiny of a people are bound together, identity and destiny are never the same. Cultural identity, that elusive object of ethnological inquiry, is the work of an imagination that can only be traced in the lineaments of tradition and in the signs of the reality that attests to it.

Music as the work of the cultural imagination

As a quasi-text in which the lineaments and traces of the cultural imaginary can be read, tradition can serve as the object of a methodologically specific mode of inquiry. Yet cultural reality, as I have argued, is no mere datum but is instead the work of a poetic imagination. Cultural identity is itself only realized through the mimetic operation by virtue of which a prospective reality becomes a present one. In the final analysis, the experience of belonging in its strongest sense surpasses all attempts to bring that which is at the heart of a tradition or a cultural way of life fully in front of us. The fundamental condition to which this hermeneutics of tradition attests is one to which the mimetic power of music also replies. Does music's power to represent a meaning not have an analogue in the mediating activity of the cultural imaginary? And does the mimetic representation in music of a temporal imago of a world in the making not have as a possible counterpart the power of the cultural imaginary to transfigure the history of a people in the light of their ownmost possibilities?

The mimetic configuration which in the work of music raises the time of the everyday above itself, in my opinion, answers to the perplexities and aporias to which all authentic cultural works reply. Why would we attribute a cultural significance to the musics of the world if we have not acknowledged that the self-representations to which they contribute are interpretations effected through the detour of cultural signs and works? And why would we seek to understand music as a cultural phenomenon if we have not already recognized in its aesthetic efficacy the power to enlarge our own self-understandings through new and different experiences?

Is it not because we recognize in the phenomenon of music an aesthetic mediation of the condition to which all human existence is subject, a condition to which the cultural imaginary also replies?

The aesthetic phenomenality of music and the reality of culture have their most fundamental significance in the replies they give to the aporias and perplexities that raise problems of the meaningfulness of human existence even to the point of putting it radically into question. As a *mimesis* of the time in which our effort to exist is made more meaningful through a work which is specifically human, music has as its counterpart the efficacy of the cultural imaginary. If music is on the one hand an aesthetic figure in which the time of human existence is mimetically represented, the reality of culture on the other hand is inseparable from the concretizing *work* of the cultural imagination. Could we not say, therefore, that music as a cultural work bears a resemblance to the *work* of the cultural imagination? And is the aesthetic figuration of a temporal cadencing in music not related iconically to the structuring of reality itself? Ricouer asks us whether the iconic element in figurative presentation is "so alien to semantic considerations" (1991B:82) that we cannot recognize in mimetic representation the iconic augmentation of reality (see Ricoeur 1981: 292). We would have to say, then, that the *mimesis* in music of a temporal cadencing effects an increase in being that by making the time of human existence appear in a way that is higher than it is augments the experience of time by augmenting the time of experience iconically.

In view of this temporally iconic augmentation, perhaps music, because it is a *mimesis* of the time of being, has a privileged place in cultural life. As an art of time, music is the aesthetic imago of a *poiesis a se* that in reality is the concretizing work of the cultural imaginary. The self-actualization of a people through their self-representation in cultural works and traditional practices converges with such a poetics of the cultural imaginary.

Could we not say that in its most radical sense, the musical *poiesis a se* is a temporal icon of the realization of a cultural self-representation beyond the hegemony of an instrumental world? The freedom of culture would then be the freedom of a people to determine their own destiny in the light of their ownmost possibilities that their uniquely individuated way of life holds out.

Yet no cultural work in modern society, and few if any works in cultures which have experienced the effects of modernization, I would venture to say, are entirely free of the pathological dissimulation that has become an instrumental force of its technological spirit. The coercive power and hegemonic distortion of ideology, in short, is a part of the reality in which we live. In the service of its purposive function, the culture industry, whose basic principle Adorno identifies as the "affirmation of life as it is" (Adorno 1989: 37),[7] perhaps poses the greatest and most formidable threat to the immanent life of traditional musics in a contemporary world. Yet the threat of the rational administration of culture, while it is exercised in the reification and expropriation of cultural works and practices, is directed foremost against the uncoerced formation of cultural identities and the possibilities that they hold out. As the hegemonic function of the culture industry advances in accordance with its own instrumental purposiveness, it subverts the work of the cultural imaginary. By projecting a phantasmic imago in which the seemingly perfected illusion of reality as it seals off the perplexities and aporias of our existential condition, aporias and perplexities to which the cultural imaginary replies, the culture industry reifies the order of power that it at the same time enforces. Through its instrumentally purposive rationality, the culture industry forecloses the horizonal structure in which the reality of the future is one of as yet undecided possibilities, a horizonal structure to which every living culture and tradition attests. Its coercive reconciliation of the present with reality as it is services its most anti-utopian function. In its most insidious guise, the technology of the culture industry is directed ultimately against the cultural imagination itself, co-opting the very moment in which cultural identity is at the same time an open question concerning the ownmost possibilities of a people in the light of their unique heritage and their aspirations, a question to which only the cultural imaginary can authentically respond.

Yet if the pervasive reach of the culture industry touches on virtually all cultural works, works of culture transcend the hegemonic purposes of the culture industry. Music, Bloch tells us, "belongs extensively to the insistent disquiet and dawning possibility which are lodged in reality" (Bloch 1985: 219; cf. Bloch 1986 vol. 3: 1080). However much the culture industry seeks to extinguish the productive force of the cultural imaginary, the emerging possibility that in reality cultural works subvert its instrumentally reified vision is reason for hope. Apart from the cultural imaginary in which the self-representation of a meaningful way of life attains the stature of a cultural imago, the reality of culture is sheer phantasm. Yet not the hypostatizing image of an instrumentally purposive life world, but the imaginations of culturally specific peoples, holds open the utopian possibility of freedom in the light of the present reality. If on the one hand the dialectic of morality can be expressed in terms of the cultural self-realization of a people, the horizons in which all cultural realities stand on the other hand are also horizons along which cultures meet. No one can presume to dictate the course along which the many cultures that confront one another in our modern urban environment merge, clash, and diverge. On the contrary, the acknowledgment that today we live in a pluralistic world of interstices and disjunctions in its most profound sense can only be an acknowledgment of the fundamental condition to which we are all subject.

NOTES

1. The displacement of aesthetics from its traditionally contemplative standpoint toward an understanding of the efficacy of the work counterpoints this shift in focus from an object to be apprehended in an attitude of aesthetic disinterest toward a work to be interpreted in the light of the possibilities it offers. The world of the work is a world that by putting ordinary references into suspense gains a productive reference by redescribing reality. Hence the world unfolded in front of the work is a world which I could appropriate as my ownmost possibility.

2. The hermeneutical insight that the autonomy of the art work, or the text, is attributable to a productive distanciation from its originary horizon is no lesser an insight into the way that cultural works escape their original context. The recontextualization of such works in new cultural situations, in fact, is itself an instance of the fusion of cultural horizons through which a new cultural self-understanding is enriched by a cultural work which was initially alien.

3. The distanciation of the real from itself is not the least significant distanciation effected by the art work. By opening a space in which reality as it is understood is put into question, the work offers a different reading of reality itself. This reading has as its counterpart the dialectic of disappropriation and the appropriation of a new understanding in front of the work. For a further discussion of the hermeneutical function of distanciation, see Paul Ricouer's essay in *Hermeneutics and the Human Sciences*.

4. This aesthetics is evidenced in postmodern repetitive music where the compositional process is one of patterned displacement of repeating motifs. This structure of repetition levels any sense of a temporally unfolding whole by paradoxically raising the sense of time it configures to that of a quasi-eternal present. This time of sempiternal presence has as its correlate a process of aestheticization in which the deontological "play of difference" takes the place of the representation of a temporally unfolding whole.

5. Clifford Geertz, who espouses a semiotic concept of culture, recognizes the primacy of this symbolic mediation of reality. In his discussion of the Balinese cockfight, he argues that the symbolic significance of this cultural practice surpasses its literal one in that the "cockfight renders ordinary, everyday experience comprehensible by presenting it in terms of acts and objects....where their meaning can be more powerfully articulated and more exactly preserved" (Geertz 1973:443).

6.   The problem of ideology is universal to the same
      extent as is the crisis of modernization and industrial-
      ization. Ideology, however, has an integrative func-
      tion which is more primordial than its distortive one.
      Inasmuch as utopia is ideology's counterpart, the
      utopian imago of an ideal cultural self-representation
      counterpoints this integrative function. In this sense,
      every cultural self-understanding is animated by the
      play between an ideological self-representation which
      in its most pathological guise tends toward the
      reification of existing structures of power and the
      subversive force of alternative utopian visions. (See
      Ricoeur 1991A:169 ff; see also Geertz 1967. For a
      fuller discussion of the phenomena of ideology and
      utopia, see Ricoeur 1986.)

7.   For a fuller discussion of the culture industry, see
      Adorno's essays on the culture industry and mass
      culture in *The Culture Industry* (ed. J.M. Bernstein.
      London: Routledge, 1991). The essay "The Culture
      Industry: Enlightenment as Mass Deception" in *Dia-
      lectic of Enlightenment*, written with Max Horkheimer,
      provides a seminal discussion of the role and function
      of the culture industry in the context of the dialectic of
      Enlightenment (Adorno and Horkheimer, *Dialectic
      of Enlightenment*, trans. John Cumming. New York:
      Continuum, 1972).

1976   *Philosophical Hermeneutics*. Translated by
        David E. Linge. Berkeley: University of
        California Press.

Geertz, Clifford.
1973   *The Interpretation of Cultures*. New York:
        Basic Books.

Ricouer, Paul.
1991A   *From Text to Action*. Translated by Kathleen
        Blamey and John B. Thompson. Evantson:
        Northwestern University Press.
1991B   *A Ricouer Reader. Reflection and Imagina-
        tion*. Edited by Mario J. Valdés. Toronto:
        University of Toronto Press.
1986   *Lectures on Ideology and Utopia*. Edited by
        George H. Taylor. New York: Columbia
        University Press.
1981   *Hermeneutics and the Human Sciences*. Trans-
        lated by John B. Thompson. New York: Cam-
        bridge University Press.

REFERENCES CITED

Adorno, Theodor W.
1991   *The Culture Industry*. London: Routledge.
1989   *Introduction to the Sociology of Music*.
        Translated by E.B. Ashton. New York: Con-
        tinuum.

Adorno, Theodor W. and Max Horkheimer
1972   *Dialectic of Enlightenment*. Translated by
        John Cumming. London: Continuum.

Bloch, Ernst.
1986   *The Principle of Hope*. 3 vols. Translated by
        Neville Plaice, Stephen Plaice, Paul Knight.
        Oxford: Basil Blackwell.
1985   *Essays on the Philosophy of Music*. Translated
        by Peter Palmer. Cambridge: Cambridge
        University Press.

Gadamer, Hans-Georg.
1991   *Truth and Method*. 2nd revised ed. Translated
        by Joel Weinsheimer and Donald G. Marshall.
        New York: Crossroads.

INTERPRETING METAPHORS: CROSS-CULTURAL AESTHETICS AS HERMENEUTIC PROJECT

Angeles Sancho-Velázquez

THE TOPIC "MUSICAL Aesthetics in Los Angeles" offers an excellent opportunity to raise a timely question: Is an aesthetic approach suitable to address cross-cultural musical phenomena? For some time, scholars have expressed the difficulty (McAllester 1954) or the total inadequacy (Merriam 1966) of using aesthetic concepts in ethnomusicological research. Others have argued that the universality of systematic philosophies of music (Marshall 1982) or the existence of a universal basic musical grammar (Lerdhal and Jackendoff 1983) support the possibility of cross-cultural aesthetics.

In this paper I will argue that cross-cultural aesthetics is indeed possible. This claim will, however, not be made from an epistemological position (like the projects based on the search for universals), but from an ontological one. Simply stated, ontology gives priority to ways of being in the world, while epistemology prioritizes ways of knowing. To adopt an ontological approach means, in short, to assert that knowing is always derivative of a mode of being.[1] The considerations exposed in the following pages are drawn for the most part from the philosophies of Hans-Georg Gadamer and Paul Ricoeur, whose hermeneutic works are built upon such an ontological understanding. They also owe much to the ideas of Roger Savage, whose work in music criticism and aesthetics also belongs to this hermeneutic tradition.

The purpose of this paper is twofold: first, to argue that the supposed incompatibility between ethnomusicology and aesthetics is the result of the narrow views of how both disciplines are to be defined. Secondly, to suggest that Paul Ricoeur's philosophy in general, and his thoughts on the creative process in particular, provide an appropriate theoretical framework for developing a new aesthetic theory. This aesthetic theory could, I believe, meet the challenges of cross-cultural research and of contemporary reflection on art in general.

I will proceed as follows: in the first part of this paper I will critically comment on those concepts of traditional Western aesthetics that have been found inappropriate for cross-cultural research. I have chosen Alan Merriam's discussion on Western aesthetics in relation to ethnomusicology as a connecting reference for this first section. Merriam's account of the incompatibility between Western aesthetic concepts and ethnomusicological research in his *Anthropology of Music* is, to my knowledge, the most comprehensive statement of this idea in a major ethnomusicological work. Furthermore, because of the great impact Merriam's approach has had on the field of ethnomusicology, his discussion on aesthetics calls for continued discussion. Analysis of his account will allow us not only to take some critical distance with respect to traditional aesthetics but to also consider critically the perspective on aesthetics represented by Merriam's anthropological orientation. In the second part of this paper I will consider some aspects of Ricoeur's philosophical work and suggest that their elaboration in relation to aesthetics could provide answers to the problems exposed in the first section.

TRADITIONAL AESTHETICS AND CROSS-CULTURAL RESEARCH

In the chapter dedicated to aesthetics in *The Anthropology of Music,* Merriam delineates what he calls "six factors" which comprise the "total Western concept of the aesthetic." The factors analyzed by Merriam as consubstantial to the Western aesthetics are: psychic distance, manipulation of form, decontextualization, concept of beauty, purposiveness, and presence of a philosophy. Merriam comments on these six aspects and compares them with his own ethnomusicological findings drawn from research on the Congo Basongye and the Flathead Indians. After showing the non-applicability of these so-called fundamentals of Western aesthetics to these music cultures, Merriam concludes that Western aesthetics cannot be used cross-culturally.

Merriam's assessment that the factors discussed are not applicable for cross-cultural research is, in my view, incontestable. The problematic aspect of his argument lies in what is implicitly inferred from this inapplicability, namely that cross-cultural aesthetics is a self-contradictory term. How can this inference be critically challenged? I would suggest, first of all, that the concept of Western aesthetics discussed by Merriam is bound to specific theoretical frameworks which are only a part—not the whole—of the Western tradition. Secondly, I would suggest that the problems Merriam has with cross-cultural aesthetics stem from the underlying assumption of his anthropological approach that cross-cultural studies cannot be anything but a strictly scientific enterprise. In what follows I attempt to explicate these suggestions more fully beginning with a discussion of each of the six factors mentioned by Merriam.

Psychic distance

The first characteristic factor of Western aesthetics proposed by Merriam is *psychic or psychical distance.* He describes this as "detachment and isolation...What is meant is the ability of the person interested in music to remove himself from it, to hold it at arm's length as it were, and to examine it for what it is" (Merriam 1964:261). Merriam, however, does not situate this notion historically. The origin of the concept of aesthetic distance is found in Kantian philosophy. For Kant, the fundamental characteristic of the work of art was its beauty, and its main purpose was to be pleasing. Accordingly, an aesthetic experience was one of detached enjoyment of art's beauty. In Kant's words, the aesthetic attitude should be "disinterested and free, since we are not compelled to give our approval by any interest, whether of sense or of reason" (Kant [1790] 1987:52).

Merriam convincingly argues that this detached attitude is not universal, and cites the examples of the Basongye and the Flathead for whom the experience of music is always integrated into a cultural context. From this Merriam concludes, "if psychic distance can be accepted as one of the factors in the Western aesthetic, neither the Basongye nor the Flathead hold aesthetic attitudes in this respect" (1964:263). But following this line of reasoning it could also be said that the original audiences of Bach's religious music did not have aesthetic experiences, since for them the main purpose of this music was to induce or reinforce a profound spiritual state. Likewise, as Merriam acknowledges, Western folk and popular musics (which, incidentally, in so many instances have inspired Western "art" music) should also be left out of the aesthetic sphere, since they are seen as closely connected to their cultural contexts.

Another example would be much of Western "art music" written in the first decades of the twentieth century and later. As Theodor Adorno (1949, 1962) has shown, the shock value of the works written by Arnold Schoenberg, and others influenced by him, was central to their aesthetics. The concept of aesthetic value employed in Adorno's analysis radically departs from an attitude of serene, detached contemplation.

We are left, then, with approximately a century and a half of European art music to which this concept of "detached" aesthetics seems to apply. But does it? I, for one, find it hard to believe that involved listeners of Beethoven's sonatas, Verdi's operas, or Wagner's music dramas had, or now have, an attitude defined by "psychic distance." The problem here concerns the inadequacy of certain theoretical constructs to deal with what has been called "the aesthetic."

The marked separation between conceptual knowledge, aesthetic experience, and ethical concerns in Western philosophy since the Enlightenment seems to be more the result of theoretical constraints than a direct reflection of how people of any particular culture actually think about, create, and experience art. As will be shown later, Paul Ricoeur, in his reflections on creativity, seeks to overcome this separation between conceptual and aesthetic knowledge. All questions relative to psychic detachment in aesthetics appear utterly obsolete in light of Ricoeur's insights.

Manipulation of form

The second of Merriam's factors is *the manipulation of form for its own sake*. He writes that for the Flatheads and Basongye music is given to them by superhuman beings in a kind of "unconscious" process, while the Western composer "sits to his task, deliberately selects aspects of music structure which serve his purpose, and strives to compose something which is a recombination of elements of form" (1964:264). This description does, perhaps, apply to some developments in Western "art" music. However, to generalize this notion of Western compositional processes is to accept the narrow view characteristic of traditional formalist approaches.

It is noteworthy that in his assessment of the creative process of the Western composer, Merriam himself echoes the aesthetic approach he is criticizing. He talks of what the Western musician "does," when the thrust of his argument depends on a *specific conceptualization* of what the composer does. The notion Merriam has of Western musical composition is rooted in the formalistic musicological tradition which has treated stylistic innovation as a mere manipulation of musical form. This tradition disregards the cultural and social contexts within which the Western composer—inevitably—writes his or her music. It also disregards the non-rational, and not totally conscious, elements which form part of the process of artistic creation. Interestingly, Merriam fails to look at the Western composer with the eyes of an ethnomusicologist. Instead of this, his reflections on Western compositional processes are acritically made with the conceptual tools and assumptions of the traditional aesthetics he intends to critique.

Decontextualization

The third factor of Western aesthetics Merriam discusses is *the attribution of emotion-producing qualities to music conceived strictly as sound*. This factor is related to the traditional notion that musical sound alone has the capacity to stir emotions, abstracted from any context and free from any referential value. This notion, Merriam tells us, is also found among the Basongye who affirm that musical sound itself can induce emotions. But for Merriam an important difference is that "while in Western society we can state flatly that a minor mode or a particular key induces emotion, it seems doubtful that the Basongye can since for them 'a piece of music always has a set of social and cultural associations which automatically go with it'" (1964:265).

The concept that a key or a mode have by themselves the capability of stirring emotions is, once again, a concept with roots in the eighteenth century. Enlightenment thinkers considered classical music as a *lingua franca,* a universal language that any rational being could understand. There also existed a "doctrine of affections," which established fixed relationships between musical formulae and specific emotions. This musical language was supposedly capable of communication as clear as that of any spoken language. Aesthetic theories developed through the nineteenth century abandoned this "doctrine of affections" but, by failing to acknowledge the culturally relative value of Western art, they preserved the basic assumption which attributed universal value to a music.

The introduction of semiotic analyses in musicology has been instrumental in showing that Western art music is as culturally dependent as any non-Western or popular musical tradition. Furthermore, it has recently been argued that the claims of universality and abstractness in Western art music conceal various forms of domination (Attali 1985, Shepherd 1991, McClary 1991). Within contemporary philosophy, hermeneutics has provided a platform for the critique of any claims of universality by considering that works— as well as the interpreters of their meaning—are always historically situated and dependent on tradition.

Beauty

Merriam's fourth factor is the category of *beauty*. He states: "The concept of beauty as applicable to the art product or process is an integral part of the Western aesthetic. Beauty is irrevocably tied up with art" (1964:266). In contrast, Merriam tells us, neither the Basongye nor the Flathead Indians employ concepts in their definitions of music that might be translated as "beauty" in the Western sense.

In the West, beauty in art has been considered an abstract, self-contained value only since the Enlightenment period. The lack of clear-cut boundaries between the categories of beauty and practical aspects of life found by Merriam and other ethnomusicologists in the musical cultures they study was also characteristic of European culture in the Middle Ages. In his historical account of the relation between art and ethics, B. R. Tilghman writes:

> It is characteristic of more modern times to put asunder what in earlier ages was united, and by the eighteenth century the idea of beauty had begun to be restricted pretty much to the sensuous appearance of things so that the notion was eventually totally absorbed into what later philosophers called the aesthetic and lost altogether its connection with utility. (Tilghman 1991:23)

If beauty was considered an independent and fundamental artistic value in the eighteenth century, this notion has been abandoned by major Western composers and musical critics since the beginning of the twentieth century. Arnold Schoenberg, for example, declared a preference for good craftsmanship to the former metaphysics of beauty,[2] while Theodor Adorno elaborated his aesthetic theory on the basis that art has no aesthetic value if it is not socially significant (Adorno 1962).

In sum, the category of beauty has not been consistently linked to the Western concept of the aesthetic. At the same time, it is quite possible that the idea that many non-Western musical cultures lack a concept of the beautiful is not completely accurate. This notion may be due to the absence of an equivalent in some cultures of this eighteenth- and nineteenth-century Western concept of the beautiful or, as Jean-Jacques Nattiez suggests, to the influence on ethnomusicologists of narrowly functionalist currents in anthropology (Nattiez 1990:105).

Purposiveness

As a fifth factor involved in Western aesthetics Merriam cites the *purposeful intent to create something aesthetic*. This is explained as follows:

> The Western artist sets out with the deliberate intention of creating an object or sound which will be aesthetically admired by those who view or hear it, and this

element of conscious striving reemphasizes the abstractibility of art from its cultural context. (Merriam 1964:268)

Merriam goes on to comment on the slight emphasis the Basongye place on compositional processes. Their emphasis is on collective activities, such as listening to music, rather than on an individual activity like music composition. He concludes that neither the Basongye nor the Flathead seem to have "a pattern of purposeful intent to create something aesthetic" (1964:269).

I will distinguish two aspects involved in this interpretation. First, the assertion that the Western artist creates in order to be aesthetically admired confuses the actual creative process of the artist with the explanation of creativity given by traditional Western aesthetics. The notion that the creation of music is due to the artist's wish to be admired aesthetically is, on the side of production, the counterpart of the notion of art as merely pleasing on the side of the reception. In this sense, the basic critiques of this factor have already been addressed in relation to the first four points discussed above.

A second aspect concerns the topic of authorial intention. This has been a topic of considerable debate in recent decades, and still remains so in aesthetics and art criticism circles. The importance of authorial intention for art criticism was central to nineteenth-century Romantic aesthetic approaches. In an attempt to reach objectivity without using positivist methodology, Romantic authors like Wilhelm Dilthey substituted formal analyses of the work with psychological explanations of its author. The emphasis on biographical accounts and on reconstructions of what the author meant were supposed to free theories of art from both the narrowness of formal analyses and the looseness of subjective interpretations. Gadamer and Ricoeur have shown the fallacy involved in this Romantic approach, and have pointed out that the link between author and work is much more distended and complicated than psychological accounts suggest

(Gadamer 1976, 1986; Ricoeur 1981). From a hermeneutic perspective, therefore, even if the purpose of some Western or non-Western "composers" was to be aesthetically admired, this would not substantially affect the critical evaluation of their works.

Philosophy

The sixth and final of Merriam's Western aesthetic factors is the *presence of a philosophy of an aesthetic*. He bases his argument on a demonstration that, unlike in Western culture, the Basongye and Flathead do not have an aesthetic philosophy. Merriam explicates this pointing out that the Western aesthetic is primarily verbal, and by referring to the "verbal jungle" which "has grown up around the aesthetic." Later, he states that "what distinguishes the Western ideas and ideals of form and beauty is a definite 'language of the aesthetic', and it is precisely this which is lacking in both Basongye and Flathead societies" (1964:269).

One problem of the line of thought followed here by Merriam is that it seems to imply an essentialist dichotomy between literate and nonliterate societies. Christopher Marshall (1982) has pointed out this problem and has argued that this dichotomy is false. Marshall attempts to dissolve the dichotomy by suggesting that non-literate societies do have systems of aesthetic thought, which have been overlooked by ethnomusicologists because they are not the same as Western systems.

Central to the problem of Merriam's argument is, once again, the failure to situate the concept of "Western aesthetics" historically and philosophically. This failure leads to the assumption that what is described as "the Western concept of the aesthetic" is the *essential* way Westerners approach art. It also leads him to count the presence of a philosophy as a part of "Western aesthetics" when something very different is the case: it was the presence of a philosophy which gave rise to what *he considers to be* Western aesthetics.

This sixth factor also points to Merriam's basic scientific orientation, which in the beginning I counted as one of the main problems of his discussion on aesthetics. By considering the presence of a philosophy in Western aesthetics and the absence of such a philosophy in other musical cultures as part of the argument against applying aesthetics cross-culturally, Merriam is implicitly reminding us that his concern is not exploring the possibility of cross-cultural aesthetics, but the possibility of *scientific* cross-cultural aesthetics. He is, of course, aware that the lack of aesthetic discourse among the Flathead cannot be counted as a token of the inadequacy of others employing aesthetic discourse on their music, any more than the absence of an ethnomusicology among the Flathead would imply the illegitimacy of Merriam's own ethnomusicological investigations.

Merriam's analysis of "Western aesthetics" is, therefore, aimed at deciding if this aesthetics is a universal phenomenon, in order to determine if its study can be included in the scope of ethnomusicology. He concludes that neither is the case. It is not this negative conclusion that I find problematic. Rather, it is the character of the investigation. To analyze the concept of the aesthetic scientifically, which is Merriam's primary concern, would still shed little light on aesthetic phenomena, even if problems in his argumentation were solved by situating historically the concept of the aesthetic he analyzes and, consequently, by making room for a redefinition of the aesthetic which could be applied cross-culturally.

Underlying this problem is the nature of the relationship between social sciences and humanities. I believe that the kind of bridge between them which Merriam establishes is unsatisfactory. The following statement is especially telling in this respect: "Is ethnomusicology, then, a social science or a humanity? The answer is that it partakes of both; its approach and its goals are more scientific than humanistic, while its subject matter is more humanistic than scientific" (Merriam 1964:25). While Merriam is here touching on an important topic in need of discussion—the bridging of the sciences and the humanities—the particular type of relationship he suggests between anthropology and aesthetics is not satisfactory in my view. A study of a humanistic topic with the approach and goals of science, as Merriam puts it, is still an eminently scientific project, just as to study scientific discourse with the approach and goals of the humanities would still be a humanistic project. To illustrate this with a somewhat exaggerated example: to contend that a study of geological formations using the approach and goals of aesthetics would constitute a bridge between science and humanities would be exceedingly problematic. Similarly, a scientific approach to art does not necessarily make the scientific approach more humanistic. A productive bridging between social sciences and humanities should seek, it seems to me, a more profound relationship between both types of inquiry—one that overcomes the limitations of traditionally narrow views of science and humanities. The union proposed by Merriam does not allow for this step. When he considers aesthetics as a possible subject matter for the social sciences, and not as a discipline with its own approaches and goals, he is suggesting the subsuming of the humanities under the perspective of the scientific approach, not the establishment of a balanced bridging between them.

Conclusions

As already mentioned, a main problem of Merriam's argument is his failure to situate historically and philosophically the aesthetic concepts he discusses. This failure results, in the first place, in an inaccurate identification between what he calls "the aesthetic," and aesthetics as a discipline. What Merriam understands as "the Western concept of the aesthetic" is, more correctly, an aesthetic approach rooted in specific philosophical traditions of the eighteenth and nineteenth centuries. It is true that this concept of the aesthetic has been predominant in the history of aesthetics as a discipline. But it is also true that the philosophical assumptions upon which this aesthetics is grounded have been the object of thorough criticism since the end of the nineteenth century. This critique has cleared the way for new conceptions in Western aesthetic thought.

Secondly, Merriam's failure to situate the concepts he analyzes historically and philosophically gives rise throughout his argument to a confusion between "the aesthetic" as a way of creating and experiencing art, and as a way of conceptualizing art.[3] His discussion focuses on differences between the approach toward art in the Western tradition and in some non-Western cultures. However, while Merriam's knowledge of the experience of music among the Basongye and the Flathead Indians is drawn from his own ethnomusicological research, his knowledge of the "Western aesthetic" comes from his reading of (Western) aesthetic treatises. There is, thus, a slippage in his argument from actual judgments concerning Western aesthetic theories to judgments on Western processes of artistic production and reception.

In relation to the difficulty arising from the scientific character of Merriam's project I would suggest that the conclusions that can be drawn from his study on aesthetics are only valid if they answer the following question: Can aesthetics be an object of scientific scrutiny? The problem is that in the context of Merriam's approach this question equals another: Can aesthetics be a part of ethnomusicological study? What Merriam actually shows is that aesthetic concepts, because they are not universal, cannot be an object of scientific research. I do not discuss this premise but the idea that ethnomusicology can only encompass those aspects of music which can be approached scientifically.

The main conclusions I draw from my reading of Merriam's discussion are: 1) The theoretical frame which has come to be known as traditional Western aesthetics is not suitable for addressing cross-cultural phenomena. 2) Cross-cultural aesthetics cannot be grounded in scientific anthropology. Neither of these conclusions by themselves invalidate the claim that cross-cultural aesthetics is viable. The remainder of this paper moves beyond

the critical moment and suggests that the work of Paul Ricoeur is a productive ground for such viable cross-cultural aesthetics.

METAPHOR AND WORK OF ART: TOWARDS A HERMENEUTIC AESTHETICS

What follows is not an attempt to offer solutions to the problems of traditional aesthetics discussed above. It consists instead of a brief exposition of the philosophical ground upon which such solutions could be elaborated. The theoretical framework suggested for this purpose is Paul Ricoeur's treatment of creativity and imagination presented in the context of his studies of metaphoricity.

One justification of an aesthetic project drawing on Ricoeur's theory of the metaphor is offered by Ricoeur himself. He writes:

> If the problem of creativity cannot be approached directly and as a whole, perhaps it can be treated in a lateral and fragmentary fashion. Metaphor constitutes one of these limited approaches, insofar as the productive imagination assumes the form of a *semantic innovation*. The imagination operates here on the verbal level to produce new configurations of meaning, at the cost of extending the polysemy characteristic of natural languages. (1981:39)

The claim that metaphor can be considered a paradigm of creativity in the human sciences is supported by Ricoeur when he argues that there exists an analogical relation between metaphor and work. Ricoeur establishes this analogy through a discussion of the characteristics which work and metaphor share. These characteristics are the basic features of what he calls "discourse." Insofar as metaphor and work can both be considered "discourses," it can be said that metaphor is a "work in miniature," and a work "an extended metaphor" (Ricoeur 1981:167).

Ricoeur considers both work and metaphor as loci of the mediation effected by what he calls "the productive imagination." It is in this sense that the term "work of art" is employed in this paper. This concept departs from the Romantic (and ethnocentric) distinction between works of "fine art" or "high art," the purpose of which was to be contemplated, and works of craftsmanship, or "low art," considered as having a more practical and culturally bound function. In the expression "work of art," as used here, the emphasis is on the concept of "work," while the concept of "art" is considered a secondary category. As "works," a piano sonata, an American Indian song, and a ritualistic ceremony have much in common, whether or not they are classified as "art." These works, identifiable as singular totalities, are the product of the social imagination; they are "workings" through which the identity of a culture is negotiated. By regarding the work as metaphor, following Ricoeur's insight, we will be better able to understand works not as objects whose finality is to be contemplated, but as "workings," with a practical function.

Ricoeur's treatment of metaphoricity draws from some basic aspects of modern theories of metaphor as formulated by Monroe Beardsley, I. A. Richards, Max Black, and others. Ricoeur highlights the significance of these theories by comparing them with the former treatment of metaphoricity by rhetoricians. Traditional theories of rhetoric considered metaphor a trope, that is, a word used in place of another word or concept by analogy or resemblance. According to this theory of substitution the function of using words in a bizarre way was to embellish language. Ricoeur expresses it as follows:

> [In traditional rhetorics] to understand the metaphor, then, is to restitute the term which has been substituted...Therefore it is possible to give an exhaustive paraphrase of a given metaphor. From these presuppositions, it follows that metaphor offers no new information. It teaches nothing. For the same reason, metaphor is a mere decorative device. It has no informative value; it merely adorns language in order to please. It gives color to speech, it

provides a garment to cover the nudity of common usage. (Ricoeur 1991:76–77)

Far from considering metaphor a merely decorative device, Ricoeur recognizes its ability to introduce a semantic innovation. This means that the fundamental function of metaphor is not to state in an interesting or beautiful way something that has already been stated but, rather, to say something that has not been said before. Thus, for Ricoeur, metaphor is a semantic phenomenon. It produces a new meaning by putting together two concepts usually separated. For instance, when Merriam used the expression "verbal jungle" to describe a certain aesthetic philosophy, he was not just stating a previously expressed idea in a decorative way. Instead, he was offering us the possibility of thinking differently about the philosophy he was describing. The disparate terms of a metaphor do not cancel each other out. Instead, each illuminates the other, revealing aspects of both that were before concealed.

These insights into metaphoricity open new and productive ways of reflecting on poetic language and on creativity at large. The semantic innovation introduced by the clash between the two disparate terms of the metaphor points to a consideration of the cognitive power of poetic language, which in traditional rhetorics had been disregarded. It also gives full recognition to the power of new metaphors to shatter the established boundaries of language. The potential consequences of these reflections for aesthetics at large are considerable. The work of art, like the metaphor, says something new about reality. Combining elements of tradition with innovation the work, as a metaphor in miniature, makes sense while shattering established meanings.

It might be argued that the concept of musical work as extended metaphor that effects a semantic clash and thus a new meaning is only appropriate in the context of Western art music, in which the element of innovation has been emphasized more than in other musical cultures. In any living musical tradition, however, change is always present. Keeping a tradition alive does not mean a simple repeating of what has been sedimented in the past, but a bringing to life of that tradition by means of a dialectic between sedimentation and innovation. This dialectic is always operating in a tradition, although the degree of emphasis in one or the other term of the dialectic may vary greatly among cultures. In this sense, works considered as the workings of the productive imagination, and not as reified reproductions of sedimented forms, are always introducing new meanings. There is still another sense in which music, and creative work in general, can be thought of as metaphors introducing novel meanings. This is the case when creative works are conceived of as introducing a new meaning which clashes, not only with prior works, but with the everyday life of a people. No matter how slowly a musical tradition may change over time, the music being created and performed always adds something to the lives of the people sharing that tradition. The claim being made here is that creative works are more than embellished reproductions of what exists in other spheres of life. Instead of being only a reproduction or reflection of social structures, works *produce new meanings and new understandings.*[4]

I will now sketch some aspects of Ricoeur's work which could offer a theoretical alternative to the six aspects of traditional aesthetics discussed by Merriam.

Appropriation: "Making Ours"

The problems of traditional rhetoric highlighted by Ricoeur in his discussion of metaphoricity are strikingly similar to the problems of traditional aesthetics criticized by Merriam. Traditional aesthetics considered works of art just as rhetoric considered metaphors—as beautiful objects without cognitive value. A basic assumption underlying both traditional approaches was the radical separation between the realms of the cognitive and the aesthetic.

The notion of the metaphor as introducing a semantic innovation overcomes this dichotomy.

Accordingly, an aesthetics based on the analogy between work of art and metaphor would be able to bring together aesthetic and cognitive values. Such an aesthetics would consider music as saying something about reality that cannot be said in any other way. Consequently, the relationship between listeners and music would not be conceptualized as detached contemplation. Instead of psychic distance aimed at appreciating beautiful sounds by themselves, the aesthetic attitude would be characterized by the willingness to attempt to understand what music is saying to us.

The relevance of this new definition of aesthetic attitude and experience depends upon how "understanding" itself is defined. For Ricoeur, understanding requires appropriation, not in the sense of *expropriation,* but as the process of "[making] what was alien become one's own" (Ricoeur 1981:113). As appropriation, as "making ours," all understanding entails a self-understanding. The claim being made by Ricoeur, following Gadamer, is that one does not authentically understand unless in the process of understanding one's self is transformed. Appropriation, therefore, involves a risk—the risk of losing one's self in the process. It is only after having risked and lost the self that the self can be recuperated and enlarged by the apprehension of the world proposed by the work.

Ricoeur's theory of interpretation includes as well a moment of distanciation, or structural analysis of the work. Appropriation and distanciation are in a dialectical relationship, but appropriation has ontological priority with respect to distanciation and, consequently, is the culmination of the process of interpreting. This hermeneutic approach to the work of art is far from the notion of psychic distance characteristic of traditional aesthetics. In fact, it opens doors for the overlapping of aesthetics and ethics, and places aesthetics on a common ground with other forms of knowledge and every day communication.

Redescription of Reality

If art makes ethical claims, and if it has cognitive value, what then is its differential characteristic? Like the metaphor, the work of art not only says something new about reality, it says it in a unique way. Speaking of metaphors Ricoeur says that "no paraphrase can exhaust them, they are untranslatable. They say what they say and what they say cannot be said in another way" (Ricoeur 1991:80). Gadamer explicates the distinctive characteristic of the work of art as an excess of meaning (Gadamer 1976:102). Ricoeur makes a parallel claim in relation to the metaphor. For him the difference between metaphorical, scientific, and ordinary languages is that, unlike the others, metaphorical language does not avoid polysemy, that is, the ability of words to mean more than one thing (Ricoeur 1991:65–85).

It is through this excess of meaning that art and metaphorical language have the power to redescribe reality. But why would humans engage in this activity of redescribing reality? Ricoeur comments on this question in relation to language by saying:

> Why should we draw new meanings from our language if we have nothing new to say, no new world to project? The creations of language would be devoid of sense unless they served the general project of letting new worlds emerge by means of poetry. (Ricoeur 1981:181)

According to this view, the creation of a work of art is a much more complex phenomenon than a mere manipulation of form. Ricoeur explicates the creative act with the Greek word *mimesis,* signifying not *imitation* of reality, but *redescription* of reality. In other words, instead of considering art as a beautiful or unusual duplication of reality, it is regarded as a creative reconstructing of reality.

This different concept of artistic creation implies a different explication of stylistic change. Unlike the traditional explanations of style focusing on mere formal innovations, Ricoeur, following Granger, defines style as the adequacy between the singularity of a problem and the singularity of

the solution a work provides to that problem (Ricoeur 1988:162).

Context

The characteristics of polysemy in metaphorical language and of excess of meaning in artworks lead to another important aspect of aesthetic reflection. Since traditional rhetoric considered metaphor essentially a case of deviant denomination, the study of metaphoricity was to be made at the level of the words. Ricoeur, following modern theories of metaphor, contends that the appropriate level to study metaphoricity is at the level of the sentence. Words by themselves, he argues, cannot be metaphorical; only sentences can. It is only at the level of the metaphorical sentence that a new meaning emerges.

This is so because the ambiguity that results from polysemy would mean an insuperable barrier for understanding if the polysemic word was taken out of context. In this sense, Ricoeur states that the counterpart of polysemy in metaphorical language is its sensitivity to context. In a similar manner, it is the sensitivity to context which renders significant the excess of meaning of artworks.

A hermeneutic aesthetics, then, would reject the notion that sounds by themselves have the power to stir emotions. It would assume instead that in order to be meaningful sounds need to be considered in relation to the musical work of which they are a part. Furthermore, it would contend that works themselves cannot be meaningful if considered out of context. This context is understood by Ricoeur as the totality of the *mimetic* process, which encompasses three moments: *prefiguration, configuration*, and *refiguration*. Roughly stated, the moment of prefiguration refers to the world of the author; configuration refers to the immanent structures of the text; and refiguration is the moment of productive reference, which concerns the world of the reader (or listener). At the level of aesthetic reflection it would be an understanding of the complete *mimetic* process that would explicate the meaningfulness of the musical work. This process implies that a hermeneutic approach to the work of art, although basically an ontological project, would include a structural analysis and an aesthetics of reception.[5]

Meaningfulness

It is the meaningfulness of the work of art, and not its beauty, which would constitute the primary focus of a hermeneutic aesthetics. This does not underestimate the importance of beauty and play in art. On the contrary, a reflection on beauty in art linked to a reflection on art's meaningfulness would acknowledge the cathartic experience that art is able to provide.

The resistance to including the category of beauty in ethnomusicology, as well as in twentieth-century aesthetics and musical criticism, is rooted in the connotations of the concept of beauty in traditional aesthetics. In metaphysical positions beautiful art was understood as the reflection of eternal truth, while formalist analysis placed the value of a work of art exclusively in its formal correctness. As already noted, these traditional concepts of beauty had a relatively short (and exclusively ethnocentric) life. Opposed to these traditional approaches, a hermeneutic aesthetics would focus on the capacity of the work to say something.

The consideration of art's cognitive value, however, does not render beauty unimportant. Rather, it places the question of beauty's significance at a different level. Beauty should not be left out of aesthetic concerns but, in order to avoid former problems of traditional aesthetics, it should be redefined in terms of the dialectics between what the work says and how it says it.

In sum, aesthetics would not primarily be a theory of the beautiful in works of art but, rather, a theory of their *meaningfulness*. Such an aesthetic theory, chiefly concerned with the question of how artistic or cultural works are meaningful—what it is that they say to us—would fall entirely within the aims and goals of a theory of interpretation as proposed by contemporary hermeneutics.

World Proposed by the Work

One of the factors Merriam commented on was the purposeful intent to create something aesthetic. As mentioned earlier, Gadamer and Ricoeur have pointed out the fallacy involved in emphasizing the role of authorial intention in the interpretation of a work. But, after this critique, how can a movement back to formal or purely subjective analyses be avoided? Ricoeur raises and answers this question as follows:

> If we can no longer define hermeneutics in terms of the search for the psychological intentions of another person which are concealed *behind* the text, and if we do not want to reduce interpretation to the dismantling of structures, then what remains to be interpreted? I shall say: to interpret is to explicate the type of being-in-the-world unfolded *in front of* the text. (1981:141)

Instead of the aesthetic intentionality Merriam counted among the factors of Western aesthetics, a hermeneutic aesthetic would focus on the efficacy of the work. This does not mean that the creative process is disregarded. On the contrary, the reconstruction of the creative process is a necessary moment, but it would focus on the strategies employed by the authors, not on their intentions.

The importance given to the world unfolded in front of the work is tied to the notion of the work as the locus of the mediation of reality. Our works give us a world. Or more emphatically stated: our works make us who we are. Just as old metaphors—which originally introduced a semantic clash—now appear as definitions in dictionaries, since they have become part of our linguistic reality, so the works of art of past generations, along with other human works, are now part of our identity—they constitute our reality. It is up to us to contemporize this reality by means of our own works. An interpretive approach to these works, in turn, would facilitate the understanding of the new worlds projected by the works.

Interpretation

To acknowledge the role of works of art in shaping reality entails as well a recognition of the importance of a philosophy of art. The categorization of art as merely ornamental has had an impact on the way studies related to art have been regarded in academia. The scholars that subscribed to the traditional approaches were contributing, ironically, to their own marginality with respect to other disciplines. They were defining themselves as devoting their intellectual efforts to the study of merely pleasing objects, the importance of which they were unable to justify theoretically.

This self-inflicted wound of aesthetics—its lack of relevance relative to other fields—had the same roots as the problems found in traditional theories of the metaphor: the isolation of aesthetics from the spheres of knowledge and praxis. I previously noted how Ricoeur suggests a link between aesthetics and conceptual knowledge in his treatment of creativity. The link between the sphere of aesthetic reflection and the sphere of action that his approach establishes should now be more clear: to understand differently, to be able to conceive that things could be different is what triggers action which effects change. This is not simply another aspect of Ricoeur's work. As R. I. Valdés points out, the cornerstone of Ricoeur's theory of interpretation is the return to the world of action (Ricoeur 1991:9). Ricoeur sums up the relationship between poetry (or art), knowledge, and action when he writes:

> If it is true that poetry gives no information in terms of empirical knowledge, it may change our way of looking at things, a change which is no less real than empirical knowledge. What is changed by poetic language is our way of dwelling in the world. From poetry we receive a new way of being in the world, of orientating ourselves in this world. (Ricoeur 1991:85)

It is not surprising, then, that the counterpart of Ricoeur's theory of metaphor is a theory of social imagination or productive imagination. This approach to art is very distant from the "verbal jungle" Merriam saw in traditional aesthetics. Ricoeur, in fact, is well aware that the question of creativity and social imagination leads to the idea of a philosophy in contact with anthropology. Interestingly, while Merriam's scientific approach led him to reject the inclusion of aesthetics in his anthropological project, Ricoeur's theory of creativity is inextricably connected to a philosophical anthropology. Ricoeur is also clear about the dangers involved in a hermeneutic philosophy out of touch with the social sciences. He states this case by saying:

> The project of a philosophy of the productive imagination constitutes in no way an alternative to a theory of interpretation concerned to pursue the dialogue with the social sciences. It can only be a deepening of this same theory, but conducted at a level of radicality where the epistemology of the social sciences would rejoin the ontology of human reality. (Ricoeur 1981:39–40)

CONCLUSION: UNDERSTANDING THE MUSICAL METAPHORS OF LOS ANGELES

What are the musics made in Los Angeles saying? Why are the people of Los Angeles making the musics they are making? What can we learn from the relationship between the traditional backgrounds of these musics and their current configurations? What are these musics telling us about ourselves? In sum, what does it mean to understand these musics, and how can this understanding affect the way we live?

These are some of the questions a hermeneutic aesthetics would ask. Such an aesthetics would aim at interpreting the different ways of being in the world these musics are unfolding in front of us. But it should also aim at an understanding of the worlds these musics are *inventing*. The tension between the ideological identity provided by the sedimentation of tradition, and the utopian invention of possible worlds that constitutes innovation is, as Ricoeur has insightfully shown, unsurpassable. To understand who we are and to imagine who we might be are two inseparable sides of the interpretative aesthetic task.

It is the role of aesthetic reflection to facilitate this understanding. To reflect on the musical aesthetics of Los Angeles, thus, should concern what it means to be in Los Angeles in relation to the traditions from which we come, and in relation to the future that we are constructing. Ultimately, as any musical aesthetics, it should not shy away from asking the big question: what it means to be.

In September 1992 the *Los Angeles Times* published an article under the following headline: "Can the Arts Heal L. A.?" Not surprisingly, the newspaper's article lacked what I see as the key to answering this question—an in depth reflection of what is meant by art, and what is meant by the notion of healing through art, that is, of aesthetic redemption. Roger Savage has summed up the terms for this reflection well:

> Aesthetic redemption is not a fictitious solution to the antagonisms and injustices of a world given over to its instrumental purposes. On the contrary, it is the disclosure of a reality through the work of art that gives to us the possibility of understanding the world in which we live in a different way. (Savage 1993:32–33)

ACKNOWLEDGEMENT

This essay grew out of work completed under the direction of Roger Savage, who has made important contributions towards developing the main lines of the hermeneutical approach to a musical aesthetics I propose here. I would like to thank him, and the participants in his seminars, for many stimulating discussions. I would also like to thank Steven Loza for his work on the musical aesthetics of Los Angeles, work which has been the main inspiration for this paper. My husband Dennis Claxton provided insightful revision and helped me make my ideas clearer and my English more readable.

NOTES

1. The philosophy of Martin Heidegger marks the ontological turn which forms the basis of Gadamer's and Ricoeur's approaches. See Heidegger's analysis of the work of art in his essay "The Origin of the Work of Art" (1971).

2. Cited by Carl Dahlhaus in *Esthetics of Music* (1982).

3. To make this distinction does not imply ignoring the constant interrelation between theory and "real life."

4. Steven Feld (1988) draws from Ricoeur's concept of metaphor in his study on the music of the Kaluli. While Feld employs this concept mainly to discuss a linguistic metaphor the Kaluli use to define their music, in this paper the music itself is considered to be metaphorical and, therefore, to be more than just an echoing of already existing social relations and environmental conditions. Feld asks: "How might apprehending [the Kaluli metaphor] 'lift-up-over sounding' change our way of sensing sound?" (1988:78). My question is: "How might apprehending the music of a people as a metaphor introducing a semantic innovation change our way of understanding reality?"

5. Although Ricoeur's *mimetic process* might resemble Jean-Jacques Nattiez's tripartitional model (Nattiez 1990), these are two basically different projects. While Nattiez's is a semiotic project, Ricoeur's is primarily a hermeneutic one.

REFERENCES CITED

Adorno, Theodor W.
    1989 [1962] *Introduction to the Sociology of Music*. Translated by E. B. Ashton. New York: Continuum.
    1980 [1949] *Philosophy of Modern Music*. Translated by A.G. Mitchell and W. V. Blomster. New York: Seabury Press.

Attali, Jacques
    1985 *Noise*. Translated by Brian Massumi. Minneapolis: University of Minnesota Press.

Dahlhaus, Carl
    1982   *Esthetics of Music.* Translated by William Austin. New York: Cambridge University Press.
Feld, Steven
    1988   "Aesthetics as Iconicity of Style, or 'Lift-up-over-Sounding': Getting into the Kaluli Groove." *Yearbook for Traditional Music* 20.
Gadamer, Hans-Georg
    1986   *The Relevance of the Beautiful.* Translated by Nicholas Walker. Cambridge: Cambridge University Press.
    1976   *Philosophical Hermeneutics.* Translated by David E. Linge. Berkeley: University of California Press.
Heidegger, Martin
    1971   "The Origin of the Work of Art." *Poetry, Language, Thought.* Translated by Albert Hofstadter. New York: Harper & Row.
Kant, Immanuel.
    1987 [1790] *Critique of Judgment.* Translated by Werner S. Pluhar. Indianapolis: Hackett Publishing Co.
Lerdhal, Fred and Ray Jackendoff
    1983   *A Generative Theory of Tonal Music.* Cambridge: MIT Press.
Marshall, Christopher
    1982   "Towards a Comparative Aesthetics of Music." In *Cross-cultural Perspectives on Music,* edited by Robert Falck and Timothy Rice. Toronto: University of Toronto Press.
McAllester, David
    1954   *Enemy Way Music.* Cambridge: Peabody Museum.
McClary, Susan
    1991   *Feminine Endings.* Minnesota: University of Minnesota Press.
Merriam, Alan P.
    1964   *The Anthropology of Music.* Evanston: Northwestern University Press.
Nattiez, Jean-Jacques
    1990   *Music and Discourse.* Translated by Carolyn Abbate. Princeton: Princeton University Press.
Ricoeur, Paul
    1991   *A Ricoeur Reader.* Edited by Mario Valdés. Toronto: University of Toronto Press.
    1988   *Time and Narrative,* Vol. 3. Translated by Kathleen Blamey and David Pellauer. Chicago: University of Chicago Press.
    1981   *Hermeneutics and the Human Sciences.* Translated by John B. Thompson. Cambridge: Cambridge University Press.

Savage, Roger W. H
    1993   "Aesthetic Criticism and the Poetics of Modern Music." *British Journal of Aesthetics* 33: 2.
Shepherd, John
    1991   *Music as Social Text.* Cambridge: Polity Press.
Tilghman, B. R
    1991   *Wittgenstein, Ethics and Aesthetics.* Houndmills: Macmillan Press.

IDENTITY, NATIONALISM, AND AESTHETICS AMONG CHICANO/MEXICANO MUSICIANS IN LOS ANGELES

Steven Loza

WITHIN THIS PAPER MY aim is to examine a cross-section of musical forms incorporated and stylized in a movement by contemporary musicians and their audiences representing the Chicano/Mexicano culture in the city of Los Angeles, California. The styles examined include rhythm and blues/rock, rap, mariachi, and banda. Theoretical issues discuss and address identity expressed through nationalistic motives, vogues, or trends in these styles, by which I mean ethnic affirmation through an interaction of the traditional and innovative.

Ultimately, such artistic "movements" must be considered from an aesthetic viewpoint, understanding that the development of new, emerging aesthetics in the four styles examined here represents various points of dynamics and a diversity, as Los Angeles is diverse, of changing expression and the cognition of such expression. The guiding principle that I will use to explore aesthetic frameworks is the concept of tradition as a cyclical, regenerative process involving the experiences of both reinterpretation and innovation (Loza 1992:15–16)

The anthropologist Jacques Maquet has helped develop a field called aesthetic anthropology. Maquet (1979) issues a basic argument concerning the exclusive use of empirical data for the assessment of cross-cultural aesthetics. Maquet's principal admonition is that we consider not only the collective patterns and processes of any culture,

but that we also assess the specific character and thought of the *individual* artist when probing art as a cultural product. Maquet also suggests that the aesthetical domains of culture be evaluated from a "material culture" framework built on the foundation of the productive, societal, and ideational factors involved in the making of art. The issues of identity and nationalism, as I have used them in this critique, have correlated to the three levels of Maquet's triad.

In this essay (project) I continue to develop a concept I employed in an article that I wrote assessing the reinterpretation of a regional Mexican style by a popular Los Angeles group of Chicano musicians, Los Lobos (Loza 1992). In that study I designed a circular model that could serve as an indicator of the aesthetic process among societies that have experienced a dual locus of culture—in this case, the Mexican American experience as expressed through what I referred to as the "sonic power" of musical expression. Through the cyclical movement of tradition, reinterpretation, and innovation, I offered the hypothesis that musical groups such as Los Lobos represent an intense artistic motive to reaffirm tradition through a variety of reinterpreted yet fresh innovative art forms. The cognition of this turn of events is not necessarily one that is primarily conceptualized verbally; it can be a predominately "sonic" metamorphosis and style development. Thus, the aesthetic becomes an active, *art performed* form of analysis, much superior to any concept of formal aesthetic considerations through verbal communication. When I talk and write about this exciting process I have also referred to it as one of "cultural reclamation." The issues of identity and nationalism certainly fit into this conceptually, as they do into the four styles that I have briefly critiqued in this paper.

RHYTHM AND BLUES/ROCK

The question has arisen frequently: Why have Chicanas and Chicanos, especially in L.A., adapted so heavily to black music? Responses to this question have included rationales ranging from the two cultures' affinities for dance improvisation and singing to the value of socialization—the notion that much Mexican music has functioned in much the same way as the musical rank in African American society. Other conjecture has focused on the sociopolitical relationship of Mexican and African Americans. Many musicians, however, have not detected this connection, insisting on the "primal" aesthetic of the music (see Loza 1992:223–224).

The musical styles of rhythm and blues (R&B) and rock have been, through the last fifty years, among the major musical ambits of Chicanos in the U.S., especially so in Los Angeles. Jump blues evolved in the 1930s and '40s from bands like those of Cab Calloway, Count Basie, and Louis Jordan. By the end of World War II, Los Angeles artists such as Roy Milton, Joe Liggins, and Johnny Otis had gained national popularity. Milton recorded a national hit, "RM/Blues," on the Los Angeles-based Specialty Records. He was among the many swing artists who became major influences among Mexicans in Los Angeles. In 1952, black saxophonist Chuck Higgins attained a major national hit with his instrumental single "Pachuco Hop," originally aired by Los Angeles disc jockey Hunter Hancock. Mexicans in East L.A. began listening to Hancock daily, especially after he switched to KGFJ radio station, the first to broad-cast exclusively the music of African Americans (Guevara 1985). Jump blues and doo wop were becoming part of Chicano musical vocabulary. By 1958, the influence of these styles would metamorphose into events such as Chuck Rio's (Danny Flores) national number one hit "Tequila," a hybrid of Latin and the R&B/jump/rock matrix.

To outline the diversity of identity among Los Angeles Chicanos as personified through the styles of R&B/rock, I have chosen two examples: Li'l Ray Jimenéz's recording "I (Who Have Nothing)," recorded during the early 1960s, and Teresa Covarrubias's "The Cry," recorded by her with the group The Brat in 1991.

Li'l Ray Jiménez, originally from Delano, California, had been a vocalist for the original Thee Midniters before gaining considerable recognition as a soloist in East L.A. He was offered a recording contract with Motown Records and had also been scheduled to record with Sam Cooke. Neither opportunity ever materialized, and "I (Who Have Nothing)," recorded on Eddie Davis's Rampart label and which attained successful regional radio play in Southern California, was the closest Jiménez ever came to attaining the national recognition many believed he was worthy of. "The Cry," recorded by Teresa Covarrubias almost thirty years after Jiménez's local hit, provides another example of high quality Eastside rock that never really left Los Angeles. The Brat competed with some of the most popular punk, new wave, and hard rock bands in L.A. during the 1980s, but national distribution eluded this group also, in spite of the fact that the CD it was included on, *Act of Faith*, was produced by the highly respected and influential Paul Rothchild, producer of another former L.A. band, The Doors, the first rock band to achieve five successive albums with each selling over one million units.

Blues is an element that has certainly become part of the fabric of American music. Throughout the diverse musical repertoires developed by Chicano artists, the blues element has served as a basic cultural referential point from Los Lobos' classic recording of their Ellingtonesque "Kiko and the Lavender Moon" to Poncho Sanchez's adaptation of James Brown tunes over Latin R&B rhythms. "The Cry" of The Brat references the blues as much as Li'l Ray's "I (Who Have Nothing)" and both songs denote the metaphor or emotional expressions of "a cry" in a special way. This notion is further examined in my book *Barrio Rhythm* and refers to the formation of a "Chicano" musical style in Los Angeles demonstrative of "certain commonalties" among the artists:

> Vocal and instrumental tone and inflection, improvisational motives, harmonic progressions, rhythmic references and preferences, training in technique, and vocal/instrumental voicing all exhibit some specific commonalties that frequently cross-identify the styles of various Chicano musicians; that is, they apply to the venue of tone and inflection as in the case of singer Li'l Ray Jiménez and his nephew, Mike Jiménez. Both possess a wide range and have a lyrical "cry" quality in the higher register, especially at the ends of phrases in ballads. Improvisationally, a commonality often exists in terms of melodic solo passages imitative of Mexican or other Latin American styles. Harmonic progression in English ballads (or "oldies") is often similar to Mexican *bolero* standards from the 1940s to 1960s. (Loza 1993:271–2)

Thus, in my estimation, there exists an interactive influx and outflux of time and space in the factors of identity, adaptation, and the aesthetics of African American musical practice as interpreted and defined by Chicano musicians. Such intersection can be culturally evaluated from both social and musical bases of analysis. These bases, in effect, can support each other formidably in developing related hypotheses of how and why Chicana and Chicano musicians have responded so intensely to the ambit of R&B and rock.

Rap

One of the most intriguing, and to me, exhilarating phenomena to occur in urban America within the past fifteen years, and especially in Los Angeles, is that of the rap "movement." The "gangsta rap" as associated with Los Angeles has shifted the political boundaries of the rap genre and hip hop culture largely to that city. "Given the recent political events such as the Rodney King verdict and the 1992 rebellion, L.A.-based rappers have become important in terms of their critiques of both life in Los Angeles and American society as a whole" (Alvarez and Santiago 1994). Chicano rappers in L.A. have been an essential link in this movement.

One of the first Chicano rap artists to achieve both local and national recognition through his recording has been Kid Frost (Arturo Molina). His initial 1990 hit "La Raza" is a classic example of the U.S. Latin infusion of the rap format through a bilingual setting. Not only did the bilingual format of "La Raza" affirm the Latin engagement with rap, but the recording enlisted a third generation reinterpretation of a tune composed and originally recorded during the early 1960s by Los Angeles jazz musician and band leader Gerald Wilson. It was then reinterpreted and recorded a second time by the group El Chicano in 1970, at which point it became one of the various rallying anthems of the Chicano movement in Los Angeles. Finally, Kid Frost's 1990 reinterpretation expanded the instrumental yet political metaphor with the addition of a text overtly dedicated to the expression of the Chicano struggle, epitomized through the referents of life centered on both the humor and tragedy of gang warfare, but juxtaposed with the exclamation of Chicano pride.

Kid Frost's creative work, however, cannot be assessed solely through his "La Raza." On a subsequent album he collaborated with other Latino rappers in a project called Latin Alliance. One selection from the album, "Latinos Unidos," laces a mosaic of Latin-R&B musical texture (both sampled and instrumentationed) and rhythmic flavor; bilingual historical referents and interpretations of the Mexican southwest, Puerto Rico, and Nicaragua; and direct commentary on issues related to minority politics and intercultural conflict. Other compositions on the album include themes based on reflections on American identity, lowrider/boulevard culture, the political wars of Central America, and gangsta raps imaging violence, discrimination, incarceration, immigration, the Border Patrol, and romance.

In assessing the issues of cultural identity and ethnic nationalism, the aesthetics of rap expression emerges as a highly charged vehicle among a constantly growing corps of young Chicano/Latino contemporary rap artists. Although the aesthetic of rap has webbed itself internationally as a preferred expression of youth culture in a variety of languages, its relationship to Latinos in the U.S. as part of African American music is not simply an artistic interaction, dialectic, or experiment. Rather, it is reflective of living quarters such as South Central Los Angeles, almost exclusively populated by Latinos and African Americans where cultural turf may not meet in private households, but certainly does on the streets. Rap has been a point of synthesis and inevitable value to the young members of this geographic sector of a so-called city whose assumed power brokers in the media consistently not only ascribe marginal labels to the inhabitants of South Central and the Eastside, but who literally fear entrance through the portals of these neighborhoods. The Harbor and Pomona Freeways are not the favored city ways of many a record executive or even record buyer.

Mariachi

Mariachi culture in Los Angeles is yet another example of what I will refer to as a "movement." One of the distinguishing characteristics of this musical style in L.A. has been the innovative establishment of various restaurant-based "show" mariachis, epitomized by the most prestigious ensembles such as Mariachis Los Camperos de Nati

Cano, Los Galleros de Pedro Rey, Sol de México de José Hernández, and Uclatlán de Mark Fogelquist. Contrasting this highly lucrative ambiance of musical spectacle, however, live the hundreds of freelance, *al talón* mariachis, many of them lining the street curbs of the donut shop corner of Boyle Avenue and First Street, known as "La Boyle," where a kiosk is planned to be built in recognition of this Mexican tradition reinterpreted and re-enacted from places such as Mexico City's Plaza de Garibaldi.

Two practitioners of the restaurant based mariachis provide an informative juxtaposition of both contrasts and parallels. In his development of Mariachi Los Camperos, director Nati Cano, who emigrated to Los Angeles during his twenties and is now some sixty years of age, has been largely credited as the first to reap extensive success from the dinner show format. Los Camperos is considered to be one of the finest mariachis in the world. Cano's musical philosophy has been one of "purism"—his goal has been to maintain the mariachi traditional style while innovating the context of its presentation to a constantly growing Mexican and non-Mexican public. As a recipient of the NEA's National Heritage Award, he has been given national recognition as an artist fostering one of the major traditional art forms in the country.

In many ways contrasting with Nati Cano is José Hernández, the mid-thirties-aged director of Mariachi Sol de México. Although an adherent of the traditional repertoire of Mexican *sones*, *rancheras*, and other forms traditionally performed by the mariachi, Hernández has chosen to also highlight his mariachi format with the interpretation of songs representing another aesthetic layer of the bicultural Mexican American context—indeed *his* context. Hernández's arrangements of and adaptations of songs such as "New York, New York" and other English-texted popular tunes attest to this innovation—one that has attracted a special brand of attention especially among many of the "baby-boom" Chicana and Chicano afficionados who consciously identify with and appreciate the juxtapositions of such styles—in effect, an aesthetic molded bilingually, bimusically, and biculturally.

On the line of parallels, however, it is also significant to highlight the similarities in the musical and business strategies of Cano and Hernández. They are proactive cultural entrepreneurs. Both have established restaurants with mariachi shows, both have recorded and performed with Linda Ronstadt, both have instituted scholarship foundations for young musicians, both have participated as performers and clinicians in the major mariachi festivals throughout the Southwest, and both have lauded the "renaissance" of mariachi among the young Mexicano/Chicano musicians north of the U.S.-Mexican border. These are conscious actions to provide economics and extend the radius of audience and the pool of artists concurrently.

The youth emphasis of the latter movement ultimately, explicitly addresses the issues of identity, nationalism, and the emerging aesthetic among young Chicano musicians and audiences in the U.S. The proliferation of student mariachis at the high school, middle school, and even primary school levels is another contemporary phenomenon taking place in every major city of the Southwest and beyond. A tradition once scoffed at by many an identity-complexed Chicano youth thirty years ago has landed in a current niche of time and space that must be regarded as a movement of rapid reversal, cultural reclamation, and aesthetic liberation.

Banda

Finally, I arrive at a most recent phenomenon in Los Angeles—one that still bears a necessary period of evaluation—but one that has exploded on the scene in a most unexpected fashion. As I completed the final drafts of my book *Barrio Rhythm* five years ago, banda music in L.A. was just a beginning "craze." It is now a colossal wave. As a media and social force, it is reminiscent of another major movement among people of Mexi-

can heritage in the last forty years—that of the Chicano movement. Certainly, the banda craze in Los Angeles bears a resemblance to the mambo/ cha cha craze of the 1950s in New York City, there largely generated by the Cuban and Puerto Rican sector, although many non-Latino afficionados eventually also became associated with that movement.

The "banda craze" in Los Angeles is one of a more specific nationalist character—namely, a Mexican character. The banda ensemble format can be traced historically and stylistically to the traditional *banda sinaloense*, originally developed at the turn of the century in the state of Sinaloa, Mexico. It is rightfully one of the long recognized and colorful styles in the ample variety of regional music in Mexico. Consisting primarily of woodwind and brass instruments, the distinctive instrumentation of the Sinaloa style has become the standard of the contemporary banda. It has, of course, undergone major innovation. A lead vocalist is now a standard element in the formerly traditional instrumental format, and electric bass usually replaces the traditional tuba. A modern drum set and Cuban-style *timbales* are now situated as the percussion section, formerly characterized by a battery or *tamborazo* of marching band cymbals, bass drum, and snare drum (although *timbales* and congas had already been in use in the Sinaloa style).

The dance aspect of banda, referred to as *la quebradita* is, according to observations, the real heart of this socioartistic experience. Although the *quebradita*, the tango-like "break" choreography executed at many of the banda night clubs and dances throughout Los Angeles, is usually the focal point of discussion, I have noted that the essential dance steps conform somewhat to combinations of the genres performed by the banda, ranging from polka beat to tropical rhythms to traditional Mexican *sones*. A dance style has emerged that is at times a hybrid of *cumbia*, *norteño/* Tex-Mex, and *zapateado*. At many dances the actual *quebradita* is never actually executed because of space limitations.

In assessing the factors of identity, nationalism, and the emergence of a collective aesthetic in the making of the current banda phenomenon, it has been useful to think in terms of both the movement's social force and its artistic representation and regeneration. One of the principal reasons for the international media exposure of this style is the ascension of banda-*ranchera*-formatted radio station KLAX, known as "La Q" and spearheaded by disc jockey Juan Carlos Hidalgo. In August 1992 KLAX moved into the number one spot according to Arbitron ratings for the city of Los Angeles, surpassing the syndicated KLSX morning talk show hosted by Howard Stern, which had previously held the number one rating. The radio industry immediately reacted in an almost bewildered manner (the terms "shock waves" in the industry were used by *Music Connection* magazine), not only unable to explain this demographic "alarm clock," but also unable to develop immediate and competitive marketing strategies to regain top ratings. The Spanish-speaking public of L.A. is simply not part of the mainstream radio industry. Almost two years since the rating changed over, KLAX still retains the top Arbitron ratings for Los Angeles.

Aside from this debate over the commercial success of banda, the more important question arises as to why this style has captivated so many so quickly. Unlike in culture and character when compared to the older waves of European immigrants, and no longer a racial minority, the estimated 41% Latino population of Los Angeles is not so different from other cultural masses that frequently feel the need for renovation in art, fashion, and other stylistic and philosophical pursuits. Primarily a working-class people, both Mexican immigrants and U.S.-born Chicanos have opportunized the moment to "jump on the banda wagon," a vogue in which they are not vulnerably pressured to assimilate to a North American musical style, but where they can reclaim and renovate their own tradition while defying the commercial

seduction and standards of MTV and its related industry. As I said in an interview with Rubén Martínez for a cover story in the *Los Angeles Times Magazine*:

> People are saying that we don't want to look like Prince or Madonna. We can wear our boots and hats. The Vaquero style is important as a symbol. When a Mexican puts on the suit, just like in the old days you put on a zoot suit, you can walk into that club and be proud that you're a Mexican. (Martínez 1994:12)

Another issue reinforcing the social and aesthetic needs of the Mexican/Chicano afficionados of banda is the current heavy dose of anti-immigration rhetoric being used to blame immigrants for California's economic problems. Politicians have been largely responsible for much of this rhetoric which resonates with those in search of easy answers to complex social and historical problems. As Martínez so aptly wrote, "While Governor Pete Wilson, Senators Barbara Boxer and Dianne Feinstein and many other pols in the state rant about the 'immigration problem,' the more pertinent issue might be this: When will they learn to dance the *quebradita*?" Recently, KLAX disc jockey Juan Carlos Hidalgo announced his mock candidacy for governor of California, referring to his incumbent opponent as "Pupi Wilson."

Forging a Collective Analysis

In the brief presentation I have made here covering four distinct musical styles utilized by Chicanos/Mexicanos in Los Angeles, I have attempted to highlight some basic issues of identity, nationalism, and aesthetics as both social and artistic motives, and to offer the viewpoint that these two motives are interactive in the current movement.

The four styles, or "movements," represent a diversity of artistic form, "content," and expression. This variation should not surprise those of us involved in the study of Chicano/Mexicano culture in the United States, especially when centered on diverse societies in Los Angeles, itself a mammoth, interacting framework of both cultural integration and segregation. An important fact that we must realize as scholars of Chicana/o Studies is that Chicano society itself has continually diversified according to growing differences in age, gender, sexuality, social and economic class, religion, politics, immigration status, identity, and language. The dynamics of these sometimes artificial divisions often go well beyond such categories and logic. The explanations, for example, for why one second-generation Chicana, living in Los Angeles, immerses herself in the banda cultural network while another second-generation Chicana refutes the style and embraces rap have yet to be explored. As I sat and watched ten-thousand Mexicanos and Chicanos dancing to live bandas at the Sports Arena in Los Angeles in April 1994, I found myself reflecting on how culturally engaged I felt, yet at the same time, how actively disengaged. The context was not part of my present social or musical network in spite of my cultural relationship to it.

Indeed, much of the media has recently described the city of Los Angeles as a riot-torn, burned-out, mud-slid, smog-laden, earthquaked, drive-by-shot remnant of twentieth-century civilization. *Time* magazine recently featured on its cover the question, "Is the City of Angels Going To Hell?" New Yorker David Rieff has written a book entitled *Los Angeles: Capital of the Third World* (1991). My reaction to much of this is a suggestion. Let us not think of Los Angeles or any other world city as either "third world" or "first world." The changing pattern of cultures and multicultural ambits in contemporary society simply is occurring too rapidly, and at an increasing pace, to set such limited description for the human race. The Mexicans in Los Angeles have begun a "reclamation" of much more than music. But music speaks loudly, and the Mexicans may hold some answers for not only the City of the Angels, but the imminent reality of a multicultural world.

NOTES

1. It is important to point out that Wilson had become directly involved with Chicano/Mexicano culture. He married a Mexican woman and became actively engaged with Mexican culture, especially that of bullfighting. "Viva Tirado" was named in honor of Mexican bullfighter Juan Tirado.

2. I do not suggest that banda will compete politically with the intensity and dynamics of the Chicano Movement, initiated during the 1960s. As a popular movement, however, banda has penetrated a level of media influence that is unprecedented. Additionally, its political force and stature is still a matter of metamorphosis; but banda *is* highly political.

REFERENCES CITED

Alvarez, Milo and Josefina Santiago
    1994   "Los Angeles Rap Music: Historical Aspects and African-American/Chicano Case Studies." Unpublished term paper, UCLA.

Guevara, Rubén
    1985   "The View from the Sixth Street Bridge: The History of Chicano Rock." In *The First Rock & Roll Confidential*, ed. David Marsh and the editors of *Rock & Roll Confidential*: 113–26. New York: Pantheon.

Loza, Steven
    1993   *Barrio Rhythm: Mexican American Music in Los Angeles*. Chicago, Urbana: University of Illinois Press.

    1992   "From Veracruz to Los Angeles: The Reinterpretation of the *Son Jarocho*." *Latin American Music Review* 13(2):179–194.

Maquet, Jacques
    1979   *Introduction to Aesthetic Anthropology*. Malibu: Undena Publications.

Martínez, Rubén
    1994   "The Shock of the New." *Los Angeles Times Magazine*. January 30:10–16, 39.

Rieff, David
    1991   *Los Angeles: Capital of the Third World*. New York: Simon & Schuster.

    1993   "Is the City of Angels Going To Hell?" *Time Magazine* 141(16) April 19:26–31.

Widran, Jonathan.
    1993   "The Spoil of Victory: KLAX." *Music Connection* 17(14):21.

SELECT DISCOGRAPHY

The Brat. 1991. *Act of Faith.* Time Bomb Music Company.

Kid Frost. 1990. *Hispanic Causing Panic.* Pump Records.

East Side Revue: 40 Hits by East Los Angeles' Most Popular Groups. 1966 [1969]. Rampart; distributed by American Pie as LP3303 (includes "I (Who Have Nothing)" by Li'l Ray Jiménez).

El Chicano. 1970. *Viva Tirado.* MCA.

Los Lobos. *Just Another Band from East L.A.: A Collection.* 1993. Slash/Warner Brothers, 9 45367-2.

Los Lobos. *Kiko.* 1992. Slash/Warner Brothers.

Mariachi Los Camperos de Nati Cano. *Canciones de Siempre.* 1992. Peer Southern Productions, Inc. (Polygram Latino), 314 519 712.

Mariachi Sol de México. *New York, New York.* 1991. Discos Fenix.

Wilson, Gerald. *The Best of the Gerald Wilson Orchestra.* n.d. World Pacific Jazz Records.

THE EVOLUTION OF BANDA MUSIC AND THE CURRENT BANDA MOVEMENT IN LOS ANGELES

Carlos Manuel Haro
and
Steven Loza

THIS PAPER IS AN EXTENSION of the article, "Identity, Nationalism, and Aesthetics Among Chicano/ Mexicano Musicians in Los Angeles," by Steven Loza. The earlier Loza work examines a cross-section of musical forms that represent Chicano/ Mexicano culture, including rhythm and blues/ rock, rap, mariachi, and banda. The present effort focuses on the recent "banda movement" that has exploded on the airwaves of Los Angeles and generated a following of over one million listeners. The earlier paper provides a theoretical framework for studying the different musical styles and issues of identity as related to nationalistic motives, vogues, or trends. The newest musical style, and the one that requires extensive investigation because of its sociocultural and political impact, is banda music. This piece reviews the musical heritage of banda music and its evolution to what is currently heard in Los Angeles, as well as a review of several bandas and their recorded music.

The banda movement in Los Angeles closely parallels the rise of the Los Angeles Spanish language FM radio station, KLAX 97.9. This station made radio history by gaining the rank of number one station in the most competitive and important radio market in the country. Never before had a Spanish language station dominated the airwaves in Los Angeles. In addition, a point that must be acknowledged, the radio station had been "created from the ground up" in August 1992; it was, therefore, a new station that claimed the number one ranking in fall 1992. Alfredo Rodríguez, the general manager of KLAX, established the station and included banda music as part of the format in 1992. Banda was played along with *rancheras con mariachi*, *norteñas* with accordion, and music with tropical rhythms such as *cumbias*. The format was not wholly banda music, nor is the KLAX music format totally banda two years after it's establishment, but banda is what has given the station it's identity. Today, in Los Angeles, KLAX and banda music are identified as one.

The ascension of KLAX to the number one ranking has been dramatic, and the Arbitron survey ratings show a strong and continuing listening audience for the radio station. The Los Angeles area's top ten stations and their Arbitron ratings, and the percentage share of the listening audience of persons over age twelve, is provided below. The Arbitron rankings are as of the fall 1993 survey, ending December 1993; each survey period is a quarter year.

			-----PERCENTAGE OF LISTENERS-----		
ARBITRON RANKING	STATION	FALL 1992	WINTER 1993	SPRING 1993	SUMMER 1993	FALL 1993
1.	KLAX-FM	5.3	7.2	5.7	6.6	7.0
2.	KPWR-FM	5.1	5.0	5.0	4.9	4.8
3.	KOST-FM	5.1	5.5	5.1	4.7	4.4
4.	KFI-AM	3.7	4.3	4.5	4.1	4.3
5.	KROQ-FM	3.8	3.9	4.3	3.9	4.2
6.	KIIS-FM	4.1	4.3	4.0	3.8	4.2
7.	KLSX-FM	3.6	3.8	3.6	3.2	3.5
8.	KKBT-FM	3.1	3.4	3.1	3.3	3.4
9.	KRTH-FM	4.4	3.7	3.9	3.3	3.4
10.	KBIG-FM	3.7	3.5	3.2	3.2	3.2

The shares, as a percentage of the listening audience of persons twelve years of age and over, may be deceiving. There are two important points provided by the data. First, KLAX has maintained its number one position over the five surveyed periods. Second, the 7.0 share that KLAX gained during the fall 1993 survey equals 1,114,500 persons listening to the station at any given time. The size of the population affected has prompted significant local and national coverage of the radio station, its music, and the banda dancing that has become so popular.

However, the number of people listening to KLAX is not the only significant figure. For example, Los Angeles banda concert/dances are now regularly offered and have been drawing 15,000 people; there are an estimated 30,000 members, between the ages of eight and thirty, in 800 banda dance clubs; after school dances now attract 500 students to dance to banda music, with no rock and roll or rap; small dance clubs are returning to Los Angeles to meet the demand for live dance music; and the banda aficionados, who listen and dance to banda music, are a growing population that has purchasing power.

The sociocultural impact of the music and dance requires extensive investigation. Newspaper articles have noted the broad following of banda music and dance. It cuts across different generations and age groups, different economic status groups, and individuals with different life experiences. For example, the recent arrival from Mexico, the third-generation Chicana/o born in the United States, the monolingual Spanish speaker, the bilingual, the working class laborer and the corporate executive despite their diversity, all seem to be tuning into KLAX, buying the music, and going to banda dances.

Alfredo Rodríguez and the morning DJ, Juan Carlos Hidalgo, both noted that KLAX had something for all listeners, "for all the good, hard working people of Los Angeles," and that the philosophy of the radio station was to communicate "positive values." The station has not hesitated to deal with critical social issues such as "immigrant bashing" and the condition of poor people in Mexico. In the morning program there may be humorous criticism of California Governor Wilson and his policies; the following morning, questions may be raised regarding the lack of basic necessities for workers in Mexico.

Station management and the radio personalities understand that they are limited in what they can do, but they also understand and are willing to use radio for education, social awareness, and action for the good of the community. This and other topics should be investigated, including, for example, what social, cultural, and political impact banda music and banda dancing have had on Los Angeles.

PART 1. BANDA MUSICAL EVOLUTION

The musical sound of current bandas is derived from the *banda sinaloense* or *banda con tambora* sound that can be identified in commercial Mexican music from the 1940s to the present. This was primarily Mexican regional music as played in the Pacific coastal states of Sinaloa, Nayarít, Jalisco, and Michoacán. The music, however, was recognized as *banda sinaloense* and played throughout Mexico and parts of the United States where people of Mexican descent reside (particularly in California and Arizona). The traditional bandas are large groups, of fourteen to sixteen musicians, dominated by brass and woodwind instruments with a tuba and *la tambora*, a marching bass drum, providing a characteristic sound to the music. The traditional *banda sinaloense* offers strictly instrumental renditions without vocal accompaniment.

The origins of the *banda sinaloense* sound have typically been traced back to Europe. One popular theory is that Germans introduced Bavarian bands and European brass and woodwind instruments to the major trading seaport town of Mazatlán, Sinaloa. A second theory is that the instrumentation could have been introduced by the Europeans at various points in Mexico and that regional styles, with Sinaloa being one of them, quickly evolved. A

third theory regarding the origin of Mexican banda music is that the instruments were introduced to various regions of Mexico by Mexican military bands that were modeled after European military musical groups.

During the initial introduction of the instruments there would have been Europeans playing them at different social functions, but Mexicans quickly adopted the instruments and musical style and spread them to various parts of Mexico. In some instances, there were regional adaptations that changed the instrumentation; for example, Zacatecas has a version of the *banda sinaloense* sound, *tamborazo zacatecano*, that has no tuba. The use of the European brass and woodwind instruments, and what may have been a Bavarian band sound, has been transformed over a period of more than a hundred years and is now identified as a uniquely Mexican musical style.

Phase 1. The Traditional Sound: *Bandas del Pueblo*

Prior to the commercialization and recording of the *banda sinaloense* sound there existed *bandas del pueblo*, groups that would come together to play for municipal functions, fiestas (*jaripeos*), concerts at the town plaza, and other local social functions. Given the economic situation of most smaller Mexican pueblos, it can be concluded that the bandas that played in those towns were formed by resident nonprofessional musicians. Another possibility is that local military bands were used to provide music at social functions in rural towns. Regardless of how they were formed, the bandas played the *sinaloense* sound and introduced it to Mexicans in various regions. *Bandas del pueblo*, local musical groups, exist today and play for rural town functions, providing a continuing source of entertainment to Mexicans living outside of the heavily populated centers.

Phase 2. Commercialization of the Traditional *Banda Sinaloense* Sound

Professional *banda sinaloense* musical groups

evolved in the twentieth century, and their music was recorded for much wider distribution. The audience for banda music appears to have been primarily working class Mexicans; middle and upper class Mexicans preferred popular music with vocals (much of which could be traced to European or United States popular music). The *banda sinaloense* groups appear to have been more common in cities and towns of the Mexican coastal states than they were in other parts of Mexico.

An example of a commercially successful group that set the standard for the recorded traditional *banda sinaloense* sound, and one that continues to perform and record, is the group El Recodo de Cruz Lizarraga. With recordings dating back to the 1950s, this group has varied in size over its long existence, but it has typically included sixteen musicians, fourteen wind instruments and two drums. Another commercially successful group, La Banda La Costeña, has been in existence for several decades and has continued to interpret music in the traditional *sinaloense* sound. As is the norm with traditional *banda sinaloense*, these groups play instrumental arrangements and do not have vocalists. The recordings are punctuated at points when all of the instruments play simultaneously (*tutti*) to create the unique and energetic sound of *la banda sinaloense*. These are not "polka bands," but are orchestras that interpret a broad range of music.

A sample of the traditional banda of the 1950–1970 period is provided by the album, *Banda Sinaloense "El Recodo" de Cruz Lizarraga* (1976 RCA Records). This album contains primarily Mexican compositions, such as "El niño perdido," as interpreted by the *banda sinaloense*. The album jacket clearly shows the instruments used by the group, whose members all appear to be Mexican *mestizo*; they are Mexican musicians playing Mexican music. Unlike contemporary Mexican popular musical styles, where the entertainers reflect a European or American influence, *bandas del pueblo* and commercially successful groups reflect a Mexican identity.

As part of their commercialization, traditional bandas began to interpret music from various sources, including United States popular music and rock and roll. These continued to be large bands with the same instrumentation. The music continued to be strictly instrumental interpretations.

A sample of the music from this phase of the evolution of the banda sound is provided by *Bazaar de exitos con la banda sinaloense 'El Recodo' de Cruz Lizarraga* (1986 RCA Records). This album contains adaptations of such 1970s hits as "I Just Called To Say I Love You," by Stevie Wonder.

Phase 3. The Banda Sound Adopted by Vocalists

A major transition in the *banda sinaloense* sound took place as it moved away from the emphasis on instrumentals. Singers began using banda groups to accompany them as they sang songs that were primarily composed in Mexico; the "banda version" might have been a "cover" for a song (typically a *ranchera*) that had already been a hit with a mariachi accompaniment. This was a move away from the regional sound to a music that would become more popularized and accepted by larger numbers.

This transition was seemingly prompted during the 1980s by Antonio Aguilar, a major Mexican film and recording artist, who began recording albums accompanied by a *banda sinaloense*. As an established artist who had attracted a public following based on his sung interpretations of Mexican *rancheras* with mariachi, Antonio Aguilar was able to successfully market his singing with a *banda con tambora* accompaniment. His success expanded the audience and appeal of the *banda sinaloense* sound throughout Mexico and into the United States.

However, Aguilar was not the first major Mexican artist to utilize a *banda con tambora* to accompany his singing. José Alfredo Jiménez, for example, recorded an album of several of his compositions with the backing of a banda: *José Alfredo*

Jiménez, "Viejos Amigos," con la Banda Sinaloense El Recodo de Cruz Lizarraga. The album includes the well known Jiménez compositions, "Viejos amigos" and "Tu recuerdo y yo." The version of "Tu recuerdo y yo" with banda accompaniment gained national popularity, and it became established as one of the great composer and singer's most acclaimed hits. A second artist that predates Antonio Aguilar singing with a *banda con tambora* is Luis Pérez Meza, who was singing in the 1950s, and produced albums with banda accompaniment in the 1960s. Pérez, Jiménez, and Aguilar were each exponents of *rancheras* sung with mariachi. They expanded their repertoire by adding the traditional *banda sinaloense* sound to some of their music.

These singers used traditional bandas; Pérez sang with Banda La Costeña, Jiménez sang with El Recodo, and Aguilar sang with a group that had the full banda instrumentation, including the tuba. In addition, these vocalists interpreted primarily Mexican compositions, mainly *rancheras*, when they sang with banda.

The transition in the banda sound, for example, the change by Antonio Aguilar from singing *rancheras* with mariachi to singing with banda, can be appreciated by listening to two albums, *Rancheras del relaso* and *Exitos con banda*, both by Aguilar. Two examples of Luis Pérez Meza singing with a banda are *En la onda con banda* and *El gran trovador del campo: con la Banda La Costeña.*

Phase 4. The Traditional Bandas Incorporate Vocalists

Soon traditional bandas were adding vocalists to their regular members. These bandas were still large musical groups, rooted in the *banda sinaloense* style, with the same instrumentation, but having singers allowed the bandas to interpret the words and music of a vast array of popular songs, along with original music composed for bandas. These groups form an important link between the traditional *banda sinaloense* music played by El Recodo

and La Costeña, and the music heard from current groups in what has come to be known as techno-banda.

One reference group for this phase of the evolution of banda is Clave Azul, and an example of the music is provided in *15 Exitos con tambora sinaloense.* This large group of fifteen musicians has the typical *banda sinaloense* sound, they play instrumentals, but they also have several outstanding vocals, such as "Los dos amanates," and "El pescador nadador." Banda Sinaloense La Tunera, with fourteen musicians, is another example of a traditional banda that offers a vocalist, although of limited singing range. A third group, Banda Los Cachorros, played behind Joan Sebastian, a well known composer and singer of Mexican *rancheras*, when Sebastian began to interpret his music *con banda* in the 1980s. Los Cachorros also has fourteen musicians.

These groups link the traditional banda sinaloense sound with the techno-banda by incorporating vocalists; however, they remain "traditional" with their instrumentation in that they have maintained the tuba.

Phase 5. The Techno-Banda Period

The final phase in the evolution of the *banda sinaloense* sound is the techno-banda period. Musical groups, while maintaining the sound, incorporated vocalists and revised the instrumentation. Electric guitars and other instruments were introduced, but the most significant innovation was the use of the synthesizer. These changes allowed for much smaller groups than the traditional *sinaloense* bandas and the reduction in the number of instruments used (including the elimination of the tuba). The "electrified" techno-banda can be as small as five or six musicians, but their instrumentation gives them flexibility and range, and they are able to imitate the sinaloense sound.

A precise date for the beginning of the techno-banda period or contemporary banda music cannot be given. According to KLAX's Alfredo Rodríguez, the current banda sound originated in

Mexico in the late 1980s. A record producer in Guadalajara had existing musical groups, not *sinaloense* bandas, record music that imitated the *sinaloense* sound. These groups had vocalists and did not include the traditional *banda sinaloense* instruments. Through their experimenting, tropical music and *rancheras* were given a *sinaloense* sound.

One of the early contemporary bandas that adopted the *sinaloense* sound was Vaqueros Musical. Their 1989 album of the same name offers *rancheras* and *cumbias*. Around that time, Ranchero Band also produced albums, but with a greater emphasis on *bailables* (dance numbers), and had a greater singing range, with two female singers included in the eleven-piece group. These bandas offer few instrumentals. They emphasize the vocal interpretation of their music, which is composed in Mexico.

The early offerings had limited success in Mexico. According to Rodríguez, it was not until banda music became identified with Los Angeles that the banda sound gained popularity. In fact, Los Angeles is recognized as the hub of this musical style, not only in terms of radio time for the music, sales of records, or venues for the bands, but also in terms of the recording and production of the music.

PART 2. THE CURRENT BANDA SOUND, THE 1990s

Four fundamental characteristics define the current banda music. First, and most obvious, the music adopts the *banda sinaloense* sound. Second, banda is an interpretation and mixture of various Mexican musical styles. Third, the music is energetic and danceable. A cursory review of the music offered by bandas indicates that the majority is *musica tropical*, music with Latin American tropical dance rhythms. Fourth, it is performed live, in venues ranging from small dance clubs to large arenas that accommodate 15,000 dancers. The public, the banda aficionados, demand that the music be played live for dancing, and that the musicians dress in a *vaquero* style and perform dance routines while on stage.

The current banda sound is a hybrid, *una mezcla*, a combination of different Mexican musical sounds. The recent explosion of interest in banda music from 1991 onward, and as promoted by the popular Los Angeles FM radio station KLAX 97.9 and other radio stations, has fostered the birth and proliferation of many musical groups. Some groups have moved from playing *norteño* music and have adopted aspects of the traditional *sinaloense/ tambora* sound. Other popular Mexican singing groups that have existed for years have included music with banda accompaniment in their recent albums. It also appears that Mexican rock and roll groups, and groups that feature *cumbias* and tropical music, are adopting the *sinaloense banda con tambora* sound. And like Antonio Aguilar, a growing number of *ranchera* vocalists, most notably Joan Sebastian and Carmen Jara, are utilizing *bandas con tambora* as accompaniment, not only for one song, but for entire albums. This has ramifications for their live performances; for example, when Aguilar gives a concert, he uses both a mariachi group and a *banda con tambora*.

The flow of musical influence is not one-way. The existing standard Mexican musical styles feed the current banda movement, and the current banda sound feeds the standard musical styles. While the musical tradition of the current bandas is primarily the *banda sinaloense/banda con tambora* sound, there is now adaptation of music across musical styles. Bandas adopt *rancheras* that have been played by mariachi; they incorporate *norteño* music (particularly the country and western sound and the Texas-Mexican style polka); bandas play tropical/*cumbia* music (some bandas will sound, for example, like Sonora Santanera or Central American groups); and bandas incorporate Mexican popular and rock and roll music (including United States rock and roll that is "covered" in Mexico, for example, "The Night Chicago Died"). The *banda mezcla* has allowed for experimentation, cross-fertilization, and innovation.

The graph below shows the different Mexican musical styles that influence the current banda sound.

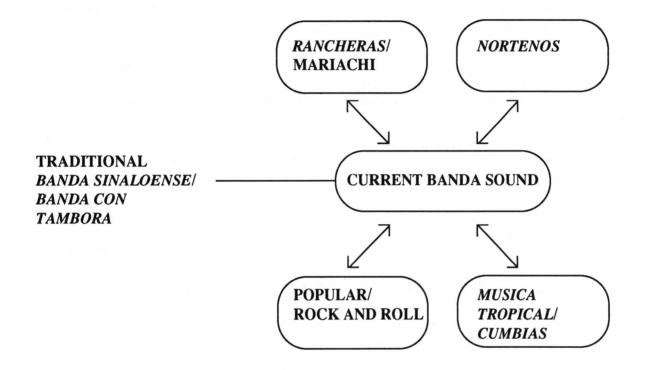

Bandas may play *rancheras*, *corridos*, *charangas*, *zapateados*, *sones*, *cumbias*, *merengue*, *boleros*, polkas, and waltz music. The groups will still play instrumentals, but these will typically be in a "country and western style," or what is called *"al estilo vaquero,"* *"al estilo* western," *"al estilo* de cowboy," *"al estilo ranchero,"* etc. This would be a major difference between the traditional *banda sinaloense* instrumental and the current banda instrumental. The *vaquero*-style instrumentals and the polkas played by bandas are drawn from *norteño* music, including Tex-Mex music. Country and western music and polkas have been performed by *norteño* groups for decades, so this is not a new phenomenon. In addition, mariachi groups, particularly those with ties to northern Mexico and to Texas, regularly perform country and western music, as well as polkas.

The country and western style instrumentals also appear to be related to the rodeos and *jaripeos*

that are popular throughout Mexico. Four examples of *vaquero* instrumentals recorded by bandas are "El Ultimo Rodeo," by Banda Vallarta Show, "Corazón de Texas," by Clave Azul, and "Arreando la Mula" and "Jinete's Country," by Banda R-15.

An important factor in the growth of interest in banda music in the Los Angeles area has been the contributions of *norteño* musical groups and their popularization of the current banda dance craze. *Norteño* groups have their own following and they have stimulated broader appeal for banda music and dance. A primary example is the song by Los Huracanes del Norte, "El vaquero guero," a novelty hit that deals with the "cowboy" dress and the dancing that is part of the banda phenomenon. This *norteño* song also notes that banda dancing is to be found in Chicago, in Texas, in California; "El vaquero guero" and other songs underscore that banda music and dance is not a regional phenomenon. Other *norteño* groups have recorded songs that comment, usually in a humorous way, on aspects of banda dancing, and they have added to the growing interest in the banda music.

Lorenzo de Monteclaro, a longtime exponent of *norteño* music, has been successful with his interpretation of songs with a banda accompaniment. His success in this area has spread the banda sound into northern Mexico and Texas. Lalo Mora, another singer drawn from the *norteño* musical tradition, has produced songs with banda. On his latest album, *Regresa el Rey de Mil Coronas*, he is accompanied by Banda La Costeña.

On the popular music side, there are growing examples of musical groups that feature music that is popular in Mexico and Central America adopting the banda sound. The music of "Los Bukis," "Bronco," "Los Caminantes," "Los Freddys," etc., is usually romantic ballads or soft rock; however, these groups are now using the *banda sinaloense* sound on some numbers (Los Caminantes have an entire album *con banda*). For example, one pop group, La Industria del Amor, had one banda number in an album, *Rey de oros*, but that was the song that received the most attention and recognition. It is a popular banda song, but it is dramatically different from the romantic numbers that are offered on the same album. As a consequence of producing records to meet the demand for banda music, popular music groups are not only adopting the *sinaloense* sound, they are also broadening the appeal of the banda sound and dance.

The current bandas play songs that may be arranged into several categories:

Love songs and romantic ballads (*"cariño y amor"*)

Lost love (usually about *"la mujer que pagó mal"*)

Satirical/novelty songs (including songs related to *la quebradita*, dancing, the *vaquero* style of dress, drinking)

Mexican nationalism/regionalism (*"Soy puro mexicano,"* *"Vengo de Nayarít"*)

Social commentary (*El Indio, mestizo* roots,

ills of Mexican society, plight of the immigrant).

The banda categories of love songs and lost love include songs that originated as rancheras or cumbias, or they are drawn from Mexican popular music. The songs dealing with nationalism/regionalism, as well as the songs that provide a social commentary, are also found in other Mexican musical styles. However, much of what can be categorized as banda satirical/novelty songs are uniquely "banda" because of the relationship of these songs to *la quebradita* and to a banda dance style. The "banda music" and the "banda dance" are interdependent; banda dancing, including *la quebradita*, has become popular because of the banda music, and banda music has gained in popular appeal because greater numbers are dancing in what has been identified as a banda dance style. Most afficionados cannot dance *la quebradita* because it is difficult and dangerous (the female partner can easily be dropped). So banda dancing for most means combinations of *cumbias*, polkas, *zapateados*, etc. But it is not uncommon to hear, "Yo bailo banda," or "I dance banda." A similar phenomenon occurred in the late forties and early fifties with the mambo; the mambo music and mambo dance were identified as one. The music generated interest in the dance, and mambo dance enthusiasts demanded the music.

The novelty songs also include references to those things that have become identified with bandas and banda dancing. Songs identify the *vaquero* western/cowboy dress for both men and women dancers, as well as accessories that identify the home region or Mexican state from which the banda aficionado comes (or their family origin). The *vaquero* dress includes the Texas-style hat, western boots, shirt, vest, and belt with belt buckle. Accessories include a *correa*, a leather strap with the name of the home Mexican state engraved; a bandanna in Mexican national colors or with the name of the state; and a *cuarta*, a short version of a horsewhip that is used in some of the dances.

The novelty songs dealing with banda dance and customs may be the primary new musical contribution of the current bandas. The novelty songs are contemporary and usually original compositions introduced by a banda musical group. The lyrics are not derived from standard Mexican musical areas such as *rancheras, cumbias*, and Mexican pop.

Current Bandas: Five Successful Groups

Five successful banda groups among current performers are reviewed here. They include:

1. Banda Clave Azul
2. Banda Machos
3. Banda Vallarta Show
4. Banda Superbandido
5. Banda R-15

Although the five groups are representative of commercially successful banda groups there are others that can be identified with the late 1980s transition, for example Vaqueros Musical, Ranchero Band, and Banda Movil. The Movil hit, "El quebrador," is an excellent example of the banda novelty song; it is a "danceable" song in a *norteño/ cumbia* style that is a mainstay of the current bandas. The song relates to the dance, *la quebradita*, to the western/cowboy dress associated with the dance, and to banda music in general. *El quebrador* is the male dancer who symbolically "breaks" the back of his partner while "dipping" her during the dance.[1]

Banda Clave Azul

Of the five groups, Clave Azul most closely resembles the traditional *banda sinaloense* musical style and sound. It is possible that the musicians in this group had "traditional" banda experience before they moved into the current banda phase. On their album, *15 Exitos con tambora sinaloense*, the instrumental, "La isla del capri," is a good example of Clave Azul playing in the traditional banda style. The song, "Arráncame la vida," blends the *banda sinaloense* sound with the addition of limited lyrics. The instrumental, "Corazón de Texas," is an example of the western theme as interpreted in a *banda sinaloense* style.

The Clave Azul album contains several appealing interpretations of old and well known songs, for example, "La feria de las flores." There is a drinking song, "Andamos todos borrachos," a song about the working class, "El venadito," a polka instrumental, "La loquita," a corrido, "El pescador nadador," and "Un indio quiere llorar," about discrimination against a Mexican Indian. Although the Clave Azul version of "Un indio" was not as popular as the Banda Machos version (described below), it has the stronger *banda sinaloense* influence. A popular Clave Azul song, "Dos amantes," is a blending of the *banda sinaloense* sound with romantic lyrics.

Banda Machos

The premiere banda of the current phase is Banda Machos. Juan Carlos Hidalgo, the KLAX morning DJ, has called the group "la reina de las bandas," and KLAX is advertised as "La Reina del Radio."

Banda Machos comes from Jalisco, but the eleven band members include several musicians who have lived and worked in the United States. According to Alfredo Rodríguez, Banda Machos had been recording in Mexico but it was not until they were played on Los Angeles radio that their popularity skyrocketed. It was Rodríguez who programmed Banda Machos songs into the daily play of KLAX, and the audience response to Machos and other banda groups is now history.

The popularity of Banda Machos is underscored by their being the highest selling "banda" group in 1992–93 with two hit albums, *Casimira* (1991) and *Sangre de indio* (1992). Each album contains several singles that received extensive air play on KLAX and other Los Angeles radio stations. These two albums were produced in the LP format, and the record covers show details about the group, such as the characteristics of the banda members and their show costumes. The musicians are all *morenos* (dark complexioned), Mexican in appearance, and their dress style is *vaquero*, western/ cowboy.

The Banda Machos albums are well balanced with novelty/satire, romantic love, lost love, and songs about social ills. The group's rendition of "Casimira" is an excellent example of a banda novelty song, but the album also includes "La culebra" and "El viejo joven," two other well known banda novelty hits. On the second album, "La Secretaria," "Y la quiere Paco," and "Al gato y al ratón" were novelty songs that received significant radio time. The typical fast-paced banda love songs are exemplified by "Un cariño como tú" and "Chaparra de mi amor;" while "Mi tesoro" is a slower paced romantic number. In the lost love category is "Lena de pirul," that was adopted by the banda; the more traditional "No soy monedita de oro" and "Sentimiento y traición" are *rancheras* that were originally interpreted by other vocalists with mariachi accompaniment.

The Banda Machos songs dealing with social ills were very popular in the Los Angeles area. The *Casimira* album contains "Un indio quiere llorar," a song that depicts race and class conflict in Mexican society through the rejection of an Indian by the well-to-do woman with whom he fell in love. Given the strong public response to the lyrics of this song, it was eventually interpreted by several other current banda groups, but the Machos version was the more popular. This is followed in the *Sangre de indio* album, with the title song lamenting the difficulties facing the Indian and dark-skinned Mexican people as they struggle to improve themselves.

Banda Vallarta Show

One of the most exciting and lively banda groups, the Banda Vallarta Show appears to be a group from the state of Nayarít. The eleven piece Vallarta Show provides the spirited dance music that forms the basis for the banda dance sound. As you listen to the music you begin to respond to the energetic vocals and instrumentation. The Vallarta Show album, *Provócame* (1993), contains several popular songs, including "Provócame" and "La negra colora," two outstanding *banda cumbia* numbers.

The third featured song is "La primera caricia," a medium paced song about lost love ("the love affair has ended, but I was the first"). This was a cover version and it was originally sung as a *ranchera* with mariachi.

The second half of *Provócame* offers a variety of songs, including "El Huerfanito," a novelty/drinking song; "Besame morenita," a fast paced dance number; "A Nayarít," a Mexican regionalism song; and "El ultimo rodeo," another example of a current banda instrumental that is a very good adaptation of the *tambora/banda sinaloense* sound, with an infusion of the force and energy of the current banda. The instrumental is, again, in a *vaquero*, cowboy/western style.

Banda Superbandido

In its album, *Maldición ranchera* (1993), the ten-piece Banda Superbandido blends Mexican standards, usually about lost love, with several novelty songs that became popular in the Los Angeles area. The songs of lost love include "La ultima copa," "Trono caido," and "Al mismo nivel." "Maldición ranchera," a *ranchera*, also deals with lost love, but it is a faster paced banda dance number that makes reference to banda music and specifically to banda groups from Jalisco.

The novelty songs have double meaning and erotic themes, including "El caramelo," "El aparatito," and "Mete y saca." Each is a good banda dance number, but the novelty aspect of the songs gained them popularity.

Banda R-15

This is a true club banda. Its thirteen members play very danceable "slow" music, usually *boleros* and *rancheras* that deal with heartbreak and lost love. In the album, *Van 15 exitos con la Banda R-15,* the boleros include "Si me recuerdas," "Voy a dejarte," "Solo se que fue en marzo," and "Los ladrones." The rancheras are also in this vein and include "Como tu decides," "Adios y bienvenida," and "Ahora si va en serio." Banda R-15 novelty songs include two *cumbias*, "El bigote" and "Si tu boquita," with the latter number gaining significant popularity and air play. "Arreando la mula" and "Jinete's Country" are examples of current banda instrumental recordings with a *vaquero/western* style.

SUMMARY COMMENTS

Banda music, as it is currently being recorded and played in Los Angeles, has evolved over five phases. The traditional banda style, as played by *bandas del pueblo*, was introduced throughout Mexico. These musical groups used European brass and woodwind instruments, without vocals, and primarily played what came to be known as the *sinaloense* style. There was then a period during which traditional *banda sinaloense* groups commercialized the banda style and the recorded music provided wider distribution. During a third identifiable phase, Mexican vocalists, primarily singers of *rancheras*, used the accompaniment of bandas; this further expanded the audience. In the fourth phase, traditional bandas, groups with fourteen to sixteen musicians and traditional instruments, including the tuba, incorporated vocalists within the group. In the last phase, the techno-banda period, the *banda sinaloense* sound has been adopted by groups that incorporated different instruments, including synthesizers, and emphasized vocals. The techno-bandas can be as small as five or six musicians, but their instrumentation gives them the ability to imitate the *banda sinaloense* sound.

The banda sound of the 1990s is a hybrid, *una mezcla*, a combination of different Mexican musical styles. Bandas interpret *rancheras, norteño* music, *musica tropical*, and popular/rock and roll music. The *banda mezcla* has allowed for experimentation and innovation. Not only is there is a vast array of music available for banda to "cover," but the bandas are experimenting with unique ways of interpreting music.

Four fundamental characteristics of the current banda music have been noted. They include:
1. The music adopts the *banda sinaloense* sound.

2. The music is a mixture, a *mezcla*, of different Mexican musical styles.
3. The music is energetic and danceable.
4. The demand is for the music to be performed live.

The larger bandas, with ten or more musicians and a full complement of instruments, including brass and woodwind, electric guitars, modern drum sets and Cuban-style timbales, have been the most successful during the 1991 to 1994 banda explosion. Banda Machos is the model to emulate in terms of its instrumentation, sound, and style.

The music that is interpreted by bandas, and the musical innovations and experimentation that occurs, will be influenced by the background of the musicians. Although no conclusions can be drawn at this time, it appears that many banda musicians, *los banderos*, have experienced living and working on both sides of the Mexico-United States border. This would give them broader exposure to different musical and interpretive styles. Furthermore, as more groups are formed in California and other southwestern states, with their roots in Chicano culture, banda music will have an infusion of new ideas. For example, some banda music is being done in a "rap" style, and some songs are being sung bilingually in Spanish and English. Lastly, increasing the record production and distribution of banda music in Los Angeles and other parts of the Southwest will also change the music.

Bandas are providing social commentary on issues of our time. One group, Banda Techno 0720, primarily sings popular music, but they recorded "Verguenza maldita," a song that deals with AIDS, in a *banda sinaloense* style. The song describes how two young men, engaged to be married to beautiful women in their town, contract AIDS and, rather than return to the town, commit suicide. The song comments that "it was not drugs nor the Mexican Mafia that killed the youth."

Female musician involvement in bandas is minimal; of the groups considered here, only Ranchero Band included women. However, the *banda mezcla* and the demand for danceable music, will ultimately require the participation of female singers. Carmen Jara, primarily a *ranchera* singer, has produced two albums with banda. Angélica María has produced songs with banda accompaniment. One female singer, Rosalva, had a novelty song, "La chica de las caderas," that was popular in the Los Angeles area. There is potential for female singers and musicians to perform and expand the banda sound.

A final point to be made here is that the current banda groups will offer both serious and humorous music in the same album. Banda Degollado, a large group with sixteen musicians, is able to perform in the best *banda sinaloense* style, as shown by their rendition of "No vas a creer." This number has all the elements of the traditional *banda con tambora* instrumentation, with the addition of the vocalist. Then, on the same album, Banda Degollado performs "Serenata con banda," a parody that mocks the current bandas and the customs that have evolved around the music and the dance. Banda Degollado, apparently, does not take itself too seriously—and maybe that is a good thing, because it is a sign of the youthfulness and exuberance of banda music.

NOTES

1.   Another interpretation that has been offered by followers of the banda style is that of connotating the "break" concept (*la quebradita*) with that of the cowboy who "breaks" a wild horse.

REFERENCES CITED

Interviews

Hidalgo, Juan Carlos.   Morning DJ, KLAX-FM, 97.9, Radio Station, Los Angeles. Hidalgo was interviewed three times; November 12, 1993, March 25, 1994, and April 1, 1994.

Rodríguez, Alfredo. General Manager, KLAX-FM, 97.9, Radio Station, Los Angeles. Rodríguez was interviewed on April 4, 1994.

Williams, Robert.   Sales Manager, KLAX-FM, 97.9, Radio Station, Los Angeles. Williams was interviewed on November 12, 1993 and March 7, 1994.

Recorded Music References

Aguilar, Antonio. *15 Exitos con tambora: con la Banda La Costeña.* Musart Records, 2032.

Aguilar, Antonio. *Rancheras del relaso.*

Banda Clave Azul. *15 Exitos con tambora sinaloense.* Lobo Musical, CLM-2010.

Banda Los Cachorros. *Hijo de León.* Fonovisa, RFC-3504.

Banda Machos. *Casimira.* Fonovisa, MPCD-5161.

Banda Machos. *Con sangre de indio.* Fonovisa, FPCD-9069.

Banda Movil. *La Grande.* Fonovisa, FPC-9078.

Banda R-15. *Van 15 exitos con la Banda R-15.* Fonovisa, FPCD-9084.

Banda Sinaloense El Recodo de Cruz Lizarraga. *El Recodo.* RCA, DKKI-3366.

Banda Sinaloense El Recodo de Cruz Lizarraga. *Bazaar de exitos con la Banda El Recodo.* RCA Camden, S-1286.

Banda Sinaloense El Recodo de Cruz Lizarraga. *La Chuchis y otros exitos.* RCA Camden, S-368.

Banda Sinaloense La Tunera. *En la raya.* Fonovisa, AFC-7028.

Banda Superbandido. *Maldición ranchera.* Andrea Records, AFCD-1001.

Banda Teckno 0720. *Verguenza maldita.* Mar International Records, MIC-353.

Banda Vallarta Show. *Provócame.* Fonovisa, FPCD-9087.

Industria del Amor. *Verano de amor.* Fonovisa, UFC-2001.

Jara, Carmen. *La mujer...el nuevo folklore de México.* Fonovisa, FPC-9109.

Jiménez, José Alfredo. *Viejos amigos: con la Banda Sinaloense El Recodo.* RCA, CAMS-1427.

Los Caminantes. *Buenos vaqueros.* Fonovisa, LUC-1250.

Los Huracanes del Norte. *Con nuevos horizontes.* Sony, DIC-80847.

Meza, Luis Pérez. *El gran trovador del campo: Con la Banda La Costena.* Fono-Rex Records, FRS-14.

Meza, Luis Pérez. *En onda con banda.* Antilla Discos, AP-661.

Monteclaro, Lorenzo de. *20 de colección.* Sony, CDL-81165/2-470632.

Mora, Lalo. *Regresa el Rey de Mil Coronas: Con la Banda La Costena.* Fonovisa, FPCD-9110.

Ranchero Band. *15 Exitos de Ranchero Band.* Discos Fonorama, KTC-T.V. 01.

Rosalva. *La chica de buenas caderas.* Fonovisa, LXC-4014.

Sebastian, Joan.   *Con tambora: con la Banda Los*

Cachorros. Musart Records, EM 2114.

    Sebastian, Joan. *Bandido de amores: con tambora*. Discos Musart, CDE-843.

    Vaqueros Musical. *Vaqueros Musical*. Discos Musart, MSD-10049.

MUSIC AT THE 1993 LOS ANGELES MARATHON: AN EXPERIMENT IN TEAM FIELDWORK AND URBAN ETHNOMUSICOLOGY

Timothy Rice

MUSIC IN LOS ANGELES comes in a bewildering array of styles and is performed by enormous numbers of musicians in contexts ranging from the intimate and private to the free and public to the fantastically expensive. For a graduate course in fieldwork at UCLA in the winter of 1993, I asked a class of beginning ethnomusicology students to examine music at one of Los Angeles's many free and public events, the City of Los Angeles Marathon. Significantly for our purposes, the marathon uses music extensively to create a sense of public, community involvement in an event run by a private organization. It was to be an experiment in team fieldwork and in urban ethnomusicology, both of which were new areas for all of us. For the community, stressed by two trials in the aftermath of the Rodney King beating, it turned out to be a test of social solidarity and courage. Here, in a series of short reports, we modestly present our findings, keenly aware of the way they are circumscribed by the limits of time and experience. Yet the civic tension surrounding the 1993 marathon, and the role music played in mediating those emotions, created an important moment in the history of music in Los Angeles. And we were there.

Team Fieldwork

While fieldwork is widely regarded as the *sine qua non* for admission into the social role of professional ethnomusicologist, it remains one of the most difficult and elusive parts of our discipline to teach. If knowledge of the history, theory, and findings of the field can be unproblematically gained through reading and discussion, fieldwork, the primary source of those findings, can only really be understood by doing it. No matter how much one prepares for it by reading about other people's experiences or by practicing with the impedimenta of documentation like fieldnotes, tape recorders, and cameras, fieldwork is really understood after the fact through reflection on what transpires in the dialogue between one's self as researcher and the people one encounters in the interpersonal and social occasions generated by fieldwork.

My design for the graduate course on ethnomusicological fieldwork includes readings and discussions on five important elements of fieldwork:

1. the human element, including entering and exiting the field, establishing and maintaining rapport, ethics, and reflexivity;
2. documentation, including the writing of notes, diaries, and logs, and the making of sound recordings, still photographs, and videotapes;
3. data gathering methods, including library, archival and museum research, bi-musicality, interviewing, and participant observation;
4. the purposes of fieldwork, including an-

swering research questions, doing applied ethnomusicology, preserving traditions, and education;

5. reporting the results, in forms such as deposits to archives, musical ethnographies, films and records (videotapes and CDs), and interactive multimedia.

But a recurring problem for such courses is what kind of fieldwork project can be assigned within the time constraints of a one-quarter, 11-week course (or even a longer one-semester course) that will provide students with a meaningful experience of the human and technical dimensions of fieldwork and have some relationship to current theory and practice in ethnomusicology. One professor I know, who teaches fieldwork in a cognate discipline, grew so frustrated with this problem, and with the resistance of some students to the off-campus, time-consuming demands of fieldwork, that he recently abandoned field research projects in his fieldwork course. On the other hand, most of my colleagues would concur that the only way to learn about fieldwork is to do it (see, for example, Spradley 1980).

A typical approach to fieldwork assignments allows students to devise their own research projects based on the premise that most ethnomusicological fieldwork is done by individuals and the notion that students will do their best work on topics of direct personal interest to them (Spradley 1979, Titon 1984). In teaching fieldwork, however, I have noticed two practical limitations to this approach. First, in one quarter or semester there is very little time to complete a project, let alone to devise it and make the contacts necessary to start it. Second, students often create projects that, while doable in a short time, don't expose them to a wide range of fieldwork experiences and thus to the practical and theoretical issues and problems that must be faced in the long-term fieldwork needed to write a doctoral dissertation. For example, the fieldwork often takes the relatively limited form of a few interviews with one key informant, and thus avoids the necessity for participant observation in group in-

teraction and performance.

To overcome some of these problems, I decided to experiment with a different approach for my fieldwork class in the winter quarter of 1993. I assigned the project to the students rather than allowing them to choose it, and designed it so they would be required to engage in both interviewing and participant observation and to address the performance of music not simply as a matter of musical understanding but as productive of social and cultural meaning. The assigned project was to be a team effort, in the hope that a synergism would result from a collective focus on one musical culture or event.

Given both the ethnomusicological insistence that music is culture and its tradition of studying musical meaning for relatively small, homogeneous societies who supposedly share a history and a cultural tradition, the obvious choice would have been to examine the music of one of Los Angeles's many ethnic communities, perhaps in the manner of Kay Shelemay's (1988) student-team research among the Syrian Jews in Brooklyn, New York. I was daunted, however, by the prospect of inserting a group of ten or so students into one close-knit community setting. It is hard enough for a community to accept one fieldworker in its midst, and that intrusion itself often changes the way people behave. I worried that neither I nor the community I might choose could manage such a large group of students well. I also worried that some students in the group would avoid the complete personal involvement so characteristic of fieldwork and hide behind the machinery of documentation or the leadership and gregariousness of a few of their colleagues.

As I thought about the project, it also seemed to me that large cities challenge many of ethnomusicology's deeply held beliefs about culture and community. Although many urban ethnic enclaves try to maintain separate identities in opposition to the homogenizing forces of education, the English language, the media, advertising, and the pressures of the workplace, cities are also places where culture clash, the deculturizing effects of poverty, and intercultural negotiation often seem to overwhelm the cozy confines implied by the culture concept and the notions of cultural separation and difference that derive from it. In cities, people experience simultaneously a sense of similarity with all who share their urban fate and a sense of difference along lines of race, ethnicity, class, education, age, and sexual orientation. If urbanites possess the sense of a shared, interlocked existence, then that might create, if we employ culture theory, a kind of urban culture (see LeVine 1984 on shared understanding as a feature of culture). But those who share the urban experience come into close proximity with one another for vastly different reasons: as natives, as willing immigrants, as unwilling exiles, or as the descendants of slaves. Our comings together seem to create in urban spaces a sense of separation, distance, and alienation from one another across all manner of social and cultural boundaries. These urban experiences and their challenge to ethnomusicological theory were not things that I had dealt with in my own work, but I decided to challenge the class and myself to think and work at the level of the urban "ethnoscape" (Slobin 1992, borrowing from Arjun Appadurai) rather than at the more intimate level of a self-defined and identifiable "musical culture." The resulting project in Los Angeles and the way it is reported bears in many ways an instructively converse relationship to Shelemay's team research in New York.

Urban Ethnomusicology at the L.A. Marathon

One of the obvious places to begin the search for music operating in the urban ethnoscape is at interethnic community festivals. If ordinary life in the city brings people of various groups into conflictual relationships, community leaders seem quite consciously to use festivals of various kinds to generate positive experiences of urban life through the cooperation and interaction of those same groups. While ethnic and racial differences

often create misunderstanding, tension, and violence when unmanaged, community festivals corral them into displays of pride and invitations for participation across the boundaries supposedly created by difference. Different languages, skin colors, and experiences of justice and economic opportunity may separate us during the week, but weekend festivals allow us to know each other through cultural forms that connect us at a human level while temporarily bracketing those differences as we side by side eat tasty food, appreciate artfully made crafts, and dance to groovy music.

Festivals can either be invented for their own sake or linked to some other event or anniversary. For the past six years or so the organizers of the Los Angeles Marathon have created a parallel music and entertainment festival. Since it occurs in early March near the end of winter quarter, it seemed a good context for our class to carry out an initial foray into music-making that might have implications for a large section of the city and not just for a local community. We could spend the early part of the quarter learning a number of fieldwork techniques and contacting and interviewing the various organizers of the events, do participant observation on the day of the marathon, and have time to write up the results before the quarter ended.

When I called the City of L.A. Marathon office, I learned that they have a two-pronged approach to music at the marathon. One person creates a "marathon of music" by placing "individual stages" every mile or so along the route where a variety of bands wanting public exposure play for free. Another person facilitates a series of eleven community-sponsored "entertainment centers in different ethnic areas" along the route. The community involvement in these entertainment centers seemed to make them the preferable target for an ethnomusicological study.

The marathon begins near the L.A. Coliseum, moves north into Downtown where old Chinatown and Little Tokyo are situated, west along Sunset Boulevard through an area where many immigrants from Central America have settled, through Hollywood, south through Koreatown along Crenshaw Boulevard into the northern reaches of mixed black and Latino South Central L.A., and east along Rodeo Road to the finish line at the Coliseum. The organizers sent me a list of the entertainment centers along the marathon route:

Mile 4: Little Tokyo
Mile 5: Olvera Street, a historic early Mexican settlement
Mile 6: Chinatown
Mile 7: Southwest Voters, in what the organizers called a Hispanic area
Mile 8: L.A.'s Best, a charity for children and school groups
Mile 10: Westside Jewish Community Center
Mile 13: Hollywood Arts Council
Mile 19: Guatemalan community and consulate
Mile 21: Mid-City Chamber of Commerce, mixed black and Latino community
Mile 23: Crenshaw district, a predominantly black area
Mile 26: Intertribal Road Runners

If the list doesn't begin to exhaust the ethnic diversity in Los Angeles, it at least illustrates that the route passes through the Japanese American, Chinese American, Mexican/Chicano, mixed Latino, Guatemalan, Jewish, and African American communities. The Native American entertainment center, we learned in the course of fieldwork, did not represent a community along the route but was set up to support the large number of Native American runners in the race. Two sizable communities along the route were not represented, Armenians and Koreans, and a more extensive study of community dynamics would surely try to understand why not. The route in many ways is cleverly chosen: it covers both the geographic and economic middle of the city, leaving out the extremes of poverty and wealth that are so jarring in this city: the tony and largely white Westside, the increasingly ethnically mixed but oddly suburban San Fernando Valley, the largely Mexican East L.A., and the poorest areas of South Central L.A., now a

mixed black and Latino area.

The class consisted of a diverse group of eight first-year graduate students in ethnomusicology and a second-year student in systematic musicology. A mix of five men and four women, there were two foreign students, from India and Kenya, and a relatively recent immigrant from Italy. Of the remaining six, four were European Americans, one African American, and one Filipino American. Given that there were fewer of us than entertainment centers, I decided not to insist on complete coverage and allowed each student to choose a center he or she found particularly interesting. Because of the potential dangers of doing fieldwork in urban environments—a factor also cited by Shelemay in her design—and differences in personalities, I suggested that each person participate in two two-person teams: on one they would act as team leader in setting up interviews, on the other they would help out as requested, and they would accompany each other on pre-marathon site visits. In fact, this plan didn't really work. Some students preferred to operate as individuals, while others were not yet ready to assume a leadership role. In the end I didn't insist on my original idea, and three students ended up working as individual agents while three pairs formed functional teams, usually with one student taking the lead in establishing contacts with the community but allowing the other student the opportunity to share profitably in the fieldwork.

Unlike Shelemay, who worked extensively with the community to design the students' project, I decided not to prepare the way by making contacts for them in advance. Entering the field, explaining your goals, and establishing rapport are perhaps the most trying and delicate parts of fieldwork— the class read about it in Paul Rabinow's 1977 introspective *Reflections on Fieldwork in Morocco*—and I wanted them to experience these things in a visceral way, not be shielded from them. Predictably some inquiries were met graciously, and the students were welcomed to come for interviews. Others encountered indifference, lack of cooperation, and even resistance. Eventually, the students made productive contacts with six of the eleven organizations sponsoring entertainment centers—Little Tokyo, Southwest Voter Registration, the Westside Jewish Community Center, the Hollywood Arts Council, the Guatemalan community, and the Intertribal Road Runners. In every case but one, they were able to conduct one or more interviews with organizers or musicians before the marathon, and the results of these interviews plus their observations of these entertainment centers are included in the mini-ethnographies that follow.

The 1993 Los Angeles Marathon turned out to be an event more pregnant with meaning for the city than any of us originally anticipated. In most years it is simply one of nearly a hundred public events (see the L.A. Arts Council brochure) where citizens have the opportunity to gain some understanding of the city's ethnic arts and to observe the workings of particular community groups. The 1993 marathon, however, occurred a little less than a year after the civil unrest, looting, and burning in the wake of the innocent verdict in the L.A. county trial of the police officers who beat Rodney King and during the closing moments of the federal trial of the same officers on charges of violating King's civil rights. The whole city was shaking, not from an earthquake this time, but in nervous anticipation of what might happen if the officers were again acquitted. The marathon went right through some of the worst-affected areas of the city. The marathon organizers bravely decided to retain the route, but needed to reassure participants from all over the city and the country that they would be safe on the streets of Los Angeles. The *Los Angeles Times* quoted a woman from Oregon, who admitted of her family, "We're frightened...We're watching the news day by day and [we] figure the trial won't end by race day...if anything happens before then, we'll cancel" (Farrell 1993). The same article reported that a female runner from Kansas City decided to stay away saying, "If you're a back-of-the-pack runner like I am, you're pretty much separated from the main body of people [in the

race], and you're very vulnerable out there." After considering the possibility of avoiding the worst-hit areas of the inner city in favor of a route from downtown toward West Los Angeles, the organizers decided to retain the original route. According to the *Times*, William A. Burke, the director, said such a move would send the wrong message and besides, according to the article, "Support from the largely black communities along the homestretch of the course had been vital in building the marathon into the nation's second largest, behind New York's." Quoting Burke, "We did what we felt was socially and intellectually responsible." The heightened emphasis on the meaning of the marathon to the city as opposed to the runners was evident in the changed motto for the race: instead of the usual "The L.A. Marathon, where every runner's a winner," the new slogan claimed, "Together we win."

The city's edginess, widely felt and reported by the media, took its toll on the students. A number were extremely uneasy about going into segments of the city largely unknown to them, and their concern comes through in some of their reports. Fortunately, they bravely soldiered on, and the result is a series of reports that assume added significance as a document of the role of music in one highly charged moment in the history of Los Angeles.

Generally their mini-ethnographies establish the important role that music plays in bringing communities together and in presenting and establishing community identity. But even if their findings are predictable at a general level, their reports short, and their time in the field minimal, the reports possess a delightful freshness that accompanies most meaningful first experiences. Through their candor we not only come to understand, or perhaps remember, what it is like to do fieldwork for the first time, we also see the city through their eyes in a new way. I did not have to coach them in the new self-reflexivity demanded by modern ethnographic theory; they came to it naturally. No veneer of self-protective professionalism clouds our ability to see them working at the process of understanding the meaning and role of music in social groups. And for all their brevity, each report contains either a pointed insight into the event it describes or telling, well-observed details that open us to a new world of musical and social experience—or both.

The papers appear here in the same order as the entertainment centers they describe were encountered by the runners. At Mile 4 Jay Mendoza ponders multiracial *taiko* drumming in Little Tokyo, worries about the biases he brings to the field, questions the link ethnomusicologists tend to assume—perhaps because of the way they name themselves—between ethnicity and ethnic music, and hypothesizes that the aesthetic appreciation of music may play as profound a role in breaking down cultural boundaries as it seems to in establishing them. Jacob Edgar's and Jean Kidula's detailed reports on the activities at Mile 7 give us a strong sense of the Latino community's self-consciousness of its own identity, reflected in its careful choice of a band, touchingly called The Alienz, to represent them. Jacob's account contains good detail on the problems of establishing contacts in fieldwork, and Jean's convinces us just how important music is to the overall mood and success of such events. At the Jewish Community Center at Mile 10, Ellen Sinatra and Shari Johnston move beyond description to a critique of the way music was used. Ellen describes the scene and worries about the lack of connection to the surrounding Latino community, while Shari hypothesizes that perhaps the music thoughtlessly replicated the alienating effects of the music industry and missed the opportunity grabbed at many of the other entertainment centers to create what she calls "an aesthetics of belonging." Kimasi Browne believes that Mile 13, the halfway point of the marathon, was psychologically important to the runners, and provides a detailed account of their response to the music there. Sarah Truher, through vivid detail, and Roberto Catalano, with moving self-reflection, create richly textured reports on the entertainment center at Mile 19, which the Guate-

malan community has turned into its most important event of the year. Both view the Guatemalan center as a positive, constructive manifestation of community with implications for the entire city. Muralikrishnan, at the end of the marathon, writes about the importance of running to Native Americans and the way they use music to create a feeling of unity.

All of the students' reports contain or imply a rather optimistic belief in the power of musical and cultural performances to create positive feelings of community and of inter-community relations in opposition to the sense of alienation from community and tension between communities frequently reported in the press. In some sense they seem to imply that the answer to Rodney King's famous question, "Can we all get along?" is yes, if we just make music and dance together more often. Although after-the-fact reflection makes such an answer seem absurd, the students' event descriptions capture just how engaging, constructive, and transformative well-designed and well-managed music events can be—and how ineffective poorly managed ones are. While the non-participating, cynical critic might claim that events such as the marathon distract us from and even hide the important work that still needs to be done to overcome the problems many people along the marathon route and on its eastern and southern periphery encounter during the rest of the year, these reports provide vivid reminders that community musical events can structure experience in powerful new ways. As we allow the music of our own and other communities to play on us, to structure how we move and how we interact with other people, we experience not only the aesthetic pleasure of artistic forms but the power of those forms to shape our understanding of the world and our relationship to others. I am tempted to hypothesize, partly on the basis of the following reports, that in the rough, tough city of Los Angeles, where we face constant challenges to our physical and psychological well-being, the positive experiences created by aesthetic forms such as music and dance in community settings like the marathon are crucial to the city's and our individual health, well-being, and desire to continue living here.

REFERENCES CITED

Farrell, David
1993   "L.A. Marathon Refuses to Run From Riot Images." *Los Angeles Times*, March 4, A1.
L.A. Arts Council
1994   *1994 Guide to Festivals in Los Angeles.* Los Angeles: L.A. Arts Council.
LeVine, Robert A.
1984   "Properties of Culture: An Ethnographic View." In *Culture Theory: Essays on Mind, Self, and Emotion,* edited by Richard A. Shweder and Robert A. LeVine: 67–87. Cambridge: Cambridge University Press.
Rabinow, Paul
1977   *Reflections on Fieldwork in Morocco.* Berkeley and Los Angeles: University of California Press.
Shelemay, Kay Kaufman
1988   "Together in the Field: Team Research among Syrian Jews in Brooklyn, New York." *Ethnomusicology* 32(3):369–84.
Slobin, Mark
1992   "Micromusics of the West: A Comparative Approach." *Ethnomusicology* 36(1):1–88.
Spradley, James P.
1979   *The Ethnographic Interview.* New York: Holt, Rinehart, Winston.
1980   *Participant Observation.* New York: Holt, Rinehart, Winston.
Titon, Jeff Todd, ed.
1984   *Worlds of Music: An Introduction to the Music of the World's Peoples.* New York: Schirmer.

Musical Formation as Racial Formation: Questioning a Theory in Little Tokyo
by
Jay Mendoza

Fieldwork informs our analysis of music in a certain locality, and understanding musical formation as racial formation requires fieldwork. Michael Omi and Howard Winant, in *Racial Formation in the United States from the 1960s to the 1980s* (New York: Routledge & Kegan Paul, 1986), define racial formation as "the process by which social, economic, and political forces determine the content and importance of racial categories, and by which they are in turn shaped by racial meanings (p. 61)....The presence of a *system* of racial meanings and stereotypes, of racial ideology, seems to be a permanent feature of US culture" (p. 63). Race is an important factor in the image of Los Angeles as a multicultural and diverse social system, and the 1992 rebellion, a mass reaction against an unacceptable verdict in the Rodney King beating case, was an example of racial formation in action. The rebellion provided the social context in which the L.A. Marathon was held, the context in which Japanese American music in Little Tokyo was performed, and the context in which I engaged in fieldwork.

Fieldwork on music requires one to seek social relationships and to engage in diverse kinds of dialogues when operating in the field. The fieldworker must enter the social context of racial formation, which impacts a fieldworker's analysis. To do fieldwork in Los Angeles's Little Tokyo on Japanese American musics, a fieldworker must be aware of the global and local social systems impacting the ethnic community.

When I arrived in Little Tokyo, the first entertainment center along the marathon route, I saw two *taiko* groups situated a block apart from each other near the intersection of San Pedro and Onizuka streets. One group, L.A. Matsuri, had approximately thirty musicians playing on instruments that included seven medium drums, four small drums, nine smaller drums, three big drums on tall stands, nine small drums on tilted stands, one hand cymbal, two metal time-keepers on stands, and one gong. The players kept a steady drum beat—short-long, short-long, short-long—for an hour while the marathoners ran past them. The metrical pulsation appeared to energize the runners and inspire them to run. Amidst the continuous short-long pulsations the players engaged in polyrhythms and solo improvisations.

I observed three subgroups in L.A. Matsuri. One group wore Expo '92 robes, another black t-shirts, and the third blue robes. The main time-keeper was Etsuo Hongo, the director of L.A. Matsuri. The group in black t-shirts appeared to be more ethnically diverse than the other two groups and, based on physical appearance, consisted of African Americans, Mexican Americans, and European Americans. The age and gender of the subgroups also differed. The blue-robed group had male and female players from ages six to adult. The Expo-robed group had mostly female teenagers, and the black-t-shirt group contained a mixture of teenage boys and girls. When L.A. Matsuri ended their performance, they had a group meeting, recited a cheer or song-prayer accompanied by a clapped rhythm, and had a group picture taken.

The *taiko* group down the block consisted of nine young women from a Buddhist group named SGI. They played seven small tilted drums arranged in an "arrow" formation, with one big drum on a tall stand and two medium drums to the side. The ethnicity of the performers appeared to be diversified although it was predominantly Japanese.

As the above description makes clear, the impact of racial formation on me as a fieldworker biased my interpretation of what I saw there. As I observed the music making in Little Tokyo, I took notice of race and noticed interracial behavior. Combining my field observations of music with Omi and Bryant's theory of racial formation, I decided to posit the concept of musical formation as an extension of it. Musical formation is the process by which social, economic, and political forces determine the content and importance of racial (or ethnic) music, and by which the music in turn is shaped by racial meanings. For Japanese American music to exist as a genre or category implies the use of race as a social concept.

Though race theory describes the larger system, Los Angeles and the United States, in which I was situated as a fieldworker, the concept of ethnic community describes the smaller field, Little To-kyo. Ethnic community life in Little Tokyo may be partly explained by what Stephen S. Fugita and David J. O'Brien, in *Japanese American Ethnicity: The Persistence of Community* (Seattle: University of Washington Press, 1991), refer to as the persistence of Japanese American ethnicity. They contend that "while their members are becoming structurally assimilated into the institutional life of the larger society...the persistence of Japanese American ethnicity stems from elements in traditional Japanese culture that structure social relationships among group members in such a way that they are able to adapt to changing exigencies without losing group cohesiveness" (pp. 4–5).

I found this to be true during my brief fieldwork in Little Tokyo. Japanese American musics include dynamic genres that preserve tradition and cultivate change. The ethnic community supports and creates a wide variety of music including *taiko* drumming, classical Japanese dance, jazz and popular musics with Asian American and black artists, performances by the Koto String Society, and the Day of Remembrance celebrations, just to mention a few. The patronage of Japanese American musics comes from the community's voluntary associations, business organizations, individuals, and professionals. That the Little Tokyo Business Association, the organization that coordinated the performances during the marathon, patronized the event is an indicator of the social, economic, and political forces at work in the maintenance of tradition within this community. Their support of community expressions illustrates the way abstractions such as racial formation and musical formation are reified in the actual content and practice of racial (or ethnic) music.

When I sought to analyze the musical formation of an ethnic community in terms of the bias in my own racial ideology, I realized that I was surprised to see Mexican, African, European, and Japanese Americans performing *taiko* drumming side by side at the marathon. I had assumed that I would see only Japanese performing as a symbolic and practical manifestation of their ethnic or racial identity.

Obviously, the performance of Japanese music by a mixed-race group challenged my and perhaps other ethnomusicologists' biases about the processes at work in the racial (or ethnic) formation of music. Some sort of complex appropriation and assimilation of cultures was going on, but who was assimilating what?

The appropriation of one group's culture by members of other cultures creates a puzzle for the analysis of musical formation as a product of racial formation. Perhaps Japanese Americans, in allowing people of all races to participate in what was originally their cultural practice, were assimilating into a relatively new interracial and multicultural ideology that challenges older notions of racial formation in America. But why should *taiko* drumming, originally a Japanese tradition transplanted into Japanese American musical life, be appropriated by Angelenos of every race? Perhaps what I believed to be a Japanese American musical tradition may be understood as something else by the Mexican, black, and European performers of it. For the non-Japanese performers of *taiko* drumming their ethnicity cannot be denied in the equation of musical and racial formation; perhaps they practice and understand Japanese *taiko* drumming as merely another aesthetically pleasing way to make music in Los Angeles in the 1990s. Perhaps I should reinterpret what I saw during the marathon in Little Tokyo as an attempt in musical performance to break down the rigid boundaries and barriers created by the persistent ideology and practices of racial formation and question whether the dialectical relationship between racial and musical formation is the only or the most important feature of musical practice in Los Angeles.

The Alienz at Mile Seven
by
Jacob Edgar

When my alarm clock buzzed at 5:46 on the morning of the Los Angeles Marathon, the first thing I wanted to do was hide under the covers for another few hours. Then, remembering why I had set my alarm in the first place, I leapt out of bed, suddenly excited by thoughts of what lay in store for me that day. Fortunately, I had not been preparing to subject my body to twenty-six-plus miles of self-inflicted torture. Instead, I had been through hours of telephone calls, preliminary interviews, discussions, and classes designed to hone my technical and theoretical skills. After a quick shower and a bad cup of coffee, I jumped in my truck and headed off to UCLA. There I met Jean Kidula, my co-worker on the Marathon Project. We got on the 10 freeway east, and headed towards Sunset and Figueroa, the location of mile seven of the marathon route and the site of the day's fieldwork.

The organizer of Mile 7's entertainment center and volunteer brigade was the Southwest Voter Registration office in Montebello. Jean and I had contacted the person in charge of the event, Elva Sandoval, during the weeks preceding the marathon. It had not always been the smoothest process establishing a relationship with Elva. She seemed rarely to have the time or the interest to talk with two graduate students in "music" who wanted to bother her with what must have seemed a vague and ill-defined project. My own lack of clarity about goals was probably apparent to my contacts and affected their reaction to the work I was proposing. My inability to explain exactly the purpose of the project (except, of course, to fulfill the requirements of my class) made it sound ambiguous and not worth spending time on. Fortunately, my fuzziness cleared as I made more contacts and began to get a sense of the elements at work in the marathon.

The difficulty of the original contact also made me realize that fieldwork is not always smooth. I could relate to Elva: I would probably react the same way if a stranger called up out of the blue and told me about this weird project he or she was working on and would I be the guinea pig. Actually, it surprises me how open people are to answering personal questions about their history, opinions, likes, and dislikes. I could tell that I was going to have to act a little bit like a telemarketer, as I attempted to convince Elva and my other informants that they wanted to give me some of their time so I could conduct a "domain analysis" on them. I was hoping a few key words like "graduate student," "UCLA," "research project," and "at your convenience" would prove that I was trustworthy and had only good intentions.

My pitch worked to the extent that Elva agreed to be interviewed on February 26. Jean and I arrived at the Southwest Voter Registration office only to find that Elva had left the office to "run some errands" and had asked one of her assistants to talk to us. Elsa Casillas had only been with the office for about a year and she was not able to tell us much about the history of Southwest Voter Registration's involvement with the marathon. But we learned that the group chosen to play at the entertainment center, The Alienz, had played in the previous marathon.

I asked Elsa to tell me what it was about The Alienz that made them the organization's choice to play at the marathon. She said, "The reason that we chose them was because most of the people that will be attending, at least at our mile, will be Chicano, Mexican, Latin Americans, and they particularly like to listen to *salsa*, *rancheras*, *cumbias*. They [The Alienz] play a nice variety of music so that's really why we chose them."

Elsa also pointed out that her organization was definitely aware of the public-relations element of the event and the role music played in giving the organization a face to the public at large. "We are a Latino organization," she told us. "We are not partisan and we do a lot of our registration in the Latino community. We are focused on empowering the Latino community in the Southwestern part of the United States so we are not going to bring a rock band because it wouldn't reflect the community we are working with. We are going to bring a band that reflects the musical tastes of the people we are working with and that will entertain not only the people that are there, the volunteers, but also serves as a reflection of our organization. We want

it as people pass by or as the cameras pass by. We want them to understand that we are a Latino organization." Elsa's remarks provided valuable insights into the role and function of music in the marathon. While I expected this to be the case, I did not realize the extent to which those involved in the event understood and articulated the importance of music for making a political, social, or cultural statement.

After getting slightly lost on our way to the marathon, Jean and I drove up Sunset Boulevard past banners marking the various mile marks. As we approached the hill to Mile 7 we saw a crowd of people in white t-shirts on the left side of the street crowded around a gated parking lot. On the other side of the street another crowd was beginning to develop. It was 7:15 and the first of the wheelchairs racers, who start before the runners, was not due to pass for more than an hour. We pulled around the corner, parked, and rushed through a few last-minute preparations with the camera and the DAT machine we had brought to collect data.

As we walked up to the site of the Southwest Voter Registration's entertainment center I took visual stock of the scene. The parking lot served Club Bahia, a large, square building just down the hill on the same side of Sunset Boulevard. It was not difficult to imagine the type of music usually played at the club: "CUMBIA," "SALSA," and "MERENGUE" were pasted in large, colorful letters on the walls. The crowd we had seen on the way up the hill now numbered around fifty people, and they were assembled around the entrance to the parking lot. They were not being allowed into the parking lot itself, where The Alienz were setting up in front of a mobile home parked about thirty feet from the entrance.

Jean and I merged with the crowd hoping to see a familiar face. We immediately found Elsa Casillas, and she led us past the guard at the gate. He might not have stopped us from entering anyway. Jean and I did not look like anyone else in the crowd, made up almost exclusively of Latina/os of high-school age, as Elsa had predicted, wearing the white t-shirts provided to volunteers. With our camera and microphone, most people immediately assumed we were reporters and let us wander freely and ask questions as much as we liked.

After exchanging polite greetings with us, Elsa led us to a man and a woman who were standing near the mobile home. It was Mario Flores, director of The Alienz, and his fiancée Marisella. I had talked to Mario a couple of weeks earlier, at which time we had had a fascinating conversation about his band. I remembered how surprised I had been when I first called him. Expecting him to speak in Spanish, I heard instead a fake southern drawl on the answering machine that said, "Howdy, boys and girls. This here's where The Alienz live. Just leave your name and number and we'll call y'all right back."

When I finally did get in touch with Mario, he talked for over an hour. He described the origins of The Alienz and their goals as a group. He told me that his own musical upbringing in the mixed cultural environment of Los Angeles led him to feel equal affinities for everything from Tex-Mex to the blues. "We mix it all up," Mario told me. The Alienz, he explained, have kept working because they address the musical tastes of a certain segment of the population: the "Chicano ear," as he put it, one that is bicultural, well-versed in Latino and American music. He said that the four core members were not disciples of one kind of music. They like all music. They grew up with Mexican music and rock and roll. Their influences include rock, *salsa*, *norteña*, and other styles.

"We reflect from a musical perspective the Chicano experience," Mario said. The band sees itself as part of an effort to encourage the young. They want people to look at the musical part of themselves. They want the younger Chicana/os to understand "It's OK to be bicultural. There is a richness to that experience." The band originated in the political environment of the "liberation circuit," playing at strikes, rallies, and demonstrations. They evolved from what he called "César Chavez type" functions to become less overtly

political in their performances. They are political musically, Mario told me. They let the music and the energy speak for itself. Their politics are reflected in the celebration of culture that the band represents.

When I asked him how The Alienz served the purposes of the Southwest Voter Registration, he said they "fit the bill musically." He mentioned, as Elsa had, that they are versatile and can play a wide range of music that satisfies the broad tastes of the organization's clientele. He joked that the organizers could have hired Los Lobos, but his band was much more affordable!

I talked with Eddy Farias, the lead guitarist and co-director of the group. Eddy appeared to be in his late thirties or early forties, had short dark hair, and was wearing a white oxford shirt with the tails hanging out of his stone-washed jeans. As he tuned his guitar, he said that his was the generation that doesn't appear in the sociology books, the "Chicano-*cholo*-hippie type," the type of crowd that his music largely appeals to.

While the band was setting up, the volunteers prepared for the runners, filling up huge buckets with hydrant water to make Gatorade. Tables along both sides of Sunset were covered with multiple layers of cups filled with Crystal Geyser water and the slightly scary, green Gatorade. Farther down the hill, on the other side of Club Bahia, a King Taco truck was parked in another gated parking lot. A line of volunteers filed out into the street waiting for the breakfast that had been promised.

At 8:20 the band played their first number, a *ranchera*, which warmed up the crowd until the power went out halfway through the song. The power restored, the band went into a blues, then a *cumbia*. A few isolated walkers came strolling up the street as the volunteers and viewers hooted their support. Mario heckled the walkers as they passed, telling them to pick up the pace.

The music had been playing for about twenty minutes, and no significant body of marathoners had passed by yet. Jean and I took this opportunity to talk to people on the street. We approached two middle-aged women happily eating tacos and moving to the music. I stupidly asked the yes-or-no question, "Do you like the music," to which they of course responded "Yes." I asked them what they listened to at home and they said "*Todo. A mi toda la música me gusta*" [Everything. I like all music]. This was not the case with a man who stopped me and asked if I was a reporter. I said no, but he enthusiastically talked to me anyway, saying he was with a group from a drug rehabilitation center. I asked if he liked the music and he said they were okay, but he preferred rock. Someone behind him said, "You could make a request for some Queensryche." As if reading his mind, The Alienz broke into a heavier rock-and-roll number.

Soon the wheelchairs came speeding by, and Jean and I headed for the King Taco line to engage in some participant observation. While in line for food, we talked to a man who we had seen dancing to the music earlier. Dressed in a black t-shirt, black pants, and a baseball cap, he had colored his long ponytail with silver spray. He lived nearby and had been at the marathon in previous years. He said that even though he was Latino he did not speak Spanish. A lot of the more traditional styles played by The Alienz he had ignored when he was growing up but now enjoyed because he learned to appreciate them over the years. I got the impression that he was one of those "Chicano-*cholo*-hippie types" that Eddie had mentioned earlier.

For our final foray into "person-on-the-street" interviews, Jean and I interrupted a pack of giggling teenage girls who were standing by the side of the street and dancing to a *cumbia*. Our conversation stopped every few seconds so that they could cheer on one of the straggling wheelchair racers, but I managed to learn that they listened to this type of music at home. It reminded me of our conversation with Elsa a few weeks earlier, when she told us that when she was a teenager it was considered very uncool to listen to Mexican music. She pointed out that now, the younger generation of Mexican Americans listens to Mexican music most of the time.

Finally, the runners arrived. The Herculean leaders passed with an entourage of escort cars and TV crews spewing toxic exhaust into their already smog-filled lungs. The Alienz struck up what Mario called "The Marathon Mambo" and a man jumped off his bicycle, loudly honked the horn he had been pestering people with all day, put on an umbrella cap, and danced his heart out. A little boy used a piece of metal to beat on the parking lot gate. The song ended and Mario encouraged the passing runners with such unhelpful remarks as "only nineteen more miles to go!"

Soon the last of the runners hobbled by. At 11 A.M. The Alienz called it quits. The sun had been beating down on the band all morning, and they looked hot and tired. As they were striking, we talked some more with Eddie and Mario. Eddie told me that they play more traditional Mexican acoustic music as well, depending on the situation. He also stated that he hoped their music helped promote racial tolerance in Los Angeles by opening up people's minds. Mario gave us the band's card. It was silver with new-wave writing. The logo read: "The Alienz. Crossing musical borders."

The crowd slowly dissipated as the street sweepers came in to shovel up the mountains of crushed cups left by the passing herd. Jean and I said our good-byes and thanked Mario, Elsa, and everyone else who had so willingly allowed us to question them. The signs that read "Entertainment Center" and "Thank You Alienz" were quickly removed from the gate and Sunset Boulevard gradually reverted back to its normal state. Jean and I headed to the truck, crammed in our stuff, sighed, and drove off.

The marathon was an ideal forum for practicing fieldwork techniques. It also provided a wealth of material for analysis. Perhaps most interesting was comparing my expectations before the project with understandings reached afterwards. One of the most surprising things was the degree to which my informants conducted their own analyses of the marathon event, which led me to believe that it indeed had special significance for them.

I was also surprised by the diversity of music chosen to represent the Latino community in Los Angeles. Everything from *salsa* to rhythm-and-blues seemed to resonate with both performers and listeners. Most of the other entertainment centers used one kind of music associated with one particular community: *taiko* drumming at the Little Tokyo center; marimba at the Guatemalan center; and rock-and-roll in Hollywood. The variety of music played by The Alienz speaks to the numerous styles of music the Latino community in Los Angeles identifies with.

For me, the marathon project was a successful introduction to the struggles, pitfalls, and joys of conducting research in the field. I learned about the difficulties of establishing a working rapport with informants, the clash of expectations with reality, and the problem of determining "what it was all about" when all the tapes have finally been transcribed. This last issue—synthesizing the information into some type of logical and conclusive analysis—was the most difficult aspect of the marathon project, and I assume this holds true with any fieldwork experience. Clearly music played a multi-leveled role in the marathon. At one level, it was mere background noise; at a second level, it was a consciously chosen representation of community identity; at a third level, it was a nonthreatening attempt to affirm a sense of solidarity in a city where the effects of the previous spring's riots were still being felt.

Music as a Symbol and Agent of Unity and Diversity at Mile 7 of the Los Angeles Marathon
by
Jean Kidula

The process of studying the 1993 L.A. Marathon struck me as similar to an initiation ceremony that introduces initiates to the codes and rites of a particular social group. Like traditional initiations, this one was preceded by preparation for the actual ceremony. At the collective level, the class met once a week to discuss ways to approach the event. Then in pairs we contacted some of the organizers of the "marathon of music" to prepare for better coverage of and involvement in the event itself.

Jacob Edgar and I chose to observe and participate in the marathon from an entertainment center sponsored by Southwest Voter Registration, a group managed by a predominantly Latino/Chicano administration interested in the affairs of this community. The organizers told us they thought of the event as one in a series of calendric performances and implied that they used the marathon as a forum for promoting awareness of their contribution to society and attracting volunteers for their cause. One interviewee said,

> It's a public relations event...So we do it more than anything else for publicity and it's enjoyable....We are focused on empowering the Latino community in the southwestern part of the USA.... So we are going to bring a band that reflects our taste as it serves as a reflection of our community....We want it as people pass by, as the cameras pass by, we want them to understand that we are a Latino organization.

Their entertainment center at Mile 7 was located at 1130 Sunset Boulevard in a predominantly Spanish-speaking community, and most of the volunteers were from this community. Early in the day they put up tables, carried boxes full of Gatorade bottles, removed paper cups from cartons and set them up on the tables, and tried to fill up plastic water tanks from a fire hose. The organizers had hoped to see Hispanic civic leaders at the event, but none were present because there had been another function the day before that had gone on into the early hours of the morning. Presumably they didn't give the marathon a high priority for the recruitment of voters.

The organizers invited a band known as The Alienz to provide music. According to them, this group portrayed a strong Latino heritage while at the same time allowing for integration into the overall American culture. They had already participated in the marathon for at least two years and had fit the bill. One musician saw the band's role as awakening the general public to the existence and contribution of the cultural and ethnic community they were to represent. He also saw them as educating their own people on their musical values and encouraging a sense of belonging and appreciation of their own culture.

The Alienz consisted of four permanent members and one occasional member. The leader, Mario Flores, an original member, was a vocalist, saxophonist, and mouth-organ player. The other original member, Eddy Farias, played rhythm guitar. The others were Jessy Rangle, a bass guitarist and vocalist, Joey Gomez, the drummer, and Jaime Horta, who occasionally played congas with the band.

My contact with Latin music had been mostly secondhand. It was strongly conditioned by African appropriations of Cuban styles via the famous Zairian soukous style. Having arrived from Africa just six months prior to this event, my reaction to recordings of the original Cuban and other Latin styles was ambivalent. I was anxious to observe a performance with a Latino audience, and so have an alternative experience. At the same time, coming from a multiethnic background, I wanted to learn how Los Angeles as a multicultural city assimilates the different musics that are presented by its peoples, and how the people define their roots through their music while maintaining a sense of themselves as part of a larger whole. I hoped not only to watch the runners and to cheer them but also to document the types of activities that surround the event—and in particular, the music and its role, place, and significance in the marathon—and how all these activities contribute to establishing a Los Angeles culture.

While The Alienz were setting up their equipment in a parking lot adjacent to the Bahia club, Eddy told us that their set was usually determined by audience make-up and taste, but it was always bilingual and bicultural. At the marathon, "we will come up with a couple of songs at the beginning and then someone will call out a song and then we'll go and then someone else will call another song out. So it depends what you are feeling, what mood you are in." He saw the role of the group as a means of being a part of "the social harmony that happens here. We see the runners as people from all walks of life....We are here to have fun...to cover the seventh-mile atmosphere and to be a part of it." While the band set up and we interviewed the musicians, the police cordoned off the streets perpendicular to Sunset Boulevard. The only traffic allowed was police cars, ambulances, fire trucks, and some official vehicles directly involved in the marathon.

The Alienz started playing around 8:20 A.M. Their first number was a *ranchera*. The log we kept of their performances confirmed that they actually played in a wide variety of styles. They followed the *ranchera* with a *cumbia*, a blues piece, bebop, *norteña*, another blues, Tex-Mex, and rock in that order and then continued to mix it up after that. The first people we saw actually dancing responded to the first *norteña* number. Most of the spectators bunched themselves next to the music on the side of the road where the band was stationed. The other side was populated by the volunteers, some of whom manned the water tables while others assigned themselves the role of cheerers.

When a short circuit stopped the music at one point, the people's reaction told us that they were very aware of the music. After a few minutes, the music resumed and a sense of normalcy was restored. One lady stationed as close to the band as possible seemed surprised to be asked about the music. She had taken it for granted: "there has to be music."

The atmosphere was one of anticipation as we waited for the first wheelchair racers and the band continued to play. I thought that the pauses between the songs were long but I had been warned that, in the absence of a fixed set, the musicians had to discuss what they were going to play next. They also listened to the radio to find out where the marathoners were in order to play certain songs when they arrived. People hummed, danced, and sang along with the band as they waited.

Suddenly a group of planes appeared overhead and on the road in front of us a motorcade led by a police car heralded the arrival of the wheelchair marathoners. The street was alive with the sound of cheering. The water tables were a beehive of activity as volunteers prepared to hand cups of water to the marathoners. The band was playing a Tex-Mex polka and increased the volume as the racers came into view. Those who wanted to win the race barely even looked at the water being handed them. They wanted it poured down their backs, which had to be done quite carefully so as not to impede the progress of the others. When the polka ended, Mario encouraged and lauded the efforts of the racers. The band went on to sing several more songs, and, as the racers trickled by, the beat got slower until they were singing the blues quite slowly. The people were restless, and music filled the gap between racers. Between numbers, the silence was deafening.

During the lull before the runners arrived, we interviewed one of the volunteers we had earlier seen dancing. He turned out to be a regular participant. We asked how the band reflected the community's ambiance.

> The band itself plays a lot of different kinds of music, a lot of Mexican music…rock and roll music, jazz, blues, a mixture of everything which is pretty much what Latino people are. They are a mixture of everything. People have a certain idea of what Latino people are like and they find out it's not because we like all sorts of things…I guess it's just a different kind of mix of musical styles. It's a very versatile band.

Although he did not know all the songs, he recognized the styles and danced. He had not grown up listening to Latin music; it had been considered *démodé*. He had since realized that he could have a balance between Mexican culture and North American culture.

As the motorcade flanking the runners appeared around the corner, the band swung into the lilting beat of the "Marathon Mambo." It suddenly seemed as if people appeared from everywhere as spectators filled the street, cheering the runners, shouting, clapping their hands, and generally creating an excited atmosphere. It was as if Jacob and I were thrown back as the crowd surged forward to get a clear glimpse of the lead runners. They had a determined look on their faces. They did not seem to want to be interrupted by the crowd, the water handlers, or even the music. Undeterred, Mario welcomed them to the Latino/Chicano mile during the instrumental interlude. In the excitement of the moment, I forgot about the music and tried to get a view of the runners in the hope that I would spy some Kenyans and make my voice heard in Los Angeles. To my disappointment, none was in that first group so I melted back into the crowd. The band continued to play a lot of upbeat songs—tending towards some form of rock, *cumbia*, one or two *salsas*, more *rancheras*, and Tex-Mex—that reflected the mood of the crowd and the speed of the runners. More people responded to the music by dancing as they waited for the thousands of slower runners to make an appearance. Soon a huge throng was making its way up the street to the cheering of the crowd and the encouragement of the musicians. The slower runners sometimes acknowledged the musicians by waving to them and even dancing, and occasionally a segment of the crowd broke into loud cheering as a runner they recognized passed by and waved back at them. The street was littered with colorful paper cups. In the silence between numbers, all one heard was the sound of the runners' feet on the paper cups like the sound of heavy rain. It was a relief to hear the music start again and in some way restore a type of order. As the number of runners diminished, the music became slower and slower, and the crowd dwindled until the street was almost as empty as when we arrived.

The musicians, who had played without a real break except to drink something once or twice in the blazing sun, were pleased with their performance. They explained that they had started with a *ranchera* because they felt the style reflected Latino-ism in Los Angeles to both insiders and outsiders to the community. At the same time Latinos are a bicultural community with exposure to what is considered mainstream American music. The band therefore played a variety of other styles not Latino in origin. The diversity of their repertoire made it hard for them to be categorized under one label.

The various people we talked to before and during the marathon all seemed to want the music at the marathon to be representative of the diversity of cultures in the Latino world. The music filled the gaps when the people were waiting for the action. The music chosen tended to correspond also with the general atmosphere in that it got faster for the racers and slower for the joggers and walkers. The band leader, while applauding the efforts of the competitors, took the role of community spokes-man. I was interested to hear that some of the organizers, volunteers, and spectators had grown up not listening to Latino music, as if there was something wrong with it, only to find later in life that they needed it as part of their cultural identity. Participation was a way of identifying. Having an entertainment center in this community acknowl-edged the presence of these people as a part of the Los Angeles community with a cultural identity of their own.

The Alienz and the music they played repre-sented an ethnicity that outsiders may consider homogeneous but actually has a wide range of cultures within it. For me, the band tended to stress a Mexican heritage, but the group wanted to in-clude everyone, and this they did by playing a wide variety of music. The group did not just say "we are Latinos" by singing only in Spanish; they also sang in English to give themselves a wider identity and audience. When Kimasi Browne (a class member

of African descent) said they sounded as if they were black, it confirmed Mario's desire to sound as authentic as possible. The Alienz clearly had an idea of what kind of image to portray to the rest of the world. They sought to advertise their ethnic roots yet still be seen as part of the North America mainstream. For the musicians, music emerged as a strong agent in the creation of individual identity at three levels: as performers, as Latinos, and as part of the North American conglomerate.

It is amazing that a music performance like this can provoke so many thoughts and impressions. Follow-up would be necessary to verify or deny some of my impressions. However, it is clear that many people recognize music as a source for creating unity. The character of the city derives from an amalgam of cultures, each with its indi-vidual identity but contributing to the way Angele-nos and outsiders perceive Los Angeles. Like other large urban centers, the city also represents the make-up of the United States: a conglomerate of cultures that have blended in many respects and yet retain diverse individual characteristics.

Music for the Westside Jewish Community Center at Mile 10
by
Ellen Sinatra

The wheelchair marathoners, looking like spin-dly, silhouetted tarantulas from outer space, sped towards us on Sunset Boulevard, the street made shiny by the sun. Their arrival signaled the begin-ning of the L.A. Marathon for those of us at Mile 10, the corner claimed by the West Side Jewish Community Center. As they approached, we heard the music from "Evita" blasting away from a small white tent on the sidewalk. A few minutes later, the first runners came bravely up the hill as Ari, one of the musicians, shouted "Welcome to the Westside JCC" over the PA system. People were milling about, talking with one another, drinking coffee, and reading the paper. Some were watching the runners and looking down the street to see who was coming next, but few appeared to be listening to the music or watching the musicians. In fact, the music at that corner was at times pre-programmed and recorded rather than live. If it had been entirely recorded, would anyone have noticed or cared? How was it that the people from the Jewish community, with its strong musical tradition, were so easily able to ignore the music representing them at this public event?

The Westside Jewish Community Center is located in Los Feliz, a pretty neighborhood that has fallen into some disrepair over the past twenty years. Graffiti is everywhere, on sidewalks, buildings, and some of the roadwork signs on the corner. A neighbor was painting over graffiti on his garage door as Shari Johnston and I arrived the morning of the marathon. The JCC has had to install locks on their doors and big iron gates around their buildings for safety. The people who live in this neighborhood are primarily Latino. They also watched the marathon at that intersection, lined up across the street from the JCC, but there was no interaction between the two groups. As Carrie Jehovitz, the JCC organizer explained to me, they decided to sponsor an entertainment center for the marathon to help encourage the runners, not apparently to promote community interaction.

Huge welcome signs and brightly colored balloons decorated the fence lining the street, and people occasionally remembered to blow one of the noisemakers they had been given. At one point, a cotton candy wagon with plastic blowup snakes crossed the street and drove slowly by the crowd. As the morning progressed, people from the JCC, who had come from seven Jewish Community Centers around Los Angeles to be with their friends for this event, brought chairs from the JCC out onto the street, to watch the race and continue their conversations. Inside the JCC, decorated for the upcoming Purim Carnival, food and drinks had been prepared. Coffee, water, and orange juice had to be fetched from the building, so drinks were not readily available for the musicians, the runners, or the spectators.

The "Fantastic Duo," Rick and Ari, played for the event. They specialize in Yiddish and Jewish music, but also play Greek and Latin music. Rick plays saxophone, clarinet, and synthesizer, and Ari plays the accordion and acts as master of ceremonies. Carrie heard them play at the JCC's senior center and hired them for the marathon. They played under a white tent with walls on three sides, which effectively cut them off from the viewers on the sidewalk. Later they complained about this situation, but from what I saw, they didn't do very much that was interesting to look at anyway. In fact, almost nobody walked over to see them or interact with them in any way, although some girl scouts selling cookies on one of the four corners stopped what they were doing to dance the *hora* a couple of times. Some of the runners stopped and chatted briefly, thanked us for cheering them on, and in some cases even danced to the music.

The musicians and their music did not seem particularly related to the community. They didn't concentrate on traditional Jewish music, but played their whole repertoire of ethnic and popular music. It sounded bouncy and upbeat, except when they took a break and set their synthesizer to play pre-recorded music selections that were general and undefined. Ari seemed to enjoy his role as emcee, and frequently welcomed the runners to the JCC entertainment center. Perhaps the most noticeable feature of their music and announcements was its loudness. At one point, while I was talking to them, Ari told me to stand farther away from the speakers; he was concerned that I would hurt my ears. Both musicians were fully professional, both in how they presented themselves and how they played their music. They were there to provide this corner with lots of pep and energy.

Although Shari and I were there as fieldworkers—students from UCLA, writing our notes during the event and talking to people—I was interested in how comfortable it was for us to be there; we were just part of the crowd. Although the major objective that morning for people from the JCC was to get together with friends from other JCCs in Los Angeles—and as a consequence they presented the image of a very closed community—they were very friendly and nice to us. But everything and everybody else was extraneous to their primary desire to socialize with friends. Outsiders and outside events were rated according to their entertainment value and lack of intrusion on their real purpose for being there. The runners were interesting only for a little while. Shari and I were somewhat welcome, because we were friendly and unobtrusive. The music was entertaining, although a bit too loud for them. The people across the street were simply ignored, as was the graffiti.

The music seemed to have little relation to their Jewishness or anything else related to their culture. Ari and Rick could do whatever they wished, so long as it wasn't too loud or obtrusive. I think Ari and Rick understood this situation, but I suspect the JCC entertainment center, with its lively but generic party music, was not one of the more memorable ones for the runners. They came from another universe, silhouetted by Chinatown in the background, up the shiny street, passed through the Jewish Community Center party, and then moved on, eventually disappearing into Hollywood, another planet in Los Angeles.

An Aesthetics of Belonging at the Los Angeles Marathon
by
Sharilee Johnston

As a result of my attempt to document music at the 1993 L.A. Marathon, I have begun to understand the different ways music groups and music-making impact a community. I suggest that two types of music-making occurred at the marathon and probably occur in other social settings in Los Angeles as well. The first type is what Theodor Adorno (1989) refers to as music that serves the culture industry. The second type generates what I term an aesthetics of belonging.

At what Jean-Jacques Nattiez (1990) calls the productive level, or the *raison d'être* for the music making, it is useful to analyze how these two types

of music diverge and what sorts of social structures they generate. I propose that the community entertainment centers at the L.A. Marathon, when produced as a community action, were extremely valuable forums for community interaction and empowerment of the individual voice.

Ellen Sinatra and I worked with the Westside Jewish Community Center (JCC) on Sunset Boulevard and the musicians they hired to play for the L.A. Marathon. The musicians were professionals who had learned that to "stay alive in this town you [have] to do just private parties and stuff." They do what is appropriate for the situation and present themselves on behalf of their employer. They are a commodity.

As members of the community of bands staying alive in L.A., this group represents a cultural scene of survival. This is not a scene in which the members speak directly to or for a community or ethnic voice. It is one in which the musicians for hire are constantly aware of the hegemony of patron tastes. In this respect, the voice of the community is implicitly acknowledged through hiring practices and the types of events that require live music.

When Ellen and I first met the group, they were playing Greek music for a Bat Mitzvah on a weekend before the marathon. They had understood from us that we were interested in "ethnic music," so they wanted to assure us that they could do that. They also assured us that they were not limited to one ethnicity—"from Greek music to Israeli music to Latin music. Whatever we do it sounds authentic so it's always a challenge and it always sounds good, sounds authentic." For them diversity translated into more job possibilities. Authenticity seemed to refer to recognizability.

Though they told us their music was traditional and authentic, I think it was in an effort to assure us we had found what they thought we might be looking for. We asked about their involvement with the Jewish Community Center. Ari responded, "They [the JCC] hired us to primarily play and show support for the Jewish Community Center where if the Greek community wanted to hire us, we could just as easily have performed that as well, you know…We do have limitations, don't get me wrong."

At the marathon, the musicians supported the runners vocally, but this was the only sign of personal interaction between the audience and the band. They played Jewish, Greek, Latin, American pop, and movie music at the marathon, but nobody seemed to notice. There was no interaction between the band and the JCC marathon audience, although they did open with some Jewish-sounding tunes that seemed to satisfy the woman who had hired them. They were employees of the JCC, not community-involved musicians.

Their lack of involvement came across even more strikingly when we realized the extent to which the synthesizer played a key role in their music-making. Rick had sampled and preprogrammed all of their selections. On the job, the musicians accompanied the MIDI track. This enabled them to sound like a large band, to play a wide variety of tunes "authentically," to put out music fairly continuously for a three-hour period, and to be slightly removed from the content of the music.

It seems that two forces were at work for the musicians: the hegemony or power structure of patron tastes and their enjoyment of the personal contact with their audience. Survival musicians respond to an unspoken pressure to satisfy their audience and employer by playing the familiar, comforting, and pleasant. They have chosen to do this not by promoting their own sound, expression, voice, or musical style, but by adapting to as many situations as possible. For these musicians, their music does not represent either their personal or community identities; it represents their professional survival techniques. They play gigs, not their own music, as they cater to the make-up of their current audience and employer.

In the power structure between the musicians and their patrons, the musicians serve the needs of the employer and represent the employer publicly. The personal interaction between the musicians and the audience does not generate community involvement or group interaction. The musicians are almost always outside the community they play for and yet represent. They step into an event as employees. The ethnic diversity of their music is profitable to them, and the ethnic references, authenticity, appropriateness, and flexibility are key factors in their survival. Though Ari and Rick, on a personal level, have the satisfaction of relating to individuals in the audience during a performance, their music, developed to placate, to appease, to be recognizable and therefore comforting, and to meet the needs of their patrons, serves the same underlying ideology as the culture industry. Such music, from Madonna to TV commercial music to "Achy Breaky Heart," appears to serve the social need to belong while simultaneously perpetuating a false utopian vision of belonging. It never addresses any issue that might feel disruptive or confrontational or suggest a response. From conception to production, it serves a hierarchy of employer and culture-industry tastes.

The *Los Angeles Times* made a point of discussing the community interaction the sponsors hoped the marathon would inspire, especially in light of last year's riots. But to what extent does the identity of the performers affect the feelings of community interaction and belonging, especially when several of the neighborhoods along the marathon route were disrupted less than a year before by civil unrest? Not having the resources to answer this question through fieldwork, I would like to respond philosophically.

The hierarchical social structuring of survival-bands in relation to patrons can be contrasted to the interactive social structuring of community music to create what might be termed an aesthetics of belonging. An aesthetics of belonging generates a voice of the people—spoken by the people and addressed directly to their ethnicity, community, and position within the culture of L.A.

Reflecting on Nattiez's (1990) tripartite model for musical aesthetics as well as on the work of Adorno (1989), Jacques Attali (1989), and Paul

Ricoeur (1981), I think it is possible to construct an aesthetics of belonging in which music-making communicates a powerful message about what society has been and could become. Music born of community or cultural identity suggests a degree of social awareness. The music is a response to a perceived need in the community; it satisfies that need, either metaphorically through the structuring of the musical performance or literally through the message of the lyrics.

Such music addresses, confronts, and enlightens real people. It may or may not be happy, positive, or easy to listen to, but it responds to the needs of individuals within a community. The music, through physical and metaphorical structuring, addresses interaction and empowerment within a community. This interactive music-making offers people on both sides of the music—performer and audience—the possibility of hearing each other and deriving a sense of community from the shared interaction.

In the case of the marathon, I hypothesize that many of the community entertainment center performances fulfilled this vision of music—to speak effectively to the needs of society and be a voice of the individual. Whether the styles were centuries old or contemporary, music-making at many of the centers escaped co-option by the culture industry. It instead structured a meaningful way of interacting as a community. The music my classmates saw and heard seems to have developed as a response to a group's need to be heard. At some of the entertainment centers, music-making may have channeled negative and violent emotions into a more productive behavior, to be heard by others as the voice of a community. Such music-making offers something for both insiders and outsiders to appropriate precisely because it offers an image and practice of lived experience as a member of a community.

If the musics at many of the entertainment centers along the marathon route differed in style, they shared, at the conceptual level, the need of people to communicate experiences. The music at the marathon reflected a need by the people of Los Angeles to find a voice that is interactive, challenging, and offers a sense of belonging. Not only did the music entertainment centers represent a particular community, they spoke to the possibility of overcoming cultural, political, and social boundaries. The music at many centers invited people from many different communities to participate and interact with one community through the act of shared listening to music. By accepting the invitation, individuals were touched, altered, and empowered as they experienced the community structure that the music structures.

The L.A. Marathon fieldwork experience was extremely productive for me, as I'm sure it was for my classmates, who witnessed community involvement, appreciation, and interaction less than a year after the civil unrest of 1992. This is not to say that the violence that exploded during the riots has been successfully channeled into music or washed away in a year's time. The violence of last year was only a small eruption of the underlying anger and alienation in our society. Much culture-industry music merely projects the anger loudly enough to gain media attention. In contrast, community music-making provides a productive response to those same feelings of anger and alienation by structuring an experience of belonging.

REFERENCES CITED

Adorno, Theodore W.
    1989   *Introduction to the Sociology of Music.* Translated by E.B. Ashton. New York: Continuum.
Attali, Jacques
    1989   *Noise: The Political Economy of Music.* Translated by Brian Massumi. Minneapolis: University of Minnesota Press.
Nattiez, Jean-Jacques
    1990   *Music and Discourse: Toward a Semiology of Music.* Translated by Carolyn Abbate. Princeton, NJ: University of Princeton Press.
Ricoeur, Paul
    1981   *Hermeneutics and the Human Sciences.* Edited and translated by John B. Thompson. New York: Cambridge University Press.

**The Circle of Reciprocity between Runners
and Musicians at the Halfway Point of the
L.A. Marathon
by
Kimasi Browne**

During the eighth annual Los Angeles Marathon on March 7, 1993, complimentary and opposing forces, the mobile runners and the stationary musicians, engaged in a collaborative relationship. More than twenty thousand runners ran through the streets of Los Angeles and made a left turn at the corner of Hollywood Boulevard and Orange Drive at the Hollywood entertainment center, located at Mile 13. This paper seeks to show the reciprocal relationship between the runners, the musicians, and their songs, as well as the way this entertainment center, like all of them at the marathon, asserted the cultural identity of the surrounding community. Hollywood, as a mythic place for the making of movies, promotes the melding of cultures, races, and economic classes, just as the marathon does. Consistent with Hollywood's image, the style of music chosen for the entertainment center, rock, appeals to an equally wide range of people.

The rock band, the Monte Carlos, provided the music. According to band leader Billy Chiofi, their goal was "to inspire the crowd to inspire the runners." The musicians selected music that would excite and inspire this diverse group. Melody, tempo, and harmonic rhythm reflected the level of athletic performance of each group of runners. Each song generated a specific response in the runners. Their ability to respond to the music was aided by the fact that the runners ran towards the stage rather than along side it, and thus were in contact with the music for a longer period of time than at the other entertainment centers. As Nyla Arslanian, president of the Hollywood Arts Council, put it in a pre-marathon interview (she and her project coordinator, Laurie Fookes, were the primary sources of information during the preparatory phase of this project):

For one thing, we are set up in the middle of Hollywood Boulevard. The street is normally closed for the stage to be set up and it has to be pulled down as quickly as possible after the event to allow traffic to continue. With the stage set, they have the runners running at them, as opposed to what happens in the other centers where the runners run past them. So they are entertaining the twenty thousand people running and what the music is, [is] to bring spectators out—be they council members, tourists, or street people—to participate together, to cheer the runners, and to just have fun as a community.

Arslanian also pointed out another unique thing about her center: it is at Mile 13, the halfway point of the marathon and a crucial psychological point for the runners.

I asked Billy Chiofi just prior to the band's set-up whether he had prepared a program or list of songs from which the band would perform. He responded, "We've been playing together for a long time, so I just call 'em off the top of my head. I like to hang fast and loose." Chiofi later confessed, "I ran in the 1986 marathon....Playing in the marathon is the band's favorite event....Most of the musicians brought their wives and kids." Kirk Arthur, the drummer, said that the band had been together for over five years. He introduced me to the other band members: Larry Rasberry, guitar; Jim Blazer, organ; Michael Clark, lead vocals and keyboard; Phil Krawzak, tenor saxophone; Harry McKittrick, trombone and baritone saxophone; and Billy Chiofi, lead vocals and guitar. Ritt Henn, although not a regular member, joined them on bass.

The announcement came, "The race has started late. They are on Figueroa now. The wheelchairs should be arriving soon." At 9:24 A.M., the band began playing without announcement shortly before the first wheelchair participants came whirring by. The musicians took turns playing improvised solos. Billy Chiofi screamed into the microphone, "We are the Monte Carlos. How ya doin'? We're here for one reason, to encourage the runners, 'cause they are working very hard for themselves and for the city. So from now 'til about twelve, we're gonna clap, and clap loud and scream for them!" Then the band played "Up On the Roof," and the crowd went wild with dancing and cheering. As the race wore on, it became obvious that the themes of the songs were appropriate to the occasion in the sense that they all referred to physical activity such as knocking, walking, and dancing. Most of the songs were love songs, which matched the mood of the day, but there were no slow ballads. I also divided the runners into three groups. The band may have, too, since their music seemed to change with the arrival of each group.

The first group, the self-motivated runners, were the earliest to arrive. Extremely well developed physically, this group had energy and resilience; they did not pant. Mostly men, none was obese. Determination and resolve emanated from these athletes. Well prepared and well paced, they did not demonstrate any wear and tear at the halfway point and seemed to have no anxiety about running the remaining thirteen miles. As they reached the turn at Hollywood Boulevard and Orange Drive, they heard "Knock On Wood," a song about the bravado of a successful lover who appreciates the "good thing that he's got." These runners were like front-line warriors, ahead of the crowd, scouting untraveled territory. The medium tempo was not geared to the runners, but the lyrics, "Think I'd better knock [knock] on wood, baby" and the band's musical simulation of a knock-knock-knock on a door were equivalent to the "high five" hand-sign that can be interpreted as "you are going great, keep going, we are proud of you." Although the runners seemed extremely confident and self-motivated, they acknowledged the cheers and applause of the spectators, waving back as they turned the corner and continued. Those behind the lead runners acknowledged the musicians, who, warmed up now, were really pumping out the music to the runners in return. Billy Chiofi con-

tinually shouted to the runners during the songs, "Hey runners, you're looking good! Hang in there! We're with ya!"

The second group, approximately thirty minutes behind the first, was physically fit, but not homogeneously so. Some were overweight, although not obese. They seemed to be approaching exhaustion; a grimace of resolve was on their faces. They seemed to be concentrating on the finish line. This group, mostly men, also included women, walkers, and even a few wheelchair participants. The band played "Your Love Keeps Lifting Me Higher" as they arrived. These runners were not as responsive to the music as some in the first group, probably because they were not as physically fit. Many were panting and seemed oblivious to the songs, deep in the concentration necessary to continue. Since many in this group were walkers, "Walking the Dog," as well as the encouragement of the crowd and Chiofi, seemed to motivate them, the song taking on new meaning as the runners nursed their tired feet ("dogs") at the halfway point.

The third group, the largest in number, comprised the slowest and least motivated runners, who seemed to need the inspiration of fellow runners and the cheers of the spectators. Jovial, laughing, and appearing to be having a good time, they seemed to view their participation in the marathon as a social occasion. Women, children, and walkers dominated this group. Several of them dropped out of the race for a breather, and then continued with the run. This group arrived near the middle of the song, "Do You Wanna Dance?" This early 1960s classic was played at a faster tempo than is customary. The runners responded over and over with "Yeah! I wanna dance!" This group tended deliberately to encourage the band. They began to dance in place and twirl in the streets as they ran. During the song, "Satisfaction," the most recognizable reciprocity occurred. As the runners responded to the song—they lifted their legs high like trotting horses, waved their arms back and forth above their heads, and shouted "Yeah! Way to par-tay!"—the band quickened the tempo and began to play a vamp, a chord progression repeated ad infinitum with improvised riffs above the chords. The bass drum was pounding, thump-thump-thump-thump, about 130 beats per minute. The runners, walkers, wheelchair participants, children, women, old and young men, all seemed to identify with the music. The runners sang the lyrics and trotted in time to the music. They transformed the race into a raucous block party.

The musical style and songs at this station provided an obvious link to the Hollywood show-business image. The movies made in Hollywood seem to present an America and a world divided by many cultures, races, lifestyles, economic levels, and religions, and yet one united by a hunger for certain heavily advertised commercial products and one dominant musical style, rock. The moniker "Entertainment Capital of the World" captures the slickness and commercial approach of the Hollywood entertainment center—the setting included the television cameras and crews of KCOP-TV Channel 13, complete with hydraulically extended cameras and boom microphones—as well as its desire to appeal to a broad and diverse group of spectators. The Hollywood center was not linked to a particular ethnicity, but was oriented toward the runners themselves and the larger world beyond Hollywood that they represented. The halfway point of the marathon was a perfect point for the runners to encounter the zenith of their marathon experience. Here the reciprocity between runners, musicians, and spectators came to fruition.

Una Trajectoría musical en Los Angeles: Music at the Guatemalan Community Center
by
Sarah Truher

It's 9:20 A.M. and about an hour has passed since Roberto Catalano and I arrived and began to absorb the feelings of anticipation around the Guatemalan Community entertainment center. César de León, the bass player and leader of the marimba band

Grupo Murmullos Chapines, is helping a few official-looking types set up equipment on the bandstand facing Catalina Street. The bandstand forms one side of the entertainment-center plaza set up in the parking lot behind the old Ambassador Hotel. The other three sides are bounded by about twenty *casillas de alimentos/informaciones* bustling in preparation; I can already smell the incredibly soft, fresh corn tortillas on the *parrilla*. Maybe puréed black beans and sharp white cheese will be served with them later in the day.

The sights, sounds, smells, and other sensations of the center remind me of a morning several years ago I spent wandering around the market at Chichicastenango, Guatemala: rising early, here in Los Angeles, to the first beautiful spring-like day after all the rain and clouds; seeing the red-tile roof of the Ambassador against the deep blue of the sky; and listening to the eloquent Spanish I associate with Guatemalan speakers, a word or two of an indigenous Mayan language from the women slapping round balls of dough against their palms, and the sizzle of the *parrilla*. My reverie is interrupted when a monstrous heap of a car pulls into the unpaved, deeply rutted parking lot, kicking up dust and spewing thick plumes of carcinogens. As I walk by a row of booths, one of the working women calls out, "Señora, señora!" Back in Chichi, I was overwhelmed by the din of voices calling out to me, the colorful textiles, and the smells of dozens of dishes being prepared. I found my way out of the labyrinthine market place toward the steps of the town Cathedral, a spiritual center, well known to tourists and locals. I was in search of a quiet spot where I might set myself to the more tranquil business of transcribing the elaborate flute-and-drum music being played by two men on the vertiginously high roof above me. But that moment of peace was brief. Soon after I sat down on the steps, a pair of young boys approached me with burning incense and an emaciated chicken in a cage, wanting to know—their English was perfect—did I want to make a sacrifice?

As I scribble away here behind the Ambassador,

perched on what I thought was an unobtrusive spot on the wall next to the parking lot, a man passes by saying, "make sure you represent my people well!" I guess he knows exactly what I'm doing. From this vantage point I can see an environment in transition. A couple of dozen people, crowded around the bandstand, listen to a man, apparently the main organizer, thank people for their help and support in making the event possible. Yellow police tape has just been put up. A young Latina female Explorer scout in uniform is giving a teenage kid the security spiel. Groups of young men stand in circles in the plaza behind the bandstand, shifting their weight from one foot to the other, not looking at the beautiful woman with long black hair and a short skirt who walks by. More people trickle into the bandstand crowd. Families with little kids arrive to seek places on the curb. A group of shiny high-school girls with beauty pageant sashes over their up-dated *mulas* and traditional wraps is buzzing around, doing some kind of PR thing that involves selling tickets. A *paletería* pushes his white refrigerator cart down the sidewalk; I hear the little bell and I remember the dysentery I got the last time I had a *paleta de coco*.

Roberto and I meet briefly with César. He introduces us to the musicians from the marimba band, Mi Guatemala, from Antigua, and then disappears. César de León is a very friendly and gracious man who was eager to talk to Roberto and me over the past few weeks about his band and about the importance of the marimba band in Guatemala and in the Guatemalan community in Los Angeles. He told us that he felt very fortunate and proud to have represented Guatemalan culture in some important events around the city. This morning César is more rushed with us; he has a lot to do and none of his band members has shown up yet. Roberto and I take a few photos and shoot some video footage of the members of Mi Guatemala introducing themselves. Two weeks ago we taped interviews with the seven members of Murmullos Chapines. They were all confident and very articulate interviewees. Each one spoke about

the marimba's African origins, the popularity of the instrument in Guatemala, and their own experience with marimba music. Our success with Murmullos Chapines before the marathon prompted our request to Mi Guatemala that they introduce themselves and tell us whatever they would like about their musical background. To my initial surprise and discomfort, this morning a couple of older gentlemen were somewhat shy and obviously felt quite awkward. However, the group's female vocalist, Ana Miranda, an attractive, gracious woman, made direct eye contact with me as the tape rolled. She spoke about the community's enthusiasm for the music and her pride in being part of the group.

At about 9:45, the center seems to throb with anticipation. The Antiguan band has begun to play, and John Ulmon, the Guatemalan consul and our first contact person for this project, introduces Don Mateo Flores to the crowd. Flores, a champion marathoner from 1952, is a well-loved national hero. The first wheelchair racer passes by and the crowd turns its attention to the street, giving up a cheer complete with Arsenio Hall-type woofs and arm pumping.

By 10:30 César is worried because his band hasn't shown up yet. It doesn't present too much of a disaster logistically because the two bands were going to play together anyway. But there are four marimbas on stage and only enough musicians to play two of them. The two marimbas brought by the Antiguan band are stunning and I notice Roberto taking some pictures of them. They have enormous rectangular box-shaped resonators; their diamond-shaped tips point at the ground and suggest to me the gourd resonators of the West African xylophones. The marimbas' intense buzzing sound contrasts with the clear quality of the singers' voices. The band is getting an enthusiastic response to some very familiar numbers; several couples dance below them in front of the bandstand and everyone sings along with the group's two vocalists: "*todos los dias pasaban.*" People gather around to watch Don Mateo Flores, looking fly in his blue warm-up suit appliquéed with rainbow strips of Guatemalan woven cotton, dance with a young partner. Two women eagerly point out Flores to me. Beyond him I notice a young girl in traditional dress unknowingly evoke a smile of approval from a middle-aged woman.

A cheer from some distance down the street pulls the audience toward the curb and tells us that the first runners are approaching. They pass! Helicopters, small planes, motorcycles, cop cars, camera trucks, and the lead van create a chaotic commotion around two or three skinny guys in sweaty shorts. A Mexican runner approaches and gets a rousing cheer. The first Guatemalan passes by and for about a half a block is escorted, fed oranges, and doused with water by two young men carrying two enormous blue-and-white Guatemalan flags. John Ulmon announces the Guatemalan runners' names as they pass, and each runner gets the same replenishing escort. People in the crowd call out to the runners in support.

As more runners pass, people continue to dance and sing along with the band. César returns with a drummer we haven't met before and one of his marimba players. The three join the Antiguan band on the stage, filling out the sound a great deal.

After many runners pass, the combined band takes a break. I get a quick chance to talk to Ana Miranda, the singer, as she shoots some photos of the runners from the stage behind the marimbas. She gives me the names of the band members and elaborates on the statements she made earlier about the Guatemalan community and the importance of the marimba. Ana Miranda introduces me to Arma Ronelas, the daughter of Rene Molina, the band's leader. Arma tells me that she has been chief hostess and cook for the band for three marathons prior to this one and that this is the first year she has been able to come to the event. She gives me her phone number and tells me she is very interested in talking about her community. I take a couple of pictures of her and her Dad. Sometime later, a man I haven't met yet greets me from the stage and invites me to come over anytime to see his videos

of Guatemala; he is Arma's husband and is as helpful as she is.

It's 12:00 noon and Jay Mendoza joins Roberto and me. We buy a delicious cholesterol-laden lunch at one of the *casillas*, and discuss the event a little, mostly in terms of problems or successes with our equipment—and in terms of food. As Jay leaves to find Murali at the Native American entertainment center, one of the satin-sashed young women hits us up for a raffle ticket. It's a deal: we buy the ticket and she gets the chance on a prize.

Marimba music blasts over the P.A. while the musicians take a break. People are resting, sitting around, eating and talking, and there isn't nearly enough shade to go around. The women at the *parrilla* must be dying. The crowd thins out quite a bit, though some devoted supporters cheer on the few runners straggling by. The *paleteria* rolls by and I go for it. Disgusting chocolate; I'll probably be dead this time tomorrow. We are in the company of families, street vendors, and a few groups of young men here on this strip of grass lining the street under the trees. I get a shot of the *paleteria* and then put on the zoom lens for a shot of a woman selling some kind of mystery snack—yellow stuff in baggies—from an umbrella cart across the street.

César walks by. I catch up with him to ask a couple of questions, but he looks disappointed and apologizes to me for the fact that his band didn't show up. There was a mix-up about the location and parking. I thank him and tell him that he need not apologize to us. As I attempt to ask a few more questions about the music and the event, it becomes rapidly clear that he wants to end the conversation. We run into John Ulmon, the consul; César gallantly introduces me to Ulmon and then disappears.

John Ulmon is eager to talk about the Guatemalan community and this event. He hopes that this event can help boost the reputations of Guatemalans here in Los Angeles. Ulmon feels that Latinos have a reputation they don't deserve, that they have been stereotyped because of the riots and gangs. Most people don't know anything about Guatemala, according to Ulmon, even though there are about 300,000 to 500,000 Guatemalans in the city. Ulmon says that everyone comes out to have a good time and show their pride in who they are. "We can get to know each other," he says, and I take this in the larger sense to reference all the different communities in Los Angeles. I remind him that I am interested in the music, and he tells me that he chose the groups himself because they are thought to be the best. He says that after the race the Guatemalan runners are going to be presented with prizes at a festival which is to begin around 3 P.M. The festivities will include traditional dancing. Mr. Ulmon winds up our conversation by introducing me to a woman from San Antonio Aguas Calientes who has been brought to L.A. specifically for this event. She has been making tortillas all day. She tells me about her work in a craft cooperative making clothing and about the enthusiastic response she gets for her crafts and food from the people of Los Angeles during the marathon. This is the third year she has participated in it.

Roberto and I are wandering around the center in the blistering heat waiting for the dancing to begin. It's 2 P.M. and I'm kind of frustrated and bored after having been passed from person to person and having been unable to find any of the musicians to talk to. I'm thinking about getting something to drink but I don't feel like spending a buck on a Coke. Some interesting-looking characters are leaning against an R.V. with a blue tarp awning; they inspire me to think about doing another interview. We walk over toward this bunch because they started waving to us; perhaps they caught me sizing them up as possible sources for "cover terms." I ask the three men and one woman if I could record our conversation and to my relief they decline; they just want to talk to us. One of the three men, the one most likely to be under-age, hands Roberto and me each a brew from a plastic bucket of ice, and we begin to relax a bit.

We talk about living in L.A., about how for some people it's hard just getting by and for others life is good. One of the men tells us about some of the beautiful areas around Guatemala, saying about one place in particular that, "they've gone in there and really made it nice." This kind of statement usually alarms me but I don't pursue it. Roberto's and my attempts to discuss the music kind of fall flat, though we are told again that the marathon is an event that the whole Guatemalan community comes out for.

The dancing has just begun in the center of the plaza behind the bandstand. The street is no longer the focus of anyone's attention though an occasional runner can be seen straggling by. Our interviewees give us their phone numbers and we promise to send prints of the photos we've shot. Roberto and I join the dense ring of spectators around the dancers. I snake my way into the circle's interior like an annoying anthropologist to get a good spot from which to take the last six pictures on the roll. The music is canned and does not feature the square rhythms of the electric bass and traps nor the references to American and Mexican music of the live music from this morning. A children's dance and a humorous belt dance, in which a man pursues and "captures" a woman with a long woven cotton belt, evoke appreciative comments, laughter, and applause from the audience. These dances are followed by a line dance from Quetzaltenango, performed by five couples moving through a series of formations to a bass-heavy recording of marimba and drums. All the dancers are dressed in colorful traditional clothing; alas, I have forgotten the regional distinctions between the patterns of embroidery and weaving.

As three costumed kids line up in the "wings," one holding a bird-cage sort of thing, Roberto and I simultaneously decide to start packing it in. It's three o'clock and we begin to run around to say our *graciase*s and our *que le vaya muy bien*s. From the bandstand I get one last bird's-eye view of the intricate shuffling step the dancers are executing. Roberto and I wearily go over the events of the day briefly before heading west down Wilshire Boulevard. Given our limited experience with the hardware we have been carrying around all day and with the Guatemalan musical tradition, we agree that we have been productive today.

***

At the marathon, L.A.'s Guatemalan community comes together to share and celebrate its rich cultural heritage and to present proudly that heritage to the city. In my mind, the aural and visual image of Don Mateo Flores, the champion runner who inspired generations of runners after him, dancing gracefully to the murmur of the marimba band vividly portrays the many different kinds of expression that make up L.A.'s Guatemalan cultural tradition. This image, along with many others of the day, brings up some questions for me. The Guatemalan community here is made up of various groups of people who can claim different musical traditions as their own. How does the marimba tradition as it was expressed during the event come to be claimed by so many of the Guatemalans who came to the entertainment center? Several people spoke to us about the riots of 1992 and their hope that marathon day would provide an opportunity to mend the relationships between the different communities of a city ripped apart by violence and despair. We spent the day watching people dance and sing and cheer together in the street behind the old Ambassador, people who might not have had the privilege to do so in their own conflict-torn nation of origin. As the hours passed, I wondered if the marathon and the festivities at the Guatemalan community's entertainment center may have provided, for a day, a way to begin healing the wounds that many Guatemalans may have suffered both in Central America and here in Los Angeles.

A Day in the Life of Los Angeles at
the 1993 Marathon
by
Roberto Catalano

I was reasoning within myself that early Sunday morning, March 7, 1993, while driving on an almost empty freeway. I was nervous, trying to fight back the doubts and fears that arose in me at the prospect of fieldwork among a million people in an unknown part of L.A. We do not know our city, nor do we really bother to. We say it's too big, too spread out, and (blame it on the media) most of us have the utmost fear of it. Could many of us say that we have ever been to South Central, to East L.A., Compton, Watts? As everyone knows, in these troubled neighborhoods desperation, underdevelopment, and struggle are everyday reality. After the 1992 civil unrest, the voices of its citizens still shout loud and clear, calling for reforms against the too-optimistic statements of recovery from the media and those who have an interest in declaring these areas of Los Angeles to be rebuilding themselves. An imbalanced social system, sick to the bone and too inflexible to understand, too blind to see, closed in an obtuse arrogance and disturbing indifference generates anger, ignorance, violence, children handling guns instead of lollipops, and pollution in the air and in the minds of people. Is that all there is out there? Is this all we know about our city? Can we say that we know its people? These and other thoughts clouded my brain on a bright and sunny morning on my way to meet Sarah Truher, my companion in this fieldwork at the 1993 L.A. Marathon, to observe the competition as well as the Guatemalan marimba ensembles.

Although my biases were difficult to suppress, I was hoping to carry out this project the best way I possibly could. After all, this was my first ethnomusicological assignment. I needed to concentrate as much as possible on the job to be done and on the questions to ask the musicians. I wanted to know more about the Guatemalan marimba, or maybe just sit back, relax, and try to see things through the eyes of the people. In any case, I needed to mingle with the people and watch their reaction to the marathon and to the music.

Much to my surprise, my throat-gripping thoughts about being in either a pitiful or a mean part of town dissipated as we arrived at the site chosen by the Guatemalan community. Not a million people but rather about a hundred men and women worked at their stands, some preparing food and crafts, others arranging last-minute details at a quiet and relaxed crossroads on Catalina Avenue and in an adjacent parking lot partially shaded by a line of trees. The peaceful atmosphere and the happy anticipation of a special day reminded me of the times I used to set up my instruments to play at a *festa di piazza* back in my native Sicily. On a makeshift stage—a flatbed truck about 35 feet long shaded by an awning—the musicians assembled their instruments and amplification. The stage paralleled the street and closed off the parking lot. During the race the players faced the street and the onlookers; once the race was over, they turned their instruments to face the parking lot for the after-marathon party. Soon the stage was crowded with four beautifully carved marimbas: a tenor, featuring big conical resonators on the bass keys, two altos, and one soprano. Two of these instruments belonged to the ensemble "Mi Guatemala," a group of proud, older musicians brought in from their country exclusively for this important occasion, and the other two to "Murmullos Chapines," a Los Angeles-based Guatemalan ensemble. Drums, electric bass, three horns (trumpet, alto and tenor saxes), and a female singer completed the ensemble. People danced merrily to their music almost the whole time we spent there.

If it is true that the greatest distance between people is not space but culture, there are two things in this world that can sensibly reduce that distance: music and sports. When these two elements happen to come together within a single occasion, there must be more reasons to celebrate than just the spirit of a competition. Social events like the L.A. Marathon usually bring news of peace and understanding and create an all-too-rare opportunity to touch people of different nations, cultures, creeds, colors, ages, and shapes. Watching the runners interact with each other and the spectators along the route was particularly moving. It made me want to get up and run with them. I saw an

L.A.P.D. officer on a motorcycle mirror the excitement of the race with a "hundred-teeth" smile while inciting the crowd to laugh and cheer by energetically rotating his right arm *á la* Arsenio Hall. Where and when can we witness such a wonder on a normal L.A. day? And in a neighborhood such as this one? The distance between people diminished even before the race started. There was room only for recognition, respect, and appreciation for one another. For once, Angelenos were joyfully living on the streets instead of in their cars. There was not a single reason to feel afraid or insecure. To me, those were excellent reasons for celebration.

The marimba played almost incessantly as first the wheelchair racers and later the runners went by. The sound of the marimba accompanied the whole celebration from 9:00 in the morning until sundown. For the Guatemalans, as well as for many other communities, a fiesta like the one we witnessed is never complete, nor valid, without the presence of live music—in this case, the marimba ensembles. Recorded music is not the same. When the marimba dedicated a happy tune with a syncopated, catchy rhythm to all of the Central American participants in the marathon, some runners turned their attention toward the stage and seemed to adjust their pace to the rhythm of the music. Was it coincidence or did they know the tune? In any case, it was a fleeting but significant moment that hit me deeply. At a seemingly unconscious level, music caused a momentary detour and directly possessed these human beings. I saw a small group of young Guatemalans offer water, ice cubes, and orange slices to the runners. A girl positioned herself so that she could spot any approaching Guatemalan runner. At her signal, three young boys, one of them holding the Guatemalan flag, escorted the participants, to the accompaniment of patriotic shouts and cheers, along the 700 to 800 feet of this improvised Guatemalan territory. A little girl about three or four years old stood by the curb and offered her open palm to the passing runners for a high five. So many unknown hands met her playful request that she continued her game for at least an hour. Sarah and I were seeing the way sports can draw people together; that day the marathon was the cathartic element for these immigrants who had created a little Guatemala on that narrow street.

Around lunch time, as slower runners and joggers went by, the marimbas stopped their music for a while as the attention of the people shifted to the food stands. We talked with a few people in the crowd and, much to our surprise, we learned that the L.A. Marathon is the biggest event of the year for the Guatemalan community. Not a religious festival, not a music festival, but the marathon. In fact, the party was going to continue into the evening, long after the race was over. The Guatemalan runners were going to be awarded and celebrated. More marimba music and dances would be performed. Just before the end of the competition, we saw some dances performed in the parking lot by a group of dancers from the Guatemalan region of Quetzaltenango. The feeling I got watching people enjoying these pretty and colorful dances was that they knew their meaning and the stories tied to them. It was good to see parents teaching their children about a cultural heritage so important for every "Chapin" (the nickname for a Guatemalan). Virtually every mother and father seemed to call the attention of her or his child to the action taking place during the dance—a reassuring sign of a still-very-much-alive cultural awareness. For the Guatemalan community, marathon day is their most important event of the year. Their perceptions of themselves as a people, their sense of belonging, and their awareness of communal unity are refueled. We often heard the word *orgulloso*, "proud," during our interviews with people and musicians alike. The marathon and its associated activities made them proud to be who they are, proud of where they come from.

We left our post late in the afternoon just as the slowest marathoners, walkers with numbers on their chests and backs, crowded the sidewalks and the streets were returned to the dominion of cars and trucks. On the stage, the musicians turned their instruments around and prepared for the evening. As we left, I realized we had seen something very different from any other sporting event I had ever attended. Soccer games and Olympic competitions pit one person or team against another. The marathon, on the other hand, was a complete human experience: everyone—racers, the crowd, and amateurs—brought themselves there and participated in one way or another. Whether or how fast you ran was not the point; rather the marathon was a manifestation of human solidarity and understanding. I was deeply moved by the wheelchair competitors. They, more than anyone else, reminded us of how much nobility and dignity there can be in simply carrying on in the face of misfortune. The spectators reacted to all the participants' efforts with gestures of support, help, understanding, and their very presence. The marathon was a healing, relieving process. The runners of the L.A. Marathon did what they did to challenge themselves, but their individual efforts had undeniably positive repercussions for the community at large. All along the course, musicians, although paid little or nothing, shared their music with their communities and with the visitors drawn there by it for many long, hot hours. Both the runners and the musicians represented those usually ignored but wonderful people who dignify the meaning of human life by giving unconditionally to the rest of us.

Now I understand why so many cities around the world sponsor events involving huge numbers of citizens. As disturbing as it is, it seems that only these kinds of events can bring people of different cultural backgrounds together to create a feeling of togetherness. As long as we live in these inhuman cities, only radical events of great magnitude seem to relieve their citizens' chronic feelings of alienation and despair. Civil disobedience and riots are one such type of event, the marathon another. Living in this urban reality, I feel we would need a marathon a week to bring some peace and understanding among us.

The Role of Music for the Native American Community at Mile 26 of the L.A. Marathon
by
Muralikrishnan

On the March 7, 1993, the day of the L.A. Marathon, Los Angeles was transformed temporarily into a new city: feelings of togetherness, of safety, and of friendliness between people prevailed. Late in the day, streets filled with water bottles, paper cups, and hats provided visual evidence of the festival-like atmosphere created by the marathon. As different ethnic groups played their music and bystanders cheered the runners, the entire scene provided me with a major cultural shock. This was the first time I had witnessed such community activities since I moved to Los Angeles six months earlier, bringing with me fears of the problems faced by large cities of the United States. The Los Angeles Marathon gave me a new outlook on the city.

At Mile 26, the Intertribal Road Runners organized a performance by Native American Indians. Their entertainment center was situated in a large expanse of grass at the northwest corner of Exposition and Menlo, near the Natural History Museum. They set up a white *tipi* and two groups performed alternately, one from the northern plains called "Wild Horse" and the other from the southern plains called "Eagle Spirit." Each group had its own canopy, under which the musicians, who also sang, sat on chairs in a circle around the drum. There was enough space between the two groups for the costumed dancers to dance. About seven male musicians made up "Wild Horse," while "Eagle Spirit" consisted of three male musicians. The dancers were both male and female, and there was a master of ceremonies common to both groups.

My main informant for this fieldwork was Ben Hale, the leader of the southern group. I conducted a number of interviews with him before the marathon, and learned that music at the marathon provided more than mere entertainment for the runners. When I asked him why his and the other group

were playing at the marathon, he said that they perform not only to entertain but also to educate people and to present their culture in a positive manner. He added that running was an important part of his culture and that about 55 Indian runners would participate in the marathon; the music would make them feel at home when they passed this center.

The southern group, however, did not have microphones, and, although I was standing very close to the performers, the music didn't seem particularly loud. I wondered whether the runners could even hear them from the street? I suspect that, perhaps more than the music, it was the presence of the Native American groups, the scene with its *tipi*, and the costumed dancers that the runners found symbolically supportive. The music seemed to play the additional role of generating community feeling among the Native American Indians who were present there; it was played for the entire community, not just to entertain the runners.

In a multiethnic society, every community tries to find opportunities to communicate its identity, uniqueness, and difference from others; cultural performances are one important way to do this. I saw many young kids dancing. What do they know about these runners? Parents brought them to the marathon scene to experience and bring life to their cultural identity. The music at Mile 26 of the marathon provided an opportunity for parents and children to create a feeling of unity and oneness among the members of the Native American Indian community.

Realizing how important community-sponsored events can be to creating a sense of ethnic identity within a multicultural city like Los Angeles, I wondered why other communities, like those from South and Southeast Asia, did not provide music to support their runners, at least some of whom I saw at the marathon. Do they not feel the need to support the runners from those communities? Did they not receive an invitation from marathon organizers? Do they tend to live in other areas of the city, far from the marathon route? Was their music not suitable for this type of setting? Obviously more research would be needed to answer these questions.

In conclusion, music at the Los Angeles Marathon seemed an important means for many of the communities to create a sense of togetherness and cultural identity. Each community's sense of well-being created a positive chain reaction throughout the city. Peoples' attitudes seemed to change, as they experienced the diverse cultures of Los Angeles. As opposed to the impression one gets from the local news of a polluted city full of cars, carjackings, riots, kidnapings, and shootings, the marathon erased those images at least for a day and projected a new, fresh picture of Los Angeles.

MUSIC IN THE CHINESE COMMUNITY OF LOS ANGELES: AN OVERVIEW

Guangming Li

IT IS CLEAR THAT MUSIC has been a dynamic factor in the Los Angeles Chinese community since the time the community was established and continues to play a vigorous role in the daily life of the community more than ever. However, other than reports of some scattered records from the past and of present-day musical activities in Chinese newspapers, detailed documentation and research still remain to be done.

As a Chinese musician residing in Los Angeles, I have had the opportunity to familiarize myself with the community and to be involved in various musical events and community groups. As a student of ethnomusicology, I have made field observations and interviewed a number of Chinese musicians and leaders of Chinese organizations. This essay is primarily intended to describe some highlights of the music I have learned and personally experienced in Los Angeles; no conclusive interpretation on the subject is pursued herein.

The framework of this essay is as follows: 1) a general introduction to the community, 2) music in the community, in which I describe various musical events in relation to responsible institutions, 3) music and commodities, 4) music and media, and 5) a summary and some closing remarks.

THE CHINESE COMMUNITY

Referring to historical background, overall cultural characteristics, and geographical distribution, the Chinese community of Los Angeles County may be divided into two sub-communities. One is the Los Angeles Chinatown and the other encompasses the city of Monterey Park and other suburbs. Below are brief descriptions of these two areas.

Los Angeles Chinatown

The first registered Chinese in the city of Los Angeles appeared in 1852. A Chinatown around Union Station on Spring Street became identifiable in 1870 (Cheng and Kwok 1988:39). Most of these early immigrants were male and mainly worked as laundry men, market gardeners, agricultural and ranch workers, and road builders (ibid.). The Los Angeles Chinatown that people refer to centering around North Broadway today, however, is the one that was built in the 1930s when the original Chinatown was displaced from its location by the construction of Union Station (ibid.:40). Differing from Chinatown America, this new Chinatown was the first that was completely owned, planned, and built by the Chinese (ibid.:39).

Today's Chinatown is not only an attraction to tourism, like the old Chinatown, with numerous notable Chinese restaurants and gift shops, but is also a center of the American mainstream with various modern commercial and public facilities and services. There are about twenty banks and financial institutions operating there, some of them owned by Chinese; the Chinatown Branch Library contains some 300,000 books, magazines and newspapers in Chinese, English, Spanish, and Vietnamese; the Castelar School on Yale Street has a major student body of Chinese descendants; the Chinatown Service Center provides medical services; and the Chinatown Senior Citizen Service accommodates many Chinese senior citizens and various social and cultural organizations. In the late 1980s, it was estimated that Chinatown had 10,000 residents and 20,000 business people, visitors, and tourists during each day (Lew 1988:59).

The Chinese population of Los Angeles Chinatown increased considerably after 1965, and Chinese from mainland Southeast Asia began entering Chinatown in the mid-1970s. Today, a considerable number of businesses are owned by Vietnamese Chinese.

The awareness of Chinese cultural heritage is strongly felt in Chinatown. The Golden Dragon Parade during Chinese New Year's days may date back to the very early days of the community and Moon Festival events were recorded several decades ago; however, they have been discontinued at various times during the past years. Since the late 1980s, these two events have been held each year on a large scale and with great programmatic variety. Thousands of people of different cultural backgrounds have attended. In 1988, the Chinatown Cultural and Community Center was planned and The Chinese Culture and Community of Greater Los Angeles, Inc. was formed. A new cultural project, the Los Angeles Chinatown Heritage and Visitors' Center, has presently been proposed by the Chinese Historical Society of Southern California. In addition, this cultural awareness is consistently reflected by the statements of the Chinatown Pageant queens.

As with their counterparts in San Francisco and New York, the early Chinese immigrants in Chinatown were Cantonese speakers from Guangdong province of China. Although more Mandarin-speaking residents have moved into Chinatown within the past forty years, Cantonese is still the language most commonly used in social settings and cultural events. Many Vietnamese Chinese, in fact, have been descendants of Canton.

In terms of religion, Christian churches have played an important role in Chinatown since very early days. While many Chinese people attended church services, Chinese Buddhism does not seem to play as significant a role. It appears that, up to the mid-1970s, the number of Chinese Buddhists was insignificant when compared to Christians, and there was still no Chinese Buddhist temple in Los Angeles County at that time (Wu 1974:76–8).

Chinese Community in Suburbs

A suburban Chinatown emerged in Los Angeles some twenty years ago. This came after the United Nations' recognition of the People's Republic of China in 1971 and discussions between the British and the Chinese about the return of Hong Kong in 1997. A new influx of Chinese immigration from Hong Kong, Taiwan, and mainland China into the United States took place in 1970s (Fong 1994:28). Many of these newcomers came to Los Angeles and Monterey Park, a city about eight miles east of Los Angeles in the San Gabriel Valley. The Los Angeles area was one of the three most favored destinations along with New York and San Francisco. From 1983 to 1990 Monterey Park and Alhambra (an adjacent city on the north side of Interstate 10) ranked second in the number of Chinese immigrants among the three most popular urban sectors in the U.S. The number of Chinese immigrants has increased rapidly, and in Monterey Park alone the Chinese population reached 21,971 in 1990, representing 63% of the entire Asian population in the city at that time.

Many of the early Chinese newcomers to Los Angeles suburbs were well educated professionals and adapted well to Los Angeles (Fong 1994:48). Since the mid-1970s, business people from Taiwan and Hong Kong started to arrive, first at Monterey Park. They were real estate people, merchants, heavy investors, and frequently wealthy, often bringing hundreds of thousands of dollars in cash. Soon much of the area was owned by these wealthy Chinese newcomers. "The Chinese Beverly Hills" and "Little Taipei" have been two terms used by Los Angeles Chinese residents to refer to the area. At present, it is estimated that in Monterey Park about 70% of all business enterprises are owned by Chinese (Fong 1994:44). Some fifty Chinese restaurants, more than thirty realtors, at least eight Chinese supermarkets, numerous professional offices, bookstores, herb shops, bakeries, and small specialty services among other businesses are operating. It seems that because of their somewhat superior financial position the merchants have appeared bolder and more agressive. Unlike their professional counterparts, they often do not show much interest in the American mainstream. Few of these merchants have spoken English, even though most of them understand it, and they have not often been in agreement with certain American conventions of doing business. Recently, many Chinese have moved to other areas, although Monterey Park is still the central area for most Chinese immigrants.

As the newcomers settled, social, commercial, and cultural facilities and services were established and then expanded. According to the Chinese Yellow Pages (Southern California), there are in the suburbs more than a dozen Chinese newspapers produced and distributed (some of them with international distribution), about ten TV stations/ production enterprises, six Chinese radio stations, about forty various kinds of social and political associations, and some forty Chinese language schools (only three in Chinatown). There are also more than one hundred Catholic and other Christian churches and organizations, twenty Chinese Buddhist temples, organizations, and shops that are operating. Among the temples is the International Buddha Progress Society, the largest Buddhist monastery in the West. Increasingly, different kinds of cultural events and activities, including music, have been presented and/or hosted by or at these social and cultural institutions.

In contrast to Los Angeles Chinatown, Mandarin is the most commonly used Chinese language in the suburbs. This relates to the fact that a majority of the new immigrants are from Taiwan and mainland China. For instance, from 1983 to 1990, 2,479 Chinese immigrated from mainland China, 2,328 from Taiwan, but only 768 from Hong Kong, the latter representing less than 14% of the newcomers (Fong 1994:32). Although some of those from Taiwan speak Taiwanese, Mandarin is the most common language in working places and is used for communication in most business and community settings.

Nevertheless, in spite of such differentiation, Chinatown and the Chinese community of the suburbs have been closely in touch. The modern transportation systems make it easy for them to visit each other and participate in events and activities in other areas. Also, through the Chinese media, namely the newspapers and local broadcasting systems, they constantly share the same ideas and experiences.

MUSIC IN THE COMMUNITY

Musical genres and styles that are heard in the Los Angeles Chinese community are of great variety, including Chinese traditional, Western classical, popular, imported, and other ethnic music. They are presented in concerts and social and cultural events by various performing groups, often sponsored by social, cultural, and business organizations.

Based on the contexts of differentiation between the two communities, I would like to discuss the musical genres/styles of Los Angeles Chinatown and the suburbs separately.

L.A. CHINATOWN: MUSICAL EVENTS AND LOCAL PERFORMING GROUPS[1]

Musical events in Chinatown present music of most of the categories mentioned above. Included are Chinese opera, instrumental music, popular music, imported music, and other ethnic music.

Chinese Opera

CANTONESE OPERA
The most popular genre in Chinatown is the

Cantonese opera, a regional theater in the Guangdong (Canton) province of China. Although it has its own features in various aspects, it may be easy to identify by its theatrical Cantonese speech and its accompanying ensemble which consists of Chinese *erhu, yangqin, dizi, houguan, ruan* (connected with an electric amplifier),[2] and some Western music instruments such as saxophone, banjo, and electric guitar, among others.

There are two active Cantonese opera clubs in Chinatown, the Yuet Sing Music Club and the Victory Music Club. The former was established in 1964 and the latter in about 1980. Their members are local Cantonese-speaking Chinese (including some from Vietnam). They are officially two different groups having their own directors, bylaws, and permanent venues. However, they have no rules prohibiting members of one club from crossing the boundaries of the institution to participate in activities of the other. Except for a few, most of the members are not professional artists with traditional training but amateurs. They are business owners and other professionals, especially in the Chinatown area. While senior citizens are important especially in the leadership of the clubs, many instrumentalists and singers are in their thirties and forties.

The activities of these two clubs have been primarily within Los Angeles Chinatown. Some years ago Yuet Sing Music Club rented a place in Monterey Park, as the owner of the original venue in Chinatown went bankrupt, although the group has now returned there. Of the two, the Yuet Sing Music Club meets more regularly, rehearsing twice a week, Wednesday evenings and Sunday afternoons, for about three or four hours each time. The Victory Music Club does not hold regular meetings nor rehearsals until a scheduled performance is approaching. In addition to regular membership fees, donations to the club are definitely encouraged. For example, at the current venue of the Yuet Sing Music Club, donors' names and the amount of the donations are written on red paper and posted on the wall.

Each year the two clubs present a number of concerts/performances on varying occasions, including community gatherings, fundraising for social programs, and traditional Chinese festive celebrations. The program of these performances usually comprise highlights of traditional Cantonese opera. The rendition of an entire play is sometimes given for special occasions such as celebrating the anniversary of the club, which usually takes place late in the year, and/or as participation in the Chinese Art Festival of Southern California, an annual event planned and sponsored the Chinese Culture Center.[3]

Performances have been primarily held in Chinatown. While other venues have hosted the events, the New Won Kok Restaurant and the Cinemaland Chinese Theater are usually the venues hosting major performances. For each important performance, colorful posters are always produced and posted widely. Although tickets may cost twenty or thirty dollars, or even more, the concerts are well attended, usually by Cantonese speakers, although some younger people and children not as fluent in the language may attend as well.

A pursuit of authenticity and professionalism in the opera clubs is evident in their activity. Their repertoire, make-up, and costumes are always conventional and so is their style of singing and speech. The accompanying ensembles are also of conventional instrumentation, which combines Chinese instruments: the *erhu, yangqin, qinqin, houguan,* traditional percussive set, and Western instruments such as saxophone and electric guitars.[4]

The local Cantonese opera artists have kept the tradition of worshipping ancestors, gods, or guardians of the Cantonese opera by asking for successful performances and livelihoods. At the Yuet Sing Music Club's venue, facing the entrance is an altar for two ancestral teachers—Master Guanghua and Master Tianbao of the Cantonese opera. As learned and believed by the artists, Master Guanghua was the one who taught singing and acting, while Master Tianbao taught acrobatics and military-scene music (with percussion ensemble). Also, two other divinities guarding the Qianliyan (or the "Far-sighted") and Shunfeng'er (or "Far-heard") are also worshipped (see Figure 1, Appendix II).

OTHER STYLES

In addition to Cantonese opera, other traditional Chinese operatic genres have been presented. For instance, the Kwan (Kun) Opera Society was once invited to perform for the Chinese Moon Festival. Their performances were well received by the audience and critics.

Instrumental Music

CHINESE ENSEMBLE

The "Guangdong Yingyue" or "Cantonese music" is a popular Chinese instrumental style. However, no Cantonese music ensembles independent from local Cantonese opera clubs are known. Although derived from Cantonese opera, many Cantonese opera instrumentalists can play a diversity of Cantonese music, although such is not their focus of interest, and, they do play Cantonese instrumental music on varying occasions.

Other Cantonese instrumental music has been introduced into the community. During large scale cultural events, such as the Moon Festival, Chinese instrumental musicians of classical and different regional traditions have come to Chinatown to perform their instrumental music. For example, the 1991 Moon Festival, which was co-sponsored by two active Chinatown organizations (the Chinese Chamber of Commerce and Chinese Historical Society of Southern California) and the City of Los Angeles Cultural Affairs Department, invited two Chinese instrumental music groups from Los Angeles suburbs to play varying genres and styles. On May 14, 1994, the Chinese Cultural and Community Center of Greater Los Angeles, Inc. held the first annual "Chinatown Spring: A Festival of Music" at Chinatown's Alpine Recreation Center. At this event a workshop was presented as a general introduction to Chinese musical instruments after the presentation of some Cantonese opera performances.

It should also be noted that the dragon dance, performed during the Chinese New Year Festival, makes use of conventional Chinese percussion music.

WESTERN ENSEMBLE

The only Western instrumental music heard in Chinatown is band music. Although it has been performed in the community for a long time,[5] the principal occasions where band music is heard today are usually during the Chinese New Year Festival. Also, Chinese funeral processions usually hire a marching band, with some Chinese percussion instruments mixed in.

Choral Music

Christian churches and organizations have been part of the life of the Chinese since early Chinese immigrants came to Los Angeles. The Chinese United Methodist Church and The Catholic Chinese Center are particularly significant to Chinatown.[6] Although various church choirs exist, no professional church choral group is known in Chinatown. In 1993, a children's church chorus was initiated and has performed at social gatherings. The repertoire of the choir includes both folk and religious songs.

Popular Music

It appears that karaoke contests and some social gatherings are common contexts for popular music. However, the essential repertoire popular in the community continues to be Cantonese folk songs and Cantonese opera arias. Once, as I was dining in the Golden Dragon Restaurant, a big banquet party for senior citizens was being held and I saw people singing karaoke Cantonese folk songs. Also, I am told that a Chinese lady has held several karaoke contests at the New Won Kok Restaurant and the repertoire was essentially Cantonese folk songs and Cantonese opera selections.[7]

Imported Music

Chinatown has not usually accommodated performing troupes from overseas. It is only the troupe of Cantonese opera from China that is occasionally invited when convenient. For instance, members of the community have arranged performances for the troupe in Los Angeles during the group's tours to San Francisco.

Music of Other Nationalities

There are also music performances of other nationalities in Chinatown. During the last five years, the Moon Festival has invited Korean, Native American, and Filipino musical performances. The Chinese Chamber of Commerce, the organizer of the festival this year, is planning to invite more music of different nationality or ethnic background, such as African American music, into the event.

CHINESE COMMUNITY IN SUBURBS: MUSICAL EVENTS AND LOCAL PERFORMING GROUPS

Chinese Opera

Beijing opera is the dominant traditional theatrical genre.[8] Beijing opera has distinctive characteristics in various aspects, for instance, a highly stylized speech which developed from combining various regional languages, and the instrumentation of its accompanying ensemble which features three stringed instruments: *jinghu, jingerhu,* and *yueqin;* and percussion instruments: *danpigu, ban, naobo, daluo* and *xiaoluo.*[9] Also, it has a number of recognizable schools established by famous actors from the past.

There are more than a dozen Beijing opera clubs in Los Angeles County, and most of them are based in Monterey Park.[10] While two of them are officially registered organizations, many of them are essentially private gathering assemblies. Some professional Beijing opera artists (including highly accomplished ones in their home countries) may

either belong to some of the clubs or make guest appearances in their performances. The essential membership of all the clubs' *piaoyiu* or Beijing opera amateurs[11] are retired senior citizens who emigrated from Taiwan in the 1970s–1980s. While there are some members in their fifties and occasionally late forties, it is unusual to encounter anyone under forty.

All the clubs have a leader or president, many of them have bylaws, and some have nominal administrative staff such as a secretary. They meet either weekly or biweekly. While some meet in a private home of a member of the club, many meet at public facilities such as Monterey Park City Hall, Los Angeles Chinese Culture Center and other public recreation centers.

Each year, these clubs present a number of concerts of traditional opera highlights.[12] Professionalism and authenticity of the performances are conspicuously pursued in these concerts. The instrumentation of the accompanying ensemble is standardized, including all the essential instruments. To assure the quality of the accompaniment, professional musicians and recognized accomplished amateurs are invited and paid to participate in the ensemble by the club. Not only is their repertoire conventional by general definition, but performances must also correspond to the style of the traditional schools.[13] Also, *qingchang* (singing without costume, makeup and acting) and *zhezixi* (performance of sections or highlights from Chinese operas with costume, makeup, and acting) are two common formats of performance besides rendition of an entire drama. Local artists never mix the two formats in one concert as it is not a conventional practice of presentation.

At present, the Dehan Tinsen Chinese Culture Club is the largest and most active club.[14] It has about twenty-five regular members and three permanent professional musicians teaching and advising for performances.[15] The club presented six formal shows (with or without collaboration from other clubs) in various locations of the suburbs in 1993 alone. Other well known clubs such as the

Chinese Opera Club of Los Angeles and the Southern California Chinese Opera Association may present one or two times each year, either highlights or complete plays of traditional repertoire.[16]

The concerts of Beijing opera always seem very well attended. However, the audience is primarily made up of Beijing opera amateurs and their families and friends (see Figure 2, Appendix II).

Besides these Beijing opera clubs, there is a club of Kun opera. This is another major traditional Chinese theatrical genre. Kun opera has a history of more than four hundred years. It is known for its highly refined singing styles, elegant and sophisticated lyrics, and actors' lines. It used to be frequently associated with literati and scholars.

The Kun Opera Club was formed in 1980 in Monterey Park and was named the Kwun Opera Society in 1989. Most of the members are amateurs. The teachers, however, are top professional Kun opera artists from China. The group meets once a week at home of Mrs. Jing-ying Cheng Yu, the founder and the previous president of the club. Many members live in the Monterey Park area while some live in other suburbs, necessitating for some considerable freeway commutes to rehearsals. The essential membership consists of people in their thirties and forties; however, there are also younger people in their twenties. Other than a mandatory membership fee, the club does not have restrictive bylaws.

Collaborating with other performance organizations, the club has given one performance each year at various cultural events. The repertoire is traditional and so is the style of acting, speech, and instrumental accompaniment.

Instrumental Music

CHINESE ENSEMBLES

There are several Chinese music groups. The Chinese Music Orchestra of Southern California, The Spring Thunder Chinese Music Association, the Cheng-Hsin Chinese Zither Orchestra of Los Angeles, and the San Fernando Valley Chinese Music Ensemble are specially active in performing activity.

Among these four, the Chinese Music Orchestra of Southern California is the oldest, begun in 1974. This group meets on a regular basis and has performed at various concerts and cultural events. The group has a leader and nominal bylaws but not membership fees. Most of the members are local amateurs, although professional musicians have been invited to join in their performances.

The Spring Thunder Chinese Music Association was formed by a group of Chinese music afficionados (most of whom were newcomers from Taiwan) in 1980 and has become the best known ensemble since then. This ensemble has a president and some key members, but no bylaws nor membership fees. The members meet once a week at the home of the president. Although the majority of the membership of the ensemble consists of middle-aged and younger musicians, it does have some retired senior members, including the president.

Other than performing in various cultural events in the community, the Spring Thunder Chinese Music Association has put on annual concerts of Chinese music since 1986, and they have pursued professionalism in modern Chinese music. In 1982, the ensemble appointed Mr. Lui Pui Yuen, a well known virtuoso of Chinese lute (*pipa*) and zither (*qin*) and music director in Hong Kong; and several years ago Mr. Qiao Fei, the former director of the Guangdong Music and Dance Troupe in China, was appointed to direct the ensemble. Also, a substantial number of professional musicians have been invited to participate in their performances. As a result, in their concerts of recent years the ensemble has been able to present more pieces composed for modern professional ensembles, which require complex instrumentation and sophisticated performing techniques.[17]

The San Fernando Valley Chinese Music Ensemble was formed in 1988 by a group of middle-aged Chinese professionals living in Northridge and adjacent cities. They have met weekly or bi-weekly. Except for a few, most members did not have significant music background. The ensemble welcomes anyone interested in the music and it also encourages teens to join. It does not have any restrictive bylaws other than mandatory membership.

Each year since 1989, the San Fernando Valley Chinese Music Ensemble has participated in a major cultural event, the Asian Pacific Heritage Night, in the San Fernando Valley. Pursuing professionalism in modern Chinese music, the ensemble has hired four professional musicians to teach different instruments and conduct ensemble rehearsal. The ensemble can now play some music composed for modern Chinese ensembles.

The Cheng-Hsin Chinese Zither Orchestra of Los Angeles specializes in the *cheng* (or *zheng*), the Chinese bridged long zither. Established in 1989, the Cheng-Hsin Chinese Zither Orchestra of Los Angeles has participated in various cultural and social events and presented a major concert, which was held at the International Buddhist Progress Society, in 1992[18] (see Figure 3, Appendix II).

WESTERN ORCHESTRAS

Several Western orchestras emerged in the 1980s, but there are only two currently in existence. The Olympia Philharmonic Orchestra was formed in Monterey Park in 1988 and has been steady in reaching the general public. All musicians are professionally trained instrumentalists. The purpose of this orchestra is primarily to promote interest in Western classical music, especially children within the community, and to encourage Asian talents in the performing arts. Although established as an official orchestra, there are no permanent employees and no rehearsal meetings are held until the time of preparing for concerts. The Orchestra has bylaws and a board committee but no permanent director. Directors are invited when it is time to give a concert. Chinese musicians form the base of the orchestra. However, musicians of other nationalities have participated in their performances, especially in

the wind section.

Funded by various sources, the orchestra presents approximately two concerts each year, mostly in the eastern suburbs of Los Angeles.[19] Except for a few works by Chinese composers, most of the orchestra's programs feature works by master composers from the classical and romantic periods such as Mozart, Beethoven, Vivaldi, Saint-Saens, Mendelssohn, Rossini, Liszt, among others (see Figure 4, Appendix II).

The Buddha's Light Youth Symphony Orchestra was established as a cultural program of the Buddha's Light Hsilai School, an affiliation of the the International Buddha Progress Society. It has a permanent Chinese director and some forty young Chinese musicians from ten to twenty years of age. The orchestra rehearses every Saturday afternoon. Its repertoire consists of classical symphonies, compositions in Chinese style, and Buddhist themes. The orchestra's first concert was performed at the Buddhist temple in January 1994 and another was presented at the Chinese Culture Center in Rosemead in June of 1994. The orchestra has participated in various Buddhist activities and other cultural events in the community.

OTHER WESTERN MUSIC EVENTS

In addition to the orchestras, other local organizations have sponsored events and activities of Western instrumental music. The Music Teachers' Association of California is a conventional American music organization established about one hundred years ago. At present, 99% of the members of the West San Gabriel Valley Branch are Chinese teachers, including the president of the Branch. Each year the Branch holds a Branch Honor Recital in which young Chinese students taught by members of the Association perform. All works performed are by Western composers, mostly of the baroque, classical, and romantic periods.

The Taiwan Benevolent Association of California has held annual music contests at various locations since 1990.[20] The contestants must play Chinese songs (a list of the songs are specified by the organizer) while they may play music of Western and other traditions at their choice. Young musicians under the age of eighteen may participate in the contest. Although these contests have been only for the piano and violin,[21] the number of contestants is quite large, varying between 112 to 158. About two-thirds of the contestants perform piano while the others are violinists. Repertoire comprises a cross-section of Western genres, from baroque to contemporary. Since the latest contest on the second weekend of May 1994, a requirement has become established that each contestant choose one of several Chinese compositions selected by the contest committee.

Choral Groups

There are a number of choruses in the suburbs, including Melodia Sinica, the Jupiter Chorus, the Southern California Chinese Catholic Choir, the Yue You Chorus, among many others. Usually these chorus groups are well organized, some having formal bylaws and some not. While most members of these choir groups are amateurs, it is usual that leaders are professional musicians such as conductors, soloists, and pianists.[22]

Among these choir groups, the Melodia Sinica appears to be the most accomplished. Although based in the San Fernando Valley, it has members from many of the suburbs, including about 40% from places such as Monterey Park, Pomona, Hacienda Heights, Palos Verdes, and even Ventura County. Some of the homes of members may be two hours or even longer in freeway driving time from the San Fernando Valley. Established in 1989, the Melodia Sinica has given two major annual concerts, the Annual Concert and the Christmas Concert, as well as performances for other cultural and social events. The performance of the group has reached a considerably professional level, and they have not only been invited to perform at the Los Angeles Music Center, shown on television, but also were the first Chinese choir to perform at Carnegie Hall in New York (in May 1994).

The programs of the choruses may present a variety of genres and compositions of Western, Chinese, and other traditional styles. Also, programs may or may not include songs with religious themes. The program of the 1993 annual concert of the Melodia Sinica held at the First Baptist Church of Canoga Park on June 19 is an example that includes religious themes (in contrast, the Jupiter Chorus does not present religious themes). The program presented genres/styles by modern Chinese composers. While works by Chinese composers such as "Folksong of Picking Lotus," "Mountain Climbing," and "A Kang-Ding Love Song," are not religious, most of those by Western composers are frequently of Christian themes, e.g., seven songs of "Gloria" by Vivaldi, "Just A Little Talk With Jesus" by Derricks, "Eternal Life" by Dungan, and the Negro Spiritual "Ride the Chariot" (see Figure 5, Appendix II).

Popular Music

The karaoke contest appears to be the major event of popular music performed by local community members. The Sing Young Karaoke U.S.A. has held five karaoke contests sponsored by various Chinese businesses in the past several years. In the concerts, music lovers bring their own favorite repertoire which may range from a wide variety of Chinese popular songs in Mandarin, Taiwanese, Cantonese, and English. There are also other karaoke contests. Sponsored by the Diamond Squire (a Chinese shopping center in Rosemead) and Sprint, the Sprint Diamond Children's Karaoke Singing Contest has been going on since February 5, 1994. After auditioning, any child between ages six and twelve may participate in the contest which is held every Saturday afternoon.[23] The songs that these children sing reflect a great variety of currently faddish and popular songs in various languages, like those from other contests presented by Sing Young Karaoke. Also, during other social events such as the celebration of Chinese New Year, popular songs may be presented on stage by local music talents (see Figure 6, Appendix II).

There have been only a few local pop music groups, and no concerts given by them appear to be known or documented. The "L.A. Boys" is a pop music group located in Irvine. It consists of three young American-born Chinese. However, it appears that they are better known in Taiwan than in Los Angeles. They have toured in Taiwan and have impressed younger generations there with Taiwanese and Mandarin-translated American raps.[24]

Imported Music

Chinese performing artists from Hong Kong, Taiwan, and mainland China have been brought to Los Angeles, sponsored by various business organizations. The genres and styles of these artists have represented a great variety. They have ranged from various Chinese traditional theater (including Beijing opera, Kun opera, Cantonese opera, Taiwanese opera, etc.), to dance, instrumental music, and contemporary pop songs.

However, pop music stars from Taiwan and Hong Kong have been constantly invited to present concerts, while visits of comprehensive performing arts troupes from mainland China have become more frequent in recent years. Two popular music concerts were held in April 1994. The Charity Night, a song-dance concert at the Pasadena Civic Auditorium and sponsored by the Wenxin Weiyuan Hui ("Warm and Fragrant Committee"), was presented on April 1, and featured a pair of very well known and popular young singers from Taiwan. Fang Jiwei, the female singer, is called "Junzhong Qingren" ("Lover in the Army") and Lin Zhiying, the male singer, is known as one of the "Sida Tianwang" ("Four Great Heaven Kings").[25] Two weeks after the Pasadena concert, a karaoke concert was held at East Los Angeles College Auditorium on April 16, presented by Hollywood Dynasty, Inc., and co-sponsored by various Chinese businesses. The headings of the playbill for that concert read "'94 Karaoke Night, a Concert of Red [meaning very popular at present] Singing, Movies, and TV Stars of Hong Kong, [with] First Class

Orchestra." Under the three pictures are the names of the three singers and their nicknames in brackets: "Prince Huang," "Fat Mom," and "Sexy Female Singer" (see Figure 6, Appendix II).

In March 1994, Interntex Company, a Chinese business, presented a "Night of China" at Pasadena City College, featuring a troupe from mainland China. The concert consisted of simple creation, comical Chinese dialogue, song, dance, traditional opera, acrobatics, and other forms.[26] Less than a month later, Pan Pacific Performing Arts, Inc. presented two concerts billed as "The Best of Chinese Ethnic Minority Performances" at Santa Ana High School and Pasadena City College. The concerts contained music and dance of various Chinese minorities and magic shows[27] (see Figure 7, Appendix II).

Music of Other Nationalities

Music from non-Chinese communities are also presented in the Chinese community. The Asian Pacific Heritage Night provides one example. This is a major cultural event hosted by the San Fernando Valley Chinese Cultural Association and the China Institute Southern California at California State University, Northridge, usually in May. Although it is primarily a Chinese event, the local Japanese Gardena Drum Ensemble and Japanese theatrical artists, in addition to Cambodian, Pilipino, and Thai musicians and dancers have been invited to perform in the concerts each year.

MUSIC COMMODITIES: LOS ANGELES CHINATOWN

Bookstores

There are about eight bookstores in the Chinatown area. Many of them carry music material of various kinds. The music found at most of these stores is mainly audio cassettes and CDs of various styles of popular music, both in Mandarin and Cantonese from Taiwan and Hong Kong. Although much smaller in quantity, there are some recordings in Chinese style, most of which are Cantonese opera and Cantonese instrumental ensemble music. They may also have in stock some popular music in English. Some bookstores such as the China Book Store and the Happyland Company also sell music books of "old songs" from the 1930s to 1960s, mostly in Cantonese.

The Limin Book Company is a store specializing in music commodities from mainland China. It has two departments. The one on Hill Street in downtown Los Angeles is a book department and sells various types of publications, including books, journals, magazines, encyclopedias, and reference publications on all subjects, among which are music theory and Chinese and Western music published in mainland China. The other is a stationery department which is located on Chung King Road. Besides Chinese stationery supplies and other artifacts from mainland China, the department sells various music products and rents videos.

Music Stores

I have encountered only two music stores in Chinatown. One is the above cited department of the Limin Book Company on Chung King Road.[28] It sells various kinds of common Chinese musical instruments, such as *erhu, dizi, pipa, yangqin,* and Beijing opera percussion instruments, but no non-Chinese musical instruments. Although some music stores in Los Angeles County may occasionally carry a few Chinese musical instruments and have services in ordering such instruments, the Limin Book Company department appears to be the major supplier of Chinese music instruments in the entire county. The department also rents videos and sells music cassettes, principally recordings of traditional, modernized, or Westernized Chinese music, and some Chinese rock and roll.

The other music store in Chinatown is the New Sound Karaoke.[29] It was opened in Chinatown Plaza on North Broadway in 1993. Sold are karaoke equipment and music videos, cassettes, and CDs. The music in stock is very much similar to that found in the bookstores, namely popular songs from Taiwan and Hong Kong, Cantonese opera, and English language songs.

MUSIC COMMODITIES: CHINESE COMMUNITY IN SUBURBS

Bookstores

There are more than sixty Chinese bookstores in Monterey Park and neighboring areas. Although only a few specialize in music, many of them carry music cassettes and discs and some song books.

Many bookstores carry music cassettes and/or CDs.[30] The most common genres and styles on these cassettes and CDs are pop songs from Taiwan followed by those from Hong Kong. Cassettes and CDs of traditional Chinese musical genres and styles and European popular music are also found, although considerably rare. In addition to these music recordings are song books including those of popular songs from the 1920s to 1940s.

While most other stores are selling cassettes and CDs from Taiwan and Hong Kong, Monterey Books & Stationeries, which has operated for about ten years in Monterey Park, primarily carries various kinds of music material from mainland China. The cassettes are of different genres of traditional music (e.g., Beijing opera) and modernized folk songs, while the books specialize on theory and notation from various Chinese and Western traditions. The store also rents video tapes of Chinese movies and traditional music styles and other entertainment performances.

Western music material is also found in some of the stores. The Song of Song, Inc., which was opened in 1984 on East Garvey Avenue in Monterey Park, serves as a particular example. Other than books of classical piano music, which are the main items sold by the store, stock also includes collections of music for violin, electronic keyboard, guitar (such as classical, popular melodies, ballads, and jazz) and books of various vocal genres/styles (such as hymns, folk songs, art songs, and campus songs), Western music appreciation, theory, and teaching manuals and methods.

Also of significance are various religious bookstores. The Alleluia Christian Audiovisual & Literature Center (which opened in 1985 in Monterey Park) and the EFC Bookstore (which opened in 1993) in Rosemead are two bookstores carrying Christian material and music. The recordings include music of vocal and instrumental genres. In addition to conventional hymns and instrumental pieces, there is much music composed by both American and Chinese musicians with religious themes. A great variety of commercial cassettes of Buddhist music (including Buddhist chant and compositions and performances of Buddhist themes) are available through many Buddhist organizations and stores, such as the Global Buddhist Association (in Monterey Park), International Buddhist Progress Society (in Hacienda Heights), and Lin Ca Foo Company (in Alhambra).

Music Stores

There are some thirty-three music shops in the suburbs accessible to the Chinese community.[31] About two thirds of these stores are owned by Chinese and a third by non-Chinese.[32] Although a few may stock Chinese music instruments and provide ordering services for them, Western and popular music instruments such as piano, violin, band instruments, and karaoke equipment are their primary business.[33] Most of these stores have opened since the late 1970s. For instance, the Bryan Lee Music/Piano Warehouse opened in Torrance and Monterey Park in 1979 and in 1989 respectively; the First Music Instrument, Inc. opened in Monterey Park in 1983, King's Music Center[34] in Rosemead (1985), Joseph Liu Violin Maker (1985), and Sing Young Music World, the major karaoke specialty store in Pasadena/Monterey Park (mid 1980s).

Piano stores tend to have the largest business and are the ones that buy full page ads in the Chinese Yellow Pages.[35] There are six major piano stores; the pianos these stores sell are principally those of prestigious brands and trademarks such as Germany Petrof, Steinway and Sons, Schimer, and Schimmel.[36] These stores also sell other keyboards and other instruments.[37] Most of these stores also offer music classes in which most students are children and teens studying piano performance and Western music theory.[38] For instance, the New Happy Tune Piano store offers a series of courses preparing students of all levels for subjects of the scheduled examinations of the Royal School of Music in England. In addition, the stores provide services such as tuning, maintenance, and rental.

MUSIC AND MEDIA

Televison and Radio

Chinatown and the suburbs share the same television and radio broadcasting stations. However, all the TV and radio stations and producers have been located in the suburbs since the 1980s, and the number of TV and radio stations has been increasing. Until the present, about 10 TV stations have been producing and broadcasting Chinese programs located in various suburbs.[39] Broadcasting schedules vary, ranging from limited hours, twelve hours, or even twenty-four hours during weekdays or seven days a week. Chinese languages in the broadcast are those commonly spoken in the Chinese community, namely, Mandarin, Cantonese, and Taiwanese. The programs range from news, various cultural and social events, political issues, to sports, and entertainment, both domestic and international. Regarding music programs, however, while some are produced in America, most are either adapted or relayed from Taiwan, Hong Kong, and mainland China. At present, musical programs produced and/or broadcasted by ACTV (the American Chinese Television Station)[40] on Channel 62 and Panda TV[41] on Channel 18 may reach the widest audience.[42] ACTV presents two major regular musical programs. "Regional Opera" is a one-hour show of Chinese traditional opera in the afternoons, Monday through Thursday. The program has been mostly performances of Beijing opera recorded in Taiwan. On week day afternoons "Bright Rhythm" is aired, an MTV type of Chinese popular music show produced in Taiwan.[43] The program introduces hit songs and new songs of well known pop singers.

In contrast to ACTV, Panda TV broadcasts musical programs from mainland China. Panda TV used to have a one-hour program on Sunday evenings named "Zongyi Daguan" (or "Overview on Arts"), which contained segments of performing arts which were frequently shows of Chinese MTV presentation. During Chinese annual festive seasons or holidays, such as the New Year and the Chinese Spring Festival, all broadcast time is devoted to relaying the seasonal concerts, mostly of music and dance, recorded by national TV stations in mainland China. Currently, Chinese performing arts are present in Panda TVs weekday afternoon programs.[44]

There are at least eight radio stations in the suburbs. Like their Chinese TV counterparts, Chinese radio stations broadcast various kinds of programs in Mandarin, Taiwanese, and Cantonese. Regarding music, they offer different menus from the TV stations; however, different stations have different emphases in their programming. The N.C.A. Broadcast Company, established in 1987, has two sets of Chinese programs, Mandarin and Cantonese. Both programs present varying genres of Chinese music. Although popular songs from Hong Kong and Taiwan represent a considerable portion of the broadcasting, Cantonese opera is also found in the programming.[45] In El Monte, the Overseas Chinese Broadcasting System has been operating for the last five years. Music programs have primarily consisted of Taiwanese and Mandarin Chinese songs in addition to some occasional Japanese songs.

Newspapers

Chinatown and the suburban Chinese communities share most of the Chinese newspapers. Major newspapers include the *Chinese Daily News*, *In-*ternational Daily News*, *Sing Tao Newspaper* (L.A.), *Ta-Kung-Pao*, and *Wen Wei Po*. The first three are Los Angeles local newspapers located in Monterey Park and adjacent areas and established during the last twenty years. The other two are newspapers from Hong Kong. They are widely distributed to private homes and found at bookstores and supermarkets, as well as newspaper stands.

All these newspapers have special sections presenting reports and articles about various musical events and stars. The *Chinese Daily News*, *International Daily News*, and *Sing Tao Newspaper* (L.A.) provide information about music in Los Angeles. Reports of stories and scandals concerning the stars of popular music in Taiwan and Hong Kong take most space in the papers. Almost anything that has recently happened overseas can be quickly publicized to the Chinese community in Los Angeles. Also, these newspapers contain news about entertainment stars of the American mainstream.

A few Chinese newspapers appear to mainly be distributed in Chinatown. For example, San Francisco's *Chinese Times* has popular distribution in Chinatown but not in the suburbs.[46]

SUMMARY AND SOME CONCLUDING OBSERVATIONS

There are apparent distinctions between the two Los Angeles Chinese communities and their musical orientations. While in Chinatown, Cantonese genres and Cantonese clubs are predominant and the band is the most visible Western instrumental ensemble, in the suburbs Beijing opera and Kun opera clubs represent the traditional Chinese opera styles. Modern Chinese ensembles and Western music orchestras also perform in the suburbs, where various contests occur, and various styles of music are imported. While in Chinatown there are music stores that sell only Chinese music instruments, in the suburbs a number of stores sell Western music instruments and offer Western music classes.

However, both communities share common experiences. Both engage in cultural heritage exchange and share with other ethnic communities. Both enjoy popular music from Taiwan and Hong Kong, watch and listen to the same music programs on TV and radio, and read the news in the same newspapers. Also, some Chinese traditional music is performed in both communities.

Needless to say, further detailed documentation and in-depth research must be carried out before arriving at any meaningful interpretive conclusion regarding the dynamics underlying the music differentiations and conformations of the communities. However, based upon what has been observed up to this moment, I believe that we can say that regional cultural background and social and economic conditions are significant factors responsible for the current differentiations. The popularity of Cantonese genres in Chinatown conspicuously results from the fact that the Cantonese-speaking immigrants were the first to settle in Los Angeles Chinatown, and Cantonese-speakers are the dominant population of the area. Correspondingly, the dominance of Mandarin-speakers in most of the suburbs is a major factor encouraging activity of Beijing opera in those sectors.[47] Although Chinese immigrants had settled in Los Angeles more than one hundred years ago and had become an economically self-contained community, it was not until the mid-1970s, when a considerable number of wealthy and ambitious investors and business people came from Taiwan and Hong Kong, that music business and media emerged and began to flourish. As a result of the economic and cultural development in the suburbs, and despite Chinatown still retaining its irreplaceable personality, there is no doubt that Monterey Park and its adjacent areas play a predominant role in various aspects of music activities.

Finally, though Los Angeles Chinatown and the Chinese community of the suburbs may be differentiated by music, nonetheless, their connections are enhanced by music as well. While common Chinese traditional styles and local Chinese media have brought them closer to each other, the music and news from their homelands are constantly reminding them of their common origin and characterizing their common Chinese identity.

Acknowledgment

I would like to express my gratitude to all who gave their support and shared their knowledge and insight with me. Special thanks to Sue Yee, Paul Wing L. Koon, Jiexian Cheng, Jingying Cheng, Wen-hsung Yeh, Conny Deng, Feng Ho, Lin Kwan, Diana Liu, Shufan Yeh, and Ying Liu.

NOTES

1. This only refers to music events and groups of the Chinese from China. Those by Chinatown's Indochina Chinese community are not included.

2. The Cantonese *erhu*, which is more commonly called *gaohu*, is a high pitched two-string-bowed lute. *Yangqin* is a Chinese dulcimer, *dizi* a bamboo flute, *houguan* a double-reed aerophone, and *ruan* a long-necked lute to which an electric amplifier is usually connected in Cantonese opera.

3. A politico-cultural agent of the Taiwan government.

4. It is also interesting to note that in addition to the electric guitar or the *ruan*, a microphone is assigned to all the instruments during the rehearsal.

5. Based on some photographs from the past, it is evident that a band was hired for celebrating the completion of the new Chinatown (Chang 1988:46), brass instruments were played by Chinese kids (Chinese Chamber of Commerce 1988:32), and a Western drum group of Chinese girls participated in the inauguration ceremony of the new building for the Chinese Consolidate Benevolent Association in 1952 (Hom and Fong 1988:53). Also, the Los Angeles Chinese Drum and Bugle Corps once existed in Chinatown but discontinued several decades ago (personal conversation with Sue Yee).

6. The Chinese United Methodist Church was established in 1887 (Hole 1990:16) and, until the early 1970s, Los Angeles county had more than thirty

Chinese-speaking churches, most of them speaking Cantonese (Wu 1974:76).

7. Modern pop music performance is not known at this point.

8. Formed in the middle of nineteenth century, Beijing opera has been commonly referred to as the "National Theater."

9. The *jinghu* and *jingerhu* are two high- and middle-pitched two-string bowed lutes, the *yueqin* the "moon lute," *danpigu* a drum, *ban* a clapper, and *naobo* a cymbal. *Daluo* and *xiaoluo* are gongs of two different sizes.

10. Once a group of active Beijing opera musicians counted fourteen or fifteen names of Beijing opera clubs in Monterey Park. It is difficult to detect if these are close approximates.

11. "Piaoyuo" is a conventional term for Beijing opera amateurs who participate in performance.

12. The programs are usually decided by both the president and the club members; the schedule of concerts by these clubs is, however, subject to the financial capability of the club members and availability of the venue host.

13. For instance, in playing a drama of the Cheng school, the actors and actresses are supposed to closely imitate that school, in speech, singing, and acting. Also, a *jinghu* performer known for his specialty in that style is highly expected in the ensemble.

14. The Dehan Tiensen Chinese Culture Club was established by Beijing opera afficionados twenty years ago in Taiwan and moved to Los Angeles five years later, when its president migrated to the United States.

15. Two of the three musicians, Mr. Gao Mingliang and Mr. Zha Changsheng, are well known senior artists from the Shanghai Beijing Opera House.

16. The Chinese Opera Club of Los Angeles and Southern California Chinese Opera Association are the two oldest Beijing opera clubs, established in the 1960s.

17. For instance, the 1993 concert had various genres including ensemble, trio, and several solos of traditional and modern pieces. The ensemble has thirteen parts featuring instruments for modern Chinese music ensemble such as the *gaohu, erhu, zhonghu, gehu,* double bass, *pipa, zhongruan, yangqin, guzheng, sheng, di,* and percussion instruments.

18. Other than its instrument specialty, several characteristics distinguish this group from others. About 90% of its membership are female musicians between the age of 20 and 35. It has claimed connection with local Buddhist institutions (the leader of this group, Mr. Liu Zuyao, has been the only Chinese musician supported by the International Buddhist Progress Society to teach at the temple so far, although I know other musicians have tried to do the same), and their program highlighted Buddhist themes. Also renditions of ancient sentimental poems give special flavors to their program.

19. Mr. Feng Ho, the president of the orchestra, told me they were also invited to perform in Chinatown once.

20. Similar events have also been held by Chinese organizations in other part of the suburbs, e.g., the San Fernando Valley Chinese Cultural Association held a Youth Music Festival music contest in 1991. The America Chinese Culture Association held an annual piano competition at the California State University Dominguez Hills in June 1993.

21. The piano and violin are the most popular Western instruments studied among young Chinese musicians. There are but a few learning other Western instruments such as cello and flute.

22. For instance, in the Jupiter Chorus, Mr. Lin Kwan, the conductor, received his vocal training in Japan and Italy. He taught at the College of Chinese Culture in Taiwan for some years before he came to America. Jenny Ren, soprano, studied at the Conservatorio di Musica "S. Cecilia" in Rome, and pianist Jean Chen studied at the Julliard School of Music in New York. Also, it is common for many of these choral groups and their members to be associated, or affiliated, with Christian churches where they meet for rehearsals and performances.

23. Six or seven children compete each time, and on the last Saturday of the month, the three highest ranked of each contest give a concert together.

24. I have not been able to get hold of this group and the information present here is obtained from conversations with Jane Chin and Conny Deng, two students from Taiwan.

25. Prior to this concert, all major local Chinese newspapers printed numerous articles, including pictures, about him and his popularity in Hong Kong. According to one report, before departing from Hong Kong to fulfill his military services in Taiwan, Lin gave a concert. Although admission was free, someone reportedly sold a ticket for one thousand Hong Kong dollars.

26. All the artists on this concert are highly acclaimed and well known on the national scene in mainland China, including the "National First Rank" comic dialogue artists, "the Queen of Chinese Folk Song," "Champion of Huangmei Opera Performance."

27. Eight of the artists were champions of national contests. The other four are (as advertised) the queen singer of the Mongols, the winner of an international festival of folk arts in Poland, the champion of a major competition in the Xizang Autonomous Region (Tibet), and one magician known for his unique skills.

28. The New China Emporium, a Chinese department store, once carried various Chinese instruments. It closed in 1992.

29. The store is not listed in either of the two Chinese Yellow Pages.

30. The shelves holding these materials are usually located by the counter of the cashier and very easy to see.

31. This figure is obtained from the 1994 *Chinese Yellow Pages Southern California*, as listed under Musical Instrumental Shops.

32. This is speculated by referring to the names of the shops. I have not checked on all of them, but my telephone contact with two stores confirmed the validity of the speculation.

33. There are stores specializing in piano, violin, and karaoke equipment and material. It is usually at general music stores where band instruments are an essential item.

34. The King's Music Center specializes in both piano and violin.

35. The next most visible ads in the Yellow Pages are ads for violin, which are much smaller in comparison with those of the piano stores.

36. Also sold are Japanese Kawai, Yamaha, Korean Samick, Young Chang, U.S. Charles R. Walter, Baldwin, East European Sangler & Sohne, Petrof, and Austria Bosendorfer.

37. These instruments include organ, disklaviers, clavinova, digital piano, digital keyboard, synthesizer, and P.A. systems, as well as band instruments and guitars.

38. Other subjects, such as Chinese instrumental music and jazz, may be available upon request.

39. For instance, American Chinese TV in Temple City was established in 1983, TVB Holdings (USA) Inc. in Alhambra in 1984, and N.A.C. Broadcast Company in El Monte in 1987.

40. ACTV is based in Riverside.

41. Panda TV began operation in Rosemead in 1991.

42. There are both cable and non-cable Chinese televisions stations and programs. Although there is no statistical evidence, it appears reasonable to assume a wide audience for Channel 62 and 18 because these are not cable channels.

43. It used to be on Friday afternoons.

44. An English program directly transmitted from Beijing began not long ago on Sunday evenings. After general news and reports, the "Cultural Corridor" section presents various aspects of the Chinese culture, including music.

45. I was also told that they have programs of Beijing opera; however, I did not find it in the regular Mandarin program schedule from the station.

46. The Chung Hing News is published in Chinatown. However, it does not seem influential in the Chinese community. I have asked two bookstores that sell newspapers on North Broadway about the Chung Hing News and they were not familiar with it.

47.   There are, of course, other contributing factors, such as international politics, as suggested by Wong (1985).

REFERENCES CITED

Chace, G. Paul
    1984   "The Chinese Theater, Law and Order in LA: Jen Ah Mow and his Congressional Testimony." *Gum Saan Journal* 7(2):1–4.

Chang, T.K.
    1988   "Congratulations Upon the Grand Opening of New Chinatown." *Los Angeles Chinatown The Golden Years 1938–1988:* 46.

Cheng, Suellen and Munson Kwok
    1988   "The Golden Years of Los Angeles Chinatown:The Beginning." *Los Angeles Chinatown The Golden Years 1938–1988.*:39–47.

Chinese Chamber of Commerce
    1988   *Los Angeles Chinatown The Golden Years 1938–1988.*

Crew, Noemi and Timothy Chan
    1990   "A Pictorial History of the Catholic Chinese Center in L.A. Chinatown, 1940–1990." *Gum Saan Journal* 8(1):1–23.

Fong, Timothy P.
    1994   *The First Suburban Chinatown: the Remaking of Monterey Park.* Philadelphia: Temple University Press.

Frances Yu-Tsing Wu
    1984   "Mandarin-Speaking Aged Chinese in L.A. Area." Ph.D. dissertation, USC.

Hole, D. J. Wesley
    1990   "History of the L.A. Chinese United Methodist Church." *Gum Saan Journal* 8(2):11–19.

Hom, Beverly M. and Lillian Fong
    1988   "Los Angeles Chinatown 1958–1968." *Los Angeles Chinatown The Golden Years 1938–1988.*:51–58

Kao, Alan
    1994   *Chinese Consumer Yellow Pages.* San Gabriel: Chinese Overseas Marketing Service Inc.

Kwok, Munson
    1990   "Chinese Moon Festival Success." *Gum Saan Journal* 8(2):5–10.

Lew, Karen
    1988   "Chinatown—The Present." *Los Angeles Chinatown The Golden Years, 1938–1988.*:59–63.

Lew, Margie
    1990   "Moon Festival Memories." *Gum Saan Journal* 8(2):1–4.

Mazur, Audrey R.
    1988   "Music in New York City's Chinese Community." *New York Folklore* 14:89–99.

Quan, Ella Yee
    1988   "Pioneer Families Share Their History." *Los Angeles Chinatown The Golden Years, 1938–1988*:29–31.

Riddle, Ronald
    1978   *Flying Dragons, Flowing Streams.* Westport: Greenwood Press.

Song, Bang-Song
    1974   *The Korean-Canadian Folk Song: An Ethnomusicological Study.* Ottawa: National Museums of Canada.

Tom, Kim Fong
    1944   "The Participation of Chinese in Community Life of L.A." M.A. thesis, USC.

Wong, Isabel K.F.
    1985   "The Many Roles of Peking Opera in San Francisco in the 1980s." *Selected Reports in Ethnomusicology* 6:173–88.

Wu, T.C.
    1994   *Chinese Yellow Pages/Southern California.* Monterey Park: Asia System Media, Inc.

Zheng, Su de San
    1990   "Music and Migration: Chinese American Traditional Music in New York." *The World of Music* 32(3):48–67.

Appendix I

A summary of musical characteristics of Chinatown and the Chinese community in the Los Angeles suburbs.

Music in the community

Chinatown   *The suburbs*
<u>Chinese opera</u>
     Cantonese opera   Beijing opera and Kun opera

<u>Instrumental music</u>
     Band only   Modern Chinese instrumental ensemble
                                             Western orchestra

<u>Choral music</u>
     None   Many

<u>Popular music</u>
     Cantonese songs   Various popular songs from Hong Kong and Taiwan
<u>Imported music</u>
     Cantonese opera   Various kinds from Taiwan, mainland China,
                                                and Hong Kong

<u>Music of other nationalities</u>
     Various   Various

Music Commodities

Chinatown   *The suburbs*
<u>Book stores</u>
     Recordings from Taiwan,   Recordings from Taiwan,
       Hong Kong, and mainland China   Hong Kong, and mainland China

<u>Music stores</u>
     One karaoke and Limin   Many stores
     Chinese musical instruments   Mainly Western instruments
     No Western musical instruments   Few Chinese musical instruments

---

Music and Media

Los Angeles Chinatown   *The suburbs*
<u>TV and radio</u>
     None but share with the suburbs   A number of stations and producers

<u>Newspaper</u>
     Shared with the suburbs   Shared
     plus *Chinese Times* from S.F.   No newspaper from S.F.

Appendix II

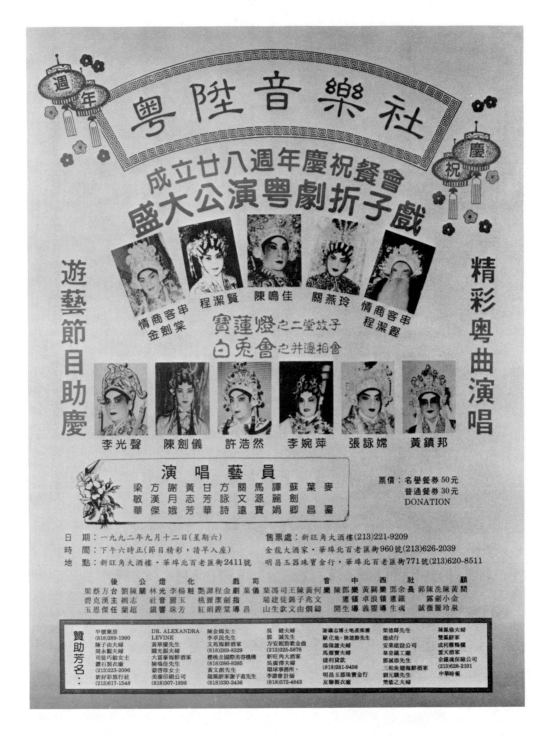

Figure 1: Poster announcing "Yuet Sing Music Club: 'Magnificent Performance of Cantonese Opera's Highlights,' the Twenty-eighth Anniversary Celebration Banquet, the New Won Kok Restaurant, September 12, 1992." Used by permission.

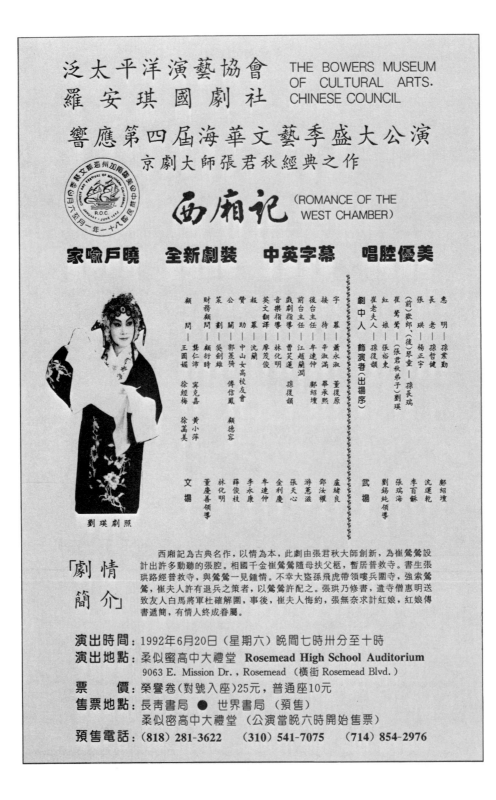

Figure 2: Playbill: "Chinese Opera Club of Los Angeles: 'Romance of the West Chamber.'
Rosemead High School Auditorium, June 20, 1992." Used by permission.

Figure 3: The Spring Thunder Chinese Music Association's Annual Concert. Courtesy of the Spring Thunder Chinese Music Association.

Figure 4: Cover page of 1992 Olympia Philharmonic Society's concert. Used by permission.

**Figure 5: Playbill: Jupiter Chorus:
The Sixth Concert at Pasadena City
College, Sexon Auditorium.
June 26, 1993, 8:00 P.M. Used by
permission.**

**Figure 6: A scene of the
Sprint Diamond Children's
Karaoke Singing Contest in
San Gabriel, California.
Photo by Guangming Li.**

Figure 7: Playbill: "The Best of Chinese Ethnic Minority Performances." Used by permission.

ELEANOR HAGUE (1875–1954)
PIONEER LATIN AMERICANIST

Robert Stevenson

I

ALTHOUGH THE RESULTS of ethnomusicologists' field investigations and on-site recordings fill columns in *Die Musik in Geschichte und Gegenwart, The New Grove Dictionary of Music and Musicians* (1980), *The New Grove Dictionary of Musical Instruments* (1984), and *The New Grove Dictionary of American Music* (1986), the biographies of ethnomusicologists and folklorists often find the doors of music lexicons closed against them. Particularly evident has been this reticence, so far as Latin American specialists go.

To cite examples of omitted leaders: (1) Henrietta Yurchenko's name appears in nearly all Middle American studies. The *Bulletin of the Sonneck Society for American Music,* xix/2 (Summer, 1993), page 15, cites her formation of a "New Interest Group, Music of Latin America and the Caribbean." (2) Carmen Sordo Sodi, the Mexican ethnomusicologist who in 1965 succeeded Jesús Bal y Gay as head of the musicological section of the Instituto Nacional de Bellas Artes,[1] published six pathbreaking articles in *Heterofonía*[2] and contributed the article, "La música mexicana en la época del Presidente

Benito Juárez" to the major anthology dealing with nineteenth-century Latin-American musical developments.[3] (3) Gabriel Saldívar [y Silva], Mexico's paramount music historian—whose ethnomusicological credentials were certified not only in his *Historia de la música en México (épocas precortesiana y colonial)* (1934; facsimile reprint, 1981) but also in *El jarabe: baile popular mexicano* (1937)—lacks a biographical entry in any music lexicon. (4) Gerónimo Baqueiro Fóster—who apart from an *Historia de la música en México* (1964) that carried forward Saldívar's history into the late nineteenth century also published a 462-page *Antología folklórica y musical de Tabasco* (1952)—eludes all biographical dictionaries.

The list of Mexicans profiled in even so specialized a vademecum as Otto Mayer-Serra's *Música y músicos de Latinoamérica* lacks such names as Daniel Castañeda, Rubén M. Campos, Alberto Cajigas Langner, Juan S. Garrido, and Paco Ignacio

---

[1] CENIDIM = Centro Nacional de Investigación, Documentación e Información Musical, located at Liverpool 16, México, D.F. 06600, became the successor to the musicological section of the INBA after Carmen Sordo Sodi's departure for Israel in 1975.

[2] "La marimba," *Heterofonía,* iv/22 (January–February 1972), 27–30; "Fenomenología religiosa de *Las danzas de Conquista*," v/27 (November–December 1972), 7–10; "La música

y la danza como expresión de protesta" (Parts I and II), v/29 (March–April 1973), 22–25 and vii/33 (November–December 1973), 12–16; "La Metamúsica de Brian Ferneyhough," vii/36 (May–June 1974), 20–21; "Antecedentes históricos de la danza de caballitos," viii/42 (May–June 1975), 24–25; "Compositoras mexicanas de música comercial," xv/78 (July–September 1982), 16–20; "La labor de investigación folklórica de Manuel M. Ponce," xv/79 (October–December 1982), 36–39; "Antropología y música: La música oaxaqueña," xv/83 (October–December 1983), 32–39.

[3] *Die Musikkulturen Lateinamerikas im 19. Jahrhundert*, ed. by Robert Günther (Regensburg: Gustav Bosse Verlag, 1982), pp. 299–325. Twelve traditional tunes serve as a musical appendix to her article.

Eleanor Hague

Taibo. If these names merely sample a roll call of Mexican *desaparecidos*, the outlook for Central and South American ethnomusicologists whose publications make possible their country coverage in dictionaries remains equally dismal.[4]

II

Not surprisingly, therefore, Eleanor Hague—the United States author who preceded all others in publishing a general history of music in Latin America[5] —still goes begging even for birth and death dates in library catalogues. Her many ethnomusicological credentials include articles on Brazilian, Mexican,

[4] In a first attempt at providing biographies of a limited group, Robert Stevenson edited an 83-page *Directory of UCLA Ethnomusicology Graduates* (University of California, Los Angeles, Program in Ethnomusicology, 1977) that profiled eleven graduates with Latin American specialties, but all eleven degree-holders until 1977 were United States persons.

[5] *Latin American Music, Past and Present* (Santa Ana, California: The Fine Arts Press, 1934) is one of the seven book entries (dating from 1914 to 1969) credited to her in the UCLA cataloging network.

and other Latin American traditional songs that began appearing in the *Journal of American Folk-Lore* as early as 1911. Her section on "Latin-American Folk-Music" continued appearing in every edition of Oscar Thompson's *International Cyclopedia of Music and Musicians* from the first in 1943 through the ninth in 1964.

Her absence from dictionaries is the more ironic, because in contrast with Nicolas Slonimsky's 374-page *Music of Latin Ameria* reviewed by Gilbert Chase with a pen dipped in vitriol,[6] Eleanor Hague's much more modest *Latin American Music, Past and Present* stimulated only favorable reviews. So eminent an ethnomusicologist as George Herzog (1901–1983), published a review in the *American Anthropologist*, xxxvi/4 (October–December 1934), page 612, that read as follows:

This book is obviously written not for the technical anthropologist, nor for the technical musician, but for the interested layman, and it should be viewed in this light. What the author sets out to do for the reader is accomplished very well indeed: to present in a popular style the musical traditions in Latin America conceived as a continuity. . . . The technically interested reader may regret that no more "meat" from the not too voluminous technical literature has been incorporated in the treatise. But he will find a good deal, nevertheless, that will assist him in his specific interest. One might mention the references selected from the old literature by Miss Hague, including pictures of musicians and dancers from codices, some of them seldom or never reproduced before, and a few suggestive prints of similar content from old sources. Pictures of modern Indian or folk dances illustrate the merging of Indian and European traits. Of especial value are the lists of dances practised today by the Spanish or the Europeanized Indians, and the bibliography which mentions many relevant works published in Latin American countries. The student must be grateful to Miss Hague, chiefly for having assembled so many valuable leads to material and sources for future study.

Since an invitation should be made attractive, the excellent format and make-up are especially appropriate to this volume, which invites the public to initial interest and the student to further research.

J. Frank Dobie's appraisal in the *Southwest Review*, xx/2 [books section] (January 1935), page 25, was no less positive.

[6] *The Musical Quarterly*, xxxii/1 (January 1946), pp. 140–143. Gentleman that he has always been, Slonimsky never retaliated against Chase's abuse.

Latin-American Music, Past and Present, by Eleanor Hague, author of *Folk Songs from Mexico and South America*, is a rarely beautiful book in format and illustration and may certainly be depended upon for scholarly information. The avowed purpose of the author is to trace out the chronological development of music in the Latin-American countries.

To be brief—and the book itself is quite brief—the historian has constructed from early chronicles a conception of the instruments, mostly drums and whistles, used by the aborigines of Mexico and Central and South America, has traced the rise of national tunes and dances following the Spanish conquest, and has brought the study down to date with a chapter entitled "The Sophisticated Music of the Present and Its Prospects."

On the misfortune side, Hague's 98-page survey coincidentally appeared in the same year that Gabriel Saldívar's 324-page history devoted solely to Mexican pre-1821 events was published.[7] Also on the debit side, she encountered for Spanish-speaking South America so extremely unreliable a monograph as Carlos Vega's misinformed *La música de un códice colonial del siglo XVII.*[8] For Brazilian data she sipped from the first edition of the one general history in Portuguese then available.[9]

Because of the defective character of the secondary material available to her at the time of writing, what chiefly supplied her with any trustworthy data concerning pre-1821 events had therefore to be travel accounts and missionary chronicles. From

Purchas his Pilgrimes (Hakluyt Society Publications [Glasgow: James MacLehose, 1906]), volume 16, pages 553–554, she derived her lengthy description of Tupynambá singing routines. Translated from Jean de Léry (1534–1611), the cited passages at her pages 46–48 include also facsimiles of the two melodies published in Léry's *Histoire d'vn Voyage faict en la Terre dv Bresil*, 3d ed. (Geneva: Antoine Chuppin, 1585), 158 and 173.[10]

At her pages 27–28 Hague quotes the sometime Dominican friar Thomas Gage (1603?–1656), who lauded the ravishing music that in 1625 he heard in Mexico City churches.[11] Concerning music in Guatemalan churches, Gage supplied Hague with the following observations:

The Fiscal or clerk must be one who can read and write, and he is commonly the master of music. . . . On the Lord's day and on other Saints' days . . . in the morning, he and the other musicians at the sound of the bell, are bound to come to church to sing and officiate at Mass, which in many towns they perform with organs and other musical instruments . . . and at evening at five o'clock they again resort to the church when the bell calleth to sing prayers, which they call *completas* [complines] with *Salve Regina*.

Continuing, Gage commented on the rivalry between nunneries. One high-ranking Guatemalan lady—a doting father's sole offspring who had in 1619 (ten years before Gage's arrival at Antigua) taken vows in a Dominican nunnery housing a thousand inhabitants—was a musical paragon adored by the entire city.

Doña Juana de Maldonado y Paz, was the wonder of all that cloister, yea, of all the city, for her excellent voice and skill in music. . . . In her closet she had a small

[7] Although she lacked Saldívar's gold mine, she did make good use of Rubén M. Campos's *El folklore y la música mexicana: investigación acerca de la cultura musical en México (1525–1925). Obra integrada con 100 sones, jarabes y canciones del folklore musical mexicano, cuyas melodías están intactas. Ilustraciones de tipos, escenas y paisajes pintorescos de antaño y retratos de músicos mexicanos* (Mexico City: Talleres gráficos de la nación, 1928 [351 pp.]).

[8] Buenos Aires: Universidad Nacional: Instituto de literatura argentina; Sección de folklore: Publicaciones. 1. ser., v. 2, no. 1, 1931 [93 pp.].

[9] Guilherme Theodoro Pereira de Mello's *A música no Brazil desde os tempos coloniaes até o primeiro decênio da república* (Bahia: Typ. de S. Joaquim, 1908 [366 pp.]) served as her most copious Brazilian source. Like Mello, she stresses the importance of Jean de Léry's Tupynambá songs, two of which she quotes at her pp. 46–47. However, she used not Mello but rather *Purchas his Pilgrimes* for her data derived from Léry.

Concerning Mello, see Manuel Vicente Ribeiro Veiga, Jr., "Toward a Brazilian Ethnomusicology: Amerindian Phases," University of California, Los Angeles, Ph.D. dissertation, 1981, p. 210: "Mello was himself a mulatto, beset however, by feelings of cultural inferiority."

[10] See pp. 191–220 of Veiga's dissertation for an authoritative study of Léry's five published melodies, followed by the history of their use and misuse by Gabriel Sagard (*Le Grand Voyage dv Pays des Hvrons* [Paris, 1632]), Marin Mersenne (*Harmonie universelle* [Paris, 1636–1637]), and Jean-Jacques Rousseau (*Dictionnaire de Musique* [Paris, 1768]).

[11] *The English American, his travail by sea and land: or, A new survey of the West India's, containing a journall of three thousand and three hundred miles within the main land of America* (London: R. Cotes, 1648 [220 pp.]); see [Thomas Gage's] *Travels in the New World*, ed. by J.E.S. Thompson (Norman: University of Oklahoma Press, 1958), p. 72: "So exquisite [is the music] in the city that I dare be bold to say that the people are drawn to their churches more for the delight of the music than for any delight in the service of God."

organ, and many sorts of musical instruments, where-upon she played sometimes by herself, sometimes with her best friends of the nuns; and here especially with music she entertained her Bishop [Fray Juan de Sandoval y Zapata, O.S.A.].

Without itemizing Hague's other citations and without unduly complaining about the heterogeneous manner in which she presented her quotations, they did at least serve Robert Stevenson (and others) with suggestions telling where to search for further useful data. However—despite the indebtednesses— at the time of writing his *Music in Mexico, A Historical Survey* (New York: Thomas Y. Crowell, 1952) neither he nor any of those who reviewed his book (Jesús Bal y Gay, Gilbert Chase, Thurston Dart, Adolfo Salazar, Moses Smith) had access to a published Hague biography.

III

Only after she died, a spinster at age 79, did biographical details finally surface in her necrologies. *The Masterkey*, xxix/1 (January-February 1955), pages 4-6, contains an obituary written by the then Director of the Southwest Museum, Frederick Webb Hodge.[12] A Life Member since May 1936 and a Trustee since 1942, she still today ranks as one of the Museum's all-time most generous benefactors. Born at San Francisco November 7, 1875, she died at Flintridge, a suburb of Pasadena, California, in her mansion at 327 Georgian Road, December 25, 1954.[13]

Already seventeen years before she published *Latin American Music* the American Folk-Lore

Society had issued as volume 10 in its Memoirs Series her 115-page volume, *Spanish American Folk-Songs* (Lancaster, Pennsylvania: The New Era Printing Company, 1917)—this volume containing her 81 transcriptions preceded by a 15-page introduction.[14] Her next book, *Music in Ancient Arabia and Spain* (London: H. Milford, Oxford University Press; Stanford University Press, 1929), was an abridged translation, cooperatively done with Marion Leffingwell, of Julián Ribera's *La Música de las Cantigas*.[15]

In 1929 when the abridged translation appeared, Julián Ribera y Tarragó (*b* Carcagente, Valencia, February 19, 1858; *d* there May 2, 1934) still remained a highly honored scholar. Elected a member of the Real Academia Española in 1912, he was three years later appointed to the Real Academia de la Historia. The review of *La Música de las Cantigas* by the paramount American Arabist, Duncan Black Macdonald (1863-1943) published in the *American Historical Review*, xxviii (1923), 530-531, contained judgments that amply justified a translation.

In this [work] he is only confirming and carrying further his thesis of ten years ago in his *Discurso*, read before the Royal Spanish Academy when he was received by it as a member in May 1912; that the key to the mechanism of the poetical forms of the various lyrical systems in medieval Europe is to be found in the Andalusian lyric, to which the *Cancionero* of Abencuzmán belongs (*Discurso*, p. 50), and that the Andalusian lyric arose in a bilingual community speaking two colloquials, Arabic and Romance, in the mixed civilization, Muslim and Christian, of the south of Spain. . . . Professor Ribera shows that the origins of Muslim music are made perfectly clear by the Arabic writers on the history of that art. These writers have also treated the art at length.

---

[12] Founded in 1907, the Southwest Museum at 234 Museum Drive (off North Figueroa Street) in Highland Park, Los Angeles (tel. 213-221-2164; fax 213-224-8223), houses a "200,000-item library of comparative anthropology, history, art and linguistics." The librarian in 1993 was Kim Walters, the Associate Librarian was Richard Buchen. For its history, see William Wilcox Robinson, *The Story of the Southwest Museum* (Los Angeles: Ward Ritchie, 1960). F.W. Hodge (1864-1956), leading ethnologist of his generation, directed the Southwest Museum from 1932 to his decease.

[13] Her father, James Duncan Hague (1836-1908), a mining engineer, is profiled in *Who Was Who in America* (Chicago: Marquis Who's Who, 1943), Vol. I (1897-1942), p. 500. From 1879 to his death he maintained homes in New York City and at Stockbridge, Massachusetts. Eleanor inherited her great wealth.

[14] Dated October 23, 1916, at Stockbridge, Massachusetts, the introduction contains a still useful survey of secular music in Hispanic California and in places in Mexico visited by her. Pedro Díaz, her informant in Oaxaca convinced her that even very "complicated types of songs" belonged to the Mexican inherited folk repertory.

[15] Although Ribera's music transcriptions erred wildly, the Joaquín Pena-Higinio Anglés *Diccionario de la música Labor* (Barcelona: 1954), II, 1875, still ranked the literary introduction as "un estudio de altísimo valor histórico." The historic portion of *La Música de las Cantigas. Estudio sobre su Origen y Naturaleza con reproducciones fotográficas de texto y transcripción moderna* (Madrid: Tipografía de la Revista de Archivos, 1922 [156+ 346 pp.]) was reissued in 1927 as *Historia de la música árabe medieval y su influencia en la española* and it was an abridgment of the 1927 history that Hague and Leffingwell translated.

Hague and Leffingwell's translation reprinted in 1969 by Da Capo earned a review by Robert Anderson in *The Musical Times*, CXI (November 1970), 1116; according to him the translation is "compulsively readable in his biographical sketches of Arab musicians whether in the East or in Spain."

So far as her dozen journal articles go: already before she gave her first series of guitar-accompanied "Folk-Song Recitals" at Berkeley in 1918 (*Bulletin of the University of California Extension*, New Series, IV/8 [September 1918]) six of her articles had appeared in the *Journal of American Folk-Lore*.

"Spanish-American folk-songs" (*JAFL*, XXIV [1911], 323–333);
"Brazilian Songs" (XXV [1912], 179–181);
"Mexican folk-songs" (XXV [1912], 261–267);
"Spanish songs from Southern California" (XXVII [1914], 331–332);
"Eskimo songs" (XXVIII [1915], 96–98); and
"Five Mexican dances" (XXVIII [1915], 379–389).

Prior to settling at Pasadena where from 1920 to her decease she spent her last thirty-five years, she had lived chiefly at her family's residence in New York City and at Stockbridge, the arts center twelve miles south of Pittsfield in the resort region of the Berkshire Hills.[16] Member of a family of great wealth, she studied privately in Italy and France, directed church choirs in New York City,[17] and was a member of the New York Oratorio Society.[18]

Her strictly musical publications began with *Folk Songs from Mexico and South America . . . piano-forte accompaniments by Edward Kilenyi*[19] (New York: H.W. Gray, 1914). After her move to Pasadena she continued with *Early Spanish-California folk-songs collected by Eleanor Hague; harmonized and set for voice and piano by Gertrude Ross*[20] (New York: J. Fischer & Bro., 1922), and "Some California Songs. Recorded by Charles Fletcher Lummis and transcribed by Eleanor Hague," published in *The Masterkey*, Pt. I, vol. 8, no. 1 (January 1934), Pt. II, vol. 8, no. 4 (July 1934), and Pt. III, vol. 11, no. 3 (May 1937). In 1946 appeared *Canciones de mi padre; Spanish folk songs from southern Arizona, collected by Luisa Espinel from her father Don Federico Ronstadt y Redondo, Translated by Eleanor Hague* (Tucson: University of Arizona, General Bulletin, no. 10 [words in Spanish and English]).

Two years before her death she prepared a 45-page typescript, "Folk Music in the Southwest," for publication in Howard Swan's *Music in the Southwest, 1825–1950* (San Marino: Huntington Library, 1952).[21] Determined to disallow any such section in his forthcoming book (laid as a cenotaph on L.E. Behymer's tomb), Swan—who was seemingly unaware that she was the author—directed that this rejection notice be sent her: "The author [Swan] feels that the subject has had adequate attention from such eminent scholars as Frances Densmore, Edna Ferguson, Eleanor Hague, Owen Da Silva, and others." This rebuff was the more painful, because Hague had herself subsidized both the publication (and the needed preparatory research) of Frances Densmore's *Cheyenne and Arapaho Music*

---

[16] In 1954 Stockbridge still remained the home of her then eighty-year-old unmarried sister, Marian Hague (1874–1971), her sole survivor. Marian's obituary appears in *The New York Times*, February 2, 1971, 40:3. In 1920 Marian had published, in cooperation with Frances Morris, *Antique Laces of American Collectors* (New York: William Helburn).

[17] Her paternal grandfather, the Rev. Dr. William Hague (1808–1887), one of the most renowned and prolifically published American Baptist clergymen of his epoch, pastored First Baptist, Boston, when her father James Duncan was born there. From 1858–1862 he pastored Madison Avenue Baptist in New York City. She was twelve when he died.

[18] Leopold Damrosch (1832–1885), founder in 1873 of the Oratorio Society of New York, conducted it until his death, whereupon his son Walter took the reins for the next thirteen years. See George Martin, *The Damrosch Dynasty America's First Family of Music* (Boston: Houghton Mifflin Company, 1983), pp. 33–37, 164–165, and 509.

[19] Concerning Kilenyi (*b* at Philadelphia, May 7, 1911; Adjunct Professor at Florida State University, Tallahassee, in 1992, after lengthy service there), see George Kehler, *The piano in concert* (Metuchen, New Jersey: Scarecrow Press, 1982), I, 666–667. His accompaniments for the ten songs require an accomplished pianist. Hague lists the sources of the ten songs on a prefatory page.

[20] Gertrude Ross born at Dayton, Ohio in 1888, lived in California from 1898 until her decease in 1940. See "Music in Southern California: A Tale of Two Cities," *Inter-American Music Review*, X/1 (Fall-Winter 1988), pp. 86, 108.

[21] Robert Stevenson reviewed the 1977 Da Capo reprint in *Inter-American Music Review*, IV/2 (Spring-Summer 1982), pp. 85–86. In Willard Rhodes's review (*Musical Quarterly* XXXIX/4 [October 1953], 630–634) he complained that the book was mistitled, that Swan grossly overdid concert attractions (thanks to Behymer), and utterly neglected folksong. The author's bias against the Mexican heritage makes the book a shameful witness to Anglo snobbery.

(Southwest Museum Papers, no. 10, 1936) and *Music of Santo Domingo Pueblo, New Mexico* (Southwest Museum Papers, no. 12, 1938). At the time of Hague's death, still unpublished remained Densmore's "Music of the Maidu Indians of Northern California"—the research for which had likewise been subsidized by Hague.

Her bounty to other ethnomusicological researchers sets her on a pedestal. At her expense Donald and Dorothy M. Cordry gathered data on site for their *Costumes and Textiles of the Aztec Indians of the Cuetzatán Region, Puebla, Mexico* (Southwest Museum Papers, no. 14, 1940) and *Costumes and Weaving of the Zoque Indians of Chiapas, Mexico* (Papers, no. 15, 1941). Apart from these publications, the Cordry Mexican expeditions yielded 196 ethnological specimens, purchased for the Museum by them from Otomí, Chimantec, Tzotzil, and Zoque indigenes. In an epoch when Museum representatives could still legally purchase and bring back archaeological finds to United States museums, she also financed the expedition to Peru and Bolivia of the Harry Tschopik couple, their Aymara Indian acquisitions (clothing, weaving, equipment, toys, pottery) totalling some 132 objects.

Reaching out beyond objects for museum display, Hague—on Densmore's suggestion—founded a Jarabe Club for youthful folk dancers headquartered from 1940 to her death at the Pasadena Settlement Association (80 West Del Mar). Eight Jarabe Club dancers from Pasadena City schools visited Washington during April of 1941 to represent the State of California at that year's National Field Dance Festival. The authenticity of their presentations so favorably impressed the Mexican ambassador, Dr. Francisco Castillo Nájera,[22] that he invited them to perform at a garden party organized in their honor. Continuing to pay all the Jarabe Club dancers' travelling expenses, Hague arranged for them to perform at Swarthmore and Mundelein Colleges on their journey homeward. At the approach of death she asked for contributions to the Club instead of flowers for her funeral.

Her memorial rites at the Pasadena Neighborhood Community Church (Curtis Beach, pastor) January 9, 1955, centered in music by Harlow Mills,

composer-pianist, who managed the Coleman Chamber Music Association 1948 to 1971, and his wife Elizabeth Morgridge Mills, concert violinist who was a protégée of world-renowned Vera Barstow. Paradoxically, Hague's own entire publication career had been devoted not to "art music" but rather to expressions now classifiable as ethnomusicological or folkloric. Moreover, her chief bequest to the Southwest Museum was a manuscript miscellany containing not masses and motets but rather *ca.* 300 dance tunes popular in Mexico before 1790.

Ethnomusicologist Samuel Martí[23] discussed these in *The Eleanor Hague Manuscript of Mexican Colonial Music* (Southwest Museum Leaflets, No. 33 [1969]). The first of his three publications devoted to the manuscript, Martí's brochure contains five music facsimiles illustrating the variety of copyists who produced the two disjunct sections of the manuscript. The same musical facsimiles—*Las Bodas Reales, Chacona De Arlequina, La Galopada, Lamarie* (preceded by a Minueto), and a page containing three Paspies (*de Princeza, de Spaña,* and *nuevo*)—reappear in Martí's Spanish-language versions of Southwest Museum Leaflet, No. 33.[24] However, Martí foundered so utterly in both English and Spanish versions that the future investigator who at last gave a coherent and reliable account had to begin by disregarding everything written about the manuscript by Martí.[25]

[22] Physician, diplomat, writer and poet, Dr. Francisco Castillo Nájera (1886–1954) had served as Mexican plenipotentiary in China, Belgium, Netherlands, Switzerland, and France before assignment as ambassador to the United States 1935–1945.

[23] Born in Hotel Dieu at El Paso, Texas, May 18, 1906, Samuel Martí died at Tepoztlán, Mexico March 29, 1975. For a traversal of his career in the United States (to 1940) see Robert Stevenson, *Music in El Paso 1919–1939* (El Paso: Texas Western Press, 1970), pp. 18–20. For his Mexican career see Stevenson's "Samuel Martí, etnomusicólogo," *Heterofonía*, 60 (May–June 1978), 3–5, an article that concludes with eleven citations of articles about him that appeared in El Paso newspapers between March 25, 1924, and December 25, 1955, in which latter year he became a Mexican citizen.

[24] "Música laica colonial," *Boletín del Instituto Nacional de Antropología e Historia*, no. 37 (September 1969), pp. 25–29; "Música colonial profana," *Cuadernos Americanos*, 168/1 (January–February 1970), pp. 99–109. The Spanish-language versions add a facsimile of folio 80 in the second section of The Eleanor Hague Manuscript (containing an *Adagio* for violin and continuo by Luis Misón [baptized Mataró, Barcelona, August 26, 1727; *d* Madrid, February 13, 1766; see his entry in *The New Grove Dictionary of Opera* [1992], III, 412–413).

[25] Trained in Chicago for a concert violinist's career, Samuel Martí never published anything without making egregious mistakes. See the account of his 383-page *Canto, danza y música precortesianos* (Mexico City: Fondo de Cultura Económica,

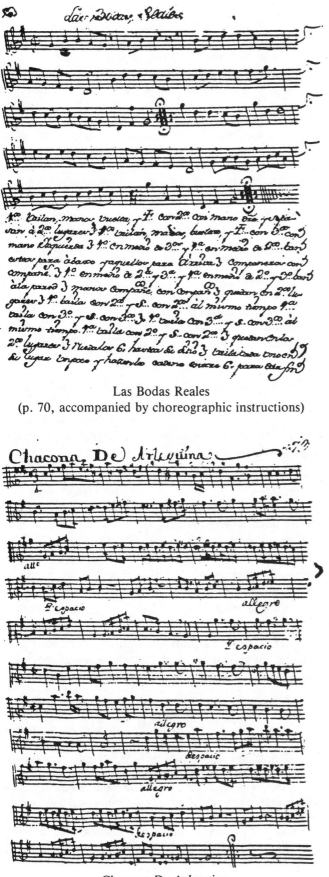

Las Bodas Reales
(p. 70, accompanied by choreographic instructions)

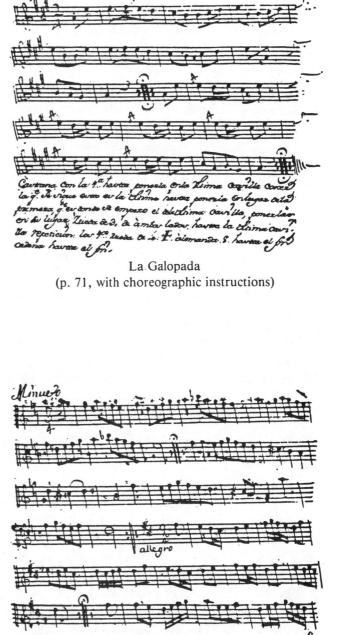

La Galopada
(p. 71, with choreographic instructions)

Chacona De Arlequina
(fol. 73)

Minuet, allegro (2/4), L'amarie
(fol. 71ᵛ)

Paspie de Princeza, Paspie de Spaña, Paspie nuevo
(fol. 69ᵛ)

IV

Craig H. Russell gave the first useful insights in his paper, "New Jewels in Old Boxes: Retrieving the Lost Musical Heritages of Colonial Mexico," read at the November 21, 1992, meeting of the Pacific Southwest Chapter of the American Musicological Society, held at California State University, Los Angeles. The data offered in the next concluding paragraphs rests wholly on "Chart 4 Eleanor Hague Manuscript, Southwest Museum" distributed as a hand-out at that November 21 session.

In this hand-out Russell traced the origins of certain dances through correspondences of 26 of the tunes. In the first section of the manuscript he found these:

1961) in *Hispanic American Historical Review*, XLII/3 (August 1962), 450–451.

Lully's "Loure pour les Pêcheurs" from his *Alceste* (1674) supplied the tune of "El Chip" at page 4; his "Premier Rigaudon" from *Acis et Galatée* (1686) provided the tune of the "Contra Rigodon" at page 112. Campra's "La venitienne" = "La Conty" from *Carnaval de Venise* (1699) equals "La Conti" at page 18. Purcell's "Jig" from his *Fairy Queen Suite No. 1* supplied the tune for "La Old Barchelor" at page 47, and Walsh's "Prince William" in his *Compleat Country Dancing Master* (1713, p. 87) equals "El Principe Guillermo" at page 142. Feuillet's *Contredances*,[26] Nos. 4 ("Le Pistolet," pp. 13–16); 7 ("le Prince George," pp. 33–38); 1 ("La bonne Amitié," pp. 1–4); and 18 ("Le Menuet du Chevalier," pp. 96–99) prove the sources for the Hague "La Mareschal," "La Prince George," "La Xameico" (= "La Buena Amistad"), and "El Minuette de los Caballeros" at pages 44, 45, 46 = 56, and 69. Ferriol y Boxeraus's *Reglas útiles*[27] ("Prosigue la gentil," p. 278; "La Charratera," p. 274; and "El Resvalon," p. 266) provided the Hague manuscript copyist with "La Charratierra," "La marcha du Roy," and "El Gallo" at pages 37, 42, and 113.

Foliated rather than paginated, the second section of the Eleanor Hague Manuscript begins with a leaf numerated "fol. 69." Feuillet's *Recüeil de dances composées par M. Pecour . . . et mises sur le papier par M. Feuillet* (1700) supplied the Hague "Paspie viejo" at fol. 70; Feuillet's catalogue of 1705 listed "La bretaña" at fol. 70ᵛ; his catalogue of 1709 itemized the Hague "Minueto de alsides" at fol. 70ᵛ; "Paysana vieja," fol. 73ᵛ; "Cherman" at fol. 74; and "Allegro," fol. 74. The catalogue of 1710 listed "La Guastala," fol. 69; the 1713 catalogue itemized "La melanie," fol. 77.

"Lamarie" at fol. 71ᵛ derives from Lully's *Ballet des plaisirs* (February 4, 1655) where it is headed "Un veillard avec sa famille." "Amable" at Hague's fol. 72 equals Campra's "Amable vainqueur" in his *Hesione* of 1700. The remaining correspondences revealed in Russell's Chart 4 read thus:

[26] Raoul-Auger Feuillet, *Recüeil de Contredances* (Paris: Chez l'Auteur, 1706); facs. repr. (New York: Broude Brothers, 1968).

[27] Bartolomé Ferriol y Boxeraus, *Reglas útiles para los aficionados á danzar: Provechoso divertimiento de los que gustan tocar instrumentos . . . Su author Bartholome Ferriol y Boxeraus, único author en este idioma de todos los diferentes passos de la danza francesa . . .* ([Málaga?]: A costa de Joseph Testore, 1745). For a description of this publication, see Felipe Pedrell, *Catàlech de la Biblioteca Musical de la Diputació de Barcelona* (Barcelona: Palau de la Diputació, 1908), I, 92–96.

No. 182
"La alemanda,"
fol. 72ᵛ

Campra, "L'allemande, dance nouvelle," *Fragments de Monsieur Lully*, 1702 [Campra].
Murcia, *Resumen*, No. 17, "La Alemanda," p. 67[28]
Murcia, *Códice Saldívar N° 4*, No. 40, "La Allemanda," fol. 78ᵛ[29]

No. 183
"Chacona de Arlequina,"
fol. 73

Lully, "Chaconne des Scaramouches," *Le Bourgeois Gentilhomme*, 1670

No. 184
"La Vacante,"
fol. 73ᵛ

Feuillet, *Contredanses*, "la Bacante," p. 113
Murcia, *Resumen*, No. 27, "La Bacante," p. 72
Murcia, *Códice Saldívar N° 4*, No. 47, "La Bacante," fol. 81ᵛ

No. 185
"Paysana vieja," fol. 73ᵛ

Feuillet, *Catalogue* for 1709
Murcia, *Resumen*, part 2 of No. 34, "La Charmant de Vainqueur," p. 75

No. 186
"Cherman,"
fol. 74

Feuillet, *Catalogue* for 1709
Murcia, *Resumen*, part 1 of No. 34, "La Charmant de Vainqueur," p. 75

No. 187
"Allegro,"
fol. 74

Feuillet, *Catalogue* for 1709
Murcia, *Resumen*, part 2 of No. 34, "La Charmant de Vainqueur," p. 75

No. 191
"Arlequina Biega," fol. 75

Lully, "Chaconne des Scaramouches," *Le Bourgeois Gentilhomme*, 1670

No. 193
"Furlana,"
fol. 75ᵛ

Campra, "La Forlana," *L'Europe Galante*, 1697
Murcia, *Resumen*, No. 11, "La Ferlana," p. 63

No. 194
"El Rigodon,"
fol. 76

Lully, "Premier Rigaudon," *Acis et Galatée*, 1686
= No. 112, "Contra Rigodon," p. 112
Murcia, *Resumen*, No. 56, "Rigodon," p. 86
Murcia, *Códice Saldívar N° 4*, No. 49, "Rigodon," fol. 82

No. 198
"La melanie,"
fol. 77

Feuillet, *Catalogue* for 1713
Murcia, *Resumen*, No. 44, "La Melanie," p. 81

No. 201
"La fustamberga," fol. 78

Murcia, *Resumen*, No. 14, "Fustamberg," p. 66
Murcia, *Códice Saldívar N° 4*, No. 38, "Fustamberg," fol. 76

Russell's identification of correspondences proves beyond cavil the European "high art" derivation of at least 59 of the 298 items in the Hague manuscript. Nonetheless, ethnomusicology still preempts this collection. So long as Rubén M. Campos's definitions of folklore can include Ernesto Elorduy's *Ella*, Manuel M. Ponce's *Estrellita*, Quirino Mendoza y Cortez's *Cielito lindo*, Juventino Rosas's *Sobre las olas*, and Narciso Serradell's *La Golondrina*, Eleanor Hague's belonging to folklorists' ranks and her manuscript's being called an ethnomusicologist's treasury, cannot be gainsaid. Except for the Latin American sacred heritage, which never caught her eye, the totality of popular secular music remained for her—as it did for so notable a successor Latin Americanist as Charles Seeger[30]—the sole division that interested her. Even today, forty years after her

[28] Santiago de Murcia's *Resumen de ACompañar la Parte Con La Guitarra . . . Año DE 1714*, the subject of Elena Machado Lowenfeld's 176-page M.A. thesis chaired in 1974 by Barbara R. Hanning at City College of the City University of New York, "Santiago de Murcia's Thorough-Bass Treatise for the Baroque Guitar (1714): Introduction, Translation, and Transcription" (Ann Arbor: University Microfilms, Order No. M-7910), was more authoritatively and completely transcribed in Craig H. Russell's "Santiago de Murcia: Spanish Theorist and Guitarist of the Early Eighteenth Century," University of North Carolina Ph.D. dissertation, 1981.

[29] *Santiago de Murcia's "Códice Saldívar N° 4": A Treasury of Secular Guitar Music from Baroque Mexico*. Russell's two-volume work scheduled for publication by the University of Illinois Press in 1994 will contain a complete transcription of Murcia's Códice Saldívar N° 4 and list of correspondences.

[30] Born at Mexico City December 14, 1886, Charles Seeger headed the Music Division of the Pan-American Union 1941–1953. According to H. Wiley Hitchcock's blurb on the back jacket of Ann Pescatello's edition of Seeger's *Studies in Musicology II, 1929–1979* (University of California Press, 1994), Seeger was "twentieth-century America's most magisterial musicologist—by which I mean that he was the most wide-ranging, deep-digging, horizon-expanding, and intellectually awesome musical thinker we have had."

Despite not mentioning Eleanor Hague in any of his publications, Seeger duplicated her value systems—at least so far as Latin American music goes. Both came from upper-crust families, both were firmly grounded in European "fine art" music. In *Notes of the Music Library Association*, sec. ser., x/2 (March 1953), p. 230, Seeger classed "the history of the fine art of Music in Mexico" as

for the most part stumbling, mongrel, epigonic, and inept. Only a few works, and those very recent, can stand beside the best work of the big world except to disadvantage. But what of the popular music of Mex-

death, Latin American music that matters to most North Americans remains within the folklorist and ethnomusicologist's domain.

ico? These are indeed pearls! And they can stand beside their fellows in any American or European country, if they do not actually stand above them.

The Editor of *IAMR* considers this myopic put-down of Mexico's historic treasury of "fine art" music humiliating and undeserved. Nonetheless, for better or worse Hague and Seeger stand on the same platform. As a result, Ethnomusicology still remains today the only academic discipline in the United States that shelters Latin American music.

THE BANDS OF TOMORROW ARE HERE TODAY: THE PROUD, PROGRESSIVE, AND POSTMODERN SOUNDS OF LAS TRES AND GODDESS 13

George Lipsitz

I was always taught to believe that music is meant to enhance life. What means something is to be able to tell a story and put wings in people's hearts.

Carlos Santana [1]

SHORTLY AFTER DARK on a Tuesday night in 1993, an excited crowd lined the sidewalks along Sunset Boulevard in West Hollywood. People came from all over Los Angeles for a performance by the band Las Tres at the Roxy Theatre. Most bands have their fans, friends, and followers, but the fervor for Las Tres was unique. A warm glow of mutual recognition and an aura of triumphal pleasure permeated the crowd. To paraphrase Doctor John, they were the right band in the right place at the right time.

Alicia Armendariz, Teresa Covarrubias, and Angela Vogel formed Las Tres in 1992. Ten years earlier they played in different local Chicana/o punk rock bands—Armendariz with The Bags, Covarrubias with The Brat, and Vogel with Odd Squad (Loza 1993: 110–112, 185–191, 265, 274). In Las Tres, they played an eclectic blend of musical styles, mixing elements of folk, rock, country, and jazz in powerful songs built around memorable melodies and intricate vocal harmonies. Their sophisticated English and Spanish lyrics touched on an extraordinary range of stories

and issues, ranging from romantic love to domestic violence, from multiculturalism to misogyny. While one could easily label Las Tres a "women's band," a "Chicana band," a "singer-songwriter trio," or perhaps a "post-punk-neo-feminist-anti-racist-Chicana-bilingual-folk-rock-country-jazz-*ranchera* ensemble," the key to their popularity lay in the ease with which their imaginations and tastes outstripped the impoverished categories that divide the music industry into distinct genres and market segments.

In the midst of a city filled with bands that seek to fill narrow commercial niches, Las Tres carved out a space for itself as something different, original, and ambitious. They combined musical virtuosity and social imagination, presenting music that taps deep reservoirs of individual and collective memory. Firmly grounded in some of the proudest ethnic and musical traditions of Los Angeles, they also presented a music in touch with tomorrow—a music that displays the possibilities of the world that is on its way, but not yet here.

Although the members of Las Tres knew each

other during their days as Chicana punk rockers, they had not really kept in contact as they went on to careers in different bands with different styles. A chance meeting between Alicia Armendariz and Teresa Covarrubias sparked the idea of getting together with Angela Vogel to play some music. "We took our guitars and started singing," Armendariz remembered, "and one person started singing lead and then someone else dropped in a harmony, and then someone else did the third, and it just felt real natural" (Armendariz 1993). It also felt good to share songwriting ideas with each other. "It takes a lot of the pressure off if you're not the only person that's putting out material," observed Covarrubias. "It makes it more diverse too. It's not the same style of music" (Covarrubias 1993).

Along with their compatibility as musicians, Las Tres also found that they enjoyed the opportunity to work with other women. "Women are more cooperative. Maybe we're just raised that way," Armendariz explained. "I feel there's a lot more cooperation than there's been in other bands I've been in. And there's a lot of encouragement. Even if you come in with a song that's not quite finished, we always take the time to nurture the song" (Armendariz 1993). The gender consciousness that the group credited for their successful musical collaboration also helps explain the emphasis in their lyrics on women's experiences and perspectives. While men and women attended and enjoyed their concerts in roughly equal numbers, the response Las Tres received from women for songs like "Happy Accident" or "Misogyny" was truly electrifying.

Part of the power of these songs came from lyrics that don't tell lies, that depict the complexities of life on this planet. Listening to Las Tres reminds listeners of how little we learn about each other's lives from most popular music, how popular culture so often works to compress the infinitely diverse ways we have of living our lives into a terribly small number of themes and motifs. But through the interplay of their music and lyrics, Las

Tres displays special gifts. The infectious rhythm of "Happy Accident" lures listeners into nodding and tapping their toes until they realize that the tensions signaled by the song's chord progressions relates to its lyrics about a woman imprisoned for accidentally shooting her abusive partner. The narrator's resolute support for defending her own life exudes a sense of self-respect that ultimately fits the upbeat tempo of the song quite well. "The women really relate to it," according to Angela Vogel, adding "and the men smirk. They know what we're talking about" (Weinstein 1993:30). Like the infectious beat of "Happy Accident," the swelling and seemingly triumphant chorus of "Misogyny" turns accusations about male contempt for women into a soaring moment of sisterly solidarity.

The Spanish language lyrics of "La Clave" issue a call for moving beyond the binary opposition between a simple ethnic assimilation whereby all people leave their cultures behind and blend into a homogeneous mass and an equally static pluralism whereby ethnic groups live in totally separate enclaves experiencing totally different cultures. "La Clave" calls for a world where difference could become a source of delight and strength, for a dynamic culture of conjuncture and intersectionality where many identities might exist together at the same time. This sophisticated and complicated stance takes tangible form in the song's structure—its Spanish-language lyrics and Mexican instrumentation and rhythms saluting a world where people of different colors and cultures work together.

The subtle interplay of music and lyrics in Las Tres allows them to be understood and appreciated on many different levels. To the surprise of the band, some people who expressed great appreciation for their music had no idea what their songs are about. Teresa Covarrubias remembered, "We were working with a guy who was going to produce us, and he didn't know what any of the songs were about. He had no idea we were talking about misogyny or domestic violence or anything"

(Covarrubias 1993). Of course, it can be a good strategy to have people on your side *before* they hear what you're talking about, and certainly one of the absolute prerequisites for success in popular music is for songs to have layers of meaning that listeners discover only gradually.

In addition, many Las Tres fans, especially women, knew exactly what the band was singing about. At times, the audience instructed the group about what themes would work. As Covarrubias explained, "I don't think when we started off doing Las Tres that we really thought, let's write about women's issues. It just sort of evolved. We've all noticed that women in the audience just seem to pick up on that" (Covarrubias 1993). Alicia Armendariz added, "When you're trying to write from your personal experiences, the fact that you grow up in a misogynist, racist society—it's just bound to pop up. And when you start writing about it and people react to it, then you realize it's something that has to be said—and it inspires you to focus on it" (Armendariz 1993).

Listeners who remember Vogel, Covarrubias, and Armendariz from their days as punk rockers were sometimes surprised to see them appear as Las Tres. They came out on stage wearing white dresses, playing acoustic guitars, and singing complex harmonies over a variety of chord progressions. But even though they were not the same people or artists that they had been ten years earlier, the members of Las Tres carried the legacy of punk rock with them in important ways. Punk elevated enthusiasm over artistry, breaking down barriers between artists and audiences by encouraging aesthetics of amateurism and emotion. Fiercely democratic, punk culture asserted that anyone could be an artist, and in its practices, sometimes everyone was.

"I feel like the essence of what we're doing now still has a punk attitude," confided Covarrubias. "We're not exceptional guitar players, but we're still playing guitars. I think the whole thing with punk back then was you don't have to be a maestro, you don't have to be an excellent player or singer.

You just get up there and you do it, and that truth and that heart is what gets your point across. And again, the same thing here [in Las Tres]. The people pick up that our heart is there and we're sincere and we're true. We don't have to be Jeff Beck" (Covarrubias 1993). Similarly, Armendariz offered, "I don't have any dissatisfaction with punk. I feel like I just grew into something else. I'm still interested in making a statement about what I feel is wrong or right with society and the way that culture or women are viewed. But now I'm doing it in a different way. I feel there's still passion, anger, emotion" (Armendariz 1993).

Part of the passion, anger, and emotion of Las Tres came from their experiences as Chicanas. Through Spanish and English lyrics, Mexican musical forms, and songs like "La Clave" that reject assimilation but embrace diversity, Armendariz, Covarrubias, and Vogel positioned themselves as one of the newest expressions of the long legacy of cultural creativity that has characterized the Mexican presence in Los Angeles. But even those elements of their repertoire that seemed totally non-Chicana/o revealed talents for fusion, adaptation, and appropriation that were deeply rooted in the Chicana/o experience.

Los Angeles was a Mexican city before it was part of the United States. In the 1848 Treaty of Guadalupe-Hidalgo, the United States government promised to respect the property, persons, and culture of Mexican Americans, but those terms were systematically violated from the start. In Los Angeles, people of Mexican origin have worked at the hardest jobs for the lowest pay for centuries. In a city with more than three-million Spanish-speaking residents, the Chicana/o presence has consistently been obscured, stereotyped, or marginalized by journalists, the entertainment industry, and politicians. As exploited workers, as second class citizens, and as artists and intellectuals with few outlets for their work, Mexican Americans in Los Angeles have struggled against great odds to define themselves and their interests.

On the level of culture, this history of conquest,

exploitation, and discrimination poses great challenges to Chicana/o artists. It has not only rendered the rich cultural life of the *barrio* virtually invisible to the rest of Los Angeles, but it has also obscured the important elements within "mainstream" culture that have distinctive Chicano origins and inflections. For example, Cheech Marin once pointed out that all of the subcultural practices celebrated within *Rebel Without A Cause* originated in Chicano communities, but that the film presented a picture of Los Angeles with no Mexican presence. Los Angeles jazz, rhythm and blues, and rock and roll owes enormous unacknowledged debts to Chicana/o artists including Gil Bernal, Bobby Rey, Chico Sesma, the Don Tosti Band, Lalo Guerrero, and Sonny Chavez, as well as to all the *cholos*, car customizers, and dancers whose dress, dance, speech and style provided the basic vocabulary for 1950s rock and roll (Reyes and Waldman 1992: 49–50).

Furthermore, discrimination and exploitation have left the community with sparse resources for supporting its artists. Sean Carillo, an artist, entrepreneur, and co-founder of the Chicano Art Network, has been trying to remedy this longstanding historical reality. He explained, "As Chicanos, as people from East L.A., we've always lacked resources. It's different from people who have equipment and studios and institutional support" (Carillo 1993). Addressing this history, Carillo has been active in promoting the work of Chicana/o artists and musicians including Las Tres. Although mainstream institutions remain woefully disconnected from the extraordinary cultural creativity displayed by Chicanos in Los Angeles, groups like Carillo's have found that audiences of all descriptions understand and appreciate the unique perspectives nurtured and honed within the Chicano experience.

For more than two centuries, the continuing migrations that have made Chicana/os both the oldest and newest residents of Los Angeles have generated an extraordinarily rich body of cultural expression in the visual arts, music, theater, and literature. Many of them have displayed what Gloria Anzaldua refers to as a *mestizaje* sensibility—a delight in difference and an ability to accommodate many different identities at the same time (Anzaldua 1988). Like the jazz critic Albert Murray who defines American culture as "inescapably mulatto," Anzaldua takes a term designed to designate racial "impurity" and turns it into a compliment. This enables her to view tensions in Chicano life between Mexico and the U.S. or between English and Spanish as productive dynamics generating a richer cultural vision.

Similarly, Anzaldua celebrates the multiplicity of allegiances and identities that all people have among their ethnicity, gender, sexual preference, and class position. For her, no one lives his or her life totally as an ethnic subject, a gendered subject, or a member of a particular class, but rather, people live all of these identities and more at the same time. For strategic and historical reasons it may be necessary to speak from any one of these positions at any particular time, but *mestizaje* consciousness affirms that every individual is a crowd, that we all have many currents of identity flowing through us.

Some postmodern critics have wrongly understood Anzaldua and other intellectuals from aggrieved racial communities to be saying that we can choose any identities we want. But the *mestizaje* consciousness articulated by Anzaldua depends upon situated knowledge, on her identity as a woman, a worker, a Chicana, and (in Anzaldua's case) a lesbian. Her concept entails appreciation of the things that people learn through struggle. Members of embattled communities have to "theorize" about identity every day; they have to calculate how they are viewed by others and how they want to view themselves.

For that reason, it is not surprising that some of the most sophisticated layering of identities and mixing of subject positions should come from the community in which Las Tres grew up—the Mexican American people in Los Angeles. The East Los Angeles Chicana/o band Los Lobos, for example, mixed together surrealistic images, jazz improvisation, Japanese instruments, and L.A rock and roll on the album *Kiko*—not as a way of denying their Mexican heritage, but rather as a way of claiming citizenship in a larger artistic and political world as *part* of the Chicana/o experience (Oumano 1992: 12–13).

Although he doesn't use the term *"mestizaje,"* the Chicano rap artist Kid Frost (Arturo Molina) also displays the delicate negotiation with identity that characterized Las Tres and many other Chicana/o artists in Los Angeles. Frost's declarations of Chicano pride utilize music, signs, and symbols testifying to the close connection between African American and Chicano youth in areas like South-Central L.A. where the population is now evenly divided between blacks and Latinos. In "These Stories Have to Be Told," one verse tells about a Chicano shunned by the community because one of his parents is Anglo ("his *plaqueazo* was *guero*, and everywhere daddy went the *batos quiren pedo*").

Frost's song "La Raza" mines Chicano collective memory in its lyrics and song samples (from El Chicano's "Viva Tirado") to present what seems like an unproblematic Chicano nationalism for the 1990s. But in the process of declaring himself "brown and proud," he makes reference to James Brown's 1968 song "I'm Black and I'm Proud," and by employing a vocal style derived from the African American rapper Ice-T, Frost pays tribute to the "prestige from below" established within hip hop culture in the 1980s. Even "Viva Tirado" by El Chicano was originally written and performed by the African American jazz composer and trumpeter Gerald Wilson. But Frost is not just revealing black-Chicano interactions or paying tribute to black culture; his intention is also to show how many things associated with black culture originated with Chicana/os. As he explained in one interview "East L.A. is a strong community, one with positive things to offer outside drugs and gangs. I want to talk about that, and I want to talk about its history. The Los Angeles low riders, the forties *pachucos* in their zoot suits. Kids don't

know how the blacks took our clothes, took our style, took who we were" (Rose 1992: 96).

Frost overstates the case: it is clear that Chicana/os and blacks in Los Angeles have long borrowed from each other in many ways with neither group receiving adequate credit for what they have created. But he is correct to point to the ways in which the Chicano origins of many elements of black culture have been erased. For example, Richard Berry's Afro-Calypso 1955 hit song "Louie Louie" was influenced by Berry's association with a Chicano Filipino band from Orange County, the Rhythm Rockers, whose members Barry and Rick Rillera introduced Berry to the music of Rene Touset whose "Loca Cha Cha" provided Berry with the model for "Louie Louie" (Reyes and Waldman 1992: 49).

Las Tres, Los Lobos, and Kid Frost stand firmly within their community's traditions as they explore worlds outside them as a spur to greater creativity. Their creations exude the sensibility enunciated by East Los Angeles artist John Valadez, who credits the "American and Latino collision" for the "schizoethnic" quality of his work. He explained, "I can look at something and see it the way I would see it as an American. No, not as an American, as the opposition. I can see both sides" (Durland 1986: 45).

In his comprehensive and definitive study of Mexican American musicians in Los Angeles, Steven Loza shows how no single genre or form can encompass the diversity of Chicana/o experience and imagination. Moreover, systematic prejudice, repression, and exclusion has often forced Chicana/o artists to prove they can master any and all musical forms simply to make a living. Over the years, this interplay of desire and necessity has left a legacy of hybridity among Chicana/o artists; the original, eclectic, and imaginative music of Las Tres built on a long tradition of Chicana/o artists skilled at mastering different discourses (Loza 1993).

The great Lalo Guerrero learned Spanish and Mexican music from his mother at home but harbored hopes of commercial success singing pop songs in English in the style of Al Jolson, Russ Columbo, Rudy Vallee, and Bing Crosby. He found his way to commercial success with this style blocked because "they couldn't conceive of a Mexican, especially one who looks as Indian as I do, sitting up there and singing Bing Crosby songs. So naturally the Anglos would get the jobs...And so I saw I wasn't going to make any money. I reverted to singing Mexican music" (Loza 1993: 158–159). But after initial success as a songwriter and singer in Mexico, Guerrero found himself shunned by Mexican entrepreneurs and musicians because he was a Chicano, and in their eyes, not authentically Mexican. Public policy and popular culture in Mexico have long derided Mexicans in the U.S. as *pochos*, a derogatory term connoting an abandonment of true Mexican identity. Guerrero and others have embraced *pochismo*, flaunting their bicultural roots in an effort to turn "*pocho*" from an insult into a compliment. In his more than fifty years of performing, Guerrero has mastered folk and popular forms from both Mexico and the U.S., while also absorbing influences from the Argentine tango wizard Carlos Gardel, and from Puerto Rican composers and musicians Pedro Flores, Rafael Hernandez, and Tito Puente (Loza 1993: 163).

During the punk era, Jesse Velo of the East Los Angeles band Los Illegals described his group's music as what would happen if Tito Puente took LSD and hung out with The Clash (Loza 1993:221). But that fusion did not make the band any less Chicano in Velo's eyes; on the contrary it enabled them to express the fused consciousness and intersectional identity that was already a part of community life. "Santana isn't the only thing you hear in the barrio, you know," Velo explained to a reporter. "You can be walking down the street at night and hear the Buzzcocks through an open window too, or Kraftwerk" (Mendelsshon 1983). Los Illegals mixed these diverse influences into their music and sang songs with both English and Spanish lyrics to call attention to the in-between-

ness of their identity. As Los Illegals member (and mural artist) Willie Herron explained to a reporter from a Texas newspaper, "what we're trying to do is feel for ourselves and bolster the bilingualness of our lifestyle. It all goes back to the way we were brought up...our culture. Our parents spoke sentences in both English and Spanish. It's important to hold on to that" (Harmon 1983:2B).

When Teresa Covarrubias was growing up in Boyle Heights, her parents listened to the music of swing bands like Benny Goodman's orchestra, while her older siblings introduced her to the rock and roll sounds of the Rolling Stones, the Beatles, and the Who. She developed a taste for artists like David Bowie and Bryan Ferry, not because they were "mainstream," but because she saw them as counter cultural alternatives to the music that most people heard on the radio. As she told Steven Loza in an interview in the mid-1980s, "I guess I was really disillusioned with everything that was happening round here and I wanted to find something different....People were just eating whatever they were showing on TV or listening to the radio and just accepting it as being 'hey, this is cool, whatever,' and I wanted to find something that I liked that wasn't following the masses" (Loza 1993:186–187).

Covarrubias later found a temporary home in punk rock with The Brat, but she has never lost her interest in expressing herself as a Chicana while still expanding her social and musical horizons. "Everything I write has some Chicano consciousness because that's what I am," she told an interviewer (Zimmer 1983:24), but she also feels a pressure "that you have to represent your ethnic background, and sometimes I think you really don't have to" (Covarrubias 1993). Or perhaps more precisely, as Alicia Armendariz added, "You do [represent your ethnic group], but you represent it in your own way. You don't have to represent it the way they want you to represent it" (Armendariz 1993).

The music industry, however, has not always held as flexible a notion of Chicano identity as

Chicana/os themselves. Raul Diaz remembers a time when Mexican American musicians like himself had to don *sombreros* and tropical outfits to get paying jobs playing during intermissions at motion picture theaters. "We wanted to play Chicano music, not come on like some clowns," he recalls bitterly (*Los Angeles Times* 1980; *Nuestro* 1979). When rock musicians Frankie "Cannibal" Garcia and the Headhunters toured with the Beatles and reached the Billboard Top Forty in 1965 with "Land of a Thousand Dances," they thought they were on the verge of mass market success. But their Chicano identity presented a problem for the record companies. "They didn't know how to market us," Cannibal later explained. "There were basically only black or white groups in the 1960s, not even many mixed groups. The people didn't even know what we were half the time; a lot of people thought we were Hawaiian or something. And with the name Cannibal and the Headhunters, most people just assumed we'd be black" (Vare 1983: 26). In the early 1980s when Los Illegals started to become popular, prospective managers suggested that they become more Mexican, suggesting that they add *timbales* and a cow bell and sing more in Spanish. "This guy from Capitol wanted to make us the Mexican Knack," recalls Jesse Velo (Zimmer 1983: 20). No doubt he wanted to answer the Knack's "M-m-m-m-m-y Sharona" with Los Illegals singing "L-l-l-l-l-a Llorona!"

This history posed problems for Las Tres. Proud of being Chicanas, they resisted being categorized as ethnic or folk artists because those descriptions did not explain who they were or what they did. A photographer asked to take their pictures in front of a mural to create a visual accompaniment to a story about the group in a mass circulation magazine. They objected, contending that such an image would be a cliché at this point. Finally they relented, and found that indeed that was the picture used to accompany their story. While the article was well written and sensitive to their actual identity, the pictures struck them as imposing a limita-

tion on how they could be perceived because they viewed the illustrations as encouraging readers to think of them only in ethnic terms.

Critics also tended to categorize the band according to gender. "People compare us to other bands that have women in them," Armendariz observed, adding "but there really isn't a comparison. There isn't a band out there that's doing what we're doing. What we're saying has not been said before. What we're doing has not been done before. It stands on its own" (Armendariz 1993). Audiences understood that, but the record industry did not. As they pursued a recording contract, disagreements about their future direction fractured Las Tres and they broke up. Armendariz and Covarrubias regrouped as Goddess 13, a band with very much the same vision as Las Tres. But whether the gatekeepers of the music industry will understand that many audiences are eager to hear a band like Goddess 13 remains to be seen.

In their efforts to be new and different, Las Tres and Goddess 13 may seem very firmly grounded in artistic modernism, in the aesthetics of formal innovation that have dominated so much of the "high art" of this century. But while they are innovative and original, their art would better be classified as postmodern rather than modern. Modernists aspire to create totally new forms of expression, while postmodernists deploy forms from the past in such a way as to problematize the present. Modernists seek escape from the everyday world by creating new spaces totally devoted to art, but postmodernists remember every place they've been and build their art out of the fragments and remains they carry with them. Modernists seek heroic unified identities capable of resisting the temptations of popular culture, while postmodernists try to build intersectional and conjunctural selves that reveal, display, and interrogate all the identities embedded within us. In philosophical terms, modernists seek a transcendent critique that will enable them to stand outside of society, while postmodernists deploy the methods of immanent critique, immersing themselves in the contradictions of their time and trying to work through them to realize the seeds of the society of tomorrow within the contradictions, ruptures, and non-equivalences of today. At a time when modernists bemoan the fall of European culture's high canon from its privileged hegemonic place, postmodernists celebrate the emergence of multiculturalism, diversity, and intersubjectivity.

In an excellent discussion of Chicano art and the "politics of representation," Rosa Linda Fregoso warns against the misidentification of traditional indigenous Chicano forms of expression as "postmodern." She shows how historical struggles for power have shaped strategies of signification among Chicana/os that privilege code-switching, parody, and indirect expression. These Chicano cultural expressions that might seem to some postmodernists simply decentered or disconnected can contain hidden historical meaning for knowing insider audiences (Fregoso 1990). Yet it is also important to see that the sensitivity to the social construction of identity and the respect for reciprocal perspectives that postmodernists labor to create as part of a critical cultural project already exist in extremely advanced and sophisticated form within traditional forms of cultural representation among Chicanos.

Las Tres and Goddess 13 offer a postmodernism grounded in concrete historical and social experiences. They see identities as constrained by power, as not infinitely open. Yet they also understand the powers of imagination and performance that are capable of creating ways of thinking and living on the terrain of culture that have not yet emerged as political forces and institutions. This progressive postmodernism speaks to old injustices and to new possibilities. For all of us who long for a world of diversity, justice, and peace, their music represents our best hopes. To borrow a title from one of their songs, their music signals the start of a *Neuvo Amanacer*—a new dawn, a brand new day.

NOTES

1. "Viva Santana," *Que Pasa* (March 29, 1991: 64). I thank Alicia Armendariz, Sean Carillo, Teresa Covarrubias, Rosa Linda Fregoso, Paulette Gershen, Michelle Pallan-Habell, Steven Loza, George Mariscal, and Jose David Saldivar for their comments, criticisms, and suggestions about this article.

REFERENCES CITED

Anzaldua, Gloria
    1988   *Borderlands: La Frontera.* San Francisco: Spinster/Aunt Lutte.
Armendariz, Alicia
    1993   Interview with Author, August 12. Los Angeles, California.
Carillo, Sean
    1993   Interview with Author, August 12. Los Angeles, California.
Covarrubias, Teresa
    1993   Interview with Author, August 12. Los Angeles, California.
Durland, Steven
    1986   "John Valadez and the American/Latino Collision." *High Performance* 35, 45.
Fregoso, Rosa Linda
    1990   "'Born in East L.A., and the Politics of Representation" *Cultural Studies* 4(3).
Harmon, Steve
    1983   "Getting Message Out Important for Los Illegals." *Laredo Morning Times*, July 29, 2B.
Los Angeles Times
    1980   October 12.
Nuestro
    1979   November 17.
Loza, Steven
    1993   *Barrio Rhythm: Mexican American Music in Los Angeles.* Urbana and Chicago: University of Illinois Press.
    1993a   "Marginality, Ideology, and the Transformative Expression of a Chicano Musician: Lalo Guerrero." *NARAS Journal* 4(1).
Mendelssohn, John
    1983   "Los Illegals Ain't Smiling." *Record* (August).
Oumano, Elena
    1992   "The Making of a Great American Band," *San Francisco Examiner* (Sunday Magazine). October 25: 12–13.

Reyes, David and Tom Waldman
  1992   "That Barrio Sound." *Pulse* (June).
Rose, Cynthia
  1992   "Kid Frost." *The Face* 96.
Vare, Ethlie Ann
  1983   "Cannibal and the Headunters." *Goldmine* (November): 26.
Weinstein, Steve
  1993   "A Sweet Sound With A Rebellious Core."
           Buzz 4(6).
Zimmer, Dave
  1983   "East L.A. Bands." *BAM* (July).

LOS ANGELES GANGSTA RAP AND THE AESTHETICS OF VIOLENCE

Steven Loza
Milo Alvarez
Josefina Santiago
Charles Moore

THE EMERGENCE OF RAP MUSIC and hip hop culture during the 1980s and 1990s has given rise to a groundbreaking musical expression that has provided a young generation of ghetto and barrio youth a voice that echoes a significant segment of its society. Through rap music, societal issues such as race/ethnic relations, political and economic disenfranchisement, police abuse, and conditions of violence are addressed by many contemporary rappers. Aspects of urban life and youth culture are expressed through an overall hip hop culture that is incorporated into musical expression. Thus, the development of this musical genre has had a tremendous influence on society, and particularly on urban youth. Specifically, rap has had a tremendous influence on African American and Chicano/Latino youth in Los Angeles, and has reflected the often violent reality of life in the ghettos and barrios. This has occurred in spite of the fact that rap music has historically been negatively interpreted by many critics, and until recently has been subject to extremely limited radio airplay. However, this has deterred neither the popularity nor the importance of rap music and the statement the art form makes about society. In fact, Los Angeles-based rap artists are among the most popular nationwide, which is reflected by the extensive sales of recordings by rap artists such as Ice Cube, Ice T,

Dr. Dre, Snoop Doggy Dogg, Eazy-E, Kid Frost, Lighter Shade of Brown, Cypress Hill, and ALT.

The purpose of this essay is: 1) to provide a specific analysis of rap music via case studies of Los Angeles based rap artists Ice Cube and ALT; and 2) to address, in a theoretical context, the aesthetic qualities of rap music as it pertains to social and urban violence. A brief historical précis on the rap movement is presented at the outset.

Historical Background of Rap Music

A brief historical sketch is important because it illustrates the cultural and social context from which rap music has emerged. Also, rap music exists as a historically conscious form of musical expression in virtually every sense. First, its musical qualities are most frequently based upon pre-existing musical formats via sampling. Second, the lyrical content is often filled with references to socially and culturally relevant historical images or events. Finally, rappers themselves are often extremely conscious of the "old school" or "O.G." rappers who originated the art form.

The origins of rap music are rooted in traditional African as well as modern African American musical traditions. As is the case with many indigenous musical forms worldwide, traditional West African music was created for the worship of societies' God or Creator. Musically, there is a heavy emphasis on the drum which is often correlated with the music as its "heart and soul." In addition, there is an emphasis on prayer and the "power of the word," or *Nommo,* which is used for the purpose of praying as well as philosophizing on life and human existence. An understanding of West African musical tradition is important when discussing the development of African American musical forms, for the Euro-American slave system largely involved the peoples indigenous to West Africa. Musically, this influence can be directly related to rap music, which at its core consists of both heavy bass via drums or drum machines, and an emphasis on lyrics through statements about "life and human existence" in the inner city.

In his article, "Performance, Protest, and Prophecy in the Culture of Hip Hop," Michael Dyson (1991:185) notes that "the modern history of rap probably begins in 1979 with the rap song "Rapper's Delight," by the Sugarhill Gang…This record is regarded as the signal barrier-breaker, birthing hip hop and consolidating the infant art form's popularity (by cracking the Billboard magazine Top 40 singles list.)"[1] In addition, this single was the first mainstream record that featured musical "samples" which would become a key development with respect to forming the basis of rap's musical development. Two of the main musical contributors to these samples are musicians James Brown and George Clinton. The basslines and drumbeats of both of these artists have been sampled on hundreds, if not thousands, of rap records and have been reinterpreted to produce many innovative sounds that have provided rap artists with a strong musical tradition on which to build their sounds. Geographically, rap music emerged on the east coast of the United States in New York's inner city. Artists such as Kurtis Blow, Afrika Bambaata, Grandmaster Flash, Funky 4 Plus 1, and the Sugarhill Gang were responsible for maintaining rap music in the early 1980s. "But the successes of the group Run-DMC moved rap into a different

sphere of artistic expression…[and] Run-DMC's stunning commercial and critical success…landed rap in the homes of many black and nonblack youths across America" (ibid.:185–186).[2]

The Emergence of Political and "Gangsta" Rap and the Expression of Violence and Urban Life

As the popularity of rap music grew, many forms of rap began to emerge. In particular, the genres of political rap and "gangsta" rap became more prominent. Consequently, "as [rap continued to evolve, it] began to reflect critically upon the terrain of its genesis, describing and scrutinizing the social, economic, and political constituents that led to its emergence and development" (Dyson 1991:185). With respect to the political rap genre, two important groups that emerged were Public Enemy and Boogie Down Productions (BDP). Both of these groups were responsible for directly incorporating cultural pride as well as a sense of history into their lyrics. In addition, both directly attacked the societal forces (e.g. the prison system, the U.S. government, the educational system) that are considered directly and indirectly responsible for maintaining Africans in America and other "minority" groups in a state of second class citizenship. Also, these rappers were on the cutting edge of developing rap music artistically by incorporating innovative samples such as political speeches, sirens, and gunshots. In other words, urban America serves as their canvas of sound from which these artists create an image through their music. These images are taken from actual life events which often involve political activism and empowerment, racial/ethnic tension, and at times violence, thus creating an aesthetic quality to urban life including violent aspects. When combined with honest and hard-hitting lyrics, the effect is overwhelming for some and empowering for others. For example, Public Enemy's LP *It takes a Nation of Millions to Hold Us Back* contains "explicit black nationalist language [which was] joined with a powerful mix of music, beats, screams, noise, and rhythms from the street" (Dyson 1991 :190). On the group's "Bring the Noise" the following is proclaimed:

> Farrakhan's a prophet and I think you ought
>   to listen to
> what he can say to you, what you ought to
>   do.
> Follow for now, power of the people say,
> "Make a miracle, D, pump the lyrical"
> Black is back, all in, we're gonna win.

With the track "Black Steel in the Hour of Chaos," Public Enemy refers to the conditions of prisons and the purpose they serve with respect to the oppression of Africans in America, without reservation:

> They got me rottin' in the time that I'm
>   servin'
> Tellin' you what happened the same time
>   they're throwin'
> 4 of us packed in a cell like slaves—Oh
>   well
> the same motherfucker got us livin' in his
>   hell
> You have to realize—what is a form of
>   slavery
> Organized under a swarm of devils
> Straight up—word 'em up on the level
> The reasons are several, most of them fed-
>   eral.

Similarly, on his LP *Edutainment*, rapper KRS-One of BDP samples conscious-raising speeches from political activist Kwame Toure (formerly Stokely Carmichael) into his cut "Ya' Strugglin'." In the cut, both he and Toure comment on the "struggles" Africans in America go through to look like their "masters" (i.e., whites) by doing things such as having plastic surgery and straightening their hair. Ultimately, KRS-One is trying to get Africans in America to be proud of who they are and that includes their physical makeup. As Toure

states, "Africans in America try to identify totally with their masters in every respect...they will go to all extremes to do it..." KRS-One raps the following lyrics:

> People change when they are ashamed
> of how they look or from which they came.
> Are you ashamed of original black?
> If not, why does your hair look like that?
> Why is your nose straighter from surgery?
> I think your really in a state of emergency.
> You're not sane to the African game,
> so you're insane and you need to obtain
> any average African sculpture
> and study it just to learn your culture.
> The blue-eyed black man to me is buggin'
> Look at yourself, man, ya' strugglin'.

Overall, the contributions of Public Enemy and BDP were critical in the continuity of rap music and in terms of insuring that rap music continued to address the social, political, and cultural concerns of Africans in America. Both groups stuck to the BDP notion of "edutainment" which is a fusion of education and entertainment.

Although the origins of the genre of gangsta rap are arguable, no other group has been as influential to the entire genre of gangsta rap than the Los Angeles-based group formerly known as N.W.A. (Niggaz With Attitude). Their landmark LP *Straight Outta Compton* was responsible for giving rise to both the genre of gangsta rap as well as Los Angeles based rap as a whole. In addition, N.W.A. began to challenge the limits of what was "acceptable" within the music industry with respect to the use of so called "foul" language and the incorporation of violent images of ghetto life. In general, the LP exposes the realities of life in the inner city such as gang violence, drugs, prostitution, and police brutality. Again, there is an attempt to discuss and address these issues through the art of rap music. The LP ominously sets the tone with the title track "Straight Outta Compton" by proclaiming, "You are now about to witness the strength of street knowledge," in addition to the following introduction by Ice Cube:

> Straight Outta Compton,
> crazy motherfucker named Ice Cube
> from the gang called Niggaz with Attitudes
> when I'm called off, I got a sawed off
> squeeze the trigger and bodies are hauled
>   off
> you too boy, if you fuck with me
> the police are gonna have to come and git
>   me
> off your ass, that's how I'm going out
> for the punk motherfucker that's showin'
>   out
> niggaz want to mumble, they wanna rumble
> mix and cook 'em in a pot like gumbo
> going off on a motherfucker like that
> with a gat that's pointed at your ass
> so give it up smooth
> ain't no tellin' when I'm down for a jack
>   move
> here's a murder rap to keep y'all dancin'
> with a crime record like Charles Manson.

This introduction not only serves to introduce the listener to the LP but also serves as an introduction to the life and mindset of the "ruthless gangsta" Ice Cube is portraying himself to be. Also, he proclaims what the consequences would be if he (or anyone from his gang or "hood") was "fucked with" and thereby expresses the territorial and violent aspect of gang culture through his art form. In addition, he boastfully claims that he has "a crime record like Charles Manson," which is an expression of his manhood as it relates to the ruthless and violent aspects of gang life. Furthermore, there exists a stark contrast between the brutal description of violent acts and the background music which for many is pleasing to the ear. This provides the music with a chilling effect. Just as with violent action movies, there exists a dialectical aesthetic to gangsta rap.

In another track titled "Fuck tha Police," N.W.A.

give their "side of the story" with respect to police brutality. The song is set up as a trial in which members Ice Cube, MC Ren, and Eazy-E give their testimonies about their experiences with the police. In one stanza Ice Cube raps:

> Fuck tha police, comin' straight from the
>   underground
> A young nigger got it bad cause I'm brown
> And not the other color, so police think
> They have the authority to kill a minority

This "reflects the brutal circumstances that define the boundaries with which most underclass black kids in Los Angeles must live" (Dyson 1991:188). Also, the lyrics expose the racially biased attitudes that many police officers have had with respect to young black men in the inner city. In addition, the importance of this example is that it provides a link between the political rap genre and the gangsta rap genre. Historically the issue of police brutality has been a volatile political issue for the African American and Chicano/Latino community. The fact that this issue is addressed by a gangsta rap group reflects a political consciousness that interacts with the political rap genre.

Overall, the development of gangsta rap fused with political rap has generated rap styles that are even more potent in their messages. Since much of this has occurred in Los Angeles, the city now serves as a center of rap music and hip hop culture. Also, given the recent political events in L.A., such as the Rodney King verdicts as well as the 1992 uprising, L.A.-based rappers have become important in terms of their critiques of both life in Los Angeles and American society as a whole. Los Angeles is thus an important city with respect to the future of rap music, and its artists warrant further investigation and study.

The following case studies are important because they bring a more focused view of the messages of influential rappers. Since both Ice Cube and ALT are L.A.-based rappers, their music reflects the city's current social and political environment, which has been one of ethnic/racial tension and urban unrest. Additionally, the fact that both rappers come from different ethnic backgrounds sheds light on the developing multiethnic nature of rap music. This, in turn, has led to rap artists developing innovative styles which essentially dominate the contemporary rap music industry.

Case Study: Ice Cube

Perhaps no other rapper is as socially significant to Los Angeles rap than rapper Ice Cube (a.k.a. O'Shea Jackson). One of the reasons that Ice Cube has emerged as a dynamic symbol is because his work epitomizes the fusion of gangsta rap and political rap. Although originally a gangsta rapper, Ice Cube's landmark LP *Death Certificate* was a successful mix of hardcore gangsta tracks with equally hard hitting politically oriented pieces that addressed many of the current social conditions of South Central Los Angeles. This was an important fusion, especially in light of the critique of gangsta rap warranting "that [mere] description [of ghetto life] is insufficient in addressing the crisis of black urban life" (Dyson 1991:189). As a response, Ice Cube's music offers solutions with respect to addressing the problems in the African American community. As was the case with Public Enemy, Ice Cube's lyrics are filled with black nationalist politics. He encourages black gangs to unite to "fight a common enemy." Also, he provides sharp criticisms of the U.S. government, the educational system, the L.A.P.D., and he does not shy away from volatile political events. An example can be found in his song "We Had to Tear this Motherfucker Up" on his LP *The Predator*, which was released just after the April 1992 L.A. uprising. In the song, Ice Cube comments on both the Rodney King verdicts as well as the uprising that occurred immediately following the first verdict. His rap is as follows:

Not guilty, the filthy devils tried to kill me.
When the news gets to the hood the niggaz
will be
Hotter than fire on pepper plus bust
Kickin up dust is a must.
I can't trust a cracka in a blue uniform,
Stick a nigga like a unicorn.
Born wicked, Laurence Powell, foul
Cut his fuckin throat and I smile.
Go to Simi Valley and surely
Somebody knows the address of the jury.
Pay a little visit. Who is it?
Can I talk to the grand wizard
Then boom, make 'em eat the barrel, modern day pharoah,
Now he ends up like Leather Tuscadero.
Pretty soon we'll catch Sergeant Koon.
Shoot him the face run up in him with a Broom-
Stick, prick, devils ain't shit.
Introduce his ass to the A-K Forty-dick.
Two days niggaz laid in the cuts.
To get some respect, we had to tear this mother fucker up.

I gotta a Mack-10 for Officer Wind.
Damn, his devil ass need to be shipped back to Kansas.
In a casket, crew-cut faggot,
Now he ain't nothin' but food for the maggots.
Lunch, punch, Hawaiian lyin' Niggaz ain't buyin
your story bore me tearin' shit up with fire,
shooters, looters, now I gotta lap top computer.
I told you it would happen and you heard, read it
But all you could call me was anti-Semitic.
Regret it, nope, said it, yup
Listen to my big black boots as I step.
Niggaz had to break you off something,
Give Bush a push, but your national guard ain't hard.
You had to get Rodney to stop me, cause you know what,

We woulda tore this motherfucker up!

It's on, gone with the wind and I know
    white men
can't talk. Now I'm stealin' bucks
and a cake from Betty Crocker, Orville
    Redenbacher
don't fuck with the Black owned stores,
but hit the Foot Locker.
Steal! Motherfuck fire Marshall Bill!
Oh what the hell, throw the cocktail.
I smell smoke got the fuck out, Ice Cube
    lucked out.
My nigga got his truck out, didn't get stuck
    out
In front of that store with the Nikes and
    Adidas
Oh Jesus, Prison Surplus got the heaters.
Meet us, so we could get the 9s and the what
    nots
Got the Mossberg with the double eye buck
    shots.
Ready for Darryl, and like Barretta would
    say
keep your eye on a barrow or sparrow.
Don't do the crime, if you can't do the time
But I'm rollin', so that's a fucked up slo-
    gan.
The Hogan's Heroes, spotted the gorilla by
    the Sizzler
hard core police killer.
A superduper nigga that'll buck.
We had to tear this motherfucker up, so
    what the fuck.
Enough.

"We Had to Tear This Motherfucker Up" is divided into three sections with each section ending with the chorus, which is the same as the title of the song. Specifically, the song refers to the '92 L.A. Uprising and it offers a justification for the actions of those who rebelled. The first sections address both the initial King verdict as well as former L.A.P.D. officers Stacy Koon and Laurence

Powell, two of the defendants in the King case. The second section begins by addressing the third officer, Timothy Wind, then makes a transition into the uprising during which Ice Cube claims, "I told you [i.e., the media and American society] it would happen." The final section of the song alludes to the activities which took place during the rebellion and its eventual end.

Lyrically, the song is an expression of the injustice that the court system had levied on the African American community via the initial King verdict. In the song Ice Cube "tries" three of the officers involved (Koon, Powell, and Wind) and subjects them to his own brand of justice, which in his eyes would have been execution. In addition, by making no apologies for the rebellion, the song justifies the rebellion as a move among the powerless to take matters into their own hands in order to achieve justice. The piece is laden with social messages by pointing out the injustice of the King verdict, while at the same time appealing to the participants of the rebellion which was the underclass (i.e., the poor, gang members) of the South Central area. Within the scenario of the pre-existing conditions of ghetto life in South Central Los Angeles, the King verdict, and the uprising, Ice Cube is relating police violence to the violence of the uprising through his art. Furthermore, the song is a reflection of Ice Cube's willingness to "stay true to the game." He raps about life in South Central L.A. (which includes the effect of the King verdict and the uprising among other issues) and does not adjust his styles to get away from what he considers his core audience. "I can't reach and try to appeal to them…motherfuckers who just bought my shit 'cause they heard it in the radio and forget about [those] that been down since day one" (Exile 1994).

Case Study: Chicano Rapper ALT

Chicano rapper ALT (a.k.a. Al Trivette) was raised in the barrios of El Monte and Rosemead, which are located about four miles east of East Los Angeles. At the age of 23 he has recorded two LPs, the self titled *ALT* in 1992 and *Stone Cold World,* released in 1994. In his brief career, ALT has come to represent the problems that young Chicano rappers face in the rap music industry, in spite of the fact that he is one of the few Chicano rappers that have been recorded by a major record label. He has stated, for example, "At first, people weren't really with it, the idea of Latinos rapping" (Brooks-Everett 1994). ALT's first LP was recorded with Atlantic Records; however, he opted to leave Atlantic to record his second LP, citing artistic freedom as a main reason.

> On the last album they made me go back and take out all the curse words. And this time again, I took them a tape which was hardcore and I told them that this is what I wanted to do. I didn't want to go through the same thing again. They told me they wanted me on their label...[but] I think they wanted me to be like Gerardo, but I'm on a way different trip then he is. I think that the real deal was that they didn't want me to release a hardcore *Latino* rap record. (Rodriguez 1994)

ALT's experience is one of many examples of what many rappers have perceived as an unwillingness of many record companies to market Chicano musicians. Leaving Atlantic Records, ALT recorded his second LP, *Stone Cold World*, with the independent label Inner City Records Inc.

With respect to style ALT classifies his music as "street."

> It's not necessarily gangsta rap. I call it real rap because what I rap about is real, and I'm being true to who I am as a person and as a rapper. These songs talk about what is really happening in the streets. If you turn your head from the problem like it isn't there, it will never go away. I want to address what's going on and hopefully, maybe one day someone will have a solution. (ibid.)

ALT's expression of barrio life and violence is evident in the following excerpt taken from his single "Heaven Can't Wait":

> Check the scenario an eighth grade class
> 'Cause nowadays kids, they grow up fast.
> But not little Johnny, 'cause he was into books.
> He never took the time to hang out with the crooks.
> When he's at home he used to read out loud.
> The kind of boy to make his mom feel proud...
> His daddy got killed in a bar room fight.
> He's down on his knees and says a prayer every night.
> And one day walking home from school with his book bag
> Rolled a car full of cholos with a big mag.
> Shot got peeled that day
> and Johnny got hit with the goddamn stray.

This rap verbalizes the irony of a child growing up in the barrio which is his home, yet not being able to escape the reality of his surroundings, regardless of how he tries to "be a good boy" and "make his mom proud." In accordance with many rappers who fall under the gangsta/political rap genre, ALT utilizes his art form to express violence in the barrio. This can be traced to the influence of other rappers. Also, it can be linked to ALT's own cultural influences considering that there exists a history in the Chicano/Mexican artistic tradition to openly depict violent images in paintings and murals, while at the same time relaying strong political and social messages.

Like many Chicano rappers, ALT represents a fusion of traditional African and African American based rap music with the realities of Chicano life and culture in the barrio. He adds his own brand of *Chicanismo* by incorporating popular "oldies" which are often listened to by barrio youth. For example, on the title track of *Stone Cold World* he uses a sample of Carole King's song "It's Too Late." Additionally with cuts such as "Tequila," he incorporates Mexican-based brass instrumentation to go along with sampled bass lines and drumbeats, giving him a distinct sound.

Towards an Aesthetics of Violence

In this analysis, one of us (Loza) suggests a radical shift from the more common methods of treating and analyzing the problem of violence. In this case, it very well may be of formidable use to consider the aesthetics of violent acts in terms of their artistic qualities, goals, and level of fulfillment. As perverse as one might interpret the notion, it is highly justifiable to observe the "art" of a drive-by shooting. In formulating such a base of comprehension, various factors can be assessed. On one level, the politics of inner-city gang life create a social network of competition and peer pressure. Fighting and murder are commonly accepted resources and recourses for gang members, not only to protect gang or individual "turf,"[3] but to do so in a manner that conforms to a particular accepted, desired, and attractive collective style. Herein lies an aesthetic dimension of the network. Much as fashion, cars, music and dance are stylistically co-opted and partially determined by gang members at certain periods of time and space, so is the "style" of violent acts. Shooting with a gun in the 1990s represents more of a "state of the art" and contemporary, and even "normative" or acceptable stylistic representation than, for example, a knifing or strangling, two methods that may represent earlier historical aesthetics of violence in gang-infested networks.

There should be some clarification at this point by citing some interpretations of such an "aesthetic." When a young gang member decides to wear a certain cut or color of clothing, a cognitive decision is being made. The symbol/icon/experience of wearing this set of clothes is in itself more than a "sign." It is a meditated, mediated form of action whereby an assortment of relationships are "secured" by the individual: acceptance among peers; social and political empowerment within a prescribed network; attainment and possession of a conditioned, stylistic mode of collective, physical expression, often one that may represent assorted levels of defiance to the dominant, commercialized norms of style and their very different uses and meanings. In assessing these possibilities, it is not difficult to ascribe a similar rationale to the development of fashion styles in the dominant U.S. market, the same market advertised on a daily basis to gang members in Los Angeles. The Calvin Klein fashion line, for example, is one that can also hypothetically be juxtaposed with the three sets of relationships outlined above. All three elements, peer pressure, sociopolitical empowerment within a group, and the possession of a collective, materialist expression, signify a comparable set of variables in the acquisition, co-optation, and manipulation of an aesthetic. The levels of cognitive experience, however, in addition to the market and the artistic organization and enactment, differ markedly.

Adapted to acts of violence, these relationships can also be observed at particular levels. Violence in the contemporary, popular culture of film and television is a standard feature, and an essential aspect of the market. "Styles" of murder and other forms of violence are constantly simulated on screen in a variety of modes. High-tech, modern weaponry is the most dominant style of murder scenes, although this context of simulation has demonstrated an assorted variety of formats, e.g., financial incentives, sexual associations, familial relationships, extortion, horror enactment, espionage, politics/war simulations, gang warfare, and mental illness. Such film simulations have most frequently been based on empirical models of violence in actual social context, although often glamorized or carnally exaggerated for purposes of sensationalism and thus, cliental lure. The aesthetic complex has thus metamorphosed from a convergence of marketing techniques aimed at the cognitive sensations of social reality. (Television and radio news broadcasts have followed similar patterns.)

A recent example of the film industry that might represent something of a divergence from the above generalizations is the film *Boyz in the Hood*, released by Columbia/Sony Pictures in 1992. Featuring rap artist Ice Cube, one of the case studies in this essay, in both an acting role and as the composer of much of the film's musical track, the movie went beyond the mere simplistic practice of exploiting the aesthetics of violence, although the latter was an inseparable factor in the story and its relation to social reality. By juxtaposing simulated acts of violence with the hard hitting rap tracks by Ice Cube, two aesthetic vernaculars converge in a manner that to many observers serves as a neutralizing metaphor. The sonic level of the sound track, comprising articulate rap and dynamic musical quality, pervades the visual sequence of storytelling in a powerful and meaningful mode of sensitized experience. Add to this the highly contemporary relevance of the film (released just before the L.A. Rebellion) and further analysis need only be turned towards a vivid memory of the film's impact—people crying in their seats and leaving theaters convinced that someone had finally touched the truth of street life in the most intense parts of Los Angeles.

Beyond this sort of analysis, three concepts can also be considered in this treatment of rap and its aesthetics: morality, the representative, and the intellectual.

Marimba Ani tells us that "art divorced from spirituality is culturally debilitating" (1994: 208). We can also recognize that spiritual ideologies have historically been highly integrated with views and dogma concerning morality. Aesthetic phenomena have been essential in the formulation of such ideologies. It is important, in assessing different ideologies of morality, that we value the cognitive over what might often be the perceptive. Ani's perception of this dialectical problem is one that she refers to as the "rhetorical ethic." She detects "a statement of value or of 'moral' behavior that has no meaning for the members of [in this case,

European] culture" (1994:312). Ani further explicates that "the concepts of traditional European anthropology are inadequate to explain the phenomenon to which [she is] referring here, as it has no counterpart in the types of cultures to which anthropologists have generally directed their attention in the past" (ibid.).

With this in mind, the textual references of Ice Cube can be reflected upon in terms of the concept of morality. On one of the tracks of his *Predator* album, Ice Cube samples and juxtaposes various commentaries by women on the expression of violence (e.g., rap lyrics). The simulation of a European American woman refers to such form as "violence," while an African American woman asks why African American rhetoric is misinterpreted. The problem of cognition/ perception is one that merits attention, and adapts interestingly to Ani's rhetorical ethic concept.

Another view that can be alluded to is one of African, e.g., Yoruba, traditional belief in the positive and negative aspects of both good and evil. Much gangsta rap includes reference to the police and their cars and helicopters. Such metaphors are often used as vehicles of abuse and corruption, in contrast to their social functions as civil protection against crime. The negative forces of the official "good" are portrayed, while the righteousness of gang life is proclaimed. Such is the form of satire developed in the previously cited "Fuck tha Police" by N.W.A. and Public Enemy's "Black Steel in the Hour of Chaos." Conversely, the positive element of the official "good" is expressed by Ice Cube as he recognizes the police car that drives by him with no incident in his "It Was a Good Day" on the *Predator* LP. Through Ice Cube's portrayal as an evil gangbanger in the film "Boyz in the Hood," the forces of both negative and positive emerge through the character at different points of emotion, tragedy, and social dynamics throughout the story.

One form of violence that has not yet been addressed here is that of sexism and misogyny. This topic also allows for the discussion of the representative—who does the art form represent? Bell Hooks, in assessing gangsta rap as social expression, has written that "the sexist, misogynist, patriarchal ways of thinking and behaving that are glorified in rap are a reflection of the prevailing values in our society" (1994: 26). She views these values as created and sustained by the dominant corporate class.

> To white dominated mass media, the controversy over gangsta rap makes great spectacle. Besides the exploitation of these issues to attract audiences, a central motivation for highlighting gangsta rap continues to be the sensationalist drama of demonizing black youth culture in general and the contributions of young black men in particular. It is a contemporary remake of *Birth of a Nation* only this time we are encouraged to believe it is not just vulnerable white womanhood that risks destruction by black hands but everyone. When I counter this demonization of black males by insisting that gangsta rap does not appear in a cultural vacuum, but, rather, is expressive of the cultural crossing, mixings, and engagement of black youth culture with the values, attitudes, and concerns of the white majority, some folks stop listening. (ibid.)

There may be counterviews to Hooks, but she raises an inevitable and precise question germane to the present essay. Is gangsta rap, with all of its various levels of aesthetic violence, a reflection of African American culture or of a larger culture? In this essay, one of the case studies signifies the emergence of Chicano rap as an outgrowth of black gangsta rap. In Los Angeles, one can encounter rap groups of Japanese American, Chinese American, Korean American, Pilipino, European American, Arab American, among numerous other ethnic and mixed affiliations. Across the U.S. and the world, rap is being produced and performed by a multicultural network of individuals either aesthetically or financially lured to the genre. A greatly significant percentage of rap recordings are purchased by white youth. One answer to the question of what culture is represented by gangsta rap coincides with Hooks's evaluation of the style as a reflection of prevailing values in society at large.

In his highly read and acclaimed book *Race Matters*, Cornel West perceives a lack of "race-transcending prophetic leaders" in contemporary black America. He adds that "this void sits like a festering sore at the center of the crisis of black leadership—and the predicament of the disadvantaged in the United States and abroad worsens" (1993:40). West believes that black intellectual leadership "discloses the cynical and ironic face of the black middle class" (ibid.). He attributes the problem of black intellectual work to two factors. First, he cites the co-optation of a substantial segment of black scholars to the standards of academe, with its "system of rewards and status, prestige and influence, puts a premium on those few black scholars who imitate the dominant paradigms elevated by fashionable Northeastern Seaboard institutions of higher learning" (ibid.:41). Secondly, West identifies black scholars representing another extreme—those who "deliberately distance themselves so far from the mainstream Academy that they have little to sustain them as scholars." The variety of "mediocrity" that ensues from this sector of marginal intellectual life outside of the university system, according to West, "suffocates much of black intellectual life" (ibid.:42).

As he does with black politicians, West proceeds to categorize black scholars into the same three categories—race-distancing elitists, race-embracing rebels, and race-transcending prophets. For the latter category, West cites the lack of current black intellectuals in the U.S. He detects neither a James Baldwin nor an Oliver Cox, affirming that "this vacuum continues to aggravate the crisis of black leadership—and the plight of the wretched of the earth deteriorates" (ibid.:43).

The pessimism of Cornel West certainly reflects much of the pessimism from whence an "aesthetic of violence," as formulated here, emerges. But has West creatively and intuitively surveyed the more possible and inclusive bounds of the "intellectual"? He has identified the lack of black leadership among politicians and scholars, separating the roles of the political and the intellectual. This signifies one of the very problems he critiques—the culturally biased standard of the academic system, which often attempts to divorce political action from intellectual purpose.

In a more inclusive conceptualization of the political and intellectual, West might also have identified the role of the contemporary artist as a significant and vital actor in the goal of black leadership in the U.S. Ice Cube (among other artists cited in this essay), in his context of social actor exploiting the contemporary possibilities and resources through aesthetic expression, fulfills the leadership role that West both hopes for and envisions as a situation transcending the older and useless limiting definition of the political and "the intellectual."

> The time is past for black political and intellectual leaders to pose as *the* voice for black America. Gone are the days when black political leaders jockey for the label "president of black America," or when black intellectuals pose as the "writers of black America." The days of brokering for the black turf—of posing as the Head Negro in Charge (H.N.I.C.)—are over. To be a serious black leader is to be a race-transcending prophet who critiques the powers that be (including the black component of the Establishment) and who puts forward a vision of moral regeneration and political insurgency for the purpose of fundamental social change for all who suffer from socially induced misery. (ibid.)

Another role that West might recognize (and perhaps he has) is that which George Lipsitz has recognized as the "organic intellectual." Lipsitz (1990) views many of the "postmodern and polyglot" musical artists of East Los Angeles in such light, and one can even question the necessity of qualifying these intellectuals as "organic." Rap artists such as Ice Cube and ALT also fit well with such description—that of *intellectuals* (who challenge a highly accepted institutional standard that society's intellectual work predominates within the established academies of "higher learning").

The good/evil dialectic also conforms to the debate of the morality of gangsta rap and its rhetoric of violence. The experiential aesthetic of violence (e.g., the witnessing of a drive-by shooting and its artful execution) becomes the basis for the artistic cognition and aesthetic energy[4] engaged in the composition and performance of a rap. The experiential corresponds to the imaging of metaphor that conveys an intellectual insight and often, a satirical tragedy or remedy, most often the former. But remedies do surface, e.g., Ice Cube's "It Was a Good Day." If the role of the intellectual is to convey some knowledge, insight, even wisdom, then perhaps we can be confident that Ice Cube has done so.

Violence presently prevades America. To divide it from the good and the wise signifies a contradiction. The U.S. leads the world in statistics of violent crime. In the Venice area of Los Angeles, seventeen murders and fifty woundings had occurred within a year as of mid-June 1994, largely due to friction between African American and Latino gangs, a situation described by one psychologist as an "urban guerilla war setting" (Crogan 1994). News networks, in light of a recent unprecedented media homicide coverage, have estimated that 1,500 women are murdered annually through acts of domestic violence.

With only 5% of the world population, the U.S. monopolizes 75% of all international serial killings (Jalife 1994). These statistics are but minuscule examples of the crime counts characterizing the country at large.

One option to the reductionist use of statistics

such as those cited above in the detection of and policy making related to social ills is the concurrent study of social values and the expression of them. Contemporary scholars owe the academy they work within the effort to assess the aesthetic dimensions of the highly sophisticated style of rap music in its various forms, and to question pervading attitudes as to whether the genre is a perverse conduit to violence, or perhaps more aptly, an intellectual deterrent to such behavior.

NOTES

1. Dyson's article is important because it serves as a general framework for an overall history of rap music. While he does not solely focus on Los Angeles-based rap music, his article provided an extremely useful basis for structuring this essay.

2. It is of interest that rap group Boogie Down Productions, on their LP *Ghetto Music: The Blueprint of Hip Hop*, recorded a song "The Blueprint" which serves as an oral history of the early days of rap music up to the point that the LP was recorded in 1989. The song was an attempt to render respect to hip hop's pioneers in addition to providing a sense of history of rap music in general.

3. *Turf* can refer to geographical territory in addition to particular women or men, material articles, colors, among other possibilities.

4. John Blacking used the terms, *artistic cognition* and *aesthetic energy*, in a public lecture that he delivered for the UCLA Program in Ethnomusicology in 1981.

REFERENCES CITED

Ani, Marimba
    1994   *Yurugu: An African-Centered Critique of European Cultural Thought and Behavior.* Trenton, New Jersey: Africa World Press, Inc.

Brooks-Everett, Natasha
    1994   "Rap's New Look." *Spice Magazine.* (April):24–25.

Considine, J. D.
    1992   "Fear of a Rap Planet." *Musician.* February: 34–47, 93.

Crogan, Jim
    1994   "Trapped by the Terror of a Venice Street War." *Los Angeles Times.* (July 18).

Dyson, Michael Eric
    1991   "Performance, Protest, and Prophecy in the Culture of Hip-Hop." *The Emergency of Black and the Emergence of Rap.* A special issue of *Black Sacred Music: A Journal of Theomusicology* 5(1): 12–24.

Exile
    1994   "Lethal." *Beat-Down* 1 (1):12–13, 28.

Hooks, Bell
    1994   "Sexism and Misogyny: Who Takes the Rap? Misogyny, Gangsta Rap and *The Piano.*"*Z Magazine* (February):26–29.

Jalife, Alfredo
    1994   "Siquiatría y politica: los matices de la criminalidad." *Exselsior* (May 10). Mexico City, Mexico.

Lipsitz, George
    1990   "Cruising Around the Historical Bloc: Postmodernism and Popular Music in East Los Angeles." In G. Lipsitz, *Time Passages: Collective Memory and American Popular Culture:* 133–160. Minneapolis: University of Minnesota Press.

Rodríguez, Pebo
    1994   "LRM Entertainment." *Lowrider Magazine* (April):24–26.

West, Cornel
    1993   *Race Matters.* Boston: Beacon Press.

SELECT DISCOGRAPHY

ALT. 1992. *Another Latin Timebomb.* Atlantic Recording Corporation.

ALT. 1994. *Stone Cold World.* Inner City Music, distributed by Par Records.

Boogie Down Productions. 1989. *Ghetto Music: The Blueprint of Hip Hop.* Zomba Recording Corporation, distributed by RCA records.

Boogie Down Productions. 1990. *Edutainment.* Zomba Recording Corporation, distributed by RCA records.

Dr. Dre. 1992. *The Chronic.* Interscope Records.

Da Lench Mob. 1992. *Guerillas in the Mist*. Atlantic Recording Corporation, distributed by East West Records.

Ice Cube. 1989. *Amerikkka's Most Wanted*. Priority Records.

Ice Cube. 1990. *Kill at Will*. Priority Records.

Ice Cube. 1991. *Death Certificate*. Priority Records.

Ice Cube. 1992. *The Predator*. Priority Records.

Ice Cube. 1993. *Lethal Injection*. Priority Records.

Ice T. 1988. *Power*. Sire Records Company.

Ice T. 1991. *O.G. Original Gangster*. Sire Records Company.

Kid Frost. 1990. *Hispanic Causing Panic*. Virgin Records.

Kid Frost. 1992. *East Side Story*. Virgin Records.

Latin Alliance. 1991. *Latin Alliance*. Virgin Records.

NWA. 1988. *Straight Outta Compton*. Ruthless Records.

NWA. 1990. *100 Miles and Runnin'*. Priority Records.

Public Enemy. 1988. *It Takes a Nation of Millions to Hold Us Back*. Def Jam/Columbia Records.

Public Enemy. 1990. *The Fear of a Black Planet*. Def Jam/Columbia Records.

Public Enemy. 1991. *Apocalypse '91...The Enemy Strikes Back*. Def Jam/Columbia Records (Sony Music Incorporated).

Run DMC. 1993. *Greatest Hits 1983–1991*. Death Row/Interscope Records, distributed by Atlantic Records.

SOCIAL ASPECTS OF PERSIAN MUSIC IN LOS ANGELES

Behzad Allahyar

A COMPREHENSIVE INVESTIGATION of the musical life of Iranians in Los Angeles would require a vast study due to the rich variety of ethnic, religious, political and social communities represented by the more than 250,000[1] Iranians living in Los Angeles and the surrounding metropolitan area. The enormous array of musical traditions that form a part of their culture is aptly illustrated by the more than fifty Iranian singers, a larger number of instrumentalists, various groups of dancers, recording studios and distributors, and Iranian music shops and cabarets flourishing in the region. Locally produced Iranian television programs are frequently entirely devoted to Iranian music while others give a substantial amount of air time to the advertising of Iranian concerts, nightclubs, new releases on cassette and CD by Iranian musicians and singers (mostly local), and classes available for instruction in Iranian music and dance. Although thousands of Iranians have emigrated and live throughout the U.S., Canada, and Europe, the majority of these musical activities occur in Los Angeles. The Iranian community of Los Angeles has such a prolific and abundant amount of musical life and traditions that it can easily be considered the capital of Iranian music outside of Iran.

Iranian music in Los Angeles experienced tremendous growth during the decade following the 1979 Revolution, paralleling a rapid expansion in Iranian media of all kinds, which continues to the present day. These include three 24-hour radio programs, several hours of daily Iranian television programs,[2] a few daily newspapers and many weekly, monthly, and quarterly magazines, all in the Persian language. These are supported by the Iranian business community whose advertisements provide a strong base of financial support for the various media. The prominence of music within the Iranian communities of Los Angeles is notable when we recall that historically, music has not been a part of daily life or of significant importance in Iran.

In the Los Angeles community, musical events have come to serve a unifying function, bringing together political and social groups that tended to be segregated from one another in Iran both before and after the 1979 Revolution.

In general, there are two main types of music readily available in the Iranian community in Los Angeles: popular and classical. Before discussing them, however, it is necessary to briefly review the historical and musical situation in Iran before and after the 1979 Revolution.

Iran: Historical Background

Iran is an Islamic country with a population of approximately 50 million, the majority of which belongs to the Shi'ite sect. Music has always been a controversial subject for religious leaders throughout the history of Islamic Iran. However, Iranian historical sources reveal a musical history dating back more than 1,400 years, to 622 A.D., the first year of the Islamic calendar. Names of songs, musical terminology, and musicians are found as far back as the period of the Sassanid dynasty (c. 262–652 A.D.). Bas reliefs displaying wind, string, and percussion instruments date back still further to the Achaemenid period (6th–4th century B.C.) (Farmer 1938). Although we have no written music or any extant sources in Iran citing specific musical examples that go back beyond the nineteenth century, there are a number of scholarly treatises written about music through the middle of the fifteenth century, and accounts from historians, travelers, and scholars that mention music and musicians and their situations at various times.

Iranian classical music as it is recognized today cannot be traced back more than a century, unless one considers the names of modes and melodies that have been used in Persian literature and musical treatises over the last several hundred years. Around the beginning of the twentieth century, a court musician, Mirza 'Abdullah (1843–1918), introduced to his students classical music that he and his two brothers had been taught orally by their father and uncle. Until this time, the oral tradition was the main method used in teaching music. It seems likely that about the time of this family, Iranian music faced a reorganization of the whole system of *maqam* to *dastgah*.

> The twelve *maqamat*, or modes, as codified by Maraqi and by Safi al-Din before him are presented in the manuscripts of the Safavid period (1501–1736). However, this codification of *maqamat* does not appear to correspond to the actual musical practice of the time. Such a contradiction between theory and practice led to the introduction of a system of seven *dastgah-ha* in place of the 12 *maqamat*. It is difficult to identify precisely the moment when the term *maqam* was replaced by *dastgah*, but it appears likely that Forsat-e-Shirazi (1852–1920) was the first to mention *dastgah*.

All this suggests that a change in terminology occurred to reflect a change in musical practice. Although the terms *maqam* and *dastgah* have been applied in part to describe a modal system and its melodic variations, and in part to the names of the modes of some melodies, these concepts are not absolutely equivalent. (Massoudieh 1978: 6–7)

In present theory, each *dastgah* (mode) contains a number of melodies called *gusheh*. The *dastgah* system will be discussed in greater depth later in this article.

Classical musicians during the nineteenth century can be categorized into two broad groups: those who belonged to the court or those who performed for wealthy aristocrats under the patronage of the Shah or members of his entourage, far from the forbidden religious leaders and the other groups which played around the city, depending on the patronage and assistance of ordinary people. This latter group of musicians consisted primarily of Jews for whom Islamic religious law was not applicable and whose musical traditions were allowed to continue (Shamin 1992). The activities of other non-court musicians were limited to weddings and circumcisions. There were no public performances.

Military music formed another significant tradition during the nineteenth century. Its origins can be traced to reign of Nasiru'd-Din-Shah-i Qajar (1847–1895), who for half a century lived in pleasure and never hesitated to prepare festivities for his own enjoyment even though the country faced deep crises and was on the verge of chaos (Shamin 1992: 442). Upon seeing a military band in France during one of his travels to Europe, he wanted the same type of music for his court and commissioned the French government later to send one of its military musicians to Iran. Alfred Jean Baptiste Lemaire went to Iran in 1882 and arranged a military music school; he taught theory, piano and all military musical instruments to selected army students funded by the government. After a few years, he was able to organize a few bands from among his students (Mallah 1975). At the beginning of the twentieth century, access to music and musical instruments in Tehran was highly restricted, limited to a very small number of musicians. Indeed as late as 1899, US. Consul Arthur S. Hardy was informed by Alfred J.B. Lemaire that there were no stores in Tehran from which to buy musical instruments.[3]

But over the next couple of decades, this began to change, due largely to the efforts of Darvish Khan (1872–1926) and a few of his colleagues, who began to arrange public performances of Iranian classical music. Probably the most renowned musician of his era, Darvish Khan received some musical training from the French teachers at the military academy and apparently took the concept of public performance from the military band's performances. A respected composer whose works have been published in a collection, he appears to have been the first musician to have worked on rhythmical aspects of Iranian classical music; one of his most important works for Iranian music was in the form of *pish-daramad* (prelude), a precomposed rhythmic piece.

Music in the Pahlavi Dynasty Period

At the time of the second Shah of the next and last dynasty (the Pahlavi Dynasty 1925–1979), classical music, which had previously been available to only a very limited audience became more accessible to the general public. Radio was established around 1940 in Tehran, offering a few hours of programming each day. Renowned Iranian classical musicians often performed live for these programs. Other musical genres were included: with the gradual expansion of radio run by the government, popular music was introduced under the term "jazz music" (*musiqi-e jaz*). By the 1950s, radio audiences were listening to various forms of popular music and Iranian music arranged in a Western style.

Western classical music began to achieve wider

popularity in Iran. Tehran's main music school, Honarestan-e Musiqi, established a Western classical music major, which was highly successful. In 1953, a Philharmonic Society was founded by several Iranian graduates of European schools. Later, this society arranged a large number of recitals and concerts by European musicians and was under the jurisdiction of an important government official, which guaranteed annual support by the government. A small symphony orchestra composed of Iranians and foreigners (mostly Russians) was initiated. A monthly musical journal, *Majalley-e musiqi*, was published by the Ministry of Culture.

Iranian classical music suffered by comparison in terms of visibility. There were up to forty Western classical concerts per year, but no advertisements for any strictly Iranian musical performances. Iranian music magazines were devoted to translations of Western music articles, biographies of Western musicians and discussions of Western classical music. Iranian music was rarely mentioned. These phenomena can be linked to the trend toward modernization—the goal of the government—which apparently included Westernization. This trend can also be observed in other fields, including architecture, development of cities, painting, sculpture, etc.

Western musical instruments were introduced to Iranian musical groups at this time, and musicians began imitating Western popular music. Combining Western musical styles with Persian texts, they created a new popular form of music.

Popular music reached its apex in Iran during the last decade before the 1979 Revolution. The improved economic situation, which was largely dependent on high oil prices, had created a new wealthy group that sought contemporary forms of entertainment. Many of them had studied abroad and were familiar with Western musical styles from firsthand experience as well as through the mass media. In order to entertain this new wealthy group, a new style known as *cabaret* that incorporated Western styles was developed, attaining its greatest popularity in Tehran. Government-run radio and television supported the Western style of pop music with Iranian texts, and popular Western singers from the United States and Europe often shared the stage with Iranian singers and musicians in Tehran's cabarets.

An international music conference took place in Tehran in 1966 with another a year later.[4] During these conferences, Iranian classical music was investigated and some noted ethnomusicologists from abroad suggested that it be preserved and introduced to the world. Before this conference, Iranian music had begun to be studied by non-Iranians; this was around the time an annual festival (Jashn-e Honar-e Shiraz) was established in Shiraz next to the ancient Iranian ruins at Persepolis, the capitol of the Achaemenids. Performances of Western classical music by internationally renowned musicians usually opened and closed this festival. But Iranian classical music also received some attention from the government.

Music in Tehran

Tehran, the capital city of Iran, has long been considered the country's cultural center. It was the source of almost all the written texts concerning music from the nineteenth century. Its importance only increased with political centralization in the Pahlavi era. A closer examination of the musical genres popular in Tehran before the Revolution is therefore important to understanding the later development of Iranian music in Los Angeles.

In general, two kinds of popular musical groups evolved in Tehran during the twentieth century. The first type used Western electronic instruments with a few brass or wind instruments. The second combined Persian musical instruments with a few Western ones, including Western stringed instruments, usually the violin and double bass, and occasionally a flute. The singer in the second type of group was known as the "people's singer," and was likely to be someone with no formal musical training who might perform in restaurants in downtown Tehran. In the last years before the Revolu-

tion, both types of music were strongly supported by government-run media; most of the singers were employees of Iranian radio or television.

Culturally, Tehran is divided north-south, with the northern region being the more Westernized. This distinction was manifested both musically and socially during the years before the Revolution. In the southern cabarets and restaurants, including the downtown district, repertoire usually consisted of music performed using Persian instruments and a few Western ones and/or music from Iran's neighboring Arab countries with Turkish, Afghani, and Indian melodies set to Persian texts. Customers of southern cabarets often encouraged the singers to perform songs with Arabic texts. No Western music was performed and dress codes tended to be rather informal. The audience was almost exclusively made up of men. In the northern cabarets of Tehran, everything was Westernized, including musical instruments, repertoire and the singers' costumes (although Arabian "belly dance" was included). Men were expected to wear a suitcoat and tie. It was customary for a singer to perform Western songs with English texts for audiences made up of both men and women.

The Iranian Community in Los Angeles

During and after the 1979 Revolution, Iranians in large numbers left home to settle in various cities throughout Europe and the West. Such a large number emigrated to Los Angeles that Iranians often term the city "the capital of Iranians in exile" or "Tehrangeles." They have become a significant force in the business community of the city. The 1993 edition of the "Iranian Yellow Pages" lists 1,008 pages of Iranian-owned and operated businesses. As a result, a foundation of support has been established for Iranian radio and television in Los Angeles.

Many Iranians who settled in Los Angeles came from the middle and upper classes, and had benefited from the improved economic situation in Iran during the last years before the Revolution. Many of them were the former audience of Tehran's cabarets and nightclubs. After the Revolution, the Islamic government prohibited popular music and allowed only traditional music. This prohibition forced a large exodus of musicians.

Cabarets

Around 1980, there were only a few Iranian restaurants in Los Angeles, and only one presented Iranian popular music on an occasional basis. In 1981, the first Iranian cabaret was established in L.A. By 1984–85, the number of restaurants and cabarets had increased quite noticeably. As the number of Iranian immigrants to Los Angeles increased and the number of Iranian businesses in the area multiplied, more and more Iranian singers, musicians, and composers moved to Los Angeles. Today there are scores of restaurants and a few cabarets operated by Iranians in Los Angeles with a substantial number of them offering live Iranian popular music. On any given night, one has several choices of where to go for popular entertainment, all advertised exclusively in the Iranian media. An evening's show in a cabaret is usually made up of several singers and other entertainment. Many of the factors distinguishing cabaret entertainment in northern and southern Tehran are paralleled in Los Angeles. However, the cabaret audiences in Iran before the Revolution continued to patronize only one type, while in Los Angeles the majority of cabaret audiences attend both types regularly.

The cabaret known as "Ofog-Talai," in the Westwood district of Los Angeles, an area frequented by many Iranians, was strikingly similar to the type found in southern Tehran before the Islamic Revolution. This Los Angeles establishment borrowed its name from the most well known cabaret in southern Tehran before the Revolution and presented similar music with the same singers. Advertisements for this cabaret were found strictly in the Iranian media. Although advance reservations were required, the cabaret operated on a first-come first-served basis.

In September 1989 I visited this cabaret on a typical evening. Among the more than 100 persons in the audience that night, only four were Americans, and the program was conducted entirely in Persian. Seating was crowded, and the music was amplified to a point where it was difficult to decipher the lyrics.

Four singers and a belly dancer entertained for approximately four hours, accompanied by three musicians playing a *tombak* (drum), *santur* (zither), and a Western violin. Three of the four singers who performed in the show had been popular in Iran. The fourth singer began her career in Los Angeles, but many Iranians compared her voice with that of a singer once popular in Iran, now deceased.

Although belly dancing belongs to Arab culture, it was popular in Iran before the Revolution and referred to as "Arabic dance." The advent of the Islamic Revolution incorporated much Arabic language and tradition. Presently, Iranian nationalists call it "Eastern dance" or "Middle-Eastern dance," terms frequently used in cabaret advertisements in the Persian media.

The performance of the belly dancer, an American using the Iranian name "Shahrzad," was not quite authentic. She danced in front of customers on both the ground and upper levels of the cabaret while men placed dollar bills of various denominations over her costume. The singers presented songs with varying themes, including some of their old "hits" from Iran. Several selections made the audience so happy and excited that they stood up to dance in the cramped space. Two of the better known singers reminded the audience of their background and encouraged them to reminisce. Between songs, the singers talked to the audience about their homesickness and homeland. Themes of nostalgia and homesickness were often presented immediately after pieces meant simply for the pleasure of the audience. One singer who had made a well known television commercial for a cooking oil (Roghan-e Qu) in Iran was requested to sing the tune from it; the audience joined in and sang it with him.

Other types of Iranian cabarets in Los Angeles are more Westernized. They frequently employ

American and Iranian musicians who use Western musical instruments including electronic keyboards, electric guitars, saxophones, and drums. A sound technician is often present for all performances. One orchestra accompanies all the singers, and the entertainment lasts about four hours. Generally, these cabarets pay their performers well and maintain an upscale atmosphere often with a strictly enforced dress code for the audience. At these "Westernized" cabarets too, the programs are conducted in Persian.

Cabaret Tehran is the most famous Iranian cabaret in the Los Angeles area and has been in existence over the last decade while other cabarets seem to only survive for a short time. The owner of Cabaret Tehran advertises by means of a thirty minute television program on Sunday evenings at midnight, featuring interviews with singers who are to perform there that week. The program format changed over the years; political discussions replaced interviews with singers and musicians. Presently, a few minutes of the program "Diyar" (Wednesday, 12:30 P.M., KSCI, Channel 18, Los Angeles) features advertisements for Cabaret Tehran. Calling it a "little Iran," they advertise it as the place where Iranians can get together to be happy and make new acquaintances. For Iranian artists making their debut in Los Angeles, it is the "house of hope."

Restaurants and Discos

Music in Iranian restaurants ranges from taped Western music to live performances of either traditional or popular music. One might hear a tape of the most recent recording of a famous Iranian popular singer, or a recording of Western light music. At some restaurants, live performances take place, usually with a singer and/or instrumentalist.

There are also a few Iranian discos which have live music; they are generally open during the middle of the week or on Sunday nights.

Popular Music Concerts

Many Iranians are familiar with cabaret and restaurant entertainment, since they frequented them in Iran. However, a new form of entertainment has emerged in Los Angeles: popular music concerts. (The term "concert" is loosely applied to any kind of performance.) Before the Revolution, singers of popular music in Iran rarely performed outside of cabarets, television, private parties, or weddings. In Los Angeles, however, one can find an increasing number of concerts of Iranian pop music as more and more Iranians emigrate, with a sharp increase in the number of such concerts occuring about 1984. Although there are currently many singers of popular music within the Iranian community in Los Angeles, only about twenty were known previously in Iran. A far greater number of singers began their musical careers in Los Angeles, many of whom are now earning a better living than those whose careers originated in Iran, as evidenced by the larger audiences they attract. They have no agents and perform in halls and hotel ballrooms that can accommodate up to 3,000 persons, with the majority of audience composed of young people. Popular venues include the Palace and the Palladium in Hollywood. Occasionally, the Los Angeles Fire Department is forced to cancel a performance because the number of tickets sold far exceed the buildings capacity. Sometimes tickets are sold for concerts which never take place. Ticket prices range upwards from $25, and in cases of overselling, tickets are non-refundable. There are no seats, but there is a platform for dancing and a bar. Doors usually open at 8:00 P.M. Tapes of popular Persian music play until 11:00 or 11:30, when the singer appears on stage. The live program can last for one to two hours. Persian television often broadcasts a singer performing one of his or her hits which serves as an advertisement for an upcoming performance in a cabaret or a new cassette. Until 1987–88, Iranian popular performances in Los Angeles were relatively simple and usually employed only Iranian musicians. As the community grew, the performances began to emulate Western rock concerts. The use of lighting and other visual effects, especially steam effects, became increasingly more common. Backup singers and dancers, usually Americans, are now often used. Iranian pop singers frequently employ Americans to accompany their performances with electronic keyboards, guitars, and drums. (Iranian singers believe that they can pay American musicians less and have less hassle in their professional relationship.) They also frequently use American dancers with erotic dress and dancing styles, claiming the audiences prefer them.

Most lyrics are sung in Farsi and deal with the subject of love. They are performed in the 6/8 rhythm common for Iranian dancing. This rhythm predominates throughout popular music. At the Persian restaurant Shiraz in July 1993, the keyboard entertainer, equipped with four keyboards and a rhythm box, played the tune "Happy Birthday" in 6/8; later on that same evening, Dave Brubeck's "Take Five" was also played in 6/8. A noted Iranian composer arranged some Persian folksongs that were in 5/8 meter in 6/8, including the folk tune, "Chashmha-ye Yaram" for a female singer in Los Angeles. When questioned why he made the metric alteration, he responded that the singer was more comfortable in 6/8.[5]

While love is the most frequent theme, song lyrics occasionally deal with more serious issues: the political situation in Iran, the Iran-Iraq war, or the homesickness, sorrows and melancholy of the Iranian community living outside the homeland. Rhythm and melody type, however, are the same as in the songs that deal with lighter subjects. Thus it is possible to find an Iranian in Los Angeles dancing to a popular song whose text deals with a more serious subject. For example, the text of one very popular song begins with a description of the singer's life back in Iran—traditions, environment, family left behind, with a special emphasis on the singer's longing to see his mother. As the song goes on, the singer says he ruined his life by staying here and also expresses his desire that the Iranian flag will one day be his shroud. Although the lyrics depict a serious predicament, the music

is very lively, and one can see many Iranians dancing to such songs at private parties or cabarets. For example, one popular female vocalist sings "Havar, Havar, they have taken what we had!" But the music is for fast dancing—the singer performs with a smiling face and performs a type of erotic dance she had made famous during her career.

In December 1988, the popular singers Sattar and Shahram were interviewed on television by the host of a popular half-hour program.[6] The host had previously conducted a videotaped interview with two Iranians about their views on Iranian music in Los Angeles and their opinion of Sattar and Shahram, who were well known performers in Iran. According to these respondents, the songs were better in Iran, where listeners could sing some from memory, whereas in Los Angeles, there is no stimulation to learn songs since the texts are meaningless. The two singers offered their response to these criticisms in a bitter dialogue:

Sattar: You people yourself are the main cause for this change. I should apologize and say that you people have pushed the music to banality because, for example, when I sing my song, "Pennyroyal Flower,"[7] the people stand up and dance to it. It means they don't care or they don't understand the meaning of the song. And they never request a few songs that I have about the homeland. If I sing more than one of these, they stop me and ask me to sing something for dancing.

Shahram: Me too. If I sing just one song about our homeland, everybody protests, and they ask me to sing fast music for dancing. For example, nobody asks me to sing a song about Iran: ("If I can put the letters 'I', 'R', and 'A' together and place them next to an 'N', I would be able to make the most beautiful name. Iran...Iran...Iran...) But everybody asks me to sing, for example, "Pariya" ("Oh you, more beautiful than an angel, don't go to the alley! The boys in the alley are thieves, and they'll steal my love.")

Interviewer: Up until a few years ago, you performed with a flag of Iran near you and sang about Iran. But now, it seems that you are mostly thinking about business.

Shahram: A singer should first become famous, and then everybody will listen to whatever he sings. My style since the beginning of my career was music for dancing—pop and disco music. You people should ask those singers who began their careers here in Los Angeles to sing more songs about the homeland. It's obvious that beginners never will do that, because they know that nobody cares about these songs and they'll never become famous and successful. For example, several musicians and singers last year composed and arranged a song about Iran and recorded it. They were able to sell only a hundred cassettes, but the singers that have dance music have the potential to sell five to twenty-thousand cassettes. I promise you that you people who are watching me right now have changed up to ninety percent from what you were in Iran. If you are driving here and see an Iranian on the sidewalk who needs help, you step on your accelerator and continue your direction. But in Iran, if we saw somebody with a flat tire, everybody would stop and help them change or repair it.

The Iran-Iraq war was a problem for popular singers in Los Angeles, because many Iranians protested that concerts of this nature should not be given while people were dying in their homeland. After the 1988 ceasefire, the number of concerts in Los Angeles increased greatly.

Many Iranian performances take place on Iranian national festivals and holidays with performances on American holidays like Thanksgiving, Christmas, Valentine's Day, and the Fourth of July becoming common between 1988 and 1990. Iranian popular singers are beginning to travel to various parts of the United States, Canada, Europe, and Israel, and even to some Arabic countries in the southern Persian Gulf. This is especially true at the time of Persian New Year, *Nowrooz*, which starts on the first day of spring.

However, as their numbers in Los Angeles and other parts of the United States increase, Iranians are gradually abandoning their once fervent hopes of someday returning to Iran, hopes that had been prominent after the Revolution and during the Iran-Iraq war and heavily reinforced by the Iranian media in Los Angeles over the years. Media personalities speak less about politics in the 1990s; a popular theatrical group which formerly presented political plays on occasion now performs works of a comic nature. On one night in Los Angeles, three separate theatrical groups presented the following plays: "The Smell of Love," "The Night of Love," and "Love, Bread, and the Green Card." Advertisements for home loans appear frequently in the Iranian media. Recordings and performances of popular Iranian singers are compared to Michael Jackson, Sting, Prince and even Marlon Brando. Concerts of Iranian classical music by groups within Los Angeles and those visiting from Iran are often an introduction to it for many Iranians living in Los Angeles. However, they are introduced to this music out of its traditional performance context and acoustical nature— in large halls with electronic amplification.

Private Parties and Weddings

Private parties and weddings are two of the most important sources of income for popular singers. A performance can cost up to $5,000 per night, but one can also find singers that will come for a few hundred dollars as well. The Iranian Jewish community uses singers at their private parties and weddings and is able to pay high prices to attract the best performers. Consequently, singers try to become popular in their community. Although Iranian Jews were a part of traditional music-making in Iran during the first half of this century with some of the finest musicians and best musical instrument makers,[8] they have become high-paying listeners in Los Angeles, offering the highest remuneration to singers for performances at their social gatherings, especially weddings. In popular music, musicians and singers prefer to be paid cash. One of the reasons is to avoid bounced checks. This is mentioned indirectly by one famous singer in the media. Singers prefer to get at least 50% of their earnings before the performance and assurance that the money is valid. Musicians also prefer cash for performances and recording jobs. Most financial arrangements are not written down, but instead are conducted orally as was traditional in Iran; there is rarely a contract.

Some singers have been extremely successful simply from private parties and weddings—successful enough to open up a variety of businesses with the proceeds. They frequently achieve a great measure of acclaim, sometimes inappropriately so, according to some more conservative community members. Hydeh, one of the most financially successful singers, famous both in Iran and in the Iranian community in the United States, passed away in January 1990. Her funeral was attended by a few thousand Iranians all dressed in black, and flowers were sent from the wife and son of the late Shah. Some Iranians protested that a pop singer should not be given so much attention, referring to several national artists not as well known in the L.A. community whose recent deaths in Iran were not even mentioned by the Iranian news media in Los Angeles. They complained further that no one sent flowers to the thousands of young people who died in the Iran-Iraq war. For for three weeks after Hydeh's death, the Iranian media remained preoccupied with her life and career.

Cassettes and Recordings (The Music Industry)

There are about five Iranian music distributors in the Los Angeles area. Cassettes form the bulk of the music distributed, and every Iranian singer produces at least one new cassette each year. Recently, the lack of sufficient repertoire and the high costs of production and marketing have forced several less popular singers to join together to produce a recording. Number of copies produced ranges from 2,000 to 50,000 and the prices vary from $6.00 to $7.50. Cassettes of all types of Persian music are readily available from Persian grocery stores, many of which have large displays of Persian cassettes and posters of singers attached to their walls. Many are exported to Canada and Europe; usually Iranian companies in Los Angeles first distribute new tapes among Iranian communities in Europe, as they suspect that Iranian recordings from Los Angeles are likely to be copied and sold. Copying the tapes is an important business; cassettes from Iran can be copied by companies in Los Angeles without giving any rights to the composer or performer because Iran is not protected under international copyright law. (This phenomenon also occurs with books from Iran.) There is stiff competition among the Iranian music copying companies in Los Angeles, and often a permanent battle between them. During the Midnight Show television program on KSCI, Channel 18, in July 1993, Mary Apik, an actress who makes puppet show videos for Iranian children, said she spent $200,000 for production of her videos and is losing $50,000 to $60,000 on every video due to pirating and copying. Since 1989, Iranian music has also become available on CD in Los Angeles.

When the most popular Iranian singers go into the studio to record, they are usually supported by a single distributor who pays the composer, lyricist, players, and studio for recording time. Other singers have to come up with the total costs on their own and later give all rights to the distributor who advertises for the selling of the tape or CD. The cost of making a tape or CD can go as high as $50,000 for a new singer. For most of them, the first tape is their last.

In the Westwood section of Los Angeles, a Persian music store which offers cassettes and video tapes also serves as a ticket outlet for many concerts of Iranian music. An advertisement in April 1990, in the Persian weekly magazine *Javanan* promoted the latest cassette by the popular duet, Andy & Kouros. It featured several large photos and an article which compared the beautiful packaging of their cassette to one produced two years earlier by the international rock star, Sting. The advertisement boasts that the recording's quality "is comparable to albums of Michael Jackson, Prince and other famous American recording artists."

Some singers feel that it is necessary to revive Iranian traditional and folk music. Morteza, a pop singer and businessman, discussed this subject in an interview with the host of the TV program "Jam-E-Jam" in 1989. The host of the show asked Morteza why he sang folk music with electronic music accompaniment in a popular style, wondering if Morteza did not want to pay anyone for composing songs for him. Morteza's response to this was:

> "I wanted to bring them back to life, and I wanted to perform them with a progressive technique and technology. I wanted to give them to the young people here, and show them their culture. These musics were performed by a shepherd with a *nay* [a vertical bamboo flute] over long distances. But now, with my work, they have been revived. In Iran, many singers performed them, but when I did, these songs became more famous than ever before."

If one considers the wealth of performances and recordings of folk songs in Iran that are referred to by Morteza, one could immediately see that the repertoire he uses was not just performed by shepherds over long distances, but was performed widely by some of the most distinguished classical musicians. Morteza changed the role and meaning of these musics, adapting melodies and texts that were suitable for discos. For example, one of the songs he borrowed has a text where a person

addresses his mother saying, "Now is the time for fighting. My bullets are on my shoulder and my rifle is in my hand." Morteza arranged this text and the melody for dancing. The success of the recording only lasted a year.

Popular Iranian Music in Los Angeles

Vigen, among the first of famous popular singers who began his career forty years ago in Iran and has been living in the United States for the last twenty years (presently in Los Angeles), was called "Sultan-e Jazz." During an interview, he was questioned about the difference between Los Angeles and Iran. He answered that in Iran people would come to "Cafe Shemiran," have a drink and enjoy listening to the music, but in Los Angeles, members of his audience come to him after every performance and tell him that his singing reminded them of Iran. The interviewer, Sattar, who also is a singer, confirmed that this situation happens to him as well.[9]

As in cabarets, homesickness and nostalgia are themes for some songs and settings in both popular and classical Iranian concerts. Mo'in is the most popular singer at the present time; he is able to draw crowds of 6,000 Iranians to the Universal Amphitheater in Burbank, California. The text to one of his most famous songs is about his homeland, Esfehan, Iran:

> "I wish to go back to Esfehan, go there and sit next to the Zayandeh River and sing a song. I am here [L.A.], but my heart is there [Esfehan]. All of my desires are there…who can tell my sadness?"

All of the musical events in the Iranian community in Los Angeles—concerts of traditional and popular music, cabarets, cassettes, and their advertisements in the Persian media, are specifically designed for an Iranian audience. A significant portion of advertisements on Persian television is concerned with concerts, primarily of popular music. Most non-Iranians in Los Angeles are unaware of these Persian musical events and of the themes attached to them because they are all conducted and advertised in Persian. They are also unaware that music in the Iranian community in Los Angeles has created a variety of jobs for composers, lyricists, instrumentalists, singers, recording engineers, distributors, cabaret owners, and salespersons.

Iranian popular music is very successful in Los Angeles. There is no doubt that Los Angeles is the center for this type of music for all Iranians, those living in the United States, Europe, and even in Iran.[10] The activity of popular singers, musicians, concerts and recordings in Los Angeles has never been greater in the history of Iranian music of any type. A singer needs only a few pieces of equipment for making popular music—a synthesizer, a romantic song text and a melody in 6/8 rhythm. The complex artistic arrangements using a variety of instruments employed by musicans in Iran before 1979 have been exchanged for readily availabile synthesizers and other equipment that make the creative process easier and more profitable in Los Angeles. Occasionally, two popular singers will combine their performances to attract a larger audience. In the last few years, some popular singers have produced music videos, similar to those shown on MTV. Some earlier popular songs in Los Angeles had a social or political message, but those were unsuccessful. Iranians who are looking for messages or sophisticated poetry usually do not listen to dance music, and those who listen to this type of music rarely expect to hear profound messages while they are at a club, a party, or an Iranian disco complete with laser lights and steam.

Popular music has created many music industry jobs for Iranians as well as for some American musicians in Los Angeles. But in spite of Los Angeles's position as hub of Iranian popular music, the more than forty singers, television programs, recording studios, instrumentalists, and stores selling cassettes and CDs have neither an organization or society to represent them, nor a union to protect their interests. Musicians find it all too easy to lose a job even after playing with a popular singer for a long time.[11] Some older singers attempted to create a union for themselves, but were unsuccessful.[12]

Musical Training

Among some Iranians there is a desire to learn the traditional musical instruments of their homeland. However, it is often not possible to study and attain the level that one might achieve if one studies with a master of a certain instrument in Iran. As with most Western music teachers, teachers of Iranian music in Los Angeles often are skilled in only one instrument. However, Iranian music teachers in Los Angeles very often are called upon to teach traditional musical instruments that are not their specialty. There are two *santur* players with professional background who live in Los Angeles. For instruction in Western classical music, most Iranians prefer to have an Iranian teacher because of the convenient relationship and the ability of the teacher to communicate in Farsi with their children.

With regard to musical instruments, it is difficult to take instruments out of Iran, and it is forbidden to send them. Some Iranians in Los Angeles have attempted to make Persian musical instruments with varying degrees of professionalism, although some materials, such as mulberry wood, are difficult to obtain and necessitate modifications. Usually, musicians who come from Iran bring a few musical instruments for sale.

The most prominent musical instrument in Iranian music today is the *tar*. However, its prominence cannot be traced back for more than about 100 years (the time of Mirza Abdullah's father), as is the case with the *radif*. The musical instruments used in performances of Iranian traditional music employ ones that are not used by the Darvish and are not common to regional folk musics.

Iranian Classical Music in Los Angeles

Iranian classical music is based around the concept of mode, or *dastgah*, which as previously mentioned, can be loosely compared to the Arabic system of *maqam*. Improvisation (*Badahe-navazi*) plays a very important role in Iranian classical music. Every *dastgah* (mode) has a number of melodies (averaging around 45 per mode) called *gusheh*. The length of a *dastgah* played in its entirety averages around 40 minutes. There are seven *dastgahs* and five *avaz* derived from them which total twelve modes that are used over and over again in classical Iranian performance. When an instrumentalist knows all the *gushehs* in the *radif* (the entire repertoire of *dastgahs* and their *gushehs*), he or she is able to improvise on them. The tradition of improvisation is dependent on the knowledge and ability of the performer and plays an important role in creating music. One element which many Iranian musicians believe helps them to improvise better is a transitory moment known as *hal*, or "lived experience." It is a state of ecstasy in which the performer believes he can improvise at his best. For some Iranian musicians, *hal* also depends on having a "good" audience. Improvisation is necessary in order for the *radif* to exhibit the multitude of variation for a given melodic pattern.

Iranian classical music is traditionally a solo and private music for singer and instrument. The instrumentalist must follow the singer, and there usually is a drum accompaniment. Iranian musical instruments are designed to play complicated technical patterns; acoustically they are not designed for ensemble playing. Consequently, some instruments must be amplified in order to achieve a good balance in the ensemble. The instruments of Iranian classical music are rarely heard without amplification in Los Angeles concerts, and this phenomenon departs from the private and intimate nature of the music which has been the tradition all along. In Los Angeles, the majority of the audience has not heard acoustic performances on Iranian instruments due to all the electronic equipment and amplification that is necessary to produce a concert in a large hall.

Another important concept in Persian classical muisc is the notion of mysticism. If one closely

examines the "mystic" possibilities for Iranian classical music, one finds these to be related directly to mystical poetry rather than the music itself. Since text is the dominant part of an Iranian musical performance, the focus of the performance is on the poetry. The music must rely heavily on it. A receptive audience will be familiar with the entire text of a mystic poem and recognize it by the time the first verse is sung. Usually singers choose poems for conveying certain situations or emotions.[13] The texts of mystical poets are subject to a variety of interpretations and can be used to express sentiments relating to political situations, love, freedom, etc. The poetry used by contemporary classical musicians is associated with the non-metric part of the *radif*. The *tasnif* (a precomposed song) from the first half of this century is about love or the political situation of the time. The concept of *hal*, a transitory, internal mood, is associated with the poetry. Darvish[14] ritual uses the *daf* (frame drum) to accompany the mystical text in order to achieve *hal*. But unlike the Darvish traditions, which used repetitions of text and the rhythm of a frame drum to achieve *hal*, contemporary Iranian classical music does not have sufficient rhythmic dominance and must rely heavily on the text. The type of rhythms used in contemporary classical music do not promote excitement and stimulation when compared to those used in private Darvish ceremonies. This lack of a strong rhythmic element in Persian classical music can be linked to Islamic treatises and precepts of religious law over the centuries which were against a dominant rhythmic component.[15]

While Iranian classical music (*Musiqi-e Sonnati* or *Musiqi-e Asil*) is not in such demand as is popular music, it is nevertheless increasing in prominence and popularity thanks to the efforts of a number of skilled teachers and performers now living in Los Angeles. Even before the recent waves of immigration from Iran, *santur* player and music teacher Manoochehr Sadeghi performed frequently in Los Angeles. During the last two decades he has introduced Iranian classical music to students (both privately taught and through UCLA's ethnomusicology department), seminars, and a variety of festivals while also leading his own group of musicians. Another permanent group (with musicians on a temporary basis) started around 1985. Called "Ushshaq," it is headed by another *santur* player and music teacher, Isma'il Tehrani. Morteza Varzi, a *kamencheh* (vertical spiked fiddle) player, taught and led a group of Americans who played Iranian classical music. They are no longer active. However, the groups led by Sadeghi and Tehrani continue to perform. While their activity is limited to one or two concerts a year in Los Angeles, they are able to attract audiences of up to a thousand people.

Los Angeles also hosts concerts by Iranian classical musicians who come from Iran to perform for brief visits. These originated in 1987 when Mohammed Reza Lotfi, a noted *tar* player, appeared with another virtuoso, Hossein Alizadeh. The largest Iranian audience for classical music in Los Angeles was drawn in 1990, when Mohammed Reza Shajarian, the most renowned singer of classical music over the last 25 years, attracted an audience of more than 6,000 for three concerts, one of which was for the benefit of Iranian earthquake victims, and was held at the Music Center in downtown Los Angeles.

Concerts by Iranian musicians touring the Iranian communities in the United States have provoked many arguments and grievances over the years. Firstly, some of the classical musicians living in Los Angeles protested that those visiting musicians took audiences away from those having to make their living here. They contended that visiting artists are able to support themselves in Iran while Iranian musicians practicing their profession in Los Angeles are not allowed to perform in Iran. Another grievance arose from the pro-monarchist factions in Los Angeles who accused the visiting musicians of being opportunists at the service of the Islamic Republic who had come to collect money from Iranians in opposition to the current form of government. They were further accused of disseminating government propaganda urging people to return to Iran.[16]

On the other hand, musicians from Iran complain about their difficulties with finances and musical life in Iran. They believe it is difficult to concertize in Iran, claiming they are not free to play what they want (e.g., they avoid playing music of a joyful nature that is suitable for dance). Their profits are restricted to 30% of the total income, thus they find it preferable to travel to Iranian communities in Europe and the United States.

> With the production of some acceptable traditional music during the period 1986–88 which had government approval, there arose an interest by ordinary persons to buy cassettes of this music. Many amateurs also got into the market...There are several reasons for the decline after 1988: 1) the internal nature of the music, with its specific type of expression and quiet, calm, and stable nature cannot respond to society's various needs, especially those of the young, whose youth and energy require more movement; 2) government officials focus on traditional music and have actually ignored other types of music which consequently gave rise to numerous musicians with insufficient background who perform in the name of traditional music; 3) the cassette market is saturated many of the cassettes are similar to each other and lack artistic innovation. Officials dictate to maintain the old nature of the music. (Roshan Ravan 1990b:54)

In 1988, a number of Iranians in Los Angeles began to listen and look for Iranian classical music. Different factors contribute to the ascent and decline of popularity and interest in Iranian classical music in Iran and Los Angeles, despite their same source. Firstly, statistics on attendance at concerts would help to clarify the factors. The only concert hall in Tehran opened around 1967 and was built quickly in order to prepare for the Shah's coronation ceremonies (Massoudieh 1967). Prior to the construction of this concert hall, concerts took place in small halls at universities and elsewhere. There were only a few performances of Iranian classical music (mostly in a smaller hall next to the main one built for the Shah's coronation) as compared with the many Western classical music concerts, operas, and ballets that took place in the main concert hall. There were no concerts of Iranian classical music without a singer. The most popular of these singers before and after the Revolution was Mohammed Reza Shajarian. Attendance at his concerts over the last two decades illustrates the growing popularity of classical music both in Iran and in immigrant Iranian communities in the United States. Before the 1979 Revolution, Shajarian gave one performance in the main Rudaki Hall (1,350 capacity), another one at the Shiraz Festival and one or two performances in smaller concert halls each year. A generous estimation of the total attendance of all his concerts within a one year period is between two to three thousand. However, after the Revolution he would perform his concert ten nights in a row at the same hall. This program would then be taken abroad and performed throughout Europe and the United States. By far the largest audience he attracted was in Los Angeles. As mentioned earlier, in 1991 he repeated his concerts in Los Angeles three times. During the course of his first concert tour (Iran, Europe and the United States), approximately 50 to 60 thousand Iranians attended his concerts. The sharp rise in number of attendance after the Revolution clearly demonstrates the increasing popularity of Iranian classical music.

When comparing the situations in both Iran and Los Angeles, the factors attributing to his popularity show certain similarities and differences. In Iran, classical music is the only music sanctioned by the government, but even so, musicians and musical instruments are never shown on television although parts of their music may be broadcast. No other types of music are permitted.[17] In Los Angeles's Iranian community, where many musi-

cal styles compete for audience, classical music derives some of its appeal to evocations of nostalgia and homesickness. Some older members of the Los Angeles audience were crying at Shajarian's concerts; they felt Shajarian was able to "take them back home" and give them the feeling that they were in their motherland once again.[18] For some of the younger Iranian members of the audience, Shajarian's concert was a "renaissance" for music that heretofore had been uninteresting to them. Where previously they might have dismissed it as a "pessimistic" type of music, they came away from Shajarian's performance with a new appreciation of their musical heritage.

While the overall position of classical music in Los Angeles is positive, some problems must be noted. Classical musicians performing in Los Angeles to an audience less familiar and thus less critical may find themselves insufficiently challenged. Even though the creative process of improvisation can result in very beautiful moments when performed by an excellent instrumentalist, it is also used by many as an excuse not to practice. Sometimes the first practice takes place during the first concert. This results in concerts that have no performance pattern and are basically unrehearsed. Many Iranian musicians who perform in Los Angeles use the excuse of improvisation for abrupt changes; mistakes are often in the name of improvisation.[19] At the same time, many members of the audience are trying to experience the music in their own manner and mood.

As an attempt to generate interest, some Iranian classical musicians incorporated arrangements of regional Iranian folk musics for their classical instruments to increase the interest of an audience. When in Los Angeles, musicians from Iran decorate their stages with Iranian rugs, cushions, plants, and flowers. None of this was part of a traditional classical performance back in Iran: even the preceding generation in Iran sat on chairs and dressed in suits and ties, including Ahmad Ebadi, the son of Mirza Abdullah (mentioned earlier) and master of *setar* in Iran who appeared on stage in Rudaki Hall and on television dressed in suit and tie and stood in front of the orchestra as the soloist. Despite the fact that the acoustic nature of classical Iranian music is suited to small surroundings, a sound system is generally used in Los Angeles concerts. Because many musical instruments used in Iranian classical music do not produce loud sounds, amplification is necessary when performing in large halls. This tends to counteract the intimate nature of Iranian classical music.

Musical Behavior in Los Angeles

There are different types of behavior exhibited by musicians in the performance of Iranian classical music in Los Angeles. Performers who live in Los Angeles generally sit on chairs, sometimes looking at printed music on music stands. They wear Western attire, usually a suit and tie. Persian rugs and some type of Iranian symbols tyically adorn the stage. In contrast, musicians from Iran who perform concerts in Los Angeles generally sit on cushions covered with Persian rugs; they often close their eyes while playing. When touring abroad, Iranian musicians frequently dress in some distinct national costume which very often is a variant of some type of folk dress (e.g., Kurdish wide-legged pants), although these would not be worn were they performing at home in Iran. Audiences for these performances must be absolutely quiet. If a rare joyful piece is performed, the members of the audience must not exhibit their happiness. Should a newcomer to these type of concerts be unfamiliar with the expected modes of etiquette and exhibit inappropriate behavior such as clapping, other members of the audience, who praise the music as "divine sound" will often try to correct the offender's behavior. The performer himself may stop the rhythmic piece and continue with the *avaz* (non-rhythmic part of the *radif*) or even put his instrument on the stage, look at the audience in an angry fashion, and wait until they become quiet.

The musicians' demand for absolute respect from the audience has historical roots dating back to the first part of the twentieth century when the status of musicians declined. A commonly used derogatory term for musician was *Amaleh-e Tarab*, literally "mirmal-maker." Later, the equally problematic Arabic term for musician, *mutreb,* was employed.[20]

The low status of music and the absence of social and professional opportunity for musicians during the twentieth century created a situation which did not encourage musicians to perform their art. The lack of dignity and respect created conditions which allowed them to restrict their performance to parties, *bazm*, and smaller social gatherings. A few prominent musicians who came from religious families found it necessary to use an alias at the beginning of their career to avoid giving offense. Musicians made a concentrated effort to improve the attitudes towards them—they preferred to call themselves *musiqi-dan*, a term similar in meaning to *mutreb*, but without the negative or derogatory connotation. This behavior and other practices used by musicians during concerts were part of their strong attempts to gain back the respect and dignity they felt they deserved.

Media and Professional Relationships

The majority of programs for concerts of Iranian classical music are in Farsi and give biographical information about the performers, without explanation of the music or instruments used. Advertisements for those musicians coming from Iran occur usually on one of the Iranian television programs. There are also many daily and weekly newspapers and magazines, and three 24-hour radio programs in Farsi. Advertisements often depend on the relationships of those involved in the production of a concert with those controlling the media, and also whether the music is of a popular or classical nature. The advertisers often have interviews with the performers prior to the performance, but it is rare to find any kind of followup about these performances, including critiques. There is not a single critic in any of the Iranian media in Los Angeles for the multitude of concerts.

Perhaps advertisers in the media do not criticize because they do not want to risk losing future business.[21] Also, when one advertiser obtains the advertisement for a concert, other media do not mention the performance, even if it is a momentous event.

It seems unlikely that Iranian classical musicians are able to make a living from their concerts and the few students they instruct. (Several tapes of Iranian classical music were produced a few years ago, but were not in great demand.) It is profitable for classical musicians from Iran to come to Los Angeles for concerts and tour other North American cities with substantial Iranian populations. Musicians on tour from Iran usually stay at the homes of their enthusiasts; still the tradition exists where wealthier Iranians host them at their private parties (*bazm*) in Los Angeles and elsewhere. Oftentimes there is stiff competition between wealthier Iranians for hosting the touring musicians while in Los Angeles. Nevertheless, recent statistics show that the number of concerts of classical music is not as great as it was in the late 1980s. The audiences are also smaller. Classical musicians who depend heavily on improvisation produce artistic moments during the course of a two-hour performance, but like popular musicians, they face problems with repetition, and use body movements and stage settings to create new performances.

It is noteworthy to mention that few Iranian musicians performing in Los Angeles, whether they be from Los Angeles or Iran, have any desire to perform for non-Iranians, as long as they have strong support from their own ethnic group. Those who come from Iran have the freedom and opportunity when in Los Angeles to perform what they were not able to when in Iran. However, the freedom and opportunity rarely results in any significant innovation in the music.

During the sixty years of public performance in Iran, there were occasional amateur critiques, some of which were in actuality personal attacks (Darvishi 1988). The dearth of professional criticism is also

a problem in Los Angeles. Musicians, both popular and classical, have self-proclaimed accolades in their advertisements and published biographies. Pop singers are given a variety of titles, including: "the sun of Iranian music who rises from east to west," "rhythmic master," "the hot rhythmic pulse of the city," and the "Master of Iranian pop music." Classical musicians frequently call popular singers and musicians *mutreb*, bringing complaints from the popular music personnel who believe this derogatory term should not be applied to them because they are responsible for making people happy. For classical musicians, the term *ostad* (master) is the most desirable name which they are willing to assume. Recently, it appears that attempts to boost this term are occurring, e.g., "world master," "one of the top Iranian singers in the world," one musician from Iran performing in Los Angeles refers to himself as a "neoclassical musician," although this Western term has no Iranian equivalent.[22]

Conclusions

One can summarize then that music assumed a role of greater importance for the large number of Iranians who settled in the Los Angeles metropolitan area since the fall of the Shah in 1979 than for those living in Iran. Although popular and classical Iranian music seem to serve very different needs—one strictly for entertainment purposes, the other to evoke, deep, reflective moods—they both serve as cultural identifiers for members of the Iranian community in Los Angeles who reminisce about life back in Iran.

Popular music is the most attractive event for Iranians and can draw several thousands. This is perhaps the reason why singers call themselves the "ambassador of friendship" and Cabaret Tehran is known as "Little Tehran." In the 1990s, the less Westernized forms of music associated with southern Tehran's cabarets disappeared. Various groups have attempted to bring Iranians together for a variety of purposes, but none is as successful as those which involve popular music.[23] During the 1980s the popular singers appeared at Iranian political demonstrations and were used to attract crowds in protests against the Iranian government. Even the media used their appearance at a rally to encourage Iranians to attend. In the 1990s, however, there are almost no demonstrations. Successful popular singers are able to draw huge Iranian crowds and attain great financial success.

The strict use of the Persian language in the media and in both popular and classical concerts (even though first-generation Iranian Americans may not understand Farsi very well) assures continuity in the Iranian culture of Los Angeles. Themes of nostalgia, homesickness, sorrow, and melancholy have been prominently displayed in much of the music presented in Los Angeles.

Persian classical music, while less prominent than the various pop traditions, is also increasing in popularity among Iranians in Los Angeles, and has undergone a series of stylistic and social changes. For many older community members it evokes feelings of nostalgia, while younger audiences find in it a sense of pride in their cultural heritage.

Iranian music, whether classical or popular, now serves a unifying role, bringing together Iranians of different religious, political and social backgrounds. The huge number of Iranian media that arose in the area since the Revolution has greatly assisted in the dissemination of musical culture within the Iranian community and attests to the growing popularity of this music in its adopted homeland of Los Angeles.

NOTES

1. 1990 Census figures obtained from the U.S. Bureau of Census on October 29, 1993 listed 108,875 Iranians living in California. Census bureau officers reported that questions on ethnicity were only asked to one out of every six households, making the figure inaccurate. The number 250,000 is a conservative estimate given by the Iranian media in Los Angeles.

2. Iranian television programs began with only thirty minutes of airtime a week, but now are presented several hours each day.

3. Letter from Consul Hardy to Mrs. Brown who was looking for Persian musical instruments, April 7, 1889. *The Metropolitan Museum of Art Collection of Musical Instruments.* New York: New York.

4. See *Music Education in the Countries of the Orient: Proceedings of a Conference Held in Tehran* (1967).

5. Author's interview with the arranger, July 1991.

6. This interview was aired on KSCI, the International Channel in Los Angeles (Channel 18).

7. The text of this song is as follows:
"Pennyroyal flower, is our world sleeping? Don't you see that God is sleeping and somebody has come and under his name is beheading the love? Pennyflower, pennyflower, if my heart is bloody today, I still have my hope until it will shake the world one day."

8. John Taylor wrote to Mrs. Brown on April 19, 1900, that he could not find a single Iranian musical instrument. It was recommended that he ask Iranian Jews to bring him them. (*The Collection of Musical Instruments at the Metropolitan Museum of Art,* New York: New York.)

9. Diyar TV Program, April 2, 1993.

10. Recordings of Iranian popular music from Los Angeles are distributed illegally underground in Iran and are in great demand.

11. A *tombak* player (drum) said he lost his job with a singer after accompanying him for several years because the singer decided to begin using an electronic rhythm box.

12. Discussion by popular musicians, March 5, 1989, at UCLA.

13. Poetry has a strong meaning for Iranians. It is also used by fortunetellers, soothsayers, and ordinary persons for predictions of future actions.

14. The Darvishes are the only sect of Iranian Muslims who use music in their rituals and ceremonials.

15. For example, Ghazzali (1058–1111).

16.   Over the last three years, the Iranian government has asked people who have left the country after the Revolution to return and take their capital, skill, and education back to Iran. Most of the Iranian immigrants living in the United States are skilled and educated, and some are wealthy.

17.   The hall was named Rudaki. After the Islamic Revolution, it was changed to Vahdat.

18.   The Iranian Symphony Orchestra is still in existence and has a few programs each year, but most of its members have left the country.

19.   This response was often repeated when the author interviewed members of the audience.

20.   Personal experience of the author when performing with several classical Iranian musicians.

21.   The terms *mutreb* (musician) and *raqqas* (dancer) are still used today as insults.

22.   This author was called by a prominent member of the Iranian media as a best source for discussing two prominent musicians who were coming from Iran to Los Angeles for a concert tour. When criticizing earlier concerts of these same musicians, the media anchor abruptly ended the conversation.

23.   In 1992 a group of old masters had a concert tour in the United States, but were unable to attract large audiences. They appeared on stage in a simple manner to show how Iranian classical music had been performed over the last few decades.

24.   See biographical descriptions of Iranian musicians in the *Program Guide to the Los Angeles Festival*. August–September 1993.

25.   Between August 13 and November 5, 1989, there was an exhbition of Iranian (Persian) Art and Culture from the fifteenth century at the Los Angeles County Museum of Art. It took five years to collect all the materials from throughout the world. It was expected that huge crowds of Iranians would be attracted to this exhibit. Although the exhibit was well received by the general public, this was not true for Iranians. However, on the closing day there were performances of Iranian music and dance, and several hundred Iranians attended to participate in the festivities.

REFERENCES CITED

Barkechli, Mehdi
   1963   *La musique traditionalle de l'Iran, les systemes de la musique traditionelle de l'Iran (Radif) avec transcription en notation musicale occidentale, par Moussa Ma'aroufi.* Tehran: Secretariat d'état auz beaux-arts.

Caton, Margaret Louise
   1983   "Tasnif: A Genre of Persian Vocal Music." Ph.D. dissertation, UCLA.

Chelkowski, Peter J., ed.
   1979   *Ta'zieh: Ritual and Drama in Iran.* New York: New York University Press and Soroush Press.

Darvishi, Mohammad Reza
   1988   "Vay az in naqdha-e musiqi." *Adineh 22.* Tehran.

Farhat, Hormaoz
   1990   *The Dastgah Concept in Persian Music.* Cambridge, New York: Cambridge University Press.
   1973.   *The Traditional Art Music of Iran.* Tehran: High Council of Culture and Art.

Farmer, Henry George
   1938   *The Instruments of Music on the Taq-e Bustan Bas-Reliefs.* n.p.

Ghazzali, Mohammad (1058–1111)
   n.d.   *Kimiya-e Sa'adat.* n.p.

Kuchertz, Jozef and Mssoudieh, M.T.
   1976   *Musik in Bushehr (sud Iran).* Munchen: E. Katzbichler.

Kuchertz, Jozef
   1975(?) *Volksgesange aus Iran.* Germany: D. Reimer.

Mallah, Husein 'Ali
   1975   *Tarikh-e musiqi-e nezami.* Tehran: Tehran Intisharat-e Hunar va Mardom 1354.

Massoudieh, Mohammad Taghi
   1973   *Hochzeitlieder aus Balucestan.* Regensburg: Gustav Basse.
   1988   *Musik in Balucestan.* Hamburg: Karl Deter Wanger.
   1973   *Tradition und Wanden in der Persichen Musik des 19 Jahrhunderts.* Regensburg: Gustav Basse.
   1978   *Radif vocal de la musique traditionnelle de L'Iran par Mahmud-e-Karimi. Transcription et analyse par Mohannad Taghi Massoudien.* Tehran: Viazarat-e Farhang va Hunar.
   1967   *Majalleh-e Musiqi.* No. 112–113. Tehran.

Music Education in the Countries of the Orient: Proceedings of a Conference Held in Tehran. Organized by the Asian Music Circle and the Iranian National Music Committee,

September 7–12, 1967. Tehran: International Institute for Comparative Music Studies.

Rushan Ravan, Kambiz

   1990a   *Barrasi-e vaz'iyat-e fi'li-e musiqi dar iran,*
           No. 1.

   1990b   *Kitab-e Mahur.* Tehran: Muasseseh-e
           Farhangi-e Mahur.

Shamin, Ali Asghar

   1992   *Iran dar dureh-e Saltanat-e Qajar Qarn-e
           Sizdahum va himeh-e avale-e Qarn-e
           chahardahum-e Hijiri-e Qamari.* Tehran: 'Ilmi.

CONTEXT-DEPENDENT AESTHETICS: MARIACHI MUSIC IN LOS ANGELES[1]

Steven Pearlman

MARIACHI MUSIC IS RECOGNIZED throughout the world as one of Mexico's important cultural symbols. Its origins are in the mixture of European and indigenous forms and values. With the Spanish conquest in the sixteenth century, and the ensuing suppression of aboriginal culture through European values carried by the *conquistadores* and missionaries, aboriginal music performance faded, but was transformed structurally into the antecedents of modern Mexican folk and popular music, in a process that has continued for more than 400 years. Indigenous instruments were replaced by Spanish imports, such as the harp, guitar, and violin, and the music that developed was identifiably Spanish, but it also carried values and meanings relevant to the local populations. Evidence of the continuity of indigenous musical values and their mixture with the European is found in the new musical instruments that evolved in Mexico. Two of these were the *guitarrón* and *vihuela*, which now form the rhythmic foundation of the modern mariachi.

Current understanding of the word *mariachi* reflects the continuity of this indigenous structural view. Whereas previous etymological perspectives had the word coming from the French word *mariage*, applied during a period of occupation in the 1860s (and clearly false since several sources[2] report that the word *mariachi* appears in print at least fifteen years before the French occupation), more current approaches (Rafael 1982) suggest an indigenous origin and imply that the word *mariachi* has been applied to the various evolving ensembles from indigenous to modern times.

As this once local and regional music matured in the state of Jalisco, in the area of Cocula and Tecalitlán, it was caught up in the dialectic of Mexican political life. By the early twentieth century, mariachis in Mexico City continued the process of synthesizing and evolving, expanding repertoire to include new imported genres and eventually bridging the symbolic gap between the two classes in Mexico. Mariachis became Mexico's cultural representatives to the world and a metaphor for egalitarianism and cultural unity at the end of the Mexican Revolution. One of the ways this was accomplished was by abandoning the *calzón blanco*, the white cotton clothing that had been traditional for the musicians and identified with the rural poor, and adopting the *traje de charro*, the dress suit of the *hacendado*. This change of attire, sometimes attributed to Mariachi Vargas de Tecalitlán, enabled the mariachi to represent both rich and poor, both urban and rural, and to become a cultural symbol. It was at this point as well, in the 1920s and 1930s, that the trumpet became a standard component of the mariachi, fixing the basic instruments represented in the modern mariachi.

For the purposes of this study the mariachi is thus conceived as an ensemble that includes a minimum of four instruments (and musicians), the *guitarrón*, the *vihuela*, the violin, and the trumpet;

members of which are dressed in suits that at least represent the *traje de charro*; and whose repertoire includes several standard forms and selections that are typical of the region in Mexico where mariachi music evolved, but are not necessarily included in other regional musical styles of Mexico. This framework thus excludes many other forms of Mexican music. Despite the fact that many non-Mexicans refer to almost any Mexican music or musician as "mariachi," the term in proper usage is quite specific.

In the United States the music performed by mariachis has become an important focus of ethnic identification for both Mexicanos and Chicanos, although each of these groups brings different levels of familiarity and expectation to their understanding of mariachi music. For the non-Hispanic community the mariachi has come to be an important component of theme parties and community events designed to celebrate Hispanic culture, and this community too has its preconceptions concerning what mariachis do and what they should look like and sound like. In addition, each of these groups, Mexicanos, Chicanos, and non-Hispanics, have their own ideas as to where mariachi music should best be heard, and what constitutes "authenticity" in mariachi music. The result, in Los Angeles, is a variable aesthetic of mariachi music performance which is linked to context and performance style.

CONTEXT

"Context" in this case refers to all those features that define the performance environment. Thus context goes beyond simply place of performance and type of event to include other variables. Some of these additional salient variables of context include economic structure (and constraints) of the performance environment; corporateness of the performing group; audience composition, including ethnicity, gender, and age distributions; and performer-audience proximity and interaction.

The range of places where mariachi performance occurs includes *cantinas* and bars; restau-

rants; private parties in homes, parks, and rented halls; and concert performance in a variety of venues. In addition to regular or occasional performance at bars and restaurants, events at which mariachis perform include a wide range of life cycle markers such as baptisms, birthday parties, *quinceañeras*, graduations, weddings, anniversaries, and funerals, plus performance at music festivals or other events that emphasize ethnic understanding or identification. A variable related to place and event type is audience composition. Audiences range from being predominantly adult male, to adult mixed gender, to family groups. Apparent audience ethnicity can range from all Mexican, through mixed Latino and Chicano and mixed Latino and non-Latino, to predominantly non-Latino.

Another part of context is the proximity or spatial separation between mariachi and audience, and the degree of interaction between the two. These range from high proximity and high interaction, through increasing separation and decreasing personal interaction, to the wide spatial separation and low interaction characteristic of most concert performances of music in the United States.

Mariachis work under a wide range of economic conditions, and the structure of the economic environment is another part of context. Different economic structures or conditions include performance on a "per song" basis; performance that is remunerated on the basis of a single event, which may include regular weekly performance underwritten by a restaurant owner where all musicians earn the same amount of money, and some types of concert events; hourly compensation, most common for private parties; and salaried performance where there is a differential scale of remuneration, with checks issued on a regular basis, and which may include features of both event-based and hourly based compensation.

Corporateness, indicating the extent to which the performing group is an ongoing entity irrespective of its component members, is another variable of context. The range of corporateness among mariachi ensembles includes unnamed pickup groups that work together for an evening or event and where decisions to perform may be somewhat spontaneous; named pickup groups, where an individual prints business cards with a name, but recruits musicians on a per event basis; established, named ensembles that have a core group of members that perform most events, with outside substitutes recruited on an "as needed" basis; and institutional ensembles that have more members than actually perform at any single event, allowing substitutions for illness or vacations, and replacements from a pool of musicians who work together regularly and know repertoire and arrangements in common.

This wide range of variables produces a continuum of performance contexts with several discernible nodes, or context types, which I have chosen to label *"cantina," "chamba,"* "restaurant," "dinner theater," and "concert."

THE *CANTINA* CONTEXT

The setting of *cantina-* context performance, for the most part, is in small to medium sized beer and pool bars known as *cantinas*; it is comparable to a common public performance context found in Mexico. In Los Angeles this context is predominantly found in Mexican neighborhoods, and the audience in the *cantina* context is predominately Mexican and male. While couples and family groups may be present, the audience males are the focus of performer-audience interaction, and they become clients when they request songs. The mariachis will play at the client's location in the establishment for specific requests.

The "per song" economic basis is one of the defining characteristics of *cantina*-context performance. Mariachis working *al talón*, or on a per song basis, generally charge a fixed amount for every song played. One musician maintains a list of songs requested by the client, who is then charged the total bill when he is finished requesting songs; in cases of dispute he is presented with the list as evidence of the total number of songs performed. When one client finishes his requests, to which there is theoretically no limit and which often include five to ten selections, the mariachi moves on to another client in the same establishment, if there is one. Charges are often based on a rate schedule of approximately $1 to $2 per musician per song. Other variables which may affect the amount charged include whether the *cantina* charges a fee or percentage to the mariachi to allow them to work in the establishment and maintain their exclusive right to solicit clients there, and whether the group leader takes an extra amount "for gas" if he is also acting as chauffeur. For example, a five piece mariachi might charge $7 per song, which would include $1 each for the musicians, an extra dollar for the *cantina*, and an extra dollar for the leader to compensate him for his expenses. Nightly income under this economic basis is unpredictable. It is possible for musicians to earn as much as $100, given the right establishment and the right clientele. It is just as likely however that mariachis might spend several hours available for prospective clients, waiting, talking, eating, drinking, practicing, and end up with only $5 to $10, barely enough money for food.

Figure 1: Client participation in cantina context

Most mariachi musicians will play in the *cantina* context from time to time, but for some musicians this is the only context in which they work. Groups that work *al talón* are small, composed of four or five musicians in most cases, but sometimes more. On many occasions the groups that work *al talón* are arranged on the spur of the moment, and it is common that some of the musicians in any given ensemble on any night may never have performed previously with the others. Individuals may arrange in advance to meet at particular locations, but often temporary groups are formed from local "hiring halls." There are several locations in Los Angeles where musicians looking for temporary work congregate. They come dressed in their *trajes*, with their instruments, and play pool or talk until a work opportunity develops. There is a generally low to medium level of corporateness among groups that work in the *cantina* context.

The *cantina* context is generally characterized by high musician-client proximity, and high interaction levels. When performing for particular clients the musicians will often literally surround them, enveloping the individual at the bar or the group at a table within a wall of sound. Clients often sing with the mariachi as well, and are encouraged to do so. The structure of the environment fosters intrinsically high levels of performer-audience interaction.

THE *CHAMBA* CONTEXT

Chambas are performances of a non-recurring nature, generally private parties held to mark important life cycle events. These events may be held at homes, churches, public parks, restaurants and rented halls.

While the physical location may vary widely, the economic basis is one of the primary markers of this context. There is generally a verbal or written contractual arrangement between a mariachi and an individual client to perform for a particular period of time in exchange for a fixed fee, usually determined on an hourly basis, given a minimum of two or three hours. There is some variability in the fees charged for hourly performance in the Los Angeles area, ranging from $150 to $250 per hour

for a four piece group, through $250–$350 for a seven piece group, and as much as $500 or more per hour for the largest ensembles. Individual musicians expect to be paid between $30 and $50 per hour for *chambas*, with the leader's or organizer's share being somewhat higher.

Chamba-context performance may include strolling to play at individual tables, similar in appearance to *cantina*-context performance, but it just as often involves playing in a fixed location, for the benefit of all those in attendance. There is thus the potential for reduced audience proximity and reduced performer-audience interaction as compared to the *cantina* context. Audience composition in the *chamba* context most commonly includes both males and females of diverse ages, although for some occasions age distributions may be more limited. A range of apparent ethnicities is also found, although for many family events the audience is almost exclusively Mexican or of Mexican descent, and at some "theme" parties the audience may be entirely non-Latino.

In some cases repertoire may be fixed or established, as is common in liturgical Masses played in church. In most cases, however, selections performed are based on client request. Often the client who engages the mariachi for the *chamba* provides the mariachi with a list of songs to be played. This also serves to reduce performer-audience interaction. On the occasions when mariachis stroll from table to table interaction may be similar to that found in the *cantina* context.

While some *chambas* are performed by "named" pick-up groups, with musicians recruited by the musician with whom the original contractual arrangement was made, most performance in *chamba* context is done by groups with a higher level of corporateness: named, established ensembles. Clients who engage mariachis for such events usually have heard the group perform at some other event, and like to be assured that the group they hire will be essentially similar to the one they have heard and seen.

THE RESTAURANT CONTEXT

The restaurant context includes formal business establishments that hire mariachis to perform on a regular basis, ranging from family restaurants to nightclubs. Audiences include both males and females, and are generally more or less gender balanced. Age distributions vary depending on the nature of the establishment. They may include multigenerational family groups in restaurants, or be predominantly young adult singles or adult couples in nightclubs. Apparent ethnicity tends toward being Mexican, of Mexican descent, or generalized Latino, particularly in the nightclubs. Audience ethnicity is more mixed in the family and chain restaurants, becoming predominantly non-Latino in some areas, where mariachis become part of the ambience of a specialty ethnic restaurant rather than being a normal part of daily cuisine and cultural experience. Audience proximity and performer-audience interaction are both generally less than in *cantina* context. Both are further reduced in those instances where mariachis perform on a stage with microphones, usually in front of a dance floor, typical in some restaurant/dance club establishments.

Weekly performance that is underwritten by a restaurant adds an element of financial security to mariachi performance. Regular fixed performances, known as *plantas*, are considered permanent; some in fact last for decades. The primary economic relationship in *planta*-based performance is between the mariachi and the restaurant owner, who pays the mariachis a fixed amount of money for the entire performance period. The restaurant owner usually structures some aspects of performance to enhance his business: having the mariachi take regular breaks may allow table turnover in a busy establishment for example. Most *planta* performances pay between $50 and $100 per musician for a three to five hour engagement. Remuneration may also be related to the number of nights per week in the same establishment, the expected permanence of the engagement, and the fringe benefits, such as meals and drinks, either free or at reduced prices, which accompany the contract price. Payment is almost always in cash; establishments that pay by check are usually charged more in order to compensate for deductions and the potential inconvenience of having to cash checks. Mariachis usually play requests when asked, and accept tips, but won't ordinarily charge a fixed rate per song. Tips may add anywhere from $5 to $40 to total income per musician. This economic basis, a guaranteed payment plus tips, typifies restaurant-context performance.

In some contexts transitional between *cantina* and restaurant an establishment may pay $20 or $25 per musician for a fixed period, usually an hour, often to accompany aficionados, or those who enjoy singing with the mariachi, but still require them to be on site for four or five hours during which time they would be available to work on a per-song basis.

Besides economics, the other main identifying and structuring feature in restaurant context is group corporateness. Since restaurant owners expect continuity, and mariachis receive regular dependable income, ensembles of fixed membership, generally ranging in size from four to eight musicians, become more common. These are generally named, established groups organized around a central core of musicians, although there may be occasional substitutes. The groups accept engagements for *chambas* that don't conflict with their regular *planta* schedule, with clients for *chambas* often drawn from *planta* audiences, engendering substantial overlap in some features of *chamba* and restaurant contexts. Many organized groups will have three or four *plantas*, and will work at one or two *chambas* per week, generating dependable incomes of between $300 and $500 per week per musician for about fifteen to twenty hours of performance time.

THE DINNER THEATER CONTEXT

The dinner theater context, found in large restaurants often owned or operated by mariachis or directors of the groups, features large, institutional ensembles based on high levels of corporateness, often including eight to twelve musicians per show and a total group membership of twenty or more, performing shows of fixed length for a widely varied clientele. Shows are generally around an hour in length, and are usually followed by intermissions of an hour to allow for table turnover and new seatings. Audience composition is usually gender balanced, age distribution is broad, and apparent ethnicity is mixed, including Mexicans, Chicanos, and non-Latinos. Some of the more famous dinner theater contexts are established tourist stops on international tours, further increasing apparent ethnic diversity. There are only a few dinner theater contexts in the greater Los Angeles area.

Dinner theater contexts feature stage performance with microphones, which symbolically, if not actually, decreases performer-audience proximity, and results in low levels of performer-audience interaction. Requests are not solicited and are usually not played.

The economic basis of dinner theater context is based on salaried payment of employee-musicians. Musicians expect to perform from three to five nights per week in establishments that are open nightly. The large number of employee-musicians allows for days off, and illness and vacation substitutes. Income is based on days per week, seniority, and the director's perception of the individual's importance to the group, resulting in a wide diversity of incomes within the group, as opposed to the relative egalitarianism found in the other performance contexts. Performance at *chambas* is somewhat limited by the need for a large group to be present at the restaurant on a daily basis, but the large core of musicians ensures that some musicians are always available for outside work. Annual incomes for low seniority musicians working in the dinner theater context are thus often less than those who perform in restaurant/*chamba* contexts, but *planta*-based musicians often reach a plateau income, and within the employee structure of dinner theater context there is some opportunity for economic advancement.

THE CONCERT CONTEXT

The concert context is exemplified by contractual agreements to perform on stage for single events, for specified time periods, and is in many ways best considered a single event subset of dinner theater context. Mariachis that perform in concert context are highly corporate—named, established groups or institutional ensembles—and are usually large, ranging from a minimum of seven musicians to groups as large as twelve to fifteen or more. Separation of performers and audience is high, and there is little opportunity for interaction between performers and individual audience members. Audience composition varies, and although it is typically gender balanced, age and ethnicity distributions are broad. Concert-context audiences typically include Mexicanos, Chicanos, and non-Latinos at the same event. With the exception of economic basis and physical place, in general the context variable values for concert context are the same as for dinner theater context; in the subsequent discussion these two contexts will be considered together, and referred to as "show" context.

PERFORMANCE STYLES

Performance style includes a number of variables, some of which already mentioned, which describe the physical and aural features of performance in the various contexts. These variables include: appearance and dress, which includes such features as clothing; spatial arrangement of the performing group; choreography and synchronicity; genre distribution, i.e., relative frequency of performance of different song types; set time, or the amount of time spent in performance, including the ratio or performance time to non-performance time within sets, measuring the amount of set time spent in talking, interaction, or anything other than musical performance; average song length, including the parameters which affect average song length such as the methods by which

Figure 2a: *"Caminos de Michoacan"*—standard arrangement

Figure 2b: *"Caminos de Michoacan"*—truncated arrangement

songs are expanded and contracted and the number of songs per hour; and general qualities of musicianship and expression of musical dynamics in performance. There is a clear correspondence between performance style and context, and the range of performance styles can similarly be expressed along a continuum. Identified performance styles include the *al talón* style, the *planta/chamba* style, and the entertainment or "show" style, which correspond to the *cantina* context, the restaurant (and *chamba*) context, and the dinner theater (and concert) context respectively.

THE *AL TALÓN* STYLE

The *al talón* performance style, referring to the pattern of moving from table to table, or from *cantina* to *cantina*, and to the solicitation sometimes necessary to coax potential clients into requesting and paying for songs, is most commonly found in the *cantina* context.

Since mariachis that perform in *cantina* context are essentially pick-up bands, despite the occasional central core of musicians who may work together, there is little opportunity to develop new arrangements or to compose new pieces, nor is there incentive to do so. No outside rehearsals take place, and standardized arrangements of songs are performed only on request. There is often a particular recorded version which serves as a model for a song, and reasonably competent musicians will know its introduction, ending, and embellishments or *adornos*. In addition, however, there are standardized *al talón* versions which are also universally known. *Al talón* versions have shorter introductions and endings, often fewer verses than the versions of the same songs performed in other contexts, and are often performed at slightly faster tempi.

An example of a standard arrangement (Figure 2a) and an abbreviated performance in *al talón* style (Figure 2b) illustrates this: the song structure is intact but truncated in *al talón* style. In both these selections this section serves as the *entrada*; the first example, the standard version played in *planta/chamba* style, has four phrases, while the second, the common *al talón* version, has only the first and fourth phrases. When this introductory melody is repeated between each verse, as is common in this song genre, the net difference in elapsed time may be as much as 30 seconds.

One reason for the shortened versions is that it is to the musicians economic advantage to play as many songs per hour as possible, since *cantina*-context clients are requesting and paying for songs on a per song basis. Customer satisfaction is maintained in part by the ability to perform all songs requested, in part by the personal attention given them by the ensemble. Even when a song is requested that is not universally known, or which has no model or standard arrangement, the use of formulaic structures enable performance as long as one of the musicians knows the lyrics.

When there are no requests the mariachi will either move on to another location or wait for additional customers to come into the *cantina*. This wait time might be spent in rehearsing new songs recently released, since a certain percentage of requests will be new songs people have heard on the radio. It might also just be spent in conversation. As a result there is wide variability in percentage of time spent in actual performance, and duration of performance in *al talón*-style performance. The method of earning money is fixed, i.e., it is piecework income, only occasionally buffered by a minimum guarantee. Percentage of time spent in performance (performance ratio) may range from as little as 5% (one song performed in an hour, when no client is willing to pay for a song) to 90% (or more), wherein 50 to 54 minutes of an hour would be spent in actual performance, with the rest spent in negotiation with clients. The number of songs performed may be as high as 25 per hour. Song durations in *al talón* style average less than 2:20, and the total time spent in performance (set

time) varies widely due to the absence, in most cases, of defined sets.

On the less profitable evenings, where few songs are requested, the social aspect becomes more important than the economic. Musicians may spend their time and money between requests drinking, playing pool, and socializing. They get to know each other, discuss conditions in Mexico, and gossip about local bands and players, or musicians who have only recently arrived from Mexico.

For many of the recent arrivals, the *cantina* context and *al talón* style are preferred, particularly if they don't have local contacts. On the one hand it is a comfortable context, similar to past experience for most Mexican musicians. In addition, since most musicians play *al talón* from time to time, and since group configuration is so flexible, it is often a good way for a musician new to the area to make contacts, to get information about local performing contexts and bands, and thus expand his opportunities for finding work.

Besides the variability in income, percentage of performance times, and set times, other aspects of *al talón*-style performance are consistent from event to event. Since *cantina*-context groups generally do not have corporate existence, and show evidence of few if any of the features of group organization, dress is almost invariably simple: black *trajes* in the *charro* cut, but often without *botonadura* (silver decorations) on the pants, and often without *moños* (ties), since it is unlikely that the musicians will have the same style ties in common. This common denominator of dress allows participation by all in an egalitarian fashion. Similarly, since performance in *cantina* context is usually done by pickup groups, there is not likely to be synchronicity in bowing, articulation or phrasing, nor is attention likely to be paid to these features. In *al talón*-style performance the overwhelmingly predominant song type (see Pearlman 1984 for a discussion of genres) is the *ranchera*, with occasional *sones* and *boleros*. Other genres are infrequent in *al talón* style; plotting of genre distribution by context illustrates the usefulness of

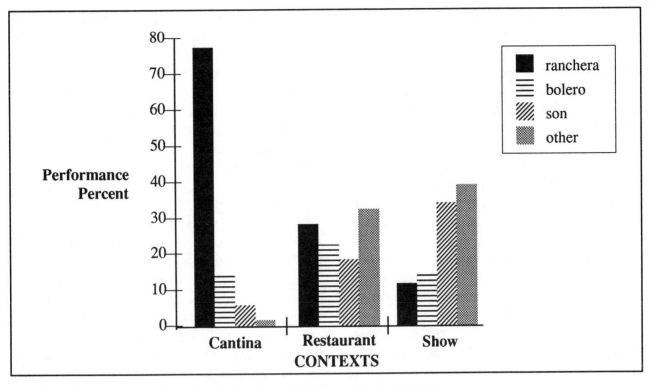

Figure 3: Percentage of performance by genre in various contexts

Figure 4: *Al talón*-style mariachi in *cantina* context

Figure 5: Transitional context mariachi at El Mercado

genre as a context/style indicator (see Figure 3).

It is clear that there are certain features of successful *al talón* performance that are very satisfying to both performer and client. It is characterized by extremely close performer-audience interaction; participation of the audience, either with *gritos* (stylized yells) or singing is expected.

While *al talón* style is primarily found in *cantina* contexts, in some neighborhoods the same style, or aspects of it, is performed in larger establishments and transitional contexts. The prime example of a larger establishment such as this is El Mercado ("The Market") in East Los Angeles. There, even though the performing groups are larger, more organized, and have some level of corporateness, the style of performance is definitely an extension of *al talón* style. Income is on a per-song basis. Song frequencies, based on the analysis of my non-random recorded sample, average about 78% *ranchera*, 15% *bolero*, 5% *son*, and only 2% other, almost identical to other *cantina* context/*al talón*-style groups. Total performance time in an hour sample has exceeded 56 minutes, or a 93% performance ratio. Mariachis performing at El Mercado (there are three that perform simultaneously in different open restaurants on the second floor) take no breaks as a group, allowing set durations of as long as thirteen hours. Thus in effect the mariachis at El Mercado represent both the ultimate expression of successful *al talón*-style performance, and the transition to *planta*-style performance and the restaurant context.

PLANTA-STYLE PERFORMANCE

A substantial percentage of the songs played by restaurant-based, *planta*-style mariachis are still standard arrangements of well known songs, but there are some major differences between the repertoires of *planta* and *al talón* styles of mariachi music. It of course remains the case that ultimately any mariachi must please its audience in order for it to be successful, and *planta*-based mariachis must play requests from restaurant clientele. But while *planta*-based mariachis may expect tips, they won't ordinarily charge customers for songs since their income is in fact from the house. Con-

Figure 6: Summary of *al talón* style

VARIABLE	STYLE> *Al talón*
income	per song
requests	important
performance ratio	90% +
group size	4–8
corporateness	negligible
dress	casual
synchronicity	low
spacial org.	flexible
set time	varies
genre	*ranchera*
avg. song length	2:20
songs per hour	up to 25
audience proximity	close

sequently there is no pressure to play as many songs as possible in a given length of time, as is the case when working *al talón*, and the possibilities of playing more involved introductions or endings to songs allows stylistic innovation. In addition *planta*-based mariachis often have the opportunity to play material not actually requested, but which can show off the versatility or musical ability of the group, because the mariachi will be expected to perform even if there are no specific requests. A *planta*-style mariachi can thus be expected to play a wider range of music than encountered in the *al talón* style, albeit with a reduced total repertoire, with an increasing tendency towards elaboration in performance, and a propensity towards the establishment of a unique group repertoire and style that sets it off from other mariachi groups in town. Distinction from other groups is also reflected in the adoption of matching *trajes* and *moños*, including replacing, in some cases, the traditional silver *botonadura* with suede decoration called *greca*, only possible with a minimum level of corporateness (see Figure 7).

Figure 7: *Planta*-style mariachi wearing a *traje* with *greca*

Genre distributions for *planta*-style performance show a much more even distribution of the main genres, with more auxiliary genres represented than in *al talón* performance. Typical distributions were 18% *sones*, 28% *rancheras*, 22% *boleros*, 24% miscellaneous, and 8% polkas. The miscellaneous category includes tangos, *popurrís*, *jarabes*, and *huapangos*, among others. The actual range of material performed by the *planta*-based band is additionally subcontext dependent. For example, the band is not as likely to play dance music in a strolling hotel engagement as it is on stage with microphones in a night club or at a wedding reception. Similarly, since the clientele is more likely to be ethnically diverse in a restaurant context performance, the attempt by the mariachi to cater to the backgrounds of the audience affects song selection and diversity. It is not unusual to find typical Mexican folk and popular material juxtaposed with an American jazz standard like "Hot Canary," a German polka, a selection from another area of Latin America (perhaps a *samba* or tango), and an arrangement of Von Suppe's "Poet and Peasant," all in the same set.

The pace of performance in the *planta* style is ordinarily more relaxed than in *al talón* style. Tempi are slower, even when arrangements are the same. Average song length is significantly greater, averaging around 2:50 per song. Set length is less variable, ranging from approximately 30 to 60 minutes, and performance ratio is substantially reduced. In restaurant and *chamba*-context performance, sets are separated by breaks of between 20 and 30 minutes, which further reduces performance time ratios. *Planta*-style performance frequently has performance ratios of between 50 and 60%, as opposed to around 90% in some *al talón*-style performances. Average number of songs per hour, including break time, is between 10 and 17, as compared to the 20+ common in *al talón*-style performance.

Audience interaction in *planta*-style performance tends to be more subdued than in *al talón* performance. Since there is an impetus to perform for all audience members rather than a single paying customer at a time, distance between performers and audience increases. Increased distance leads to linear spacing, and a standardized

Figure 8: *Planta*-**style mariachi showing linear spatial arrangement**

placement of instruments, with *armonía* (*guitarrón, vihuela,* and, where present, guitar) on stage left, and *melodía* (violins and trumpets) to their right, as indicated in Figure 8. In those restaurant and *chamba*-context performances where groups use sound systems, the performer-audience separation is augmented still further.

In sum, it is clear that there are distinct structural and contextual differences between ensembles that perform in *cantina* contexts, *al talón* style, and those that perform in restaurant/*chamba* contexts, *planta* style. The *planta*-style groups are corporately organized. Income, besides being ordinarily greater, is differently structured, being based on the regularity of job or hourly based wages as opposed to tips. The sizes of the *planta*-style groups are, on average, larger than the *al talón*-style groups. Genre distribution is both broader and more even. Percentage of performance and number of songs per hour are both less. The net result is a different manner of performance, derived from different values, which results in identifiably different performance style.

ENTERTAINMENT/SHOW

At the opposite end of the continuum from the *al talón* style is the "show" or entertainment style. This has not been a common performance style in Mexico, and there is no Spanish word used to refer to it (although mariachis in Mexico do perform in

Figure 9: **Summary/comparison of** *al talón* **and** *planta* **styles**

VARIABLE	STYLE> *Al talón*	*planta*
income	per song	hour/event
requests	important	accepted
performance ratio	90% +	50–60%
group size	4–8	4–10
corporateness	negligible	present
dress	casual	matching
synchronicity	low	medium
spacial org.	flexible	linear
set time	varies	30–60 min.
genre	*ranchera*	mixed
avg. song length	2:20	2:50
songs per hour	up to 25	10–17
audience proximity	close	medium

concert as accompaniment to singers or dancers). Mariachis in Los Angeles instead use "show" to indicate this particular context and style, characterized by relatively fancy restaurant, dinner show, venues, innovative musical arrangements, and instrumental and vocal virtuosity.

Within this style performing groups are often large, with as many as four to eight violins, two or three trumpets, plus *guitarrón*, *vihuela*, and guitar, and, rarely, harp. There are only three mariachis in Los Angeles that regularly perform with large groups such as this in stage or concert contexts, but several smaller groups are occasionally hired to play infrequent stage/concert performances as part of their ordinary cycle of work throughout the year.

Figure 10: Show-style mariachi in dinner theater context

In a concert or stage performance requests are ordinarily not solicited and usually not played. Rather a variety of song forms are played, covering nearly the entire range of genres. Song forms that are specifically dance forms, such as polkas, *cumbias*, and *danzones*, are generally not played as part of a performance in a show context. Typical genre distributions included 34% *sones*, 13% *popurrís*, 9% *huapangos*, 12% *rancheras*, 16% *boleros*, and 17% miscellaneous, including *clásicas*, *sambas*, and special arrangements. Average song length was around 3:06, with set lengths of about one hour, and performance ratios of over 90%.

Curiously, in some respects entertainment style and *al talón* style share some features, notably performance ratio, in that when an *al talón* group has sufficient requests it may also have performance ratios of over 90%. However, where performance ratio varies in *al talón* performance, it doesn't in show style, and of course in most other aspects the performance styles are quite different.

Mariachis that perform primarily in the entertainment style show a continuation of the corporate nature and of the elaboration process found in *planta*-based mariachis, and in fact are in many ways the antithesis of the *al talón* style. These groups present highly polished appearance and performances, with matching *trajes* and *moños*, precisely articulated phrasing, and synchronized bowing. They are generally affiliated with single restaurants, performing five or six nights per week in the same location. Membership in the bands is permanent, with pay being drawn from restaurant income. Musicians in these bands are paid fixed salaries, usually on a weekly basis, with occasional augmentation of regular income through *chambas*. One interesting feature of the larger house bands is that while employment is considered to be permanent, not all musicians play all the time, so that it is possible to rotate days off, and even to have more than one band performing at the same time under the same name for *chambas*. This occurs when clients request smaller groups for parties because hiring the entire group would be too expensive, due in part to the extra overhead, above musicians' pay, usually charged.

Performance of these larger house bands is very much show-oriented. Stages are often tiered, so musicians are arranged differently than in other styles. Movement of musicians on the stage is choreographed as different singers or musicians step out of the ensemble to be featured and are then reabsorbed. Some of the groups have their own arrangers in addition to the group directors, so that few of the songs are performed in their popular versions. In addition original material takes a more prominent place in performance than it does in either of the other levels of mariachis, and virtuosic singing and instrumental performance are often highlighted (as evidenced in the transcriptions of *"La Bikina,"* figures 11a and 11b), perhaps more in keeping with a North American view of what constitutes musical entertainment.

The members of the entertainment-style mariachis generally think of themselves as being the best ensembles in town, despite the removal from traditional and popular Mexican music as it is played both here and in Mexico, and there is a fair amount of prestige associated with belonging to one of these groups. Interestingly however there is a shift away from the egalitarianism common to *al talón-* and *planta*-based structures. In both of the lower-level organizational forms, pay is generally equal for all musicians, although leaders may get slightly more. In the large show-context mariachis there is often a wide diversity in income from musician to musician.

The audience that attends performances in this context is also different than in the other contexts. In show-style performance, whether in concert, or in large restaurants in a more American "dinner theater" atmosphere, there is a physical separation between performer and audience, augmented by use of a formal stage, use of microphones, and the lack of opportunity for either physical or verbal interaction. The audience tends to be somewhat more restrained, although it will applaud enthusiastically for particular performances, whether individual or ensemble. The audience, like the performers, tend to have separated from the fictional egalitarian ideal that characterizes other performance contexts and styles. Just as the audiences appear more successful financially, they tend to appreciate and expect virtuosity from individuals.

In sum, the performance motivations in entertainment style performance are quite different from the other styles. Since individuals do not pay for particular songs, there is no need to immediately satisfy particular individuals, and since income is not dependent on the number of pieces performed

within a particular time period there is no pressing impetus to truncate forms. Consequently it is the longer versions of songs that are played, and the longer forms in general, especially *popurrís*, are more heavily used than in any other context. Within the show context there is a tendency to feature a number of different solo singers, a number of different featured instrumentalists, and the technical and musical ability and versatility of the group as a whole. A major implication is that in order to successfully perform songs in this context, given the number of musicians involved and the greater complexity of material, rehearsal is necessary. When rehearsal is necessary, musicians play together on a regular basis and the musical ensembles exist as corporate entities rather than as collections of individuals gathered for a particular performance. When groups exist as corporate entities the existence of the group transcends the presence of particular individuals. One musician may leave the group; he is replaced by another who is expected to learn the repertoire and the arrangements. Over a period of several years it is not unlikely that 50% or more of a group may change. In a group that plays the majority of its performances in a show context, it is the nature of that particular performance context that allows selection of the repertoire, and it is the social context of the performing group that allows development of arrangements that may differ substantially from the generally known arrangements, whether standard or truncated, that are likely to be heard in the other styles.

AESTHETICS

That there are differences in performance contexts and style in mariachi music is certainly clear; that these are based on aesthetics needs to be elaborated.

Aesthetics is, basically, the philosophy or study of beauty in music or art, and the responses they engender. While the context-dependent aesthetics of mariachi music performance is not always clearly articulated by performers or audiences, and there

Figure 11a: *"La Bikina,"* version 1—planta-style excerpt

This song, which would be classified under genre as "miscellaneous," is a common piece in *planta/chamba*-style and show-style performances. Version 1 is a fragment of a common arrangement performed in restaurant contexts in the 1980s. Version 2 is a fragment of a show-style arrangement introduced in the mid-1980s.

Version 1 features violin *pizzicato* in the introduction, a rather plain trumpet melody line (measures 5–10) backed up by a unison violin part that takes over the end of the melody in measure 11.

Version 2, on the other hand, features a more stylized introduction with trumpets playing in parallel thirds; overlapping trumpet lines (measures 8–9 and 51–54); more complex harmonization (as present in measures 9, 25 and 17–18); a more complex violin *pizzicato* part with both interesting syncopation and chromatics (measures 11–19); and perhaps most distinctive, a syncopated and embellished trumpet solo (measures 42–48) under unison voices. These features, especially in this combination, would only be present in a show-style presentation.

Figure 11b: *"La Bikina,"* version 2—Show-style excerpt.

Vers. 2:2

are no descriptive treatises that describe mariachi aesthetics as there are for various classical musics, it is still possible to extract aesthetic values from performances in context, in conjunction with an evaluation of audience composition, response and interaction.

When the aesthetic feature or features of objects or performances are attended to in a direct way, a specific state of consciousness may ensue. Jacques Maquet, concerned exclusively with visual objects in his recent writings (1979, 1986), has called this a "contemplative state." Some of its main characteristics are absorption in the object attended to, and a suspension of ordinary awareness, particularly of temporal awareness. A similar state of consciousness, characterized by involvement, absorption, and a suspension or alteration of time perception, also may occur in audiences observing musical performance. In fact, the role of audience and context in performance has been of major importance in ethnomusicology over the past fifteen years or so. It is not so large a step to

hypothesize that aesthetic experiences in general are context-dependent and interactive, and that this may be particularly true of the relationship between audiences and performers. What is necessary is to determine the aesthetic foci, the areas of salience in performance to which audiences attend, and which musicians present, in each style.

The level of audience involvement, and the level of aesthetic success, depends on the quality of the relationship established between audience and performers. This relationship is not necessarily one of physical interaction, but rather a relation between audience expectation and the ability of the performers to meet and possibly expand on those expectations. Successful, satisfying performances are thus equivalent to other aesthetic experiences; when performer intention and audience expectation are congruent, and when the audience attends to features of performance in a focused way that fosters involvement, an aesthetic experience, a suspension of ordinary consciousness, may result, especially if the performer is able to stretch expec-

Figure 12: Summary/comparison of *al talón, planta,* and show styles.

VARIABLE	STYLE> *Al talón*	*planta*	*show*
income	per song	hour/event	weekly
requests	important	accepted	infrequent
performance ratio	90% +	50–60%	90% +
group size	4–8	4–10	8–17
corporateness	negligible	present	definite
dress	casual	matching	complex
synchronicity	low	medium	high
spacial org.	flexible	linear	tiered
set time	varies	30–60 min.	60 min. +/-
genre	*ranchera*	mixed	*popurri*
avg. song length	2:20	2:50	3:06
songs per hour	up to 25	10–17	15–20
audience proximity	close	medium	low

tations without breaking the implicit rules governing the performance. Interestingly, it is also conceivable that performances may be aesthetically satisfying even when performer intention and audience expectation are not congruent. In fact, the structural tension in ambivalent contexts may enhance some aspects of performance, and result in shifts, sometimes unintended, in the perception of meaning, or in aesthetic appreciation.

So, to return to the examples presented, clearly there is a transition of both performance intention and audience expectation, and a corresponding transition in stylistic features of performance, across the range of mariachi performance contexts. Some ensembles limit their performance to particular contexts, and there is congruence established between style, expectation, and aesthetics. Some musicians, however, and some ensembles, become adept at identifying the particular features peculiar to specific contexts, and are successful performers in a range of contexts. They can perform in a range of styles, varying the aesthetics of their performance in relation to contextual variables. Similarly many non-performers, i.e., audiences and clients, have available to them the opportunity to select between different contexts, and thus between different performance styles and different aesthetic expressions. There is clearly, therefore, an awareness on the part of both musician and audience, at least in some cases, of intentions and expectations, and choices about where to go and how to play and listen are made by each. Many musicians who restrict their performance to a particular style feel that their style is the "true" mariachi music. For example, musicians who work *al talón* feel that show-style musicians just don't have the repertory to compete in the *cantina* environment, and that highly orchestrated show-style performance is something other than "real" mariachi. On the other hand, the show-context performers feel that they are the cutting edge of mariachi aesthetics, creating new arrangements and repertoire. All in all, for those who can perform in multiple contexts, it is by understanding which features are

salient in each context, based on contextual and environmental variables, that mariachis in Los Angeles attempt to enhance the aesthetic experiences of their audiences.

The inter-relationship of context, performance, and aesthetics is thus particularly relevant to the study of mariachi music in Los Angeles because there is a continuum of contexts and performance styles along which both performance style and audience expectations of particular features of performance vary. The net result of these shifts in context, the shifts in both intention and expectation, is a variable aesthetic of mariachi music. The same basic music is performed recognizably, but there are distinct stylistic differences in different contexts. Successful performance in one context will not necessarily be successful in another context. In fact, the farther removed the style from the context, the more likely that the result will be unsatisfying, aesthetically displeasing, and unsuccessful. There is in fact a relation between context and aesthetics, and the aesthetic loci are identifiably different in each style.

Examining the *cantina* context and the *al talón* performance style it is clear that some features of *al talón* style are simply context-dependent. It is, for example, in the financial interests of the performers to play as many songs per unit time as possible. This is accomplished, as was mentioned previously, in three main ways: tempi (the overall speed of pieces) are increased, minor structural elements such as repetitions are omitted, and particular formal components such as introductions, bridges, and endings are abbreviated.

While this is a structuring and identifying feature, it is not an aesthetic focus, nor are appearance and musicianship. Musicians dressed in a fashion more appropriate to concert contexts would simply seem overdressed—they would violate the essential egalitarianism of the *cantina*. Similarly, while quality singing or playing are acknowledged, they are peripheral to the main foci: audience interaction, and depth of performance repertoire.

Audience members expect that the mariachi

will play versions of songs with which they are familiar. Audience members expect that musicians will perform all requests, and there are hundreds, perhaps thousands of songs in the active *al talón* mariachi repertoire. The mariachi tries to maximize the number of songs played in an hour in order to maximize their income, but they must do this in a way that doesn't violate audience expectation. Since there is such a direct relationship established, audience members are, in a sense, somewhat forgiving of variations in musicianship, and slight deviations from "standard" song versions, because of the personal attention given them by the ensemble. As long as the mariachi plays structurally complete songs, the audience is satisfied. When clients sing with the mariachi, the performer-audience gap is minimized, and mariachis that can accommodate the clients' intonational problems and erratic rhythms are appreciated. If the mariachi can also generate increased excitement and participation in the audience, the aesthetic experience is enhanced. The audience is successfully involved.

The intention of performance shifts along the continuum from *al talón* to *planta/chamba* performance. Whereas in *al talón* style the emphasis is on performer-audience interaction, in the restaurant context the mariachi is more directly involved in providing ambience than it is in directly serving individual clients. While the mariachi often accommodates requests, the pressures that structure performance in the *cantina* context are not present, and performance changes. Songs are longer, musical competence and innovation in musicality become increasingly valued, and in contexts with mixed audience ethnicity, repertoire begins to include songs more popular north of the border, including, when possible, songs in English. The performance environment may be more relaxed, if the intention is more to provide atmosphere than to excite the audience.

In most of the cases of *planta/chamba* performance, while the mariachi is a significant factor in the environment, the audience has not come exclu-sively for music. The expectation of the audience is not totally one of participation, as may occur in *cantina* context, but shifts towards observation. Further, since the audience does not interact as closely with the ensemble, it tends to become less forgiving and more demanding, not only in terms of music performance and repertory, but also in appearance and presentation. *Planta/chamba* style is intermediary between *al talón* and show style—while audience interaction and exhaustive repertory knowledge becomes less important, the shift of focus to synchronicity, musicianship and originality is discernible.

The show context completes the pattern of increasing separation of performer from audience. In most show-context performance, the mariachis shift away from standard arrangements and away from audience requests. In the most complete expression of show-context performance the musicians are the owners of the establishment, so there is less pressure to conform to external demand. Innovative, original arrangements and individual virtuosity, both instrumental and vocal, are highlighted, and these become part of the aesthetic foci in this context. Programs are orchestrated and paced to emphasize the versatility of the show-style mariachi.

In show performance, the separation between audience and mariachi is even more clearly demarcated. Mariachis in very large ensembles perform on a stage, with a physical and interactional gap between the ensemble and the audience. The audience comes specifically and primarily for the music, and expects high levels of musical performance and high levels of peripheral factors such as appearance and showmanship, which become more important for a less personal and less forgiving audience. The mariachi is allowed more freedom in performance, in that in show context performance it is no longer necessary to strictly adhere to the structural constraints that characterize other types of performance, yet at the same time the mariachi is challenged to excite the audience by bending without breaking the audience expectations.

Having now established that there are real, context-dependent, aesthetic differences in mariachi performance, the next issue is to determine why these differences are important, in other words, what is the meaning or significance of these differences?

Clearly the aesthetics of mariachi music performance is not constant; it varies and is shaped contextually. The issue in defining variable aesthetics thus becomes the determination of the loci of meaning, i.e., those features of performance that are most salient in different contexts, and the relationship of aesthetics and the cultural and social basis of mariachi music performance. This must be done on two levels. First, it is necessary to identify the manner in which general characteristics of performance parallel community-wide social/cultural values and structures. Second, it is also necessary to look at the different contexts to see how these values are differentially expressed, and by comparing the different behaviors in the contexts, determine the mechanism by which aesthetics become variable.

Among the cultural features or values differentially expressed in different contexts and relevant to an understanding of mariachi music performance is a general thread of "apparent" egalitarianism important to the mariachi community. Individuals strive not to appear economically more successful, or somehow better, than others. This is reflected in patterns of consumption of material goods, in participation in rotating credit associations, avoiding the implications of hoarding and of material vanity. Yet at the same time, there is a cultural value placed on individual independence and competence. There is a great deal of pride placed in individual autonomy, and in not being subject to the control of another, except to the extent that the control is relinquished temporarily and voluntarily.

It is possible to fit contexts, and in parallel, even song types, into a continuum matching this structural relationship. The mariachis that work *al talón*

are the most egalitarian; those in show contexts the least. At the egalitarian end of the scale the musicians all earn equally for equal work; at the non-egalitarian end there is income differentiation. At an egalitarian level of performance there is emphasis on the ensemble, i.e., on inclusion; in show performance the virtuosic abilities of both solo singers and solo instrumentalists are highlighted and the emphasis is on stratification and differentiation. In the egalitarian contexts the song forms with "plain" singing style (*rancheras*) are more prominent than the forms that emphasize vocal distinctiveness and embellishment found in show performance. Even the audience, integrated with the performers in *cantina* context, becomes differentiated from the ensemble in show performance; they are primarily observers rather than participants.

Thus general performance characteristics for mariachi music in Los Angeles reflect the cultural/ social values and structures of the mariachi community, plus the intersections of mariachi values and audience values in the different contexts. The expression of general structures as particular aesthetic features are context-dependent, expressed differently in different settings, transformed to match changing expectations, or even merged with values originating outside the community. When there is congruence of (musical) intention and (audience) expectation, when the individual aesthetics in the performers matches values in the audience the potential exists for an aesthetically pleasing experience. But clearly there are satisfying aesthetic experiences even if those values are derived from entirely different cultural/social sets, as in those performance situations where there is a substantial non-Mexican component in the audience. To a large extent, the aesthetics of show-style performance represents the congruence to a North American model of entertainment and virtuosity. The American value system specifically recognizes the success of the individual, in distinction to the traditional Mexican system which avoids self-aggrandizement. Mexicans in Los Angeles are caught between noncongruent structures, and they attempt to find congruences in expression; in show-style performance this involves making the mariachi/*artista* (soloist) distinction, transforming it to allow otherwise inappropriate individual prominence, and then presenting it to a hybrid audience in such a way that all can find aesthetic satisfaction, even though the value systems on which the aesthetic perceptions are based are radically different, even fundamentally opposite.

The result is that Mexicans, Chicanos and non-Latinos who attend show style performances may as well be attending entirely separate events, as can be best exemplified in the use of the *popurrí* as a genre. The *popurrí* is a medley of songs, usually around a related theme. *Popurrís* often feature key changes between song segments, marked by nontraditional segues. Each segment often features different singers, or different instruments as well. Those who know the repertoire, who know the music and traditional performance style, recognize and focus on the songs themselves; those whose expectations lie more in a North American model of music performance, primarily non-Latino Americans, focus on the transitions between song segments, and the emergence of solo singers and high levels of musicianship.

Evaluated from this perspective it becomes easy to see why musicians who perform in single contexts may regard their own style as the "true" expression of mariachi music. The *al talón* style expresses a particular set of cultural values and structures, understandable to a particular segment of the Mexican population. In ambivalent settings, however, it becomes necessary to present what are essentially ambivalent messages. One can either regard this as the healthy evolution of a form to meet changing cultural systems, or the abandonment of the particular national cognitive system that allowed the widespread popularity of the general style in the first place. Obviously this cognitive ambivalence is most pronounced as non-Mexicans or acculturated Chicanos become audience members; there is less certainty of shared structure,

hence more aesthetic tension, and the need to generate new forms. This allows the development of show-context performance as a viable performance option in the United States, and explains why it has not existed until recently in the same way in Mexico. The show-context performance aesthetic represents the sharing, or congruence, of fundamentally different cognitive structural origins, much in the same way Spanish and indigenous forms merged in the fifteenth century, and much in the same way that the modern mariachi became a potent cultural symbol for Mexico earlier this century.

In sum, it is clear that the cultural and cognitive rules governing mariachi performance, i.e., the aesthetics of mariachi music in Los Angeles, are dependent upon performance contexts. In this case, while the musicians are aware of the differences and can express them verbally, important aesthetic features are best elicited analytically. One of the results apparent through this examination is that the variable aesthetics in mariachi music performance is based, at least in part, on differences in salience and meaning expressed in and interpreted from performer-audience interaction. Mariachis in Los Angeles thus reflect, perhaps metaphorically, the structural ambiguity inherent in their lives at a multicultural intersection, yet they can manipulate this ambiguity to provide aesthetically satisfying performances for audiences of varied cultural and social backgrounds.

NOTES

1. This article is based on primary anthropological research principally conducted from 1979 to 1987 during which time the author performed with professional mariachi ensembles; it is augmented by continued performance and less systematic observation from that time until the present.

2. See, for example, the liner notes to Arhoolie release C-9051: *The Earliest Mariachi Recordings 1908–1936*. Phil Sonnichsen (1986) writes:
    Ten years before the arrival of the French, a local priest by the name of Cosme Santa Anna,

working in the community of Rosamorada, Nayarít, wrote to his bishop of the excesses committed by men influenced by gambling and strong drink. In his letter of April 26, 1852, he makes specific reference to "Mariachis" as being responsible for supplying the music which regularly accompanied disorderly dancing, drinking and gambling in front of his church during nominally religious fiestas.

REFERENCES CITED

Maquet, Jacques
   1986   *The Aesthetic Experience.* New Haven, Connecticut: Yale University Press.
   1979   *Introduction to Aesthetic Anthropology.* Malibu, California: Undena Publications.

Pearlman, Steven Ray
   1984   "Standardization and Innovation in Mariachi Music Performance in Los Angeles." *Pacific Review of Ethnomusicology* 1:1–12.

Rafael, Hermes
   1982   *Origen e historia del mariachi.* Mexico: Editorial Katún.

Sonnichsen, Philip (et al)
   1986   Liner notes to *The Earliest Mariachi Recordings 1908–1936.* Arhoolie Records C-9051.

"POPULAR PRICES WILL PREVAIL" SETTING THE SOCIAL ROLE OF EUROPEAN-BASED CONCERT MUSIC[1]

Catherine Parsons Smith

THREE HEROES REGULARLY masquerade as the sum and substance of Los Angeles's music history. In spite of their dissimilarity, their collective pre-eminence conceals more than it reveals about concert music in the period stretching from the consolidation of Anglo dominance in the 1880s until the start of World War II. In the beginning, goes the formula, there was the legend of L.E. Behymer, who embroidered shamelessly on his achievements as an impresario by claiming that he single-handedly developed Southern California's audience for concert music and opera out of the primordial ooze. He took credit for bringing the first and only "real" artistic events from the East starting in 1887 and for decades thereafter.[2] Later came the very real beneficence of William Andrews Clark, Jr., who, by founding the Los Angeles Philharmonic in 1919 and supporting it for fifteen years, lit a candle in the prevailing, near-total darkness to give the city one of its major cultural institutions. Finally, there was the somewhat belated arrival of musical modernism, mythically marked by the coming of Arnold Schoenberg in the fall of 1934, the appearance of other famous émigrés in the following years, and the inception of the Evenings on the Roof/Monday Evening Concerts in 1939.

With all respect to the real achievements of these three, the myth of their solitary activities conceals far more interesting histories, with repercussions that have carried to the present day. In this paper, I propose to explore one aspect of the story of the first of these fabled heroes. As a framework for my exposition, I shall invoke the concept of multiple narratives, as suggested by feminist literary critic Carolyn Heilbrun. In *Writing a Woman's Life* (1988) and in her detective fiction as well, Heilbrun points out that a narrative is implicit in the career, and the life history, of any individual. The most obvious events are often diversions to an underlying, concealed narrative, one that better explains the facts of the case. Discovery of the underlying narrative, she proposes in her criticism, is the job of the biographer, and, she argues in her fiction, of the literary-critic-turned-detective.[3]

Here, Heilbrun's formulation leads away from an individual, toward a broader view of a city's characteristic concert life as it was developing. I propose that the three canonized individuals in Los Angeles's music history are narrative diversions, foregrounded by the city's music critics and by current apologists for the city's musical institutions. Their mythical preeminence has distracted musicians and readers from not just one, but a complex web of other, underlying narratives, now lost or ignored.[4] For example, several concealed narratives underlie L.E. Behymer's emergence as the dominant impresario of southern California. His own claims that he was responsible for events as far back as the visits of Adelina Patti, or Theodore Thomas's National Opera Company in 1887,[5] are,

I would argue, diversionary, contradicted by the evidence of his own invaluable archive, now in the Huntington Library. In this paper, part of a larger project that explores several of these hidden histories, I propose to explore the short period of open, competitive concert-giving that took place between 1899 and 1905. In those few years, partly as a result of this competition and its outcome, a concert music tradition with particular class, race, and gender associations, distinct from the wider and older traditions of public entertainment and enlightenment in church and theater, was firmly established in Los Angeles.

* * *

In 1899, when Behymer presented one public event, a lecture, two other impresarios and three theatrical managers competed to present musical events; many other concerts took place without the benefit of formal management. By 1905, when the concert-giving landscape had taken a shape roughly recognizable as the concert life typical of much of the twentieth century, Behymer controlled the appearances of the "major" touring virtuosos and opera companies in Southern California. Distinctions such as those among visiting artists and local ones and among different repertories were widened and formalized; further distinctions along lines of class and race among audiences were likewise recognized and, to some degree, formalized. Distinctions on the basis of gender and gendering are also evident. At the end of that period the outcome was formalized by the courageous, far-reaching action of another individual who functioned here as something of a *dea ex machina*.

The facts of this first concealed narrative are straightforward. In the first six months of 1899, a period of more-or-less open competition and occasional cooperation among concert presenters, the principal music events, and their sponsors, were:

- James T. Fitzgerald, music store owner, published *The Fitzgerald Bulletin*, a flyer

promoting six visiting "attractions" that included the Kneisel Quartet, pianist Emil Sauer, and the immensely popular John Philip Sousa with his band.[6]

- Frederick W. Blanchard, another music store owner and for a time Fitzgerald's partner, presented pianist Moritz Rosenthal to open the new, 800-seat Blanchard Hall in his own new Music and Art building. Blanchard also presented at least one concert in a lyceum course offered by the Epworth League at the YMCA.[7]

- L.E. Behymer, theatrical publicist, program publisher, and ticket seller ("assistant treasurer") for the Los Angeles Theater, offered Ian McLaren, a popular lecturer.

- At the Los Angeles Theater, manager H.C. Wyatt presented the Lambardi Grand Opera Company in the Italian repertory; the Bostonians, playing Victor Herbert and De Koven; Black Patti's Troubadours; and Hi Henry's Minstrels, among other events.[8]

- In a major cooperative venture, Wyatt and Blanchard offered the Ellis Grand Opera Company, featuring Melba, Damrosch, and the New York Symphony Orchestra in two opera performances at Hazard's Pavilion, a multi-purpose auditorium used for conventions, citrus fairs and other large events. (Behymer played his usual role as described above.)

These presenters by no means accounted for the city's entire musical and theatrical life. The struggling Los Angeles Symphony Orchestra, in its second season, gave the final seven concerts in its ten-concert season at the Los Angeles Theater; it depended on the Southern California Music Company to print its programs, but was otherwise without sponsorship. The Burbank Theater offered the Wakefield Andrews Opera Company, which included among its offerings the double bill of *Cavalleria rusticana* and *Trial by Jury*.[9] At the Orpheum, the all-black ragtime opera *Clorindy*,

Will Marion [Cook] conducting, appeared among the vaudeville acts. Among many other events at a variety of locations, Blanche Rogers (later Lott) and others offered the second and third concerts in a highly respected chamber music series by local artists. Concerts by C.S. DeLano's Guitar, Banjo, and Mandolin Club; Harry Barnhart, basso; and the USC Glee, Mandolin, Banjo and Guitar Club led the list of additional concerts. Domestic music making was widespread, including that of the by-now marginalized Hispanic population (Koegel forthcoming).

Two among these presenters stepped up their activities sharply in the following seasons. Music store owner Blanchard scheduled many local artists and a few touring ones in his recital hall. In the fall of 1901 he arranged his first "Star Entertainment Course" of ten lectures and concerts, mainly booked through the Redpath Lyceum Bureau in Boston.[10] Tickets were sold by the Women's Guild of the Independent Church of Christ. The ten events for one dollar included a concert by the local Congregational Orchestra of thirty-five amateur musicians under William H. Mead; the Enoch Arden Concert Company of Washington, D.C.; and the Leonora Jackson Grand Concert Company, whose featured soloist was a well known African American violinist. This course sold out so quickly that Blanchard added a second, the Imperial Course, underwritten by an organization of USC alumni, and a third, People's Course, this one sponsored by the Ladies' Aid Society of the First Methodist Church. Each was a series of ten events, priced at one dollar for the series. The People's Course included the Los Angeles Women's Orchestra under Harley Hamilton, the Throop Institute Mandolin and Guitar Club, and the Chicago Symphony Orchestra (*Los Angeles Saturday Post:*1901a, 1901b). Behymer countered Blanchard's activity aggressively with two big-budget events, offering the Grau Metropolitan Opera in a return engagement for Melba and Damrosch, and the Eduard Strauss Concert Orchestra. The next season, 1902, he followed

Blanchard's lead, offering his first concert series package. (Behymer's concert series were always called "courses," reflecting their origin in these early educational lecture/concert series organized by his rival for church groups.) He initially offered his series as a "Star Concert Course," copying the title used by Blanchard the year before. Pressured, he quickly changed the name to "Philharmonic Course," a name he retained for the next forty-five years.

* * *

The competition between Blanchard and Behymer was based on very different approaches, both aesthetic and practical. Blanchard intended his concerts for the widest possible audiences, starting with the church and university-based groups for whom his series were initially organized, and expanding to include the relatively high proportion of the city's population that were his potential customers: teachers and students of music, amateur and professional musicians. He was already a Progressive activist for the arts in the city's everyday life. In this competition and later in his career, he seems to have acted on the belief—one that is still imbued as part of the European concert music tradition and one that he likely acquired as part of his own musical training—in the inherent educational and ethical value of "serious" music. His conviction that such music should be universally accessible is reflected in his concert ads, which frequently contained the rubric, "popular prices will prevail." As a practical matter, this usually meant that there were plenty of seats available for twenty-five cents, if not always for ten; the most expensive seats often went for no more than fifty cents.[11] Although he brought in traveling virtuosos, he also sponsored local artists such as the Lott-Krauss chamber concerts and, later, the Brahms Quintet, in the hall he had built for that purpose.

Behymer's approach, on the other hand, was launched from his background in the commercial theater as press agent and concession operator. Unlike Blanchard, he was unencumbered by the peculiar ethical freight built into formal music training. Shut out of the possibility of managing a commercial theater in 1899, he attempted to develop an audience that would support a profitable concert business.[12] Thus, he took on the management of the Symphony in its third season, and of the new Los Angeles Oratorio Society; he also became manager of the multi-purpose Hazard's Pavilion and Simpson's Auditorium, which doubled as a church. (Both were concert venues at least some of the time.) Discovering that artists such as Melba and Paderewski, as well as Californians Sibyl Sanderson and Ellen Beach Yaw, drew large audiences on their first visits under his rivals' management, he enticed them to return, offering higher fees to the artists and charging higher prices to his audiences. He used H.C. Wyatt's chain of theaters in Southern California and his connections elsewhere in the West to set up multiple appearances for his touring virtuosos, later on developing his own regional network. He bought more advertising space than his rival and promoted his events more vigorously; it seems as if he single-handedly forced the local press to expand its coverage of music events by supplying unprecedented quantities of background material on his performers. His advertising and promotions dwelt on their virtuosity and stressed their cosmopolitan, international successes.

Behymer's incessant hyperbole was frowned upon by at least one critic, who wrote: "Why will the picturesque press agent insist on talking such arrant rubbish? Everything he gets hold of is the greatest that ever was....How utterly absurd this bluster is! (Frederick Stevenson 1904). Such objections were quickly overwhelmed. Most important to his future reputation, late in 1902 Behymer swung the editorial support of the arch-conservative *Los Angeles Times* away from his Progressive rival, Blanchard, toward his own position as a musical entrepreneur. He portrayed himself as the lowly challenger of the musical "trusts" (i.e., the music store owners) in the David-and-Goliath free enterprise tradition. "Too Many Concerts," pro-

claimed the *Times* in late 1902, as the entrepreneurial competition waxed, especially "cheap concerts," which seemed to be, from the editorial, virtually anything not sponsored by Behymer (*Los Angeles Times* 1902, quoted in Swan 1952). Neither he nor his rivals could then have guessed the results of his press agentry and his editorial capture of the *Times*, which eventually outlived all its journalistic rivals. Although its editorial position has mellowed overall, it has never recovered its balance in the matter of Behymer.

* * *

The competition reached its peak in 1904. The most visible part of the battleground now was not the concerts by visiting virtuosos, however. In backing rival mixed choruses, the two entrepreneurs sought to win the loyalty of local musicians, teachers, and amateurs who formed the heart of the local audience for concert music. Although only single-sex choral societies had been able to establish any continuity in Los Angeles up to that time, mixed choral singing was close to the hearts of musicians in the community, and close to the peak of an implicit hierarchy of performance mediums. In tackling Blanchard here, Behymer took very seriously the local critic who wrote of the city's weakness in "the very highest sphere of musical exploitation...the combination of large mixed chorus, organ, and orchestra" (Frederick Stevenson 1905b).

Blanchard managed the Los Angeles Choral Society, conducted by Harry Barnhart; Behymer backed the Los Angeles Oratorio Society under Julius Jahn.[13] In May 1904, the quadrennial national convention of the Methodist Episcopal Church attracted between three and five thousand delegates to Los Angeles. Two months beforehand, Blanchard announced a series of eight events, spread over the three weeks of the convention, for one dollar, "the only authorized course": seven lectures and a concert by a chorus of 600 under Barnhart, along with a "Philharmonic Orchestra" of sixty musicians, actually members of the Symphony conducted by its concertmaster. Several weeks later, Behymer trumped Blanchard when he announced his own "Great Philharmonic Course," consisting of three musical events for three dollars, including Marcella Sembrich, the Symphony (under its own name; Behymer was by then its manager), and his 150-voice oratorio society (*Los Angeles Saturday Post* 1904a).[14] Sembrich was scheduled to appear one day before the Blanchard/Barnhart extravaganza. Both entrepreneurs suffered financially when a train wreck—or a strike, depending on which paper one reads—delayed the arrival of most of the delegates beyond the dates of the first two concerts. But Blanchard/Barnhart's "Conference Chorus" eventually won the praise of the unfriendly *Times* with a repeat performance:

> The Conference Chorus gave its final concert last evening....Few finer things have been presented here by a choral organization of any sort than "Babylon's Wave," [Gounod] as it was sung last night. Barnhart had his vocalists exactly under the sway of his baton, and out of the great unwieldy group he got real pianissimos, crescendos that rose on a graduated scale for evenness, and strenuous climacteric chords that were of surprising strength. (*Los Angeles Times* 1904b)

A duel of *Messiah*s followed in the fall. The Blanchard/Barnhart performance was scheduled for Hazard's barn-like Pavilion; and "popular prices" meant, in this case, 50¢ to $1. Behymer/Jahn's group performed in the much smaller Simpson's, with prices between 50¢ and $1.50. In December, Behymer took the offensive, announcing that "in the first place, amateurish attempts will be avoided" by his group. Blanchard countered with a fatal, unnecessary defensiveness, remarking his chorus's steady improvement and "judicious pruning" of voices.[15] Blanchard had no published reply to Behymer's claim that

there have been more applications for good

things musically, as well as medium and bad attractions, than ever before in the history of music in this city...anything playing under the name of Manager Behymer this season will bear the stamp of the best in music. (*Los Angeles Saturday Post* 1904a)

One critic afterwards confirmed the politicized nature of this contest, writing in the *Graphic*:

> In commenting upon the various musical events of the past few months professional critical opinion has run to such violently opposite extremes that one can scarce find a resting place for the foot of common-sense, everyday fact. For instance, one writer lauded the [Blanchard/Barnhart] *Messiah* to the seventh heaven, while another pretty well consigned it to the nethermost hell. Mr. Jahn's venture in the same field met a like fate. (Frederick Stevenson 1905a)[16]

After one more round in the spring of 1905, when Barnhart's *Creation* apparently outdid Jahn's *Elijah* by a substantial margin, both choruses faded from sight.[17] Blanchard abandoned the impresario field and went abroad for a year. When he returned, it was to concentrate on his prosperous music store and his role as sponsor of local events, champion of music and art as tools for community self-improvement, and occasional silent partner in Behymer's concert promotions. Behymer took over Blanchard's summer Chautauqua bookings in addition to his winter events, thereby consolidating his preeminent position in offering visiting concert attractions in Los Angeles for the next four decades.

* * *

While it lasted, this competition brought a rich variety of public performances to Los Angeles. One may certainly speculate about the outcome, had the relatively well-heeled Blanchard been as ambitious, persistent, and publicity-minded as his rival. Even though resistance to some aspects of the changes that are embodied in Behymer's triumph reappeared in the city's later history, I shall avoid such speculation here, in favor of speculating on still deeper layers of contextual narrative.[18] The layers I shall consider here deal with Los Angeles's growth and its population characteristics that relate to music in this period, and developments in commercial theater, including the appearance of commercial mass culture. Both layers suggest the implications of this competition of impresarios with contrasting goals for the underlying contests about social and economic class, nationalism, race, and gender that were central to the Progressive Era. The razing of Hazard's Pavilion and the construction of Philharmonic Auditorium, Los Angeles's major concert hall for almost six decades (1906–1964) in its place set the outcome of this competition in concrete and steel.

* * *

One of these layers, the growth and population characteristics that underlie the local context for the competition of impresarios described here, serves as background for the others. At the turn of the century, Los Angeles remained a small city and a relatively new one. Neither a seaport nor a rail center, its growth was even then legendary. In 1880, there were 11,000 people in Los Angeles; twenty years later, about the time our two impresarios' contest got started in earnest, there were 100,000. One might guess that the potential concert audience increased by at least fifty percent in the four years immediately before the twin *Messiahs*.

Unlike the cities that were ports of entry for new immigrants, Los Angeles's population contained a much smaller proportion of foreign-born persons.[19] This made for a more homogeneous population in general, but it had another consequence as well. There was a significantly higher proportion of women (47%) among Los Angeles's adult population than was the case in, say, San Francisco (39%).[20] Thus there were not only more adult women in proportion to the total population, but a higher proportion of them—those that were born in the US—may be assumed to have carried the characteristically American Victorian gendering—very different for women than for men—in matters of music as well as in other areas of their lives. These two population characteristics—a high proportion of women, more of them native-born—is exaggerated in the population of musicians and music teachers. Even in 1890, the Census reports that the number of women and men in the professions of musician and music teacher were about equal; by 1900, as both music professions boomed, 60% were women, and the proportion continued to rise in the next decade. Half or more of the male musicians and music teachers, but only about one-sixth of the women, were foreign-born.

Both entrepreneurs in this narrative were strongly affected by these population characteristics. Blanchard, a New Englander who probably studied music in Europe, cultivated the music teachers and their students as customers for his business; he viewed his concert activities as a service to his clientele as well as a way to improve the community. Behymer, perceiving the feminine gendering of music, made a virtue of his non-musical background and presented himself in another way—rather in contrast to the shortened leg and slight limp that were a legacy of childhood polio—in the stereotypically male role of entrepreneur and would-be monopolist, with concerts by visiting virtuosos as the product he offered. He soon became a prominent figure in the Gamut Club, an all-male association of musicians and wealthy amateurs of music, organized in 1904 at the height of his competition with Blanchard. (Blanchard, too was active in this group.) By emphasizing the financial risks of his enterprise, he managed to discourage at least one women's group from promoting its own concerts by visiting artists.[21] His remark in the *Record* that the audience for music in Los Angeles had to be educated about the importance of the concerts he promoted, was a put-down for the largely female, at least slightly musically educated, economically elite audience he cultivated, as well as part of his campaign to sell "his" artists as a high-priced but essential social investment. Likewise, his exhortations to attend concerts for their intrinsic ethical worth is clearly aimed at a female audience.

* * *

Concert life was very closely associated with commercial theater as the competition began. Developments in commercial theater had a tremendous influence on concert-giving, well beyond Behymer's creative appropriation of commercial marketing techniques. The reasonably friendly co-existence of touring and local performing groups, both theatrical and musical, in Wyatt's Los Angeles Theater, came to an abrupt halt with the formation of the Theater Trust at just about the moment when Los Angeles's concert competition arose. The Trust imposed its own decisions on Wyatt from the opposite coast, rendering his generally community-responsive approach impossible, and making the local owner's desires irrelevant.[22]

Underlying the move to concerts as one phase of a new "amusement" industry is the explosive appearance of commercial mass entertainment in the years of this competition. Vaudeville had first appeared in Los Angeles late in 1894, and the first kinetoscope parlor opened in 1896. The opening of the Electric Theater in 1902 and the Mason Opera House in 1903 heralded the start of a decade of theater-building, and the proliferation of vaudeville and burlesque as well as movies. Theater and the movies weren't the whole story of this new industry, however. In 1901, Chutes Park, an amusement park, opened at Washington Gardens, drawing nightly crowds of more than ten thousand. There was also the proliferation of professional sports, including bicycle racing, baseball, and prizefights, as mass entertainment. Even while pushing his "high-class" concert events, Behymer also cultivated the mass audience. He held the concession on coin-operated vitagraph machines at Chutes

Park.[23] "I make money on some of the minor amusements which I manage, occasionally—baseball games and such. I use that to make up the deficit in my grand opera receipts," he breezily claimed in 1905, after he had already begun to cultivate his myth.[24] (These were rough enough that ladies did not normally attend.) Prizefights, considered particularly disreputable, were held at Hazard's Pavilion in the years of the concert competition, while Behymer was manager there (Searight 1905).[25] As in other cities, the audience for these new, "cheap amusements," was not so much drawn from the older middle class, although "high-end" theater was also growing, but was mainly a new audience, consisting of workers who were just beginning to have leisure time because of the new eight-hour workday, coupled with increased real income. The adaptation of the business methods of commercial theater to music is very clear in the competition between Behymer and Blanchard, as, earlier on, was the close connection between commercial theater and concert life, both local and touring. Awareness of this new audience, and the distinction between it and the older theater and concert audience, may explain why it was Behymer—the non-musician—who pushed his events as "high-class" attractions; why it was Behymer who introduced the rhetoric of exclusion, morality, and duty to concert promotion in Los Angeles. He applied it most specifically to his fundraising appeals for the Symphony:

> It is as much the duty of the citizens of L.A. to see that the S.O. is supported as it is to keep up good roads and a public library....It is the duty of every merchant, every capitalist and every property owner to secure at least one season ticket to the Los Angeles Symphony Orchestra. (*Los Angeles Saturday Post* 1904d)

The application of this rhetoric, and the constant reference to "high-class attractions" such as this:

The Great Philharmonic Course this season is appealing to the better class of the amusement public—the class who take seriously the best in music and literature, and Manager Behymer has at last realized that the Los Angeles public desire only the best. (*Los Angeles Saturday Post* 1905)

confirms Behymer's careful cultivation of class distinctions among the audiences for his various offerings.

* * *

Acceptance of European visiting virtuosos meant acceptance of their European repertoire, raising the issues of nationalism and prejudice against the foreign-born that have sometimes made the symphony orchestra problematic as an elitist institution in America. Arthur Farwell's presence in Los Angeles, and his lecture to the Friday Morning Club just as rehearsals for the competing *Messiah* performances were getting into high gear in November 1904, reminds us that these were the years when the first American music movement blossomed. The *Times* quoted a member of Farwell's audience: "We are trying to develop a definite American musical art, which shall be indicative of the character of us in the same way that German music is of Germany, and Russian music is of Russia, and Bohemian music is of Bohemia."[26] Even though Farwell's presentation included music derived from Indian and African American, as well as Yankee, sources; even though his collaboration with Charles Lummis in making field recordings of *Spanish Songs of Old California*, seems a harmless enough exercise in regionalist self-identification—the question of musical nationalism, and its relationship to the peculiarities of Los Angeles's population mix, as subtexts of this competition among impresarios, is raised (Heisley 1987).[27]

Racism as well as classism was built into the new amusement industry. Some of the prizefights at Hazard's Pavilion, when it was under Behymer's management, were between black fighters, just as

black entertainers (Flora Batson, Will Marion Cook and others) had played at the commercial theaters in Los Angeles in the 1890s and much earlier. Behymer had been associated with an appearance of the Nashville Students, with Sissieretta Jones, in December 1897, probably in his usual capacity as publicist and ticket seller, but he never claimed credit for those appearances as he regularly did for Caucasian performers. In this he was no doubt deferring to the prejudices of the white middle-class clientele he was already cultivating.[28] The prizefights at Hazard's Pavilion did become an issue in the building of Philharmonic Auditorium.

* * *

It is not surprising that, in this process, the newly invented elite tradition should be endowed, in Behymer, with a hero who claimed to have bestowed that tradition from on high, and whose partly fictitious history has been accepted as real. Yet many persons strongly resisted the pigeon-holing of concert music as an elite form of entertainment, with a relatively narrow audience. In fact, resistance to the elitist aspect that came with the commodification of concert life, remained a major factor in Los Angeles's music history. It lay behind Blanchard's rubric of "popular prices will prevail"; it resurfaced most notably in the later narratives of the People's Orchestra of 1912 and the Hollywood Bowl, immediately following World War I, as well as in the Federal Music Project of the 1930s.[29]

One must look to still another narrative layer to locate the women whose presence is so clear from the census data as this grand competition of impresarios took place. Outside the area of music, they were a major reason why Los Angeles was a national center for political Progressivism, and why women got the vote in California well before the Nineteenth Amendment was adopted. Women were a major part of the church audiences for whom Blanchard arranged lyceum series and lecture courses, as well as of the elite audience cultivated by Behymer for the old Symphony and for his own concert "courses." They were firmly placed in that audience as it developed, in parallel with their emergence as a political force in California. Harley Hamilton organized his mainly female violin students into an amateur orchestra in 1892; they reorganized themselves into the Los Angeles Women's Orchestra the following year. Five years later, Edna Foy, one of the LAWO's founding members, was refused membership in the Symphony because of her sex. She then studied in London for two years; when she returned, it was to resume her place in the Women's Orchestra, but not to join the Symphony. Gertrude Barrett, another member of the Women's Orchestra, played professionally in the all-woman Boston Fadettes orchestra before returning to Los Angeles and the Women's Orchestra. Most of the women who were early members of the Los Angeles local of the musicians' union were concentrated in the low-paying "family" orchestras that played in restaurants, not in the more profitable theaters until after World War I. The People's Orchestra of 1912–1914 sought music by local composers; several women were just getting interested in the heretofore abstruse art of orchestration about the time it disappeared. The general resistance to women as professional performers and composers may help explain the substantial number of women who turned to music patronage in the following decades in order to satisfy their interest in music.

* * *

One long-enduring monument that lasted through most of the twentieth century became a not-so-silent, slightly ambivalent rebuke to the view of music as a commodity whose ethical content was to be exploited by cultivating an elite, white, middle and upper class, heavily female audience—the position that Behymer ultimately came to represent. In October 1903, Hazard's Pavilion, the auditorium where Theodore Thomas's opera company had played soon after it opened in 1887, where Melba sang, where Sousa conducted

on his regular visits, where conventions and finally prizefights were held along with the "high-class" events, was acquired by a newly formed Baptist congregation and renamed "Temple Auditorium." In the spring of 1905 it was torn down and very quickly replaced with an up-to-date 3,500-seat hall and office building. Known first as Temple Auditorium, the "Theatre Beautiful," it opened its doors to the public in 1906 with a triumphant return visit by the Lambardi Grand Opera Company, a low-budget company with low prices and strong popular appeal. It continued its function as a popular location when it was renamed Clune's Auditorium in 1915. "The Birth of a Nation" and other feature-length silent movies ran there. For a few years, it was the home of the elitist Los Angeles Symphony, as well as assorted visiting virtuosos and opera companies. In 1920, William Andrews Clark, Jr., leased it for his one-year-old Philharmonic Orchestra. Thereafter it was known as Philharmonic Auditorium, the central Los Angeles venue for symphony, opera, and visiting virtuosos for nearly six decades. Although Behymer was rather pointedly excluded from its management at the start, when it was dedicated to popular but "uplifting" morally select events, he eventually took it over and maintained an office there until his death in 1947. Throughout, it remained a Baptist church—a Baptist church that had its home in a profitable downtown real estate development. The church-based entrepreneur, who had attended theater and concert performances in Los Angeles from the 1880s but later puzzled over the morality of the theater, even of Shakespeare, who outdid both Behymer and his other competitors in the matter of successful investing but never boasted about it in the press, is, of course, as little known now as Fred Blanchard, H.C. Wyatt, or J.T. Fitzgerald. She is Clara Bradley Burdette, financial wizard, suffragist, philanthropist, university trustee, and long-time officer of the National Federation of Women's Clubs.

Burdette became involved in the acquisition and development of the Temple Baptist Church property when her husband, Robert J. Burdette, a popular lecturer who had become a preacher late in life, became the first minister of the new church. It was she, apparently, who was responsible for the idea that a downtown church would be financially feasible in Los Angeles, and provide an important public service, if its sanctuary could do double duty as a site for opera and symphony concerts, and if it also offered office space. And it was she, a woman already twice widowed, accustomed to handling her own business dealings, who traveled to New York and Boston in search of the necessary capital for her project. By 1905, when she traveled to New York, Boston, and Philadelphia in search of capital for the church/auditorium project, she intended to bypass both managerial camps, and was pushing her own candidate as manager of the new theater, Sparks M. Berry (Burdette 1905).

Burdette's name scarcely appears in the newspaper coverage of this ambitious project. Her role and the difficulty she faced in doing even this philanthropic business on Wall Street is reflected in her letters. She wrote:

> [New York] Wed. night. [April 26,] 1905…I am doing my last "do" for the Baptists. Spent the entire morning down on Wall and Broad and Broadway. Nothing doing.

> [Boston] Fri. Apr. 28th, 1905…the business I was on there was different from anything I ever went on before and I found it did not "go" for a woman to be prowling around Wall and Broad street alone. I lost self-respect every minute I was there and I made up my mind that I couldn't afford it even for the new Auditorium.[30]

Burdette got involved in the Auditorium project only a year after she had been the subject of a highly gendered, front-page, full-column attack in the Los Angeles *Evening Express*. The fact that she owned stock in that paper's conservative rival, the *Times*, presumably made her a legitimate target. But the sexism that pervades the entire episode

goes far beyond the belittling, gendered language of the attack, and perhaps gives an idea of why the role of women in the narratives of Los Angeles music history seems so small in proportion to their numbers. Some excerpts from the *Express* article:

MRS. BURDETTE ILL

Fears Expressed That She May Not Recover From Attack of Congestion of Brain

DUE TO MENTAL ANGUISH

Her Sickness Is Attributed To Ambition to Become President of General Federation.

> Lying there in her beautiful home, surrounded by many luxuries and attended by loving friends, the prominent club woman tosses in her delirium and suffers from an illness brought on, it is believed, by her unhappiness over club matters.… When Mrs. B first became identified with club life in L.A. she gained favor rapidly with women of this city. She was a bright, vivacious speaker of charming tact. So well was she liked that when the State Federation of Women's Clubs was organized she was made its first president and there was no dissenting voice. Then it was, so the story goes, that ambition seized upon her…it is possible that her ambition may cost her life. (*Los Angeles Express* 1902)

Charm was allowed, but brains were definitely off limits. Burdette's published reply was also couched in the language of Victorian ladyhood. She found it necessary to explain and defend her long-standing career as a public speaker, claiming that she traveled with her husband "to make a home for him wherever he went."

Beyond the notion of frail womanhood forced to defend itself from the charge of unladylike ambition, Burdette did not have the agency to defend herself, as a look at the mechanics of the matter shows. Did the editor who had called forth the story call on Burdette, telephone her, or write a letter of apology to her? Nothing so simple. His *wife* sent her a letter explaining that the whole thing was a misunderstanding. Burdette's *husband* appeared at the newspaper office to object and deliver his wife's reply. When the editor finally chose to respond to the storm of editorial abuse and criticism from women's organizations, he wrote a lengthy letter to her *husband*, saying that the story had been blown out of proportion. In the end, Temple Auditorium, and the fact that Burdette chaired the finance committee that made the project possible, was the best answer.

* * *

Burdette's presence, which I did not even suspect for a long time after I had found the Great Los Angeles Impresario Competition of 1899–1905, and who serves as the *dea ex machina* for this paper, illustrates the complexity and the incompleteness of the narratives that underlie the social history of music in the Progressive Era, when concert music and opera were marginalized as elite, white, confusingly gendered fragments of a much larger amusement industry. Some of these narratives, especially those whose main players are not white males, are still largely concealed. It is hard to imagine that, even with guideposts borrowed from feminist criticism and social historians, we will ever get the narrative web untangled to our complete satisfaction. Nevertheless, enough is known to question the theory of the Three Heroes of Los Angeles concert music history as it has been transmitted by the artistic establishment.

NOTES

1. An earlier version of this paper was read to the Sonneck Society for American Music, February 1993. Research was conducted with the help of a fellowship from the National Endowment for the Humanities, 1989–90.

2. See Swan 1952. His study is based mainly on material now in the Behymer Collection at the Huntington Library. Although Swan was not able to substantiate Behymer's claims about his early career, he accepted Behymer's general account as a framework; see review of the 1977 reprint (Swan 1982). For another version of Behymer's early career, see Smith 1991. Robert Stevenson refutes Behymer's account of his role in founding the Los Angeles Philharmonic (Stevenson 1988). The earliest publicly expressed doubts about Behymer's hyperbole located to date appeared in 1904. See n. 13 below.

3. See also Cross 1990:210 "His other mistake was not to realize that I look for narratives. That's my profession, not being a detective. That's the profession of every professor of literature." Likewise, in this paper, of every feminist musicologist.

4. See, for example, the concluding paragraph in the 1982 IAMR review of Swan. The initial privileging of Schoenberg's arrival in 1934 as one of the three most important events in Los Angeles's musical progress results from the virtually universal critical assumption that white male modernism was the most significant artistic value in the decades between World War I and II. It reflects the privileging of European-based concert music over other musics, and of one kind of modernism over other possible modernisms. An alternative reading might be, for example, the arrival of William Grant Still a few months before Schoenberg.

5. In 1887 a large portion of the city's adult population turned out to attend six performances, two of them added on the spot, by the idealistic, ambitious, and ill-starred National Opera Company under Theodore Thomas. The company lost money or barely broke even in most of the cities it visited, but not in Los Angeles.

6. The flyers are bound into L.E. Behymer, Scrapbook #3, in the Huntington Library. Some others artists sponsored by Fitzgerald in this time period were, according to the *Western Graphic and the Los Angeles Saturday Post*, January–June 1899: Gerome Helmont, boy violinist, at Simpson's; Mae Martinez, "In a Persian Garden," at Blanchard Hall; and Lisetta Regina Mariani, soprano. Fitzgerald, who had published some of his own music, came to Los Angeles in 1891, five years after Blanchard and Behymer.

7. The performers were the Euterpean male quartet, consisting of local singers, who were assisted by a soprano and a pianist. When Blanchard Hall opened

its fourth-floor art gallery and all its studios with a large reception, the local *Western Graphic* produced a thirty-two page special edition devoted to music and art in Southern California. Its anonymous society columnist reported that Blanchard and Fitzgerald were the two individuals most responsible for the city's flourishing concert life, although they no longer spoke to each other. Blanchard, the son of prosperous parents in Worcester, Massachusetts, attended Boston Latin School and was sufficiently trained as a musician to offer an operetta to the visiting Bostonians' company on one occasion.

8. H.C. Wyatt came to L.A. in 1884 with a minstrel troupe, was manager of Child's Grand Opera House (opened 1886) for a time, then of the Los Angeles Theater (opened 1888) from 1888 to 1903. In 1903 he moved to the new Mason Opera House, which he managed until his death in 1910. See Leavitt 1912; also Charles L. Bagley, "History of the Band and Orchestra Business in Los Angeles," published serially in *The Overture, the Magazine of the Musicians Mutual Protective Association, Local 47,* starting in 1921, especially Chapter vi, 5/2 (5/1/1925):4. According to Bagley, Wyatt lost his left arm while a drummer boy in Kemper's Brigade during Pickett's Charge on the Union lines at Gettysburg, July 3, 1863. He was then "a little over fourteen years of age."

9. The presence of Mascagni's *Cavalleria rusticana* (composed 1890) on a double bill with Gilbert and Sullivan's *Trial by Jury* (composed 1875), both offered by a small touring company, is one of many indications that Italian opera was still genuinely popular, commercially successful entertainment at this point.

10. Blanchard formed the partnership Blanchard & Venter to pursue his concert and lecture promotions. In a letter written by Clara Bradley Burdette (Burdette 1905) from Boston following a conversation with Hathaway of Redpath (Burdette Collection, The Huntington Library), Venter was said to have lost $5,000 on his talent promotions in the past year.

11. One of Blanchard's publicity promotions read, "The marked demand for seats at 'popular-priced' entertainments this season has been greater than ever, and the Star, Imperial and People's courses, blocked out months in advance, have been readily taken to by the local public." (*Los Angeles Saturday Post* 1904a).

Blanchard's claim that "ninety-five out of every hundred contracts for [lyceum] events . . . on the Coast are issued from [Blanchard & Venter's] Los Angeles office. Courses of from five to ten events have already been closed by most of the leading cities of the Pacific Coast, including about a dozen in southern California" appeared two months earlier. (*Los Angeles Saturday Post* 1904b).

12. In that year, the management of the Burbank Theater, which in its six years' existence had not been consistently profitable, came open. Behymer was passed over in favor of the younger but theatrically more experienced Oliver Morosco, who made a spectacular success of the Burbank. See *Los Angeles Record* 1899.

13. For information on Barnhart, see Bragdon 1938, especially 69–75 and 110–115; also *Western Graphic* 1899:13–14. Barnhart's appearance at the Friday Morning Club in Los Angeles in 1904 is chronicled in the scrapbooks of the Friday Morning Club at The Huntington Library. Barnhart was already associated with Arthur Farwell's American Music movement. Later he was very successful as an organizer of community choruses in New York City, Rochester, and elsewhere; he was also prominently associated with the pageantry movement. His long career prejudices this writer in favor of his work in the controversy over Messiah productions described below.

14. Sembrich performed on May 2; the Oratorio Society gave Bruch's *Arminius* on May 21 (both at Hazard's Pavilion); Watkins Mills, basso, and others appeared at "a Grand Lyric concert" at Simpson's Auditorium, on May 24. The railroad snafu prevented most of the delegates from arriving in time for Sembrich's performance, while it gave an opportunity to repeat the Blanchard/Barnhart concert of May 3 some days later. The *Los Angeles Times* (1904a) gives the soloists and the program for the Blanchard/Barnhart concert: Maud Reese-Davies, soprano; Harriet Longstreet, contralto; Spencer Robinson, tenor; Lalla Fage, violinist; Blanche Williams, pianist; Alfred Butler, organist; William Mead, flutist.

> Weber, *Freischutz*, overture (orchestra)
> Gounod, *By Babylon's Wave* (chorus & orchestra)
> Delibes, "Bell Song," *Lakmé*, (Davies & Mead)
> Reinecke, "Evening Hymn" (chorus and tenor)
> Wagner, *Lohengrin*, selections (orchestra)

Mendelssohn, "Thirteenth Psalm" (chorus and contralto)
Bohm, "Thine Only" (Robinson)
Rossini, "Inflammatus" (orchestra and Davies)
Gillett, "Loin du Bal"
Mascagni, "Intermezzo," *Cavalleria rusticana*
Mendelssohn, "Wedding March"
Handel, "Hallelujah" (chorus and orchestra)

15. *Los Angeles Saturday Post* (1904d) carries competing claims. Barnhart's chorus is called "the most comprehensive and complete organization of choral singers ever attempted in this part of the country." Behymer claimed, "In the first place all amateurish attempts will be avoided." He added, "It is the duty of the Los Angeles public to turn out and crowd the church [Simpson's Auditorium] and pay homage to the great masterpiece of Handel."

16. Frederick Stevenson (1845–1925) was an English-born composer and voice teacher of very strong convictions.

17. Stevenson made his opinion of Behymer/Jahn's production clear: "'Elijah' was, I regret to say, not one whit better than 'The Messiah.'…wherein then lay the failure? Briefly, and frankly, in the soloists and in the conductor…I would have little respect for myself and less for my readers if these columns permitted that this 'Elijah' was either the 'Elijah' of Mendelssohn or in the slightest degree representative of Los Angeles" (Frederick Stevenson 1905b). The Los Angeles Oratorio Society was revived in 1918 under John Smallman.

18. See, for example, Smith 1992; also Smith 1993.

19. As reported in the 1910 Census, 25% of Los Angeles's population, and 42% of San Francisco's, was listed as foreign-born.

20. Based on the 1910 Census, calculated for the population age 15 and over. For 1900, the calculation yields 50% in Los Angeles and 43% for San Francisco.

21. The Women's Symphony considered sponsoring a concert by Ellen Beach Yaw, a locally popular soprano with an international reputation. In this case, Behymer probably agreed to sponsor her appearance in order to keep control of his business.

22. The *Herald* (May 25, 1900) reported that the Los Angeles Theater was now controlled by Meyerfeldt, director of the Orpheum vaudeville circuit; three days later, the *Express* reported that the same theater was under the control of the Al Hayman theater syndicate. In August, the *Herald* reported that Wyatt had leased the theater from Meyerfeldt, with the proviso that he not engage in price competition with the Orpheum. Clippings in Behymer, Press Clippings Scrapbook No. 6, The Huntington Library.

23. Behymer's contract concerning the vitagraph machines is in the Behymer Collection, The Huntington Library.

24. Behymer's most obvious moves to cultivate the myth of his early achievements as an impresario began c. 1912, however.

25. The close association of professional athletics with commercial theater is suggested by the address of the manager of Los Angeles Base Ball, who also ran a billiard parlor in a building that housed the Lyric Theater, a burlesque house.

26. Clipping, probably from the *Los Angeles Times*, in album "Programs, 1903–1922," Friday Morning Club Collection, The Huntington Library. On November 4, 1904, Arthur Farwell, assisted by local artists, lectured there on the topic, "Toward American Music: A Study in National Progress, with Special Reference to the Music of the American Indians."

27. The earliest discussion so far located on folk influences in European and American music is by Edward F. Kubel (1900). He mentions Edward Everett Hale, Dvorak, and Krehbiel, but not Farwell. See Glassberg 1990 for a discussion of the social and political agendas of the closely related pageantry movement.

28. There are few reports of African American music activities during the period under consideration in this essay. See Caldwell 1988. A few years later, the Los Angeles Express (1913) reported the following: "Dr. [Charles Edward] Locke to Repeat Lecture for Negroes…'Was Abraham Lincoln Justified in Issuing the Emancipation Proclamation; or Is the Negro Making Good?'…Negroes of Los Angeles invited him to repeat it for them, at the First Methodist Episcopal church, Sixth and S. Hill…The floor of the main auditorium will be reserved for negroes until

7:50 P.M. All the rest of the large auditorium will be open to white people...A chorus of the combined choirs of the negro churches of the city, under the direction of Rev. T. J. Hill, pastor of the Mount Zion Baptist church, will sing old plantation melodies."

29.　See, for example, Smith 1992, 1993, 1990 and 1989.

30.　Letters dated "Wednesday night" [April 16] and April 28], Box 34, Clara Bradley Burdette Collection, The Huntington Library. For more on Burdette (1855–1954), see Miller 1984.

REFERENCES CITED

Bagley, Charles L.
　　1921–1925　"History of the Band and Orchestra Business in Los Angeles." *The Overture, The Magazine of the Musicians Mutual Protective Association, Local 47.*
Behymer, L.G.
　　Collection, the Huntington Library.
Bragdon, Claude
　　1938　*More Lives than One.* New York: Alfred A. Knopf.
Burdette, Clara Bradley
　　1905　Letters to Robert J. Burdette. April. Box 34, Burdette Collection, the Huntington Library
Caldwell, Hansonia L.
　　1988　"Music in the Lives of Blacks in California: The Beginnings." *Triangle of Mu Phi Epsilon* 82(4):10, 18.
Cross, Amanda (pseudonym for Carolyn Heilbrun)
　　1990　*A Trap for Fools.* New York: Ballantine.
Glassberg, David
　　1990　*American Historical Pageantry: the Uses of Tradition in the Early Twentieth Century.* Chapel Hill: University of North Carolina Press.
Heilbrun, Carolyn
　　1988　*Writing a Woman's Life.* New York: Norton.
Heisley, Michael, ed.
　　1987　*Spanish Songs of Old California.* Los Angeles: Historical Society of Southern California. Reprint of first edition (1923). Charles F. Lummis, collector and translator. Arthur Farwell, piano accompaniments.
Koegel, John
　　Forthcoming "Hispanic Music in Nineteenth-Century California: The Lummis Collection of Cylinder Recordings at the Southwest Museum." *Southern California Quarterly.*
　　1994　"The Lummis Collection of Cylinder Recordings as a Source for Hispanic Music in Southern California in the Nineteenth Century." Ph.D. dissertation, Claremont Graduate School.
Kubel, Edward F.
　　1900　*Western Graphic* (July 28) 9(4):9–10.
Leavitt, M.B.
　　1912　*Fifty Years in Theatrical Management.*:254–255. New York: Broadway Publishing Company.
Los Angeles Express
　　1902　(October 1).
　　1913　(February 11): 5.
Los Angeles Graphic
　　1904　(November 5) 21(14): 24.
Los Angeles Record
　　1899　"Morosco Has Rivals: Four Prospective Managers Contest for the Burbank...Len Behymer and Harry Mears Would Each Like to Secure the Theater" (July 2).
Los Angeles Saturday Post
　　1899　(January–June).
　　1901a　(September 7).4(10): 7
　　1901b　(November 23).4(21): 7
　　1904a　(April 30) 9(18) :10–11.
　　1904b　(October 8) 10(1):15.
　　1904c　(August 13) 10(15):11.
　　1904d　(November 19)10(21):12.
　　1904d　(December 10) 10/24.
　　1905　(October 7).
Los Angeles Times
　　1902　(November 30).
　　1904a　(May 1).6(2)
　　1904b　(May 26): 6.
May, Lary
　　1980　*Screening Out the Past: The Birth of Mass Culture and the Motion Picture Industry.* New York: Oxford University Press.
Miller, Dorothy Grace
　　1984　"Within the Bounds of Propriety: Clara Burdette and the Women's Movement." Ph.D. dissertation, University of California, Riverside.
Peiss, Kathy
　　1986　*Cheap Amusements: Working Women and Leisure in Turn-of-the-Century New York.* Philadelphia: Temple University Press.
Rosenzweig, Roy
　　1983　*Eight Hours for What We Will: Workers and Leisure in an Industrial City, 1870–1920.*

Cambridge and New York: Cambridge University Press.

Searight, Frank T.
  1905   *Los Angeles Record* (March 29).

Smith, Catherine Parsons
  1993   "Founding the Hollywood Bowl." *American Music* (Summer): 206–242.
  1992   "'Something of Good for the Future': The People's Orchestra of Los Angeles, 1912–1913." *Nineteenth-Century Music* 16 (Fall): 147–161.
  1991   "'Our Awe-Stuck Vision': The Emergence of L.E. Behymer as an Impresario." Paper read at Music Library Association Meeting, Northern and Southern California Chapters, 50th Anniversary Meeting, October.
  1990   "Music and the Progressive Movement in Los Angeles." Paper read to the Western Association of Women Historians, San Marino, California, May 5.
  1989   "Opera in Los Angeles: The Federal Music Project's 1936 Production of *La Traviata*." Paper read to the Sonneck Society for American Music, April.

Stevenson, Frederick
  1905c   *Los Angeles Graphic* (April 1) 22(9).
  1905b   *Los Angeles Graphic* (April 8) 22(10).
  1905a   *Los Angeles Graphic* (March 4) 22(5): 23.
  1904   "The Musical World." *Los Angeles Graphic* (October 29) 21(13):24.

Stevenson, Robert
  1988   "Music in Southern California: A Tale of Two Cities." *IAMR* 10(1): 51–111.

Swan, Howard
  1982   *Inter-American Music Review* 4(2): 85–86.
  1952   *Music in the Southwest*. San Marino, CA: The Huntington Library.

Western Graphic
  1899   (January–June).

OUTSIDE-IN: LOST IN L.A. WITH BOBBY BRADFORD

Grace M

Los Angeles. Avant-garde. "Free" jazz.[1] If these terms seem incongruous, one might consider the music of Bobby Bradford, John Carter, and Ornette Coleman. All spent formative years of their careers in the Los Angeles area—Bradford and Carter most of their lives. While Los Angeles is not known as a nucleus of experimental or "outside" music, there has been and still is a small group of people committed to playing and supporting the creatively improvised music commonly known as "outside" or "free" jazz. In an effort to discover more about the musical and social ideals of the members of this community, I interviewed trumpeter/cornetist Bobby Bradford in 1992 for my M.A. thesis. We spoke about a number of issues including Bradford's social and musical backgrounds, his associations with Ornette Coleman and John Carter, playing music in Los Angeles as opposed to New York and Europe, his career as an educator, the social and political aspects of his music, and his spiritual and philosophical beliefs. What emerged is an ethnological portrait of an extraordinary musician in the context of the area in which he lives—Los Angeles. The following is based on this interview and on a lecture given by Bradford at UCLA in Professor Steven Loza's class, "Musical Aesthetics in Los Angeles," during the 1993 school year.

Bobby Bradford can justly be called a phenomenal jazz artist and a major innovator in his field. His musical career has spanned over four decades and includes an association with Ornette Coleman in the 1950s and later, a life-long musical collaboration and friendship with the late John Carter which, in my opinion, produced some of the best collective improvisation in the genre. Born in Cleveland, Mississippi in 1934, Bradford actually first came to Los Angeles in the mid-1940s:

> I first came to Los Angeles in 1944 when I was just a little kid, about eight or something like that. And that was with my family moving from Mississippi, because my father did work in the airplane manufacturing industry. So we came from Mississippi in 1943 or '44 and we lived up where Dodger Stadium is now—in those days they called it Bishop Heights. We lived here about a year and a half, then my father decided we'd go to Detroit. We had relatives there and he thought he could get better work there. We packed up everything and went to Detroit. We stayed in Detroit another year but by the summer of 1946, we had settled in Texas for sure. I stayed in Texas until I graduated from high school, spent a couple of years in college, then, disenchanted with what was happening in the little college that I was going to in Texas, I decided to come back to Los Angeles.

The Los Angeles that Bradford returned to was

a city in transition, musically and socially speaking. The glory that was Central Avenue, the focal point of African American culture in Los Angeles throughout the '30s and '40s, had faded. Central Avenue played an important role for the black community in Los Angeles, providing a centralized area for socializing, a source of employment within the black community, and strengthening the pride of the community. Central Avenue attracted all the prominent black artists (musicians, dancers, painters, actors/actresses), politicians, and sports figures of the day. Leading personalities stayed at the Dunbar Hotel while in town The Black Musician's Union was located on Central Avenue, which provided a gathering place for local musicians. On any given day, Art Tatum or Bud Powell or Lena Horne or Duke Ellington might be playing somewhere on Central Avenue or doing other business in between concert dates. Central Avenue was not just a street but a community—a lifestyle—that according to saxophonist/flutist and Los Angeles native Buddy Collette began to disperse by the early 1950s and started moving west and spreading out to other areas around the city.

Music ensembles became much smaller as the big bands gave way to smaller bebop ensembles, hence the need for smaller, more intimate places to hear live music. The advent of television gave people a reason not to go out of their homes for entertainment. As pianist Horace Tapscott observed, "[one] could feel things change around [oneself], [one] could see things happening" (Tapscott 1992). The early 1950s saw the amalgamation of the two segregated musicians' unions as well as an interracial orchestra. This was the climate of the city to which Bobby Bradford returned.

Bradford worked at a day job while trying to get gigs around town at night. It was during this time that Bradford began taking private lessons with the late John Anderson, a "marvelous trumpet player" in the Los Angeles area, and began playing music with Ornette Coleman. Bradford served four years in the Army, playing in the Air Force Band, and got

married, had children, and again returned to Texas. By this time schools had become integrated, so Bradford enrolled at the University of Texas where he earned a degree in music. Bradford returned to Los Angeles in 1964 and shortly thereafter met John Carter, a clarinetist/saxophonist who had also moved to L.A. from Texas. The two struck up a friendship and started playing together on a regular basis until Carter's death in 1991. With the exception of touring and living in London for a year in the early 1970s, Bradford has remained in the Los Angeles area—he now lives in Altadena—and continues to play and compose music while teaching at Pasadena City College and Pomona College.

Because of the nature of the music—improvisation often within a small ensemble—"free" jazz affords intimate musical relationships. In addition to his own playing, Bobby Bradford can be seen in terms of two significant musical partnerships or associations, the first being with Ornette Coleman and the second with John Carter. Bradford's early musical career in Los Angeles began with his association with Ornette Coleman, arguably the most famous internationally known musician associated with the style of music known as "free" jazz. Coleman lived in Los Angeles for approximately nine years during 1950–1959, but he had a profound influence—positive and negative—on many musicians playing in the Los Angeles area at the time. Like Bradford, Coleman was a pioneer of pushing the boundaries of improvised music and musical form. Bradford first met Coleman in Austin, Texas, where Bradford attended Sam Houston College. Apparently, Coleman had come into town to serve as best man at his friend Charles Moffet's wedding. Moffet was a senior at Sam Houston College at the time and after the wedding festivities, there was a jam session where Bradford was first introduced to Coleman's music. Bradford, who went on to play in Coleman's band in Los Angeles, explained how he and Coleman got reacquainted in Los Angeles:

So I came back to Los Angeles...I was

maybe nineteen. That was the summer of 1953 and in the process of going back and forth to work and trippin' around, I met Ornette again…and that's when I began this association with Ornette Coleman. Now Ornette, unbeknownst to me, had moved to Los Angeles too, but he'd come here to marry a woman that he'd met having passed through here or something, I don't know, but she was from L.A. So we talked one day, and we had met each other on the streetcar it seems to me, on the red car—you know, taking the same car from where he lived like out on 115th or so, and I lived on about 80th, come into downtown L.A. So he said he's writing music and he'd like to try and organize a band and would I be interested, so I jumped at the chance, you see. So we'd practice at his place sometimes and we'd hustle these gigs around town and the most work that we did, of course, would be at what would amount to a bar. Not places for dancing but just a bar as the entertainment. And often we played down in the sort of red-light district of L.A., which they called in those days the Nickel—you know how people have to have a slang name for everything—this was like around 5th Street, 5th as it intersects Main and Los Angeles, that part of downtown that's actually still kind of seedy.

Bradford and Coleman were both working at Bullocks department store during the day and trying to get gigs playing music at night. In addition to playing tunes from the standard jazz repertoire, they would also play Coleman's original music, which was quite different in style and approach from the music up to this point in jazz. As Bradford tells it:

Well, we'd also play his [Coleman's] originals. Now some of them were based on the chord progressions to standard tunes, but some of them were not. Some of them were

irregular in their form, like the bar groupings did not fit 8- and 16- and 24- or 32-bar blues. And when he [Coleman] would improvise on these tunes, he often would not follow any kind of chord pattern. But he manages to sustain the solo integrity under those conditions. Now that's what attracted me to his music. A lot of guys said—I got it from everybody around—they used to say, "Man, what are you doing playing with this guy, he doesn't know what he's doing and he doesn't know music and he doesn't play the right numbers of bars and everything." Well, I was not to be swayed by any such thing as that because it was clear to me that this guy had a real serious musical attitude, a posture that was really very creative. It is daring, number one—radical, at least because what was happening is that once you decided to play a melody now and you do not follow the chord patterns, then the status quo says, "Well, what are you following up there? Are you just rambling around on the instrument not playing?"…In those days, his rationale was that the music has a kind of emotional thrust also and I can turn the emotional thing into flesh and blood of music. [Others said] "Now that's too subjective, that's too vague, we want to know if you're playing, we're playing in this key here, we go to a B^b minor 7th, that's what you ought to be playing, when we get to this bar right here." He says, "But that limits my creativity. What that means is that that much of my solo is already planned and I want it to be completely free."

And so, for the most part now, the L.A. community frowned on it. Now, there were a few guys who responded to what he was doing and thought this guy's really brilliant. And there was no question about, when people heard his tunes—linear properties—the melodic value of his music was wonderful. But there was no way to use it, you see, you couldn't take it and make it fit on your gigs because you couldn't get the piano player to play something that went with it.

It must be remembered that jazz in Los Angeles in the early '50s consisted mainly of bebop and the slower, more mellow "cool" style of jazz, so named by Miles Davis's album, *Birth of the Cool*. While "cool" jazz came to be associated with the "laid-back" California lifestyle and certainly the musicians playing this style gained acceptance and recording contracts, there were different styles of music being played simultaneously in different areas of Los Angeles—there was no one "Los Angeles" sound. Popular music venues such as Shelly's Mann Hole and Howard Rumsey's Lighthouse were fashionable locales for hearing the latest popular music. Later when Bradford and Carter approached Howard Rumsey with the idea of playing at his club, Rumsey replied, "I like your music, I know you guys are good musicians, but nobody's gonna come to the club to hear that."

Bradford was drafted into the Army in 1954, thus ending his affiliation with Coleman in Los Angeles. Don Cherry replaced Bradford as the trumpet player in Coleman's band which eventually moved to New York and made history playing and recording their unique style of music. Bradford did go to New York to play with Coleman in the early '60s but after struggling financially, he went back to school, enrolling at the University of Texas:

[I] always had intentions of getting some kind of music degree so that I could be prepared to take care of a family because I knew how treacherous the music business was, especially jazz…After having gone through the university in 1958—I was there for about three semesters—then I dropped out and went to New York with Ornette Coleman, and then I came back and finally graduated from college in Texas in 1963,

and I taught in the public schools in Texas in a little town called Crockett. Oh man, high school band director, little town. It's sort of, I guess it would be southeast Texas, about a hundred and fifty miles from Houston. And after a year of that I thought, "Oh man, I can't handle this." So then we packed up, wife and kids, and came back to Los Angeles again. Now I'm back to L.A. and it's summer of 1964.

Bradford's reasons for returning to Los Angeles revolved around his family. The first time he returned to Los Angeles from Texas was because his mother and stepfather lived in L.A.—Bradford hoped to stay with his family until he could "get a foothold" and move out. He also thought he might find what he was looking for in a city the size of Los Angeles. By 1964, Bradford had a family of his own. He had already been to New York with Ornette Coleman and saw what life was like there. For Bradford, coming to Los Angeles was an economic decision. He thought he would have a better time getting a teaching job and playing music whenever he could. Though the thought of moving to New York did cross his mind, the security of having family in Los Angeles outweighed prospects in New York.

In 1964, Los Angeles was rife with social issues waiting to explode, which did happen shortly thereafter in the form of the Watts Riots. The Civil Rights Movement was making an impact; it was a period of expansion (mental and geographical) and exploration in the arts and in life. It is important to note that the social and political movements of the time had a reciprocal relationship to the music, especially "free" jazz. When I asked Bradford about the influences of social and/or political movements on his music, he was very candid and recalled the inspiration provided by Malcolm X and various African American groups in the 1960s:

John [Carter] and I both…John was born in 1929, 1930, and I was born in 1934. We both grew up in the South and had a similar view of the world, having experienced what it's like being a black kid in a segregated state like Texas or Mississippi, where I was born. It was clear to me what that meant in the South. Well, the new black consciousness of the late '50s and '60s inspired us all you see, for somebody like Malcolm X sort of redeemed us in a way. Any black man who was in his twenties—old enough to really know what the whole thing was about, having had a family and having tried to deal with it here—had somehow reached a point where he was ashamed of who he had become. Do you know what I'm talking about now? And so Malcolm had the wherewithal to give us a chance to really back up and see who we were. And we were all angry about it at first but grateful too. It was like Malcolm who slapped [us] across the face and said, "You don't have to do that, and you can still be a man in America, right, a black one and still an uncompromising black man doesn't have to…you can be disenfranchised and segregated and discriminated against and all that stuff and you can still manage to be a man in America if you want to."

And so Angela Davis and the Black Panthers and all—though I wasn't in total agreement with the philosophy of everything the Panthers had to say or what Angela had to say or Huey or all these great people—they inspired us in that they reminded us all that we had an obligation to ourselves, to our children and even to America, and even white people around us, to prove and show them everyday who we were in relationship to them and that we had managed to survive and keep part of who we were intact.

And the music around Los Angeles—Horace was involved with, in quotes now,

"The Movement" around Los Angeles, the national spirit was all over the place, we were all caught up in this thing, this new black awareness about the validity of the black aesthetic on every level. Like this music, in other words, which had been for the longest contained in a way that only white people of certain philosophical and social attitudes could relate to caused black people to take a look at it as being a kind of esoteric music that perhaps only they and certain people could relate to because of its black burden or whatever.

So we began in this period now, to see that this music had a universal appeal and that it didn't have to be a narrow thing about just the black experience in America and this burden of the black man in America, that it could be appreciated, loved, you know, packaged and sold and understood all over the world. And what that kind of thing does, you see, is strengthen your own resolve to keep doing what you had been doing before, but everyday having misgivings and ambivalent feelings about what you were doing, 'cause there were a lot of people who were saying in the period before that, "Hey, man, this is not gonna work. Just do whatever you can that white people like and make as much money as you can and be happy." And a lot of people bought into that, you see. And Malcolm reminded us all—them included—that that was a big mistake and that you don't have to do that.

Everybody who was old enough to realize what was happening, this came out in everybody's music. We were all writing things that don't necessarily have titles like, "African Warrior." Some people expressly said, "Man From South Africa," you know, "The African Dream," and Africa this and Africa and the other. A lot of people had to have those titles, you see, to help them better see who they were—and I understand that. I didn't have to name a piece, "River in Ghana," to let me know what it meant to me. And so that was in my music, it was in John's music, it was in Horace Tapscott's music, it was in all the guys in New York too—some of them more explicit. Some people needed [that], you see, during that period a lot of people went heavy on the African garb and African hairdos and Africa this. I didn't need that but a lot of people needed those things to remind them everyday that "this is my new psychological stance." Once it was clear to me what was happening, I didn't need a *dashiki* or a *bouba* or little hat or to call a piece, you know, "African Dream," or "New Tomorrow." And I didn't knock it for people who did though. It's like saying, "I'm wearing this banner now and a red badge of courage." I didn't need it, but apparently some people did and would write tunes specifically named and sort of drawn out of some sort of African relationship.

I realized still then that I was not an African, I was still an American, clearly of African ancestry and all that business, but by and large, culturally an American—I may have been a second class American but still I would have been in big trouble now if you dropped me into Africa in 1960 and said, "Okay, Bob, this is your new home now, see if you can deal with this." I understand that they are my hereditary brothers and all that, but that's a different culture and I wasn't trying to fool anybody that I could relate to that [snaps fingers] like this.

In the midst of all this, Bobby Bradford was in L.A. working a nine-to-five job trying to support his family while seeking employment as a teacher and playing music on the weekends. When the teaching position did not materialize, Bradford went to City Hall and took a barrage of tests for any jobs listed on the bulletin boards. The first place he heard from was a job for an insurance adjuster, which he immediately accepted. It was during this time that Bradford got a call from another musician living in Los Angeles—John Carter.

John Carter had already been living in Southern California since 1960 and was looking for like-minded musicians to form a group. At the suggestion of Ornette Coleman, Carter called Bradford though the two had never met:

> He [Carter] said he had heard that I was living in the L.A. basin and that could we get a band together…even though John is from Fort Worth, Texas, which was only 20 miles from Dallas, we never met. And we worked…even though John was five or six years older than me and had already graduated from college before I even left high school, he was teaching in Texas, also. He moved to Los Angeles about 1960 and he was teaching here with his family and playing weekends and trying to get something going, too. And he happened to talk to Ornette on the phone or whatever and he said he was trying to organize a band but he couldn't find anybody that wanted to play with him or to play and Ornette said to him, "Well, Bradford's out there in the L.A. basin someplace, if you can find him." So John got my number from somebody, he called me, just sat down one night and talked about it and so he and I started a band in about 1964, or '65. And we were rehearsing, we couldn't get any gigs 'cause we were playing really hard to listen to stuff. And we started with just a bass player and a drummer.

By the mid-'60s, the "New Music" had already been established—though not necessarily accepted—as a separate musical genre. Ornette Coleman's *Something Else* and *Free Jazz* albums were released in the late '50s and two Los Angeles natives, Eric Dolphy and Charles Mingus, had been playing creatively improvised music in the late fifties, but left Los Angeles to pursue careers in New York and Europe where the music met with greater recognition and support. (Sadly, Dolphy's career was cut short when he died suddenly in 1964.) Cecil Taylor was in New York and had also been "freely" improvising since the mid-fifties. Carter and Bradford remained in Los Angeles but found getting a record deal or even a paying gig extremely difficult:

> John kept his job...teaching in the public schools and I kept this insurance job. And we rehearsed a couple nights a week, Tuesdays and Thursdays, and we tried to get the band booked but when we auditioned for people they said, "Oh, man." The standard line was, "People are not ready for that stuff." And it was frantic music, there's no question about it, but we were determined at that time to play what we wanted to play, 'cause we were already making a living wage with what we were doing....The music was new, we went to several record companies and the standard phrase was, "That's really good stuff, man, but people aren't ready for that." Warner Brothers—we went to two or three big agents, we said, "Well, maybe you could book us." And they all said the same thing: "Man, that stuff's too tough for people right now, it's too advanced, it's too this, it's too the other." And we were saying, "Man, this is good music." We used to come back and say to ourselves, "Are we crazy or what?" We practice this stuff, it's sharp as a razor, the ensembles were wonderful, the lines were well played, we thought this was good

music. But it is not toe-tapping, have-a-good-time, have-a-drink, party, go-yay, pat-your-foot-and-go-oh-baby. It wasn't that kind of stuff, you see, it just wasn't working.

Eventually, Carter and Bradford did get a record date with Revelation Records, a small, home-based type of operation run by a biology professor from Occidental College. There was no money involved but Bradford and Carter thought it would be good exposure. They were right. On the basis of that record, they attracted the attention of Bob Thiele of Impulse Records who also had his own smaller label, Flying Dutchman. Carter and Bradford recorded *Self Determination Music* on the Flying Dutchman label and both believed that the years spent rehearsing would finally be rewarded with more recording contracts and more gigs:

> We thought, "Hey, man, we're really getting ready to go now." We thought this is our big thing because we got reviews in Downbeat and we got a review in one of the big Japanese papers, got a record of the year review. We thought, "Well, man, this is it, we're on our way now!" But things just sort of sat there like that. Bob Thiele and other people say this: "Well, if you guys were in New York, man you'd work more, you'd make more records and everything better would happen to you," which was probably true. But John and I were convinced that we ought to be able to do what we were doing because we've done that much, staying here in Los Angeles. We decided we won't go to New York—not gonna pack up and go to New York—because we've just taken too long to get what we've got here together. Our kids were about the age [where] they were getting ready to go to college; some of them—his, and mine were getting to that point, too. I thought, "Hey, man, the worst is

over, so we're gonna stay here," so we decided to. He and I used to talk about that often. He'd say, "Well, Bob, what do you think would've happened if we'd gone to New York?" I'd say, "Ummm, I don't know, we'd probably be more famous maybe." But I don't know what the rest of the story might have been because New York can really do some strange things to you. You move to New York with a wife and two or three kids—this happens every day—and then everything starts to just explode and splinter in New York. It often makes you make some decisions that you didn't think you would've made; it's like coming to Hollywood. You do some things after you get to Hollywood that you didn't think you would have done before you left. So we decided not to do it, you see. So, we stayed here and we began to get a little bit more playing around town and the idea of this free-form music, now, lots of people were coming into the fray then, this is like mid-sixties. There were people popping up all over the place who were playing, in quotes now, "The New Music."

Though they did get a few more local gigs after making the record, teaching was the main source of income for both men. Disappointed by the turn of events, Bradford "went off to see what would happen in Europe." He lived in London for a year, touring throughout Europe and recording an album of his own compositions. While Bradford didn't make a huge amount of money in Europe, the audience's acceptance of music that was thought of as "hard to listen to" in Los Angeles gave Bradford the encouragement to persevere composing and playing music that was not commercially accepted in the United States:

At that point I began to think, "Hey, man, we're not so crazy. There is a place in the world we can play our own music and people are not gonna ask us to play that tune by Charlie Parker." Not that I don't love Charlie Parker's music, but they were willing to sit down and listen to all original music and be quite content that it's a valid music even though you're not famous – if it's played well. And so that is the thing that encouraged me to not yield and not look back and think about trying to do something, making some sort of compromise, you see, and that's twenty years ago right there.

It is interesting to note that many musicians who played freely improvised music in the '60s have gone abroad and returned (or became expatriates) with the feeling that their music had been validated, or at least appreciated, in Europe. Regardless of whether or not the music is to one's personal liking, if it is played well, it is recognized as such there, whereas in the United States, musical appreciation is often considered by musicians to be based more on aesthetic judgments (at least in the general populace) than awareness or recognition of the craft.

Upon Bradford's return to Los Angeles, he and Carter continued their musical partnership and their personal friendship. By this time (early seventies) Bradford had gotten a teaching job and he and Carter began conceptualizing their own school where aspiring musicians could learn about the "new music" as well as a "nuts and bolts" traditional approach to jazz. The idea was realized in the form of The Wind College, which was established by Carter with other local musicians such as Red Callendar and James Newton serving as instructors. Because the location of the school was changed from the original site, Bradford did not teach there full-time, but often gave three-day clinics or workshops as an adjunct teacher. Between their roles as educators at traditional institutions to the formation of an alternative music school (The Wind College) to their roles as musicians in the community, Carter and Bradford helped shape the future of freely improvised music. A new generation of musicians, including Steve Loza, David Murray and James Newton, who have gone on to successful careers of their own, got what was probably their most valuable education by sitting in on Sunday jam sessions with these master musicians to develop and explore the art of improvisation.

Bradford and Carter did get more opportunities to play and make recordings throughout the '70s and '80s. While they may not have gotten substantial monetary rewards, there was plenty of critical acclaim from those who could appreciate and understand their music. Both men remained in the Los Angeles area and continued to play music together until Carter's death in 1991. When I spoke with Bradford in 1992, I asked him about his relationship with John Carter. His reply turned out to be a poignant eulogy to his best friend and musical collaborator:

> Well, John and I played together for…we started in about 1964 together. And over the years, we played either duo or quartet— mostly quartet, I guess, for years and we spent a lot of time together, writing and practicing together. Practicing often when we didn't have any job on the horizon— just practicing for practicing sake. You know, trying to get technique up to a point that we used to say, "Well, we want to play this so that it scares all the musicians out there." So we were practicing things so we could play it so fast, man, and so unbelievable that the guys would think, "My god, what is this?" And that's the way we used to practice, some of those fast things we played then we practiced them so that they were just like this [hand gesture of interlocking fingers], you know? And we both liked that. We liked to play so that people enjoyed it also but we liked to play for the musicians, too, so that they thought, "Well, my god, man, if these guys can do this then we ought to be able to do it."

But we were very, very close friends—our families were, too. My children and his were about the same age and our kids, those children now, are in their thirties. But in those days we spent a lot of time together, our families, too. I had three kids and he had four and so our relationship was not only professional but it was fraternal, too— we were very close friends.…I think nobody knows John any better than I do unless it's his mother or his wife, and I may know things about him that nobody knows, you know what I mean? We were that close. I think it's safe to say John was as close to me as my brother. I have spent more time with him than I have with my own brother. And we were very compatible, we both had the same kind of view with what we wanted to do in music and our obligations to our families; we agreed on that and we never had any arguments or problems about money. We never got into any fights about who'd make the most or that kind of stuff. So that made it easier for us, too – we weren't competitive to the extent that one of us was trying to get more spotlight than the other one, you know, bigger picture, or whose name was first or any of that, you see, which could often hurt a relationship.

We also were both teachers and we would rely on that for our livelihood and we weren't dog-eat-dog out there trying to get something, which often hurts your creativity when you have to worry about who's making the most money or whose photograph is bigger, whose name comes first or who got the biggest paragraph in a review, you see. We'd get reviews sometimes and they'd rave about him and they'd say, "Well, Bradford was also there," and we'd laugh 'cause sometimes I'd get a big review and they'd say, "Well, there was a clarinet also in there, too," and we'd laugh at how that worked out; [we] didn't have any problems with that. And it was a real serious loss in my life when he died. I'm still having trouble with that.

He died Easter Sunday last year. It'll be a year this Easter. And it's been really hard...I didn't know what to do with myself, you know, 'cause we—I almost went home, wanted to call him and to tell him, "My best friend just died," you know what I mean? I find myself sometimes now, something really good happens, I think, "I'll call John, tell him I just—" then I think, "God, he's not here," you know?

I was fortunate to attend a concert in 1987 featuring Bradford and Carter in a quintet setting, playing pieces primarily from Carter's epic *Roots and Folklore: Episodes in the Development of American Folk Music.* This experience has remained with me because, as an improviser, the intensity and seeming effortlessness with which the group interacted was inspiring. This kind of interaction came not only from a technical mastery of instruments, but also from a shared musical goal and a close personal relationship and trust between the musicians, in particular, Carter and Bradford.

There is no doubt that Bobby Bradford has made an enormous contribution to the music of Los Angeles. In the classroom and on the bandstand, Bradford, together with John Carter, has taught (and continues to teach) countless students, some of whom—Steve Loza and James Newton, for example—have gone on to teach new generations of students. Ironically, many people in Los Angeles, or in the United States in general, are not familiar with Bradford's music:

I would like to have the privilege of playing more in the United States than I do, but at this point in my life now, I'm not looking to be on the road nine months out of the year, going around just clubbing and all. I'm not

totally satisfied with the work that I am doing here now in terms of how much I do play. I'd love to be able to play when they have these things at Lincoln Center, or when they have something at the Dorothy Chandler [Pavilion] here. I'd like the people in Los Angeles to get to hear my music and have some kind of acceptance, if you will, or recognition in my own country.

By remaining in the Los Angeles area, in many respects Bradford's music remained pure. Because he was not reliant on records or concerts to earn a living, Bradford composed and played music because he wanted to, not to make money. At the same time, Los Angeles offered a certain lifestyle that obviously appealed to Bradford. While music is a big part of Bradford's life, many of his life decisions were based on his obligations to his family. This strong sense of family seems to be a common thread among many musicians playing creatively improvised music in L.A., as does an obligation (often in the form of teaching) to the communities in which they live. Even though the social and political forces that helped inspire "free jazz" have transformed or dissipated, the constant impetus driving Bradford is the enjoyment he gets from playing music. For Los Angeles's sake, one can only hope that he keeps enjoying it.

NOTES

1. Because of the problems with terminology, I would like to clarify the use of the words "outside," "free" and "jazz." Jazz is used to denote a genre of music which utilizes improvisation. The word came into prominence in New Orleans in conjunction with the Dixieland style of music. Some musicians believe it is a derogatory, limiting term to describe such a wide array of music; I do not. The word "outside" refers to a sub-genre of music that goes "outside" the chord changes (utilizes notes that are not part of the chord being played simultaneously) or is outside of traditional Western harmonies. "Outside" is used synonomously with the word "free" which, when used in conjunction with jazz, refers to an expansive or exploratory quality. It should be noted that many of

the musicians who play "outside" or "free" jazz do not use these terms to refer to their music. For this reason, I will keep both words in quotation marks. It should also be noted that "outside" jazz, "free" jazz, "avant-garde" jazz, "the New Music," and creatively improvised music all refer to the same style of music.

REFERENCES CITED

Bobby Bradford
    1992   Interview with the Author. February 14.
    1993   Lecture at UCLA class: "Musical Aesthetics in Los Angeles." February 2.
Buddy Collette
    1992   Interview with the Author. February 26.
James Newton
    1992   Interviews with the Author. February 1, April 7.
Horace Tapscott
    1992   Interview with the Author. February 19.

Bobby Bradford – Selected Discography

Lost in L.A. Soul Note.
One Night Stand (with Frank Sullivan Trio). Soul Note.
Comin' On (with John Carter). Hat Hut.
Variations (with John Carter). Moers Music.
Castles of Ghana (with John Carter). Gramavision.
Dance of the Love Ghosts (with John Carter). Gramavision.
Murray's Steps (with David Murray). Black Saint.
Seeking. Revelation.
Secrets. Revelation.
Bobby Bradford and the Spontaneous Music Ensemble. Freedom.
Detail Plus (with John Stevens and Dyani). Impetus.
Love's Dream. Emanem.
Flight For Four. Flying Dutchman.
Self Determination Music (with John Carter). Flying Dutchman.
Science Fiction (with Ornette Coleman). Columbia.
Broken Shadows (with Ornette Coleman). Columbia.
West Coast Hot (compilation). Novus c/o RCA.

CONTRIBUTORS TO THIS VOLUME

Behzad Allahyar studied in the doctoral program in history at UCLA. He is an active musician and researcher of Iranian music in the Los Angeles area.

Milo Alvarez completed his B.A. in history at UCLA in June 1994. He plans to continue his studies at the graduate level.

Robert Gutierrez is a leading Chicano artist from East Los Angeles. He has had numerous exhibits in the U.S. and Mexico, has done cover art for *Fortune Magazine*, and has been associated with Self Help Graphics in East Los Angeles.

Carlos Manuel Haro completed his Ph.D. in education at UCLA, where he has held positions as Research Coordinator of the Chicano Studies Research Center and as Assistant Dean of the International Studies and Overseas Programs Division, the latter his current post.

Guangming Li previously studied at Wesleyan University (M.A., musicology) and at the Conservatory of China (B.A., Chinese music). He is currently completing his doctoral dissertation at UCLA in ethnomusicology on the use of Chinese percussion music notation in Beijing opera. He has been active as a musician in the Chinese community in Los Angeles.

George Lipsitz, a historian, has written extensively on contemporary culture and is a professor in the Department of Ethnic Studies at University of California, San Diego. Author of *Time Passages: Collective Memory and American Popular Culture*, his most recent book is *Rainbow at Midnight: Labor and Culture in the 1940s*, published by the University of Illinois Press.

Steven Loza is an associate professor of ethnomusicology at UCLA. His recently published *Barrio Rhythm: Mexican American Music in Los Angeles* (University of Illinois Press) has received wide academic acclaim. He is highly involved as a musician in Los Angeles and serves as director of the UCLA Mexican Arts Series.

Grace M is completing her M.A. thesis in ethnomusicology at UCLA on Los Angeles jazz artists Bobby Bradford, James Newton, and Horace Tapscott.

Jacques Maquet has had an internationally distinguished career as an anthropologist. Author of *The Aesthetic Experience: An Anthropologist Looks at the Visual Arts* and *Introduction to Aesthetic Anthropology*, Maquet has published, lectured, and taught extensively.

Charles Moore earned his Candidate in Philosophy degree in ethnomusicology at UCLA in 1993 and is currently completing his Ph.D. dissertation on W.C. Handy and the development of blues. He has performed and recorded extensively as a jazz artist throughout the United States and Europe.

Steven Pearlman received his Ph.D. in anthropology at UCLA in 1988, where he wrote a dissertation on the mariachi context in Los Angeles. He presently teaches at the University of Redlands, and is active as musician/manager of Mariachi Nuevo Uclatlán.

Timothy Rice is a professor of ethnomusicology at UCLA. He formerly taught at the University of Toronto and has served as editor of *Ethnomusicology*. His book, *May It Fill Your Soul: Experiencing Bulgarian Music*, has recently been published by the University of Chicago Press.

Angeles Sancho-Velázquez is a graduate student in systematic musicology at UCLA, currently completing her master's thesis on the "modern" in twentieth century music, specifically assessing the "tonal-atonal" transition. She plans to continue in the doctoral program.

Josefina Santiago is currently completing a B.A. degree in political science at UCLA.

Roger Savage is an assistant professor in the UCLA Department of Ethnomusicology and Systematic Musicology. He completed his doctorate at the University of Sussex in 1987. Among his various publications is *Structure and Sorcery: The Aesthetics of Post-War Serial Composition and Indeterminacy* (Garland Press).

Catherine Parsons Smith is Professor of Music at University of Nevada, Reno. A graduate of Smith College, she has conducted extensive research on twentieth century music in Los Angeles.

Robert Stevenson, professor emeritus of musicology, UCLA, is one of the most acclaimed scholars to have been associated with UCLA, where he has taught since 1949. He was recently awarded the *Medalla de Oro*, one of the highest honors in Spain, which has been bestowed on him in conjunction with the establishment of the *Cátedra Robert Stevenson* (a permanent scholarship foundation for university study) at the Real Conservatorio Superior de Música. In the past four years, Stevenson has received honorary doctorates at Catholic University, the University of Illinois, and Universidade de Lisboa.